Driving Forensic Innovation in the 21st Century

Simona Francese · Roberto S. P. King
Editors

Driving Forensic Innovation in the 21st Century

Crossing the Valley of Death

Springer

Editors
Simona Francese
Biomolecular Sciences Research Centre
Centre for Mass Spectrometry Imaging
Sheffield Hallam University
Sheffield, UK

Roberto S. P. King
Research and Development
foster+freeman
Evesham, UK

ISBN 978-3-031-56555-7 ISBN 978-3-031-56556-4 (eBook)
https://doi.org/10.1007/978-3-031-56556-4

This Springer imprint is published by the registered company Springer Nature Switzerland AG
The registered company address is: Gewerbestrasse 11, 6330 Cham, Switzerland

Paper in this product is recyclable.

To my beloved daughter Grace: Courage doesn't always roar; use your quite voice to remind yourself that courage is not absence of fear, it is ploughing through, despite fear; use your loud voice to promise yourself that you will never allow anyone to make you feel small; believe actions, not words, and never forget to be kind to yourself and to others. We all have only one shot at life, make yours count. You are a lioness in disguise. With endless love, mummy.
Simona Francese

To my family: Sometimes we do things not for fame or fortune, but because we truly care. The calling card of life can illuminate even the darkest of pathways and cast shadows over those that doubt you. Never be afraid to question, or dare to try. Success is what ***you*** *make it. For all your love and support, I am indebted to you. For your perseverance and guidance, I respect you. For your strength and tenacity, I admire you.*
Roberto S. P. King

Preface

High-quality, comprehensive research is undoubtedly pivotal to forensic science innovation, yet its transition into the operational domain represents a significant challenge and provides the greatest barrier to innovation.

This book serves to provide a broad and multifaceted understanding of the current forensic science innovation landscape, whilst evaluating some of the enablers, road blockers and barriers to implementation that must be traversed in order to cross the valley of death between 'idea' and its successful implementation.

It is undisputable that forensic science is central in appropriately supporting the criminal justice system. This is especially demonstrated in cold cases, where criminals are continually apprehended, thanks to the technological and scientific advances of the discipline. Notwithstanding, there is a mismatch between this unquestionable truth and the ability to efficiently translate forensic innovation into practice. This dissonance holds true across both the national and international landscapes in different ways, and at different levels, with understandable disparities between the industrial and academic environments. Nonetheless, the underlying issues are very similar and appoint to two fundamental causes:

(1) the lack of a recognition of forensic science as an actual discipline, and
(2) a fundamental lack of appreciation for forensic science as a societal priority.

As a consequence, there is a general lack of dedicated funding, or, alternatively, a misdirection of the funding which may support blue-sky research, but very rarely supports the final steps of the journey, to its implementation.

Moreover, whilst communication channels between end-users (practitioners) and innovators (academia and industry) has notably improved over the last decade, it still lacks a solid framework and structure to support the journey of innovation into the real world. Generating real impact in translating forensic science innovation into exploitable practice necessitates a profound 'bottom-up' paradigm shift, from researchers to policy makers, governmental bodies, policing and research councils.

This book, the first of its kind, is intended to act as a platform to facilitate the dialogue between key innovation stakeholders, namely academia, industry and end-users, to propose a roadmap that serves to facilitate practical developments and offer a revolutionary springboard to initiate the aforementioned paradigm shift.

The book merges the technical and scientific aspects of some of the innovations that have been implemented across forensic science within the national and international landscapes, and with (i) the necessary considerations to take into account on the road to success, such as understandings of cognitive bias, business planning, data privacy and legal and regulatory aspects, (ii) the end-users perspective and (iii) the industry perspective.

The breadth of topics is addressed in a coherent, comprehensive, unique and synergistic manner, such that the challenge of transitioning a forensic science idea to forensic science product/solution has a real opportunity to be addressed. These opportunities will serve to significantly improve the conversion rate of research endeavours into implementable tools thus impacting the criminal justice system in a positive, effective and efficient manner.

Sheffield, UK Simona Francese
Evesham, UK Roberto S. P. King

Contents

About the Editors

Simona Francese is Professor of Forensic and Bioanalytical Mass Spectrometry at Sheffield Hallam University (SHU), UK. She holds a first class honours degree in Chemistry obtained from the University of Salerno, Italy, in 2000, and a Ph.D. in Chemical Sciences awarded in 2004 by the same University. In her current role, she is Director of the Sheffield Multi-Modal Imaging Centre (SMIC) sitting across SHU's Health and Wellbeing and Research and Innovation Colleges and Head of the Centre for Mass Spectrometry Imaging (CMSI) within the SHU's Biomedical Sciences Research Centre.

She is Expert in the development of MALDI MS Imaging applications and has pioneered its development for the analysis of latent fingermarks and blood to profile offenders. More recently, she has engaged in research at the interface between forensics and clinical diagnostics using blood and sweat in fingertip smears to detect cancer and other pathologies.

Her research has been implemented in police casework in UK and Europe and has been partly funded by the Home Office, West Yorkshire Police and The Defence Science and Technology Laboratory, UK, and she is now collaborating with the UK National Health System. She engages in public dissemination at all levels and one exemplary endeavour was the delivery of a TED talk in Vancouver in 2018 on molecular fingerprinting.

Dr. Roberto S. P. King is an Innovator, Technologist and Subject-Matter Expert within forensic science. He was responsible for the product innovation and development portfolio at foster+freeman, UK, where he served as Vice President of Product, and previously as the company's Chief Technology Officer. He gained a first class honours degree in Chemistry and Sports Science from Loughborough University in 2005 and completed his Ph.D. in Chemistry four years later at the same institution. He is a versatile Inorganic Chemist with expertise in the application of chemistry within the forensic arena. His background involves the development of novel fingerprint enhancing agents for use on troublesome substrates, as well as investigation into unique methodologies for evidence recovery from document-based evidence. His current research interests involve fingermarks, body fluids, questioned document examination, trace evidence, and contact transfer. He has a keen interest in exploring long-standing forensic problems using fresh and lateral approaches that encompass all avenues of chemistry, physics and engineering.

He has presented in excess of 200 lectures at scientific events around the world, including both keynote and plenary sessions. He has published more than 30 research papers, three book chapters, and appeared on numerous television and news broadcasts in relation to his work and expertise within the field. He sits on two external Advisory Boards and has led many collaborative research endeavours as Principal Investigator, including both Ph.D. and KTP partnerships. He also holds numerous patents relating to his work within forensic science.

Abbreviations

3Ts	Time, Team, Traction—the proprietary method of Székely Family & Co. to assess maturity of an innovative company
ABFO	American Board of Forensic Odontology
ACE-V	Analysis, Comparison, Evaluation, Verification
ACPO	Association of Chief Police Officers
AFP	Australian Federal Police
AFR	Automatic Face Recognition
AI	Artificial Intelligence
ASBCPA	Anti-Social Behaviour, Crime and Policing Act
ASCLDLAB	American Society of Crime Laboratory Directors Laboratory Accreditation Board
BBC	British Broadcasting Corporation
BCG	Boston Consulting Group
BFEG	Biometrics and Forensics Ethics Group
BMI	Body Mass Index
BPA	Bloodstain Pattern Analysis
BRL	Business Readiness Level is a concept that refers to the maturity of the business considerations developed alongside the technical development of an innovation
BRR	Business Readiness Rate, an assessment method of business capabilities at organizational level, predecessor to BRL
CAST	Centre for Applied Science and Technology
CBRN	Chemical, Biological, Radiological and Nuclear
CBRN-E	Chemical, Biological, Radiological, Nuclear and Explosive
CBRNE	Chemical, Biological, Radiological, Nuclear and Explosives
CCTV	Closed Circuit Television
C-DSM Directive	Copyright in the Digital Single Market Directive
CE	Capillary Electrophoresis
CEO	Chief Executive Officer
CFC	Chlorinated Fluorocarbon
CFRA	Centre for Financial Research and Analysis

ChemCentre	The Chemistry Centre
CIP	Critical Infrastructure Protection
CJEU	Court of Justice of the European Union
CJPOA	Criminal Justice and Public Order Act
CJS	Criminal Justice System
CNN	Convolutional Neural Network
CoS	Centres of Specialization
COSHH	Control of Substances Hazardous to Heath
COVID-19	Coronavirus Disease 2019
CPS	Crown Prosecution Service
CRI	Crown Research Institute
CRM	Customer Relationship Management
CSAFE	Center for Statistics and Applications in Forensic Evidence
CSI	Crime Scene Investigator
DASA	Defence and Security Accelerator
DF	Digital Forensics
DL	Deep Learning
DMCA	Digital Millennium Copyright Act
DNA	Deoxyribonucleic Acid
DOI	Digital Object Identifier
DSA	Digital Services Act
DSTL	Defence Science and Technology Laboratory
EASST	European Association for the Study of Science and Technology
ECHR	European Convention of Human Rights
ECtHR	European Court of Human Rights
EEA	European Economic Area
EIC	Entrepreneurship and Innovation Centre
ENFSI	European Network of Forensic Science Institutes
ESDA	Electrostatic Detection Apparatus
ESR	Environmental Sciences and Research
EU	European Union
EVs	Electric Vehicles
EWCA	England and Wales Court of Appeal
EY	Ernst & Young, one of the big four multinational consulting companies
FCN	Forensic Capability Network
FDP	Forensic DNA Phenotyping
FFR	Forensic Face Recognition
FIGG	Forensic Investigative Genetic Genealogy
FINDS	Forensic Information Database Service
FMEA	Failure Modes and Effects Analysis
FMS	Forensic Management System
FORINT	Forensic Intelligence
FSAC	Forensic Science Advisory Council

FSP	Forensic Science Provider
FSR	Forensic Science Regulator
FSS	Forensic Science Service
FTA	Flinders Technology Associates
FTM	Forensic Technology Manufacturer
FVM	Fingermark Visualization Manual
GCMS	Gas Chromatography/Mass Spectrometry
GDPR	General Data Protection Regulation
GovCo	Government owned company
HFA	Human Face Analysis
HMICFRS	His Majesty's Inspectorate of Constabulary and Fire and Rescue Services
HOSDB	Home Office Scientific Development Branch
HU	Hungary
IAFIS	International Automatic Fingerprint Identification System
ID	Identification
IEC	International Electrotechnical Commission
INTERPOL	International Criminal Police Organization
IP	Intellectual Property
IPO	Initial Public Offering, the first time a company offers its shares at a stock exchange (in public trading)
IPR	Intellectual Property Rights
IR	Infrared
IRA	Irish Republican Army
IRL	Innovation Readiness Level
ISO	International Organization for Standardization
JLS	Joint Legislative Service
KCL	Kings College London
KPMG	Klynveld Peat Marwick Goerdeler Inc., one of the big four multinational consulting companies
KTH	Royal Institute of Technology, Sweden's largest technical university
KTN	Knowledge Transfer Network
KTP	Knowledge Transfer Partnership
LA-ICP-MS	Laser Ablation Inductively Coupled Plasma Mass Spectrometry
LGC	Laboratory of the Government Chemist
LOI	Location of Interest
LSU	Linear Sequential Unmasking
LSU-E	Linear Sequential Unmasking-Expanded
LU	Luxembourg
MA	Master of Arts
MIT	Massachusetts Institute of Technology
ML	Machine Learning
MO	Modus Operandi

MOD	Ministry of Defence
MP	Member of Parliament
MPDD	Missing Persons DNA Database
MPS	Metropolitan Police Service
MS-DOS	Microsoft Disc Operating System
MVP	Minimum Viable Product, the first version of a product which can be sold to customers
NAS	National Academy of Sciences
NAS Report	National Academies of Sciences Report
NASA	National Aeronautics and Space Administration
NDNAD	National DNA Database
NESTA	National Endowment for Science, Technology and the Arts
NFD	National Footwear Database
NGS	Next Generation Sequencing
NIJ	National Institute of Justice
NIST	National Institute of Standards and Technology
NPCC	National Police Chiefs Council
NPIA	National Policing Improvement Agency
NRC	National Research Council
OECD	Organization for Economic Co-operation and Development
OSAC	Organization of Scientific Area Committees
OSP	Online Service Provider
OSRD	Office of Scientific Research and Development
PCAST Report	President's Council of Advisors on Science and Technology Report
PCAST	President's Council of Advisors on Science and Technology
PCP	Pre-procurement is a procurement process phase, covering interactions with suppliers ahead of the issuing of an Invitation to Tender
PCR	Polymerase Chain Reaction
PDS	Police Digital Service
PEERS	A Horizon Europe-funded project delivering transformational change in the EU CBRN-E environment through standardization (https://peers-project.eu/)
PMI	Post-Mortem interval
PoFA	Protection of Freedoms Act
PSDB	Police Scientific Development Branch
PV	Photovoltaic
PwC	PricewaterhouseCoopers, one of the big four multinational consulting companies
QMS	Quality Management System
ROI	Return on investment
SANEs	Sexual Assault Nurse Examiners
SE	Sweden

SEL	Social Embeddness Level, new method that goes beyond Technical Readiness Level (TRL) and assesses the level of societal embeddedness. Developed by TNO
SFC	Székely Family & Co. Kft., a fully-privately owned independent, non-profit start-up studio, incubator and accelerator operating from Hungary across the EU
SGM	Second Generation Multiplex
SIG	Special Interest Group
SME	Small and Medium-sized Enterprises
SNP	Single Nucleotide Polymorphisms
SOP	Standard Operating Procedure
SPACs	Special Purpose Acquisition Companies
SRL	Società a responsabilità limitata, Limited Liability Company in Italian
STAR	Science, Technology Analysis and Research
STR	Short Tandem Repeat
SWOT	Strengths, Weaknesses, Opportunities, and Threats, a common risk assessment method (see more IEC31010:2019—Risk assessment techniques)
TAM	Total Available Market
TLOs	Technology Licensing Offices
TNO	Netherlands Organization for Applied Scientific Research
TRL	Technology Readiness Level
TTOs	Technology Transfer Offices
UAS	Universal Analysis Software
UK	United Kingdom
UKAS	UK Accreditation Service
UKRI	United Kingdom Research and Innovation
UNT	University of North Texas
US	United States
USD	United States Dollar
VLOSE	Very Large Online Search Engine
VMD	Vacuum Metal Deposition
WA	Western Australia
WP29	Article 29 Working Party
WWW	World Wide Web

Chapter 1
The Chicken and the Egg: Research and Innovation Within Forensic Science

Roberto S. P. King

Abstract The chicken and the egg causality dilemma, or chicken and egg paradox, is a longstanding idiom that stems from the observation that all chickens hatch from eggs and all chicken eggs are laid by chickens. It seeks to probe, in a metaphorical sense, situations that lack clarity in what should be considered the *cause* and what should be considered the *effect*. The very nature of the postulation depicts a process of infinite regress, whereby the consequence of one action must depend on the other, and vice versa. To that end, forensic science is widely recognised as a discipline that is fundamentally underpinned by research, upon which the end goal, or application, must be objectively substantiated. In the practical sense, the application of these forensic 'tools' are exploited through innovative solutions that typically take the form of hardware, software, physical techniques, chemical processes, etc. Accordingly, how are new product/process innovations developed in a discipline that is built on the foundations of scientific rigor? Does forensic research solely drive forensic innovation? Do the latest forensic innovations drive the next generation of forensic research? Or do the two co-exist in a symbiotic manner that serves to benefit the process as a whole?

1.1 Research and Innovation

Research is defined as *"the systematic investigation into the study of materials and sources in order to establish facts and reach new conclusions"* [1]. The process of research within forensic science has, like other disciplines, a fundamental emphasis on structured explorations into a defined subject matter(s) in order to understand the consequence of such actions and develop factual conclusions that serve to improve and increase our knowledge. Whilst remaining a relatively small contributor to the 'Life Sciences' sector as a whole, at the time of writing, there are over 50 international journals dedicated to publishing forensic science research articles [2], and, on an annual basis, an order of magnitude more forensic science conferences that are

R. S. P. King (✉)
Research and Development, foster+freeman, Vale Park, Evesham WR11 1TD, Worcestershire, UK
e-mail: drrobertoking@outlook.com

S. Francese and R. S. P. King (eds.), *Driving Forensic Innovation in the 21st Century*,
https://doi.org/10.1007/978-3-031-56556-4_1

focussed on the dissemination of such research conclusions. It is clear that suitable vehicles exist for the sharing of research outputs from forensic science, and such delivery mediums serve as an ideal opportunity for broader collaboration and iterative idea generation. For the most part, such disclosure opportunities are exploited mainly by academic research institutions and forensic practitioners who wish to share the findings of their work either for professional recognition and/or for the benefit it serves the forensic community as a whole. Less so is the involvement, either in person or via publications, of the forensic science technology manufacturer, who is oftentimes the segue between (proof-of) concept and practical exploitation, typically via productisation. Forensic technology manufacturers (FTMs) may regularly have a presence at forensic conferences that include an exhibition annexe, yet their involvement beyond showcasing their products either in the exhibit arena or during a workshop, is typically limited.

Innovation may be considered as "the creation, development and implementation of a new product, process or service, with the aim of improving efficiency, effectiveness or competitive advantage" [3]. Naturally, innovation, or the evolution of innovative offerings, is more plentiful during the embryonic stages of novel subject matter exploration, where new ground and new learnings are commonly encountered. Whilst innovation is often considered to be the fruit of commercial labour, and an opportunity for revenue generation, there exists a bounty of techniques, processes and methods utilised within forensic science that are, by the very definition, innovative. Methods that are used around the world, on a daily basis, where the primary goal is not necessarily to generate financial income, but to improve efficacy, efficiency and applicability of forensic science. Quite often, forensic practitioners must apply innovative thinking and methodology when dealing with unusual items of evidence and crime scenes. FTMs have naturally evolved over the last few decades, developing innovative technologies that serve to improve and expand the capabilities of forensic end users both in the laboratory and in field. For the most part, each manufacturer tends to specialise in one or two forensic 'value streams'—the evolutionary journey from concept to application by the customer. Other larger manufacturers provide a broader range of product offerings that usually have some degree of technical overlap (such as analytical characterisation devices): the likes of Thermo Fisher [4] and Agilent Technologies [5], for example, are recognised for their product portfolio that includes offerings suitable for forensic DNA, Mass Spectrometry, Raman and IR analysis. Manufacturers such as foster+freeman [6], on the other hand, are established as market leaders within the physical forensic sciences; that is in the search and investigation of physical evidence such as Questioned Documents, Fingerprints, Glass, Body Fluids, etc. Naturally, the broader the product portfolio, the more organisational resource required to sustain, develop and support the innovation reaching the marketplace.

1.2 The Research and Innovation Cycle

As illustrated in Fig. 1.1, the act of conducting research and developing innovation are harmonious in their association with technology development. As our knowledge and understanding of a subject matter broadens and develops, it begins to unlock technological enablers that can be built upon to yield a solution. This solution may take the form of a physical device, a piece of software, a process improvement, or one of many other innovative mediums that exist. Ultimately, in the industrial (commercial) setting, it is preferred that the resulting innovation(s) is *usually* monetised in order to directly accrue revenue. With increased revenue and profit generation, comes available cashflow that may be injected back into the business to further develop the research and development programmes that underpin the process [7–9].

Outputs from research within the industrial sector are arguably prioritised differently to those that may be encountered in academia or forensic practice. In the case of the latter, research conclusions are usually disseminated in order to increase awareness of operationally relevant material (the efficacy of traditional fingermark enhancement processes on a new substrate type, for example [10, 11]). Academic institutions, whilst also striving to influence operational undertakings through their work, commonly use their research outputs, which largely take the form of publications and conference presentations, to leverage their applicability for external funding and strengthen the overall impact and stature of the organisation in a highly competitive Higher Education landscape. As with all manufacturers, FTMs are no different in their intrinsic desire to drive revenue and grow the business. Naturally, the size, maturity and ownership structure of the FTM will dictate the specific metrics that must be achieved or maintained, but without revenue and profit generation, the business cannot exist or grow organically. Accordingly, the primary focus of an FTM is that of profitability in any innovation that they develop. The business, as a whole,

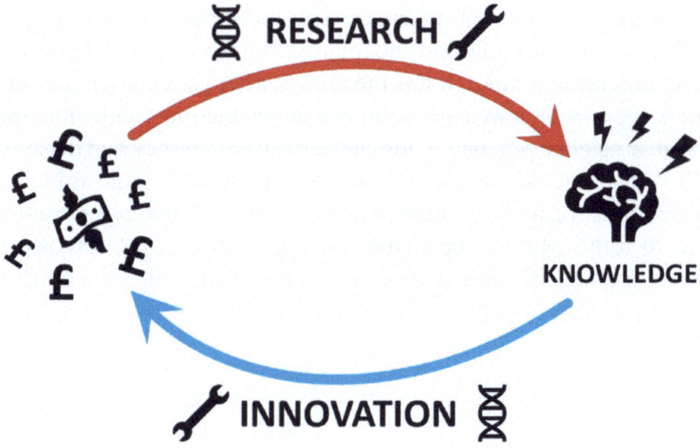

Fig. 1.1 The research and innovation cycle

must therefore work to develop product that offers a competitive edge and then seek to establish it within the market. Research outputs in the form of publications are, to an increasing extent, being recognised as important and powerful vehicles that can underpin commercially focussed ventures through provision of peer-reviewed, scientifically credible and transparent research manuscripts [12–16]. Understandably, the rigors associated with successful publication of research in peer-reviewed journals may allow FTMs to substantiate, to some degree, the credibility and viability of the product developments, whilst also facilitating informed evaluation of the work, and associated innovation, by the community that ultimately seeks to exploit it.

Whilst the benefits of peer-reviewed publications are understood by practitioner and manufacturer alike, it is often a resource limitation that hinders smaller FTMs from venturing down the peer-review journey. This, coupled with the relatively slow publication process (often months), render the prospect of manuscript compilation and submission an unfavoured activity within the commercial forensic sector. A compromise is often achieved through generation of 'white papers' or 'internal application notes' that serve to disseminate research findings via a manufacture-controlled process. Understandably, however, whilst research findings published in this way are of relevance to the forensic community as a whole, and may also be leveraged by end-users to support their technology procurement business case, the acceptance and implementation of such innovation is typically retarded given the perceived absence of independent review.

An additional road-blocker for the FTM in sharing their research and building their scientific pedigree can also stem from the negative perception of commercial participation within educational conferences. For some, the inclusion of FTM representatives within a conference agenda is construed as being too commercial, with undertones of an ulterior (sales) motive. Naturally, whilst there are commercial gains underpinning the very research being presented (and in fact it is primarily the commercial revenue itself that funds the research conducted), the researchers involved in the project(s) have a fundamental intrinsic motivation to share their findings and open-up discussion channels with the broader community. This reciprocity facilitates research evolution and relationship development between industry, academia and practitioner alike. It has the propensity to strengthen the fundamental building blocks upon which we can evolve our understandings and, more importantly perhaps, forensic science practice. Ultimately, the transparency and dissemination of scientifically robust forensic research should be supported through as many means as possible. There must be a representative demographic of research presented at such events, so as to fully appraise the shape and capabilities of the forensic landscape and strengthen opportunities for cross-functional engagement and collaboration.

1.3 Understanding the 'Customer'

The development of new forensic technologies has changed significantly over the last half century [17]. During the embryonic phases of the forensic science discipline, there existed an almost *carte blanche* of capabilities waiting to be developed that were rationalised and brought to life as the significance and importance of our forensic understandings matured. The chemical composition of a latent fingermark, for example, gave way to decades of research into fingermark enhancement reagents. The discovery of genetic fingerprinting and DNA profiling resulted in a paradigm shift across the forensic science research landscape and the race to develop new techniques and technologies to exploit the forensic capability that DNA provided, began. As the outputs of such research endeavours began to be utilised in an emerging discipline, and the resulting impact appreciated, focus naturally centred on process refinement and optimisation of these 'core enablers', rather than a quest for the next 'big thing'.

As such, some of the early FTMs were able to monopolise new process enabling innovation, by productising what would otherwise have remained a laboratory research commodity. Concurrently, these emerging manufacturers helped shape the forensic capabilities of the time. They began broadening their research ventures as a function of the emerging needs of the forensic community and their own appreciation of how technology building blocks could be assembled in a manner to provide new innovation in an otherwise sparse marketplace.

As a function of time, such technologies have naturally developed in a way that serves to automate complex or time-consuming processes and provide effective turn-key solutions. The focus has, to a large extent, been dominated by easing the labour burden on the end user and, in turn, helping to reduce evidence backlogs.

Forensic science itself, and the innovations it utilises, harnesses concepts, processes, technologies and components from wider disciplines, in a manner that is exploited for forensic application. As other more mainstream market sectors develop, so too does the potential for forensic exploitation. To that end, the transformation of forensic technologies in recent years has focussed heavily on deployable instrumentation; products that provide the crime scene examiner with laboratory capabilities. The amalgamation of forensic light sources with high end imaging technology is one such advancement that has recently begun to improve efficiency at the crime scene and help triage evidence in situ, rather than mandating it be analysed back in the laboratory [6]. The importance of arming crime scene investigators (CSIs) with previously considered laboratory technologies must not be downplayed; ensuring both parties have similar capabilities is paramount in maximising evidence recovery and detecting more evidence. An analogous example can be seen in the area of toxicology, where portable analytical devices, such as Raman Spectrometers, are now readily available and have resolving power that is suitably fit-for-purpose in the quest to identify compounds of interest, in field [18, 19].

Despite the breadth of technological offerings at the disposal of the FTM, the art of forensic innovation relies on a journey that is catalysed by a 'problem'. The 'problem' may exist in many forms: from a new class of evidence that requires better detection methods, to the deployment of a technique in an outdoor environment. The 'problem' may present itself to different stakeholders, in different ways:

- time saving
- cost saving
- regulatory compliance
- automation
- fatigue avoidance
- repeatability
- reliability
- functional suitability
- others.

It is also important to consider that quite often, the end users of the technology may not recognise that a problem exists. The daily processes that occur across forensic science are well engrained within the end users. Their familiarity and reliability of such methods may, undoubtedly, constrain their exploration of improved and/or alternative approaches. They may be unaware of synergistic technologies that have the potential to create innovative step-changes within their own discipline and, ultimately, there may even be intrinsic resistance to the acceptance of innovation, should the alternative(s) be perceived to jeopardise the importance of the roles of the individuals concerned.

In contrast, as a discreet entity, the FTM may not necessarily be aware of existing challenges or 'problems' facing their existing/potential end users. Whilst their daily operational focus is that of engineering, manufacture, marketing and sales, the research and product development agenda must be managed in a way that drives continued growth and innovation. It is typical that FTM research and development functions constantly review technology advances in other areas that may be exploited within their own. In essence, it may be considered that the FTM has the 'answers', but are looking for the 'problems', and the forensic practitioner has the 'problem', but is looking for the 'answer'.

Accordingly, it is imperative for the manufacturer to adopt a customer-centric approach to ensure that the correct innovations are developed and delivered in a timely manner and that they fundamentally address the problem(s) at hand. The customers' challenges must be clearly identified (the ***problem***) and solutions (the ***answer***) considered as a function of what is a mandatory requirement (the ***need***) and what may be preferred (the ***want***). The priority with any innovative development is that the offering is functionally capable; it is fit-for-purpose and solves the problem it was designed to. The inclusion of additional features and capabilities, whilst desirable, should not detract or compromise the primary function of the technology. This is especially true for first generation innovations, where the immediate impact should be that of functional capacity, with feature rich offerings typically emerging as iterations of the innovation develop with time.

The archetypical definition of a customer is that of a person or organisation that buys goods or services from an organisation [20]. It is widely construed as the end user; the person who actually uses the product that is purchased. As such, in its simplest form, a customer-centric approach to forensic product innovation would concern itself solely around the use case, or application, that the practitioner is to conduct. Whilst such functionality must of course be at the very heart of any product development, the FTM must also consider other stakeholders as 'customers' to the products, or services, that they develop. To bring a product to market, all facets of the business must be involved in defining the requirement specifications that the product must possess, so that the implementation and execution of technology market introduction is optimised. The product must be designed with many considerations in mind, some of which are entirely independent of the product use case:

- what are the market differentiators for the product?
- what will the sales strategy look like?
- what costing model will be applied?
- how might the forensic procurement process impact on the commercial strategy?
- how will the product be supported in field?
- are there market specific variations that need developing?
- what marketing methods will be employed?
- how will the product be demonstrated?
- what languages must be supported?
- what regulatory governance should be supported?
- how will the supply chain be supported?
- has design-for-manufacture been considered?
- what application studies are required?
- what training will be required (sales, customer support, applications, service, forensic end user)?
- what supporting documentation is required?

Whilst the list above is by no means exhaustive, it does serve to highlight the plethora of factors, and decision-making influences, that must be traversed in order to develop an effective and comprehensive forensic technology innovation in the modern era and, importantly, one that stands the best chance of being widely adopted and relied upon by the forensic end user.

1.4 Collaborative Engagement

Developing a desirable innovation for the forensic laboratory, or crime scene, should not be perceived as a process that is conducted, in isolation, by an FTM (***closed innovation***). Given the broader understanding of who the customer of the product is, the development cycle benefits significantly from a comprehensive stakeholder input to ensure the outputs are aligned to the required need(s) and use case(s). Naturally, the size of the FTM will dictate the resource allocation that is available to develop ideas and concepts internally. Larger organisations may have sufficient personnel to explore such endeavours in detail, drawing on external input at key product design

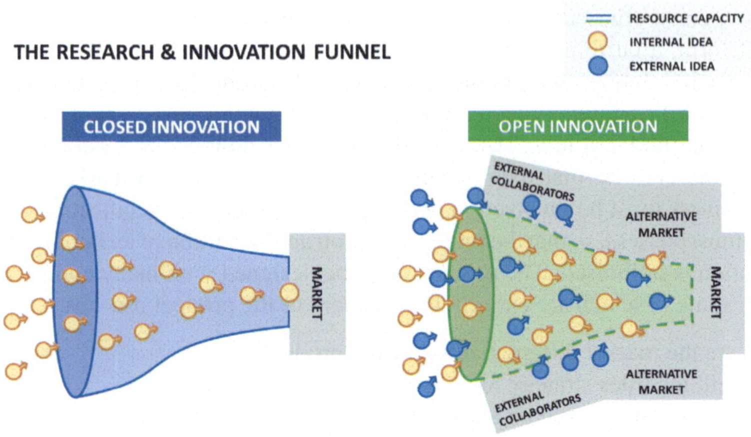

Fig. 1.2 Open and closed innovation funnels

phases where the 'voice of the customer' is critical. Smaller organisations may work more closely with external stakeholders (***open innovation***) in order to bolster their resource and knowledge pool and optimise the efficiency of their innovation process. In essence, both approaches are capable of affording noteworthy innovations, but the input of external stakeholders remains critical to effective product development and market acceptance. It ensures the technology is fit-for-purpose and has been executed with the use-case in mind. The distinction between open and closed innovation workflows, as illustrated in Fig. 1.2, is governed by the methods in which innovation is created.

The latter demands innovation be generated and controlled within the confines of the organisation, whereas and open innovation approach draws more heavily on external stakeholder knowledge and input to drive and support the innovation cycle [21–23].

The demands and benefits of each mode of action differ significantly, with closed innovation requiring the greatest minds of the discipline to be employed by the FTM. It adds significant burden (and overhead) to the manufacturer to ensure its research and development team has all the necessary skillsets and is capable of establishing itself as an industry 'thought-leader', whereby the new ideas and technology that are developed are wholly created, developed, implemented and brought to market by the FTM. The implementation of this approach can often be seen in niche technology sectors, such as forensic science, where unique innovation gives the manufacturer incontrovertible advantages over its competitors. In such instances, the FTM strives to become synonymous with their 'first-to-market' technology and can leverage that impact to substantiate the brand and develop market leadership [24–26]. Organisations that operate under closed innovation boundaries often prefer the control and exclusivity of Intellectual Property (IP) ownership, utilising protective means such as patents, publications and copyrights to deter competitors from stealing product ideas and know-how. Of course, such IP protection is not infallible, and in a discipline where the innovative exploitation of a range of complementary technologies is central to the application, and therefore harder to protect, the costs involved in developing an IP portfolio need to be balanced against the benefits they may be perceived to afford (tax relief, innovation protection, etc.).

Open innovation enables the FTM to broaden its idea generation potential through the strategic utilisation of the wider forensic community. It involves engaging with key opinion leaders and external bodies in an effort to improve the impact of the innovation itself. This may necessitate the collaboration with end users, suppliers, academia, governing bodies and sales partners to maximise the effectiveness of the innovation. Collaborative networking in this way requires extremely well managed project oversight. It is often more challenging to work to efficient timelines, given multiple contributors will likely be involved at any stage of the process. Ultimately, however, the goal here is to develop the very best technology available, by ensuring the very best resources are called upon as and when required. There is much less reliance on the skills and knowledge necessarily residing within the FTM itself. In the United Kingdom (UK), for example, schemes such as the Knowledge Transfer Partnership (KTP), governed by Innovate UK [27], exist to link forward-thinking businesses with the UK's leading academic experts to deliver innovation projects led by inspired graduates. In connecting industry with academia, both organisations benefit greatly in harnessing the complimentary skills and resources that the other possess, in turn delivering impactful innovation as a function of an open and collaborative innovation journey.

Whilst the modes to innovation will vary between FTMs and even on a project-by-project basis, there are key external innovation stakeholders that must be included during the development cycle if the resulting technology is to be effective welcomed. There is perhaps no one more important to garner feedback from than the intended end user (in this case, the forensic practitioner), after all, these are the people that will be utilising the technology on the front-line and have more experience in product application than the FTMs themselves. In addition, an FTM must consider their entire global marketplace and the region-specific needs that are regularly encountered. Product development cannot simply focus on home market requirements, without understanding the potential impact and implementation in other territories, where skillsets, knowledge, challenges, experience, and legislation are likely to be very different and may demand alternative approaches to the way the innovation is delivered.

The relationships an FTM develops with its (potential) end user base is critical to its success not only in innovation development, but in becoming a reliable and dependable source of technology within an ever increasingly competitive forensic sector. The FTM should attempt to engage with practitioners at key touchpoints along the innovation journey in an attempt to understand whether the technology concept is warranted and understood, and how it will likely fit in to, or change, the existing workflows in place. There is, of course, no obligation for end users to engage in such technology developments with an FTM, but in a discipline that strives for scientific excellence and ensuring justice prevails, the community as a whole are extremely receptive to engagement and discussion. Understandably, however, a factor that is often encountered is the requirement for practitioners to remain impartial as part of their tenure within their organisation—that is, not to give 'preferential' advice, guidance or input to a particular commercial entity over another. As such, it can oftentimes be difficult to dive deeply into concept exploration and product development feedback and improvement; the latter typically being the greatest road-blocker between the FTM and practitioner as it is these very suggestions and improvements that are central to iterative product advancements. Undoubtedly, if innovation is to be effective, timely and impactful, barriers between end users and manufacturer need to be navigated in a manner that ensures both parties see tangible benefits. Ultimately, the manufacturer wishes to develop a concept and launch it within the forensic marketplace, and the forensic end user strives to improve their practice and exploit, where suitable, the latest innovations. A certain symbiosis exists as a function of necessity, but that relationship could arguably be deeper rooted through concerted collaborative endeavours that would better arm both parties with the tools and foresight required to develop wholly fit-for-purpose technology, at the right time, with the end user application at the very heart of the product.

1.5 The Research and Innovation Funnel

An FTM must ensure that they possess a balanced product portfolio so that it is well positioned to take advantage of its current and future market growth opportunities. This strategic product roadmap typically seeks to maintain an even combination of new, growing, and mature product offerings. Product oversight using business tools such as the Boston Consulting Group (BCG) Matrix, shown in Fig. 1.3, allow an organisation to review its portfolio and understand where opportunities for improvement exist and how to maximise revenue generation [28, 29].

A balanced portfolio would ideally strive to have products within all categories (except for ***'dogs'***!), so that the ***'cash cows'*** can provide investment funds for the ***'stars'***, which in turn ensure the future success of the business and help turn the ***'question marks'*** into stars. The FTM must seek to hold, build, harvest and divest as a function of their existing portfolio and consider how their research activities are positioned to provide them with market advantage and growth as a function of time.

The research and innovation funnel is a simple concept in which an FTM can assess and review a continuous stream of ideas to ensure those that will likely be most effective and rewarding are developed further, prototyped and ultimately launched as a product. As its name suggests, this process is fed with multiple inputs (ideas) that result in comparatively few outputs (products). As such, it is critically important to feed the funnel with ideas, opportunities, applications, collaborations, etc., so that the organisation has solid foundations upon which to develop its future (forensic) innovation pipeline. A narrow focus at the idea stage, will ultimately result in limitations to innovative scope. Conversely, an over-populated idea pool requires significant

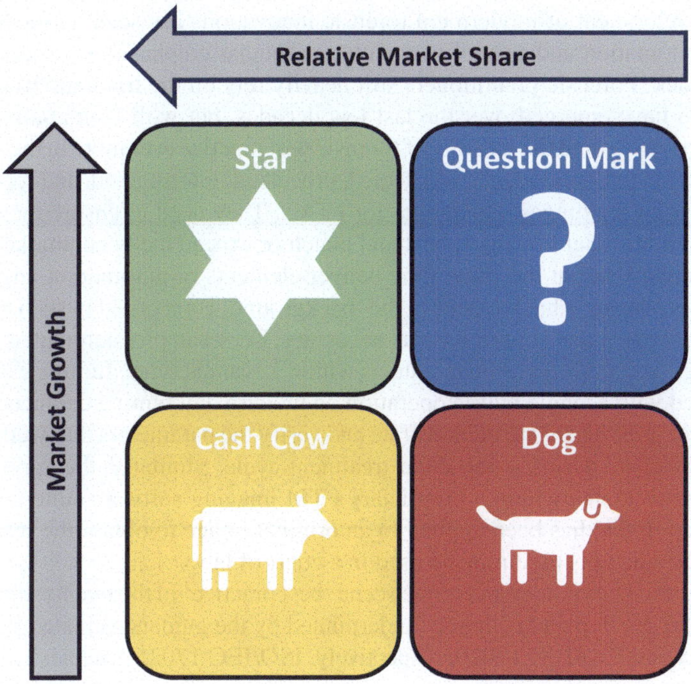

Fig. 1.3 The Boston Consulting Group matrix

resource to evaluate and triage, whilst also creating the potential to dilute impact and scope of chosen product developments.

Idea generation requires input from individuals and functional groups right across an FTMs organisation. It also necessitates inputs, either directly or indirectly, from external stakeholders. The importance of a balanced product portfolio is supported by the importance of a balanced research portfolio. They rely on each other to drive iterative products (new model variants, for example), evolutionary products (next-generation derivatives already present market innovations) and revolutionary products (first of a kind, step-change technology). For this reason, the FTM research roadmap must include a healthy mix of both evolutionary research ideas that can build on existing technology already known to the discipline and within the product arsenal of the manufacturer, and blue-sky concepts that will hopefully move forward to be the stars of the future. The research and development teams must work in unison to develop these ideas and explore them comprehensively from both a feasibility and scientific credibility perspective, given the nature of the target end user. They must also work collaboratively with the commercial arm of the business to understand the product positioning and marketing strategies that will be implemented and, as a consequence of this business alignment, determine the viability and implementation of the product idea.

The development of modern era forensic innovations has seen its focus migrate towards automation and ease of use, with a particular emphasis on process control and feedback. Forensic practitioners still heavily rely on the tried and trusted techniques that have emerged over the last few decades, but with continually inflating evidence backlogs and the scrutiny of forensic best practice ever more in the spotlight, improvements to how evidence is detected, processed, interrogated, and reported has become one of the biggest challenges for FTMs. They need to ensure their modern technologies are scientifically robust and match or exceed the benchmarked state of the art standard, but at the same time deliver elements of automation and ease-of-use, whilst ensuring what happens in the 'background' is recorded in such a way that it can be accessed and reported on as necessary. For example, automated evidence processing, such as the treatment of items within a cyanoacrylate fuming cabinet, can be executed with a single button operation on modern day fuming cabinets [26], but the end user must be able to demonstrate and verify the parameters that were effected by the instrument across a particular treatment cycle. Similarly, the application of image enhancements within a proprietary FTM imaging software suite must detail every function that has been applied to an original image to obtain the result that it subsequently outputs (and may be used in a court of law).

The rigors of laboratory and crime scene 'best practice' in the twenty-first century continues to develop and is largely underpinned by the guidance created in the ISO/IEC 17025 and ISO/IEC 17020, respectively. ISO/IEC 17025 'enables laboratories to demonstrate that they operate competently and generate valid results [30].' This standard is intended to specify the operational requirements for the competence, impartiality and consistency of the laboratory and is applicable to all organisations (falling under, or requiring, the ISO requirements) that conduct laboratory activities. In a relevant capacity, ISO/IEC 17020 specifies the 'requirements for the competence of bodies performing inspection and for the impartiality and consistency of their inspection activities.' This standard is designed to ensure in-field conformity is achieved across a range of 'inspection bodies', which, from a forensic science perspective, relates primarily to crime-scene examination (or anything outside of the laboratory environment). As these standards have evolved over recent decades, not only has the practitioner had to adapt and improve the integrity and transparency of their standard operating procedures, but so too have FTMs had to develop and enhance their technology offerings and capabilities to better align with new and best practices mandated by their end users.

Whilst it is often de facto to consider forensic innovation as a tangible piece of hardware (a new instrument, for example) the effects of ISO/IEC 17025 and ISO/IEC 17020 from an FTM perspective has required the implementation of sophisticated diagnostics and the provision of substantial amounts of data to the end user. As we strive for more automation and more capacity in the technologies we utilise, the forensic regulator understandably requires documentable confirmation that equipment/process is performing as intended (correctly). How these confirmatory checks are implemented in a product will vary from FTM to FTM and from product to product, but ultimately it must be demonstrated that technologies, whether it be physical equipment or a particular technique that is utilised, are competent, impartial, and consistent [16]. Research and development teams must develop ways to not only test and corroborate the functional outputs of their innovations, but they are encouraged to make such testing as simple as possible for their customers also.

1.6 Selling the Product—Tools for Success

The old adage that 'a good product sells itself' is (largely) incorrect, especially when it comes to the discipline of forensic science. First and foremost, there is a fundamental difference between selling products to a mass consumer market, where the customer ***wants*** the latest and greatest innovations, and a niche market that must justify the ***need*** for technology. Forensic science laboratories are, for the most part, funded through public sector money and operate under budgetary governance on a regional or national level. The allocation of funds is typically determined on a case by case, and year by year, basis, with capital equipment requests usually requiring a supportive business case to be considered. In essence, there must be a demonstratable need for new equipment to be purchased, which can take many forms, such as cost-savings, reliability, product replacement cycles, new capabilities, regulatory adherence, etc. It is not simply a case of developing a new product, marketing it and expecting it to sell. If they are to be successful, the FTM must work effectively in positioning the product in a market sector that has used the same, or similar, techniques and technologies for many years. Of course, without concerted marketing efforts, even the best products in the world will fail to get traction, as few will be aware of them. Ultimately, great products that are marketed well, will get attention, but they will not automatically sell themselves.

Forensic scientists around the world have extremely effective tools within their comprehensive arsenals, that enable them to detect more evidence than ever before. The introduction of a new product, or tool, that will be 'unknown' to the target end user, will naturally be met with interest and trepidation from a practitioner perspective. *How might this product affect their working life? What validation work will be required to utilise the product? How does it compare with reliable and existing methods?* It is perhaps easier, on an individual level, to avoid purchasing new technology until there is a wider acceptance of the product across the marketplace. In fact, having key reference sites to support a procurement application may also be pivotal in unlocking budget for such purchases. Ironically, we find ourselves back again at the chicken and egg paradox, with innovation adoption being limited by innovation adoptees, and vice versa. Consequently, it often falls to the so-called '***early adopters***' to evaluate an innovation and put it into operation. These organisations are widely recognised as progressive thought-leaders within the forensic community and have the resource base, and budgets, to consider and explore new product offerings as a function of their continuous improvement programmes.

Customer Relationship Management (CRM) [31] plays an important role in helping transition new innovation into the forensic community. The FTM must work closely with their key references to prove out the technology and critically appraise its capabilities (and shortcomings). To be effective, the evaluation exercises must be conducted in a transparent and independent manner, allowing the conclusions to be more widely accepted across the forensic community. In practice, this will predominantly be effected through product demonstrations and end user trials, upon which the FTM can expect the first purchases of its technology to be made. Once product is installed within the forensic market, its journey through practitioner validation can begin (this will vary in breadth and necessity on a region-by-region basis) and its use in active casework then becomes key in unlocking further sales. Once an innovation can be seen to be making an impact in field, so the interest and confidence in the technology increases.

Different technological offerings have differing market adoption rates that are largely influenced by the nature of the product application and how far detached from the 'norm' a solution is perceived to be. Typically, evolutionary innovations are more readily understood, and their core building blocks likely to have been previously exploited in some form. As such, it is easier for the customer to relate to the innovation and consider its added value over their existing capabilities. They will more readily be able to appreciate the integration of the new product and, as such, perceive less 'risk' in seeking to adopt it. The learning curve will likely be shallower and the business case easier to build. In contrast, innovation that challenges the *status quo* will almost certainly have to negotiate many more barriers to adoption, as practitioners seek to ensure technology efficacy is robust and the confidence in product exploitation can be substantiated.

Blue-sky forensic research, which often leads to innovation step-changes of this nature, is, as such, considered higher risk, but higher reward, given the paradigm shift it can impart on the discipline, balanced with the resistance of adoption it is likely to encounter. It becomes ever more necessary to demonstrate the credibility and validity of such innovation as comprehensively as possible, so that, amongst other things, less ambiguity is faced by the targeted end users. Moreover, this so-called developmental validation package (see also Chap. 11) is largely more attractive to the forensic practitioner as it provides them with the foundations upon which to fully validate the innovation and use it with indignation. Undoubtedly, however, validation exercises conducted exclusively by an FTM may lack the regulatory rigor or have the perceived transparency that forensic practitioners require. This seeming oxymoronicity between 'commercial' and 'science' (or, '*making money*' and '*knowledge with testable explanation*') has, for a long time, imposed significant barriers between FTM innovation and practitioner adoption. The FTM must demonstrate the capability of the innovation to entice the practitioner. The practitioner must prove the benefit and necessity for an innovation in order to adopt it. To that end, whilst the required validation exercises will vary, the associated costs and resource requirements are universally acknowledged. End users wishing to (or needing to, depending on their organisations requirements) fully validate an innovation independently of any FTM validation package, must take on the burden of responsibility for the entire validation exercise. Of course, this is easily facilitated with unrestricted use of the innovation in question, but given the very nature of the exercise at hand (which would typically precede the technology procurement itself), such opportunities are not always feasible and, again, talks to the metaphoric chicken and egg dilemma.

Whilst the end user will always be the party that decides when and how an innovation will be used, the FTM must seek to deliver a validation package that, to the best of its ability, provides evidence as to the efficacy and capability of its innovation. Details of these product positioning exercises and research programmes should naturally support any conclusions and inferences that are made, so that prospective end users can easily verify the outputs and/or further embellish them to fit more closely with their operational workflows. The transition from FTM output to practitioner exploitation, may be better facilitated with greater cohesion and dialogue between organisations in a manner that constructively allows FTM validation packages to be widely accepted and developed with the end user requirements in mind. In this way, it may become possible to increase the rate of (blue-sky) technology adoption within forensic science, whilst also optimising the collective resource available, which will in turn recognise the value of the innovation as a function of the benefits it brings to the fight against crime.

From a commercial perspective, the innovation and its associated validation package are no longer all that a manufacturer must consider when strategising market launch activities. Whilst feature laden technologies are starting to become the 'norm', and end users are inherently expecting more and more capability from any new device, the ability to help and support customers through their decision-making journey can be a key differentiator for the FTM. Here, experience (around the product, the application, the market, the procurement channels, etc.) and customer engagement, are key tools for commercial success. There is little point in developing a fantastic new technology, without the ability to qualify its worth to end users through strong positioning statements and a thorough understanding of what the customer needs. By listening to the market's pain points and realising how an innovation can create value, the FTM must then be able to show how these issues can be resolved with the technology solution they are presenting.

Naturally, the marketing of a product is vitally important so that people are at least made aware of the latest developments within the market sector. Marketing strategies will vary from company to company (and such discussion is largely beyond the scope of this chapter) but the key deliverables throughout any campaign is to present the value of the innovation to the customer(s) in a coherent manner and allow them to appreciate the benefits such a technology will bring to them and/or their organisation. The easier this message can be communicated, and ultimately digested, the more likely it is to pique the interest of the community. The more comprehensive and considered the innovation package, the simpler the perception of integration and adoption by the end user.

1.7 Technology Adoption and Cycles

Technology introduction and uptake should be considered to follow an adoption cycle that is typically exemplified by that shown Fig. 1.4.

Here, the early market activity must focus on exploitation and feedback from Key Opinion Leaders (or technology enthusiasts) in order to gain market traction and provide visionaries a step-change to their existing state of the art. Within forensic science, technology enthusiasts around the world often have very different challenges that are prioritised in very different ways. As such, it is essential that FTMs can understand their user-base so that market-driven evaluations and feedback are focussed around the appropriate key influencers. There is little point, for example, in a fingerprint department that primarily processes porous evidence types, being asked to evaluate and critique a novel technique that is fundamentally geared towards non-porous exhibits. Whilst this early market phase usually results in conservative product sales, its importance cannot be underestimated. It is essential for the forensic community to see new technology being exploited by organisations that are held in high regard and who can provide transparency and impartiality as to the value of such a commodity. The technology enthusiast adoption timeframe will vary from product to product and FTM to FTM, but it is not unusual to expect the majority of Year 1 (first twelve month following market launch) to be consumed by such activities.

Arguably, the transition from early market to mainstream market, provides one of the greatest challenges with technology adoption. There exists a natural gap, or chasm, that must be carefully traversed in order to broaden the technology user-base from the few, to the many. This chasm has the potential to engulf technological offerings that do not meet market expectations, whether that be through form, function, cost, or operational centricity. Within the (forensic) sciences, early market operational successes have the ability to provide substance to the value proposition underpinning a new product offering. This initial phase of market roll-out often sees the publication of initial research/case-study papers that can serve to support, or

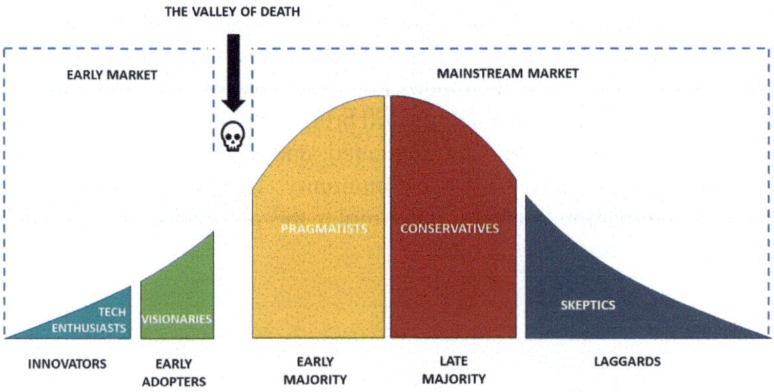

Fig. 1.4 Crossing the valley of death—the forensic technology adoption cycle

not, the adoption of the technology. With satisfactory 'buy-in' achieved, the wider mass-market interest rises, as do sales volumes and market share. The pragmatists have been able to appraise the early market feedback, acquire budget approval for purchase and obtain the technology with a 'de-risked' business case. In turn, as the mainstream market size begins to grow, and the technology starts to be considered as a 'must-have' asset, those end-users that have been more reserved since market launch (whether that be due to budget constraints, or for other reasons), begin to adopt the technology and utilise it effectively.

The early and late majority stakeholders constitute the significant majority of the mainstream and total market value. Naturally, their adoption proceeds the innovators and early adopters, whose benefit to the technology adoption cycle is predominantly one of technology acceptance and validation. With this assurance in place, the majority stakeholders may more readily, and with more confidence, seek to realise the technology offering at hand. Of course, there will always be users who decide to accept the technology much later down the adoption cycle. This group of stakeholders may be much more resource and budget limited, have a narrow operational remit and/or be intrinsically more circumspect of innovative developments within their sector. Indirectly, it becomes the role of the early and late majority users to instil the confidence in this group of individuals to accept, and ultimately benefit from, the technology being offered. For this group of stakeholders, the resistance to change is often the greatest across the entire user community, with their longstanding methods and approaches considered adequate. As a function of time and wider market acceptance and exploitation, the technology at hand becomes so impactful that the laggards openly accept its benefits and seek to exploit.

It is typical for new product introduction to reach peak market sales within years 3–5 following launch [32, 33]. After this time, sales volumes plateau and ultimately start to decline. As such, it is part of the new product development roadmap to ensure next generation product iterations are timed in accordance with such cycles. For example, there is little point launching a second-generation variant of a product within a year or so of the initial product launch. Market feedback and intelligence, used to iterate product development, takes significant time to acquire and, ultimately, benefits most from a broad user-base (which itself takes time to establish). A second-generation technology is therefore most effectively timed towards the end of this five-year cycle.

1.8 Measuring Success

The measurement of success for forensic science innovation is a metric that in many respects is difficult to quantify. From a practitioner perspective, success is largely attributed to the ability to use the technology in the desired manner and obtain the outputs envisaged. This will vary from technology to technology, but ultimately success can be captured as meeting the expectations of the stakeholders.

From a manufacturer's perspective, however, the success of new technology is ultimately measured through product sales and revenue. More successful products will sell in greater volumes. The operational successes discussed above, catalyse and accelerate the commercial revenue generation and success. Of course, FTMs hold relationships with their customers in high regard and ensuring the customer satisfaction remains high is crucially important. Additionally, it is common that most FTMs obtain significant intrinsic emotional reward from hearing of operational success stories that have been made possible by their technologies. Whilst the commercial benefits cannot be ignored, the sense of achievement and pride is something that resonates deeply across the forensic science community, and this includes the people at the very heart of innovation development.

1.9 Conclusion

Undoubtedly, the relationship between research and innovation within forensic science is a complex one. The challenges that must be addressed as part of the journey towards progressive impact are multi-faceted and, oftentimes, not controlled by any one stakeholder. From a manufacturer perspective, the ultimate goal is to create innovation that is market-leading and helps drive turnover. As a consequence of commercial reward, funds are secured to help further drive research and development, and the cycle continues. Naturally, FTMs must work closely with their technology consumers to appreciate the challenges and opportunities that exist in a highly regulated, often intransigent, discipline, where transparency and impartiality takes precedence.

For the customer, whether that be the technology end user or one of the many other innovation stakeholders, research and innovation must provide a tangible benefit upon which its business case may be substantiated. There must exist a true need, based upon a qualifiable (and oftentimes quantifiable) value. Research endeavours are unlikely to be driven by commercial factors but are almost certainly related to operational challenges of relevance. For the practitioner, the dissemination of research outputs ultimately serves to benefit the forensic community by broadening its knowledgebase and assisting in the quest for justice. For the manufacturer, however, whilst the sharing of research outputs may be fraught with risk, it serves a vital role in providing credibility and scientific rigor towards its innovation portfolio.

References

1. Oxford English Dictionary. (2010). *Research*. https://www.oed.com/dictionary/research_n1?tab=factsheet#25922908. Accessed November 20, 2023.
2. See for example: https://www.omicsonline.org/forensic-science-journals-conferences-list.php. Accessed November 20, 2023.
3. Oxford English Dictionary. (2010). *Innovation*. https://www.oed.com/dictionary/innovation_n?tab=factsheet#500709. Accessed November 20, 2023.

4. A general overview of the Thermo Fisher product portfolio may be accessed *via* the company homepage. https://www.thermofisher.com/uk/en/home.html. Accessed November 20, 2023.
5. A general overview of the Agilent Technologies product portfolio may be accessed *via* the company homepage: https://www.agilent.com/. Accessed November 20, 2023.
6. A general overview of the foster+freeman product portfolio may be accessed *via* the company homepage: https://fosterfreeman.com/. Accessed November 20, 2023.
7. Salehi, F., & Yaghtin, A. (2015). Action research innovation cycle: Lean thinking as a transformational system. *Procedia – Social and Behavioral Sciences, 181*, 293–302.
8. Yoav, K., & Shchori-Bachrach, N. (1973). The process of an innovation cycle. *American Journal of Agricultural Economics, 55*(1), 28–37.
9. Schoen, J., Mason, T. W., Kline, W. A., & Bunch, R. M. (2005). The innovation cycle: A new model and case study for the invention to innovation process. *Engineering Management Journal, 17*(3), 3–10.
10. Downham, R. P., Brewer, E. R., King, R. S. P., Luscombe, A. M., & Sears, V. G. (2017). Fingermark visualisation on uncirculated £5 (Bank of England) polymer notes: Initial process comparison studies. *Forensic Science International, 275*, 30–43.
11. Downham, R. P., Brewer, E. R., King, R. S. P., & Sears, V. G. (2018). Sequential processing strategies for fingermark visualisation on uncirculated £10 (Bank of England) polymer banknotes. *Forensic Science International, 288*, 140–158.
12. King, R. S. P., Hallett, P. M., & Foster, D. (2016). NIR-NIR fluorescence: A new genre of fingermark visualisation techniques. *Forensic Science International, 262*, e28–e33.
13. King, R. S. P., Davis, L. W. L., & Skros, D. A. (2018). The use of longwave reflected UV imaging for the enhancement of cyanoacrylate developed fingermarks: A simple, safe and effective imaging tool. *Forensic Science International, 289*, 329–336.
14. Brewer, E. R. (2020). Visualization of latent fingermark detail on fired handgun casings using forensic VMD. *Journal of Forensic Identification, 70*(3), 323–345.
15. King, R. S. P., Hallett, P. M., & Foster, D. (2015). Seeing into the infrared: A novel IR fluorescent fingerprint powder. *Forensic Science International, 249*, e21–e26.
16. King, R. S. P., McNash, B., & Wilson, R. (2023). The laboratory perspective: Confirming the integrity of fingermark enhancement reagents. *Science & Justice, 63*(6), 755–762.
17. Ramotowski, R. (Ed.). (2012). *Lee and Gaensslen's advances in fingerprint technology*. CRC Press.
18. Santos, L. P., Nascimento, M. H., Barros, I. H., Santos, N. A., Lacerda, V., Jr., Filgueiras, P. R., & Romão, W. (2022). Portable Raman spectroscopy applied to the study of drugs of abuse. *Journal of Forensic Sciences, 67*(4), 1399–1416.
19. Mojica, E. R., & Dai, Z. (2022). New Raman spectroscopic methods' application in forensic science. *Talanta Open, 6*, 100124.
20. Oxford English Dictionary. (2010). Research. https://www.oed.com/search/dictionary/?scope=Entries&q=customer. Accessed November 22, 2023.
21. Herzog, P., & Leker, J. (2010). Open and closed innovation—different innovation cultures for different strategies. *International Journal of Technology Management, 52*(3/4), 322–343.
22. Almirall, E., & Casadesus-Masanell, R. (2010). Open versus closed innovation: A model of discovery and divergence. *Academy of Management Review, 35*(1), 27–47.
23. Herzog, P. (2009). *Open and closed innovation: Different cultures for different strategies*. Springer.
24. Electrostatic Detection Apparatus (ESDA). *foster+freeman*. https://fosterfreeman.com/esda/. Accessed November 22, 2023.
25. Video Spectral Comparator (VSC). *foster+freeman*. https://fosterfreeman.com/questioned-document-examination/#workstations. Accessed November 22, 2023.
26. Cyanoacrylate Fuming Cabinet (MVC). *foster+freeman*. [https://fosterfreeman.com/fingerprint-evidence/#fuming-treatment-enhancement. Accessed November 22, 2023.
27. Knowledge Transfer Partnership (KTP). *Innovate UK*. https://www.ktp-uk.org/. Accessed November 22, 2023.

28. Mohajan, H. (2017). An analysis on BCG growth sharing matrix. *Noble International Journal of Business and Management Research, 2*(1), 1–6.
29. Boston Consulting Group (BCG). https://www.bcg.com/about/overview/our-history/growth-share-matrix. Accessed November 22, 2023.
30. Doyle, S. (2020). A review of the current quality standards framework supporting forensic science: Risks and opportunities. *Interdisciplinary Reviews: Forensic Science, 2*(3), e1365.
31. Kumar, V., & Reinartz, W. (2018). *Customer relationship management*. Springer-Verlag GmbH Germany, part of Springer Nature 2006, 2012, 2018.
32. For an insight into the measures involved in peak sales time predictions. Krishnan, T. V., Feng, S., & Jain, D. C. (2023). Peak sales time prediction in new product sales: Can a product manager rely on it? *Journal of Business Research, 165*, 114054.
33. This data results from the author's evaluation of their company's new product sales over the last twenty years. Data is confidential.

Chapter 2
A Review of Forensic Operating Models and Their Relationship to Doctrine, Service Delivery and Innovation

Mark Tahtouh and Simon J. Walsh

Abstract Forensic service providers (FSPs) are required to innovate and, we would argue, have an obligation to in order to ensure ongoing relevance, impact and trust. The economic and doctrinal forensic operating model they employ will influence the extent to which innovation is valued and supported by the FSP and by its key stakeholders. The operating model will also determine whether the focus of the innovation is solely on driving efficiency or the development of new forensic capabilities (or innovative uses of existing ones) to respond to new and emerging threats. Models that support the integration of the FSP within its operating environment are more likely to support the latter, while those more removed or beholden to economic drivers are more likely to support the former.

2.1 Introduction

Forensic science is often defined as the application of science to the law. Recently, Roux et al. have offered a more contemporary and expansive definition. It reads:

> Forensic science is a case-based (or multi case-based) research-oriented, science-based endeavor to study traces – the remnants of past activities (such as an individual's presence and actions) – through their detection, recognition, recovery, examination and interpretation to understand anomalous events of public interest (e.g., crimes, security incidents) [1].

Importantly, this work also contemplates the purpose of forensic science, including the key principle that *'forensic science has multi-dimensional purposes and contributions'* encompassing proactive approaches to policing [1]. A modern forensic science command, or service, therefore, needs to balance the delivery of quality-assured scientific examinations, that can withstand the necessary scrutiny of the judicial system, with the need to explore cutting-edge technologies and innovate to improve their capability, or tackle new and emerging threats. Furthermore, there is now a broader understanding of the role that forensic science can play in the

M. Tahtouh (✉) · S. J. Walsh
Forensics Command, Australian Federal Police, Canberra, Australia
e-mail: mark.tahtouh@afp.gov.au

S. Francese and R. S. P. King (eds.), *Driving Forensic Innovation in the 21st Century*,
https://doi.org/10.1007/978-3-031-56556-4_2

prevention and disruption of crime, and not just its detection, investigation and prosecution. This is evidenced through the evolution of forensic intelligence, which has expanded the role and impact of forensic science and ensured its continued relevance in a dynamic crime environment.

In this chapter we will reflect on the contemporary role of forensic science from the perspective of the predominant models under which forensic science services are delivered, and how those models equip us for the present operational challenges that are driving an increased need for agility and innovation. We have chosen, for the most part, to take a thematic approach to exploring operating models rather than a geographic one. We do however note a particular focus on Australasia due to (1) the authors' own experiences and familiarity with this region and (2) the availability of peer-reviewed publications with a more extensive explanation of models in use in Australia and New Zealand.

Traditionally, forensic institutions could be characterized as robust, 'brick-and-mortar' public entities, largely organized around vertical, discipline-based structures [2]. However, within this broad stereotype, there is still considerable environmental and institutional diversity that we explore at a high level.

There are also variations in the operating model, or how an organization delivers value to its internal and external stakeholders. We have classified our review of this aspect into economic and doctrinal perspectives. They are differentiated in that way as, in our opinion, this reflects both the external and internal forces that commonly interact to shape forensic operating models. From the perspective of leading forensic commands, the authors see contemplation and optimization of the operating model as an essential and ongoing responsibility to maintain the relevance and impact of forensic science services. As such, this discussion is intended to guide readers in that endeavor.

2.2 Influencing Factors

There are numerous extrinsic factors that can influence the operating model that a FSP implements. To streamline their consideration, we have categorized them broadly as *Environmental* and *Institutional* factors.

2.2.1 Environmental

We classify environmental factors as those arising from the external system or context, including societal, political, cultural, structural or criminal drivers. Of course, there are many factors and they are of varying impact and relevance. They are also subject to the impact of local or global events that can occur at any given time or place and cause short-term or lasting disruption.

To support a more focused consideration of environmental factors that have direct bearing on contemporary forensic operating models, we have identified what we see as the six key environmental factors. These are not ordered hierarchically, but, collectively, they represent the key external influences that need to be assessed and understood.

2.2.1.1 Jurisdiction

Structures and systems differ widely internationally and are themselves partitioned into different jurisdictions. The most obvious example is the distinction between local, state and national jurisdiction. There is no uniform or standard architecture to how jurisdictions are defined, or how they best intersect, but it is universally the case that jurisdictional boundaries are fixed by geographic, political and/or legal frameworks.

Jurisdiction governs other environmental factors (listed below) and will formally define the mandate and scope of forensic service providers. The corollary is that criminal and security threats are not constrained in the same way. Whilst this has been the case for a long time, interjurisdictional threats have traditionally been regarded as the exception, rather than the rule, and, for the most part, local priorities were the dominant drivers of demand for forensic services. With the increase of organized crime, cyber and technology enabled crime this is no longer the case, and such environmental changes present a challenge for jurisdictionally defined operating models. It is our view that greater partnership, information sharing, and integration is required, and we expand on these themes in later sections.

2.2.1.2 Legislative/Judicial Framework

The legal system under which the FSP operates will impact determinative factors such as the orientation of services, the relative investment and prioritization of resources and the expected role and purpose of forensic capabilities. For example, foundational distinctions such as whether an inquisitorial or adversarial system applies fundamentally affects how forensic services are organized and utilized. Parliaments shape the criminal justice environment through their administration of public funding, development and amendment of legislation and influence over judicial and official appointments. And whether we were to reflect on major interventions (such as commissions of inquiry or policy changes like drug decriminalization) or more routine or minor events (such as specific crimes with extraordinary public or political attention, or criticisms from the bench regarding forensic validity or integrity) it is undeniable that one of the most impactful environmental factors is whether the various interactions between the legal system and the forensic community are harmonious or otherwise. Fully understanding and fully complementing the needs of the legal system is an essential prerequisite for the successful provision of forensic services.

2.2.1.3 Stakeholders

Forensic science ultimately aims to reduce the impact of crime and protect the community. Depending on the jurisdiction and judicial framework under which they operate, FSPs typically service their main stakeholders, the community, via support to the courts and partner organizations in policing and national security. Within these organizations exists an even more diverse range of stakeholders including prosecutors, defense attorneys, investigators, intelligence analysts, police administrators, military and other government officials. It is commonplace for FSPs, particularly those operating at the national level, to be the sole service provider for these diverse stakeholder groups. In practical terms, this presents complexity and requires FSPs to have clarity regarding the expectations and parameters of the service agreements. It can present other tensions as well in areas such as resourcing, prioritization and the management of operational security and classifications. The breadth and diversity of requests for support is often unseen across the stakeholder group, or even at times by the organizational hierarchy who might be focused on operational outcomes and performance metrics but not appreciate the role that forensic science is playing in those achievements.

It is also important to note that forensic service providers have their own unique stakeholder community aligned to their expertise in the various specialist science and technology domains. Successfully meeting the expectations and obligations of these stakeholders can require a different emphasis to those we engage in our operational work. At the forensic command of the Australian Federal Police, both operational relevance and scientific excellence must be achieved at all times to maintain trust and influence with stakeholders across these different domains.

2.2.1.4 Demographics

The jurisdiction's population size, density and geographical distribution will help determine the commensurate scale for a FSP and whether services can be delivered by a single laboratory or network of laboratories in, for example, a hub and spoke model. It can also affect how skills, workflows, instrumentation etc. are deployed across the jurisdiction. Evaluating these aspects is critical, especially as technologies advance and present greater utility for in-field or remote acquisition and analysis of traces.

Studying factors such as age, gender, education, employment, income, religion and ethnicity within the population can help ensure the FSP workforce is reflective of the diversity within the community and the operating model caters to the needs and expectations of the community. This builds community connection and increases awareness and trust. Frontline areas of forensic science, such as crime scenes investigators, engage directly with the community, on a daily basis, and often under circumstances of significant duress and trauma. Ensuring that organizational learning includes non-technical (or non-forensic) competencies in areas such as cultural awareness, interpersonal skills, critical incident management, resilience, de-escalation and cognitive de-briefing has become increasingly important and is not only how an FSP ensures a quality service to their community and stakeholders, but also how they exercise their duty of care to their employees.

2.2.1.5 Crime Threat Assessment

The crime threat landscape within the jurisdiction that the FSP operates will influence the type and scale of forensic capabilities that are required to counter or mitigate those threats. Crime trends need to be monitored closely and continuously to ensure the FSP can respond dynamically to new and emerging threats or shift resources to manage surges in any crime type.

It is our observation that the incorporation of strategic and operational intelligence insights into capability planning is not widely applied in the forensic science field. Quantitative analysis of forensic business intelligence, or criminological trends are also rarely considered as an evidence base to reflect on the relationship between forensic capability investment or deployment, and the criminal justice outcomes that our examinations support. More commonly, change is driven through engagement with stakeholders in the academic or vendor community, and, unfortunately, might only materialize if it is opportunistically aligned to short-term injections of funding.

Understanding the current and forecasted threat picture for the jurisdiction supports a more strategic and relevant consideration of the future forensic capability requirements. It also places any identified gap or opportunity in the context of the criminal justice problem that it seeks to address. This is typically a stronger business case for investment than one based on the technology or instrumentation itself.

2.2.1.6 Digitization and Technological Innovation

Digitization and technological innovation present as both a threat (for example in the facilitation of crime and victimization anonymously, from distance and at scale) and an opportunity (to be harnessed to similarly automate or upscale forensic capabilities and services).

Digitization has "democratized" criminality worldwide, opening opportunities to any individual with ill-intent, while making their involvement in illicit activities more efficient and anonymous. Commodified into 'crime as a service' offerings, individuals have increased capacity to offend without the need for technical skill. There is also an increased nexus between digital and physical offending which generates a commensurate nexus of forensic exploitation opportunities. Examples include crimes such as dating app facilitated sexual violence where in-built features of online platforms can enable offences against the person via both digital and physical means. The volume of such offences is now very high, and rising, however the maturity of an integrated forensic response is low.

Understanding how digitization and new technologies enable crime and terrorism requires continuous and concerted efforts, and these activities need to be an integral part of crime prevention and disruption strategies. Forensic science must be proactive and adapt to this phenomenon and look for ways it can lead intelligence gathering or investigative approaches and contribute meaningful analysis to the hybrid crimes of the future [3].

2.2.2 Institutional

The authors classify institutional factors as those arising from within the authorizing environment of the organizations or agencies themselves that have had a bearing on their culture or structure. Once again, there are many such factors and we have isolated those that we consider to be most influential on the operating model of a forensic service provider.

2.2.2.1 History

The historical legacy of the evolution of forensic services in the country or jurisdiction can have an ongoing influence on the operating model of the FSP [4]. Some practices can be deep rooted and resistant to change as they exist within an entrenched organizational or departmental structure. At their origins, FSPs often emerged in situ as a result of the particular role(s) of a small number of specialists. These specialists may have been law enforcement officers, medical professionals, scientists, or researchers. Current institutions are, at times, the modern manifestation of those beginnings. This means that there was not always consideration given to the most appropriate institutional architecture within which to situate a forensic service provider.

Whether forensic services are provided by a university, government department or police command, clearly has a bearing on the organizational culture and structure and can also impact the emphasis that is placed on various elements of the service. For example, it is our experience that leading a forensic command within a national policing organization provides distinct advantages, in particular the ability to understand the criminal environment and the opportunity to integrate forensic services directly into operational strategy and activity. However, research has also shown that police organizations 'often struggle to innovate successfully' [5] and resist strategic reform [6]. As Braga and Weisburd [7] conclude:

> Police most easily adopt innovations that require the least radical departure from their hierarchical paramilitary organizational structures, continue incident-driven and reactive strategies, and maintain police sovereignty over crime issues [7].

Forensic institutions ensconced within government departments can also face cultural and organizational challenges. For example, a recent state government

Commission of Inquiry into Forensic DNA Services in Queensland, Australia recommended that the provision of Forensic services from within the Department of Health was 'an inapt fit' [8].

Where services are exchanged across departments or institutions, there is a need for some form of contract or service level agreement. Again, institutional structures will have a major bearing on those arrangements and variations in such agreements will have a determinative impact on the forensic service, its scope and emphasis.

The point is that there is no "gold standard" institutional architecture for forensic service provision. Each of the predominant structures have both strengths and limitations and will impact on consideration regarding the optimal operating model.

2.2.2.2 Role and Mandate

The role and mandate for a forensic service provider can vary widely. At one extreme, it is possible for a single FSP to service multiple law enforcement agencies and other clients (for example, border protection, military or intelligence agencies). It is not uncommon for individual FSPs to also support matters arising from both criminal and civil law (for example a forensic DNA provider that supports both the investigation of serious violent crime in the Criminal Courts and the resolution of disputed paternity matters in the Family Courts). A benefit of such a broad role is that there is space for greater operational impact and there can be a clearer and more direct relationship between the FSP and the wider policing or justice system. A disadvantage is that there are a range of diverse stakeholder expectations and the potential for operational service delivery to dominate performance expectations, at the risk of deeper, higher quality science.

At the other end of the spectrum, it is also very common for FSPs to be responsible for only one evidence class or analytical service (for example forensic toxicology), and, as a result, only be asked to provide a select array of services under a narrow range of operational or criminal justice circumstances. Naturally this presents both advantages and disadvantages as well and they are essentially a mirror image of those listed above. A benefit of a narrower, more specialized mandate is that this more singular focus can empower longer term development of scientific expertise in the specialist field of service. Conversely, this specialization leads to siloing or a reduced awareness of the external operating environment. This can compromise stakeholder relationships, particularly with more operationally focused agencies.

The authors' view is that, regardless of the scope of an FSPs mandate, they should adopt a systems-thinking approach to their environment and planning, and, as mentioned already, include as an input relevant assessment of the crime and threat environment and the operational policies or strategies that apply. It is also the authors' view that there is considerable power and potential in the forensic expertise and capabilities under our custodianship. If we occupy a narrow, confined area of the system we risk subjugating ourselves to a restricted and sub-optimal impact. The authors have found that by adopting a mindset that seeks to position forensic expertise and capability closer to the source of the operational complexity, new and highly impactful ways can be identified in which value can be derived and important outcomes achieved.

2.2.2.3 Executive Support and Leadership

Forensic science operates within a complicated system with, as previously mentioned, diverse environmental and institutional structures, stakeholders, demands, expectations, and challenges. For any complicated system to function, optimizing the connection across the interdependent areas or functions is paramount. In a practical sense, this optimization is the role of leaders, particularly around building effective bridges through partnership and collaboration, aligning, and harmonizing the efforts of different actors, and reconciling challenges or competition when needed.

Leadership in forensic science is challenging, and, arguably, an area where there is a risk of under-investment. As with other technical careers, forensic scientists establish themselves through long periods of specialist study, training, and professional application. Opportunity or promotion through the early to middle periods of a forensic scientist's career is usually offered because of technical proficiency in their field of specialization. Similarly, in operational careers (such as policing) a consistent pattern applies whereby certain roles or experiences (such as investigations) can assist an officer's promotional potential more so than others (such as forensics). However, leading people and teams within complicated or complex systems requires additional and different skills. Leading entire forensic commands within a contested, political and rapidly changing operating environment requires even greater leadership dexterity.

In any case, it is our observation that developing and delivering an optimized forensic operating model (whatever environmental or institutional factors apply) is a considerable leadership challenge. It must involve strong influencing, communication, collaboration, and change management skills. Success ultimately depends on support from others influential stakeholders (especially operational police commands and their leadership). Gaining and maintaining that support relies upon demonstrating how improved or expanded forensic services contribute to measurable improvements in operational and judicial outcomes. This, in turn, requires regular and relevant communication, including externally, to reinforce the valuable contribution that forensic capabilities make to the outcomes of the justice system that our communities depend upon and value so highly. Utilizing media and public relations channels to share forensic success stories has not been a strength of FSPs but it assists to reinforce these positive associations and the business case for continued support from leaders and partners.

2.2.2.4 Funding and Resource Provision

FSPs need to be appropriately resourced in terms of personnel and operating expenses to deliver the volume and range of services expected of them. In contrast to other operational arms of the criminal justice system, forensic science is likely to be at the higher-cost end of the spectrum, and, as such, can stand out as a "source of pressure" when budgets are being considered or allocated. Maintaining laboratory infrastructure and capability requires ongoing capital and operating investment and, due to the highly specialized technologies involved, a failure to ensure optimal service and maintenance, can risk more catastrophic impacts and higher cost rectification.

Depending on other environmental or institutional factors that apply to any FSP, it is likely that different areas of this resourcing equation will be challenging. Sometimes, it is competition for capital expenditure, or staffing, or both! Appropriation models can also be quite rigid or bureaucratic and subject to either internal or cross-agency competition. Understanding the appropriation process and the levers that might exist to influence resourcing considerations is important. In the environment in which FSPs operate, a common external lever is the formulation of a new policy proposal to government. To be successful, any such proposal needs to help the government address a particular risk or deliver upon a particular change or challenge. Positioning an FSP to leverage such opportunities requires prior investment in relationships and ensuring a level of political acumen. As already mentioned, it also relies upon an ability to situate an investment in forensic science in terms of the value or impact it will derive for the funding proposal. As will be discussed later in this chapter, demonstrating value for money or a return on investment for forensic services can be challenging. It is difficult to measure the true value or impact arising from a "unit" of forensic effort, or even who the ultimate beneficiary is for our services.

2.2.2.5 Culture

The environmental and institutional factors outlined above will impact the operating model used by an FSP, which in turn will impact the culture. Conversely, shifting the cultural identity within an FSP is an important part of changing the operating model. For example, when a reform was undertaken within the forensics command of the Australian Federal Police (AFP) to implement a more integrated and collaborative 'consultancy model' (a concept explored further in this chapter), a key leadership challenge was shifting the cultural identity of its specialists.

Like many FSPs, our expert forensic disciplines had traditionally developed as narrow silos of specialization. Obtaining expertise is understandably a lengthy and formal process that must be justified in the eyes of the criminal justice system, most notably the courts. This model influences the analytical process in that whilst multiple members may be involved at various stages, the outputs of the analysis are produced by the scientist as the 'owner' of the expertise. At an organizational level this siloing persists as specialist discipline areas are typically dispersed, either among different organizations or into different departments of the same organization. In a traditional workflow, the contribution of each discipline is deployed in a linear and sequential manner. This dis-aggregated model has had the effect of defining identity and folklore and aligning the informal status and rewards of forensic work with the individual discipline expert.

Whilst the development and application of genuine expertise is an essential component of any forensic operating model, an essential end-goal of our reform was a flexible, adaptive capability that organically combined individual expertise in an inter-disciplinary operational context. To achieve this and implement a 'collaborative' workforce, the notion of collaboration had to embody more than reporting to duty as part of a multi-disciplinary team and extend to 'collaborative' attitudes and values. The AFP forensic professional culture needed to shift from individuals and siloes to collaborative, integrated teams and base itself on an agreed shared purpose and value proposition.

Implementing this shift to a collaborative, integrated way-of-working meant reconfiguration of multiple elements of the operating model, from workflows and procedures, training and professionalization, laboratory and facility design, quality assurance and partner engagement. From a leadership perspective, the AFP forensic executive reiterated consistently the notion of "forensic first". This was necessary to elevate and unify the identity and value proposition of the command's specializations, beyond the individual specializations themselves and to their collective forensic value. To partners (in investigations, intelligence, the legal system and elsewhere), this had the effect of simplifying engagement and removing the need to attempt to orientate themselves within the nest of specializations and expertise. To members and teams within AFP Forensics, this concept allowed them to adopt a problem-centered approach to operational work that is fully collaborative and agnostic to rank or discipline. It also empowered decision-making at the "front-line" and encouraged the intended goal of distributed leadership and an increased adaptive capacity within our command.

2.3 Operating Models (Economic)

In a key contribution, McAndrew explored forensic science service delivery models through an economic lens [9]. He argues that forensic science is, in an economic sense, neither purely a public good[1] or purely a private good,[2] but rather a 'club good' that contains a degree of both the public and private. Considering forensic science in this way leads to the notion that, in creating an efficient operating model, FSPs should consider the optimal jurisdiction size and the optimal level of output of forensic services to be provided to these jurisdictions. For example, Maguire argues

[1] Private Goods are defined as Rival (One's consumption of goods and services affects the availability to others: individual preferences determine output and consumption) and Excludable (The owner of the good or service can decide not to share). Examples include a glass of wine or finite DNA analysis capacity.

[2] Public Goods are defined as Non-Rival (Shared consumption that does not appreciably change with the addition of consumers; individual preferences are not considered) and Non-Excludable (Access to service is universal). Example: National defense.

that a large number of laboratories are conducting DNA analysis at too small of a scale to be cost-effective. While they may be highly efficient in the conduct of their internal tasks, crime rates and subsequent submissions within the jurisdiction are insufficient to permit the most cost-effective delivery of services [10].

Many authors have considered whether an optimal or "best" forensic operating model exists [4, 9–13]. This generally involves consideration of the pros and cons of two extremes: public provision of forensic services by government; and entirely privatized commercial service providers. There is of course a lot of middle ground whereby there is a healthy mixture of public and private service provision or even government-owned commercial entities who have both commercial and government drivers. FSPs that are "best" will efficiently provide the quantity of forensic science output at the appropriate quality standards society desires. FSPs who give due consideration for contracting with other governments, or even privatization, may improve efficiencies from economies of scale [9].

Historically, the administration of forensic science services among developed countries has been that of public ownership at some level of government [14]. Complete privatization was largely discounted or completely overlooked as a viable alternative for many years but, after closure of the government-owned Forensic Science Services (FSS) in 2012, the U.K. Home Office uniquely explored the privatization of their entire forensic science industry [11]. Here, the authors explore three forensic operating models from an "economic" perspective: (1) Integrated, Whole-of-Government Model; (2) Hybrid Government-Owned, Corporate Fee-For-Service Model; and (3) Privatized, Corporate Model.

Some examples of jurisdictions that utilize each model are provided and some associated advantages and disadvantages will be briefly discussed.

2.3.1 Integrated, Whole-of-Government Model

In many countries, like Australia, Canada, Germany, and much of the USA, FSPs predominantly reside within the government sector; operating under police, health or justice agencies.

In some jurisdictions, the government provider may be the sole operator. In others, an integrated network of FSPs works together to provide the full breadth of forensic services required by their stakeholders.

Australian agencies who provide forensic services have traditionally maintained specialized small throughput capabilities in addition to higher throughput analyses such as DNA profiling and illicit drug analysis [2]. During a summit held in 2016, a diverse mix of practitioners, managers and laboratory directors from Australian policing agencies and forensic laboratories recognized that commercial laboratories could provide niche services not readily available within the local jurisdiction. Furthermore, they advocated for a Centers of Specialization (CoS) model in Australia and New Zealand [2, 15]. A concept paper prepared by the National Institute of Forensic Science outlines:

> The CoS Program aims to support the ability of specialist services to realize appropriate 'cross-border' economies of scale, by recognizing and linking existing Australian and New Zealand forensic science service providers and building the 'critical mass' required to operate and maintain specialized capabilities [15].

While this CoS model is an appealing prospect and could help resolve many of the scale challenges experienced by individual FSPs, its implementation has been difficult. Our experience is that, despite best intentions, extrinsic drivers such as those discussed earlier often lead FPS to focus on narrow and internally-focused goals rather than those that could be of broader (national) benefit.

2.3.2 Hybrid Government-Owned, Corporate Fee-for-Service Model

In New Zealand, the Institute of Environmental Sciences and Research (ESR), established as a Crown Research Institute (CRI) in 1992 under an act of Parliament, behaves as a 'pseudo-commercial' entity. ESR is the primary provider of forensic science services that support the criminal justice system and is required to provide an adequate rate of return to its owners (other government bodies) by charging its only customer, New Zealand Police, in a fee-for-service business model [4].

Bedford highlights that this hybrid of government and commercial models has advantages such as greatly empowering the laboratory and that backlogs are essentially non-existent [4]. Negatives include the downside of the .commercial drivers, such as the pressure on investment in 'expensive' activities, such as quality management and research and in the perception of competition between police in-house services, such as fingerprints and 'expensive' forensic science services.

Speaker argues that the ESR model demonstrates a comparative advantage over more traditional models, partly due to operational directives that invoke some behaviors of private sector business while maintaining a public sector mission [12]. Nevertheless, as Bedford concludes:

> No system is perfect. For ESR in New Zealand, the strengths of the existing model can only be maintained, and the negatives minimized if the service provider organization, police management and the people directly involved are committed to making it work. The key is the people [4].

Another example of a 'pseudo-commercial' entity providing forensic services is ChemCentre in Western Australia (WA), which is an independent statutory authority, established under The Chemistry Centre (WA) Act 2007. ChemCentre provides chemical and forensic science services for private clients (for example, the mining industry) as well as government agencies such as Western Australia Police Force.

2.3.3 *Privatized, Corporate Model*

The marketization of forensic science in England and Wales, precipitated by the decision to cease funding for the FSS, in 2010, leading to its final closure in 2012, offers a rare insight into the provision of forensic science in a competitive market and the influence this has on operating models for FSPs in such markets. Until the early 1990s, the majority of forensic science services, excluding crime scene and fingerprint capabilities, were provided outside policing by the State-owned FSS. The FSS through their seven laboratories across England and Wales, provided a scope of forensic science services to forty-one police forces outside London, who provided funding to FSS based on their relative size [16]. Other agencies and individual police forces also provided some forensic services.

> Beginning in April 1991, two key changes triggered the evolution of the landscape of forensic service provision in England and Wales, over a short period, from a totally 'free' to use, public service, into a completely marketized system. Firstly, the state-owned FSS was converted to an executive agency of the Home Office, combining all the six FSS laboratories into one organization. This gave the FSS the ability to charge customers for the forensic service they provided, and this introduced the second change; direct charging for forensic science services. These changes were triggered because of the difficulties of the FSS by that time to meet the increasing forensic demands of police forces, including the advent of DNA analysis in the 1980s. This affected the FSS turnaround time with an increase in case backlogs, which adversely impacted on the duration of crime investigations.
>
> The structural reorganization of the FSS, including its subsequent conversion into a trading fund status, and the direct charging system were, therefore, attempts to ensure that the FSS could maintain some financial independence and that police forces would be free to spend more on forensic science, allowing for forensic capacity to increase. However, this inherently led to the commercialization of forensic services; police forces could 'purchase' forensic services from both the FSS and private FSPs. As this progressed, private FSPs began to emerge, including the LGC and Forensic Alliance. As a result, some opinions indicate that the commercialization of forensic science in England and Wales was caused by accident rather than design [16].

Maguire et al. [10] advocate for FSPs to explore insourcing, outsourcing and privatization options for efficient forensic service delivery. Following the closure of the FSS in 2012, the majority of police forces in England and Wales expanded their in-house forensic science capabilities to incorporate some of the services previously provided by the FSS. Specialized services, which were outside the capacity of police forces, were outsourced to private service providers. Since then, a highly competitive and price-sensitive forensic marketplace has developed [16].

Some have argued that a free market will inevitably result in compromises to the criminal justice system and have a detrimental impact on forensic research, development and innovation [17, 18].

Regardless of the economic model applied, and whether there is a private or public institutional leaning, it is essential that sound administration and management is central to the leadership of FSPs. It is commonplace for demand to outstrip supply and, notwithstanding the paramount importance placed on the quality and integrity of the science, practices must also be efficient and productive. Regular review and evaluation of performance and the scope of services and capabilities is critical and should itself be a motivator for innovation and growth.

2.4 Operating Models (Forensic Doctrine)

Doctrine is a codification of a body of principles in a branch of knowledge or system of belief. In the context of a discipline like forensic science, a 'forensic doctrine' employed by a FSP can describe how capability and support will be delivered by the provider, through the use of specialist forensic science, technical intelligence or other specialized capabilities. Formal documentation of forensic doctrine, or even recognition as such, is not universal but may be captured in less formal ways or categorized differently (for example as an 'operating procedure', 'business plan' or 'service guideline'). For simplicity, the principles outlined in guidance documents regarding how a FSP does business, will be referred to collectively as forensic doctrine.

The intent of forensic doctrine is to provide guidance to those who provide or require forensic support. The doctrine defines the manner in which the forensic support, at the individual, functional and organizational level, is available and how that support should be engaged.

Decisions regarding forensic doctrine will be influenced by the same environmental, cultural and structural factors described earlier. Here we focus on three examples that have found application in the forensic science community: (1) Task- or Service-based; (2) Forensic Consultancy; and (3) Forensic Intelligence. It is important to note that each one is not mutually exclusive to the other. Indeed, a FSP may decide to have a certain holistic doctrine or separate doctrines for individual services or capabilities that it offers.

2.4.1 Task- or Service-Based

Investigators traditionally engage forensic science service providers at the tail-end of an investigation and dictate the forensic examinations they would like completed. This task- or service-based delivery model essentially puts the 'customer' (usually law enforcement and/or the judiciary) and their needs or demands at the center, and the forensic doctrine employed is to essentially service their needs or demands.

This model can be advantageous in ensuring that investment in capability deployment is commiserate with actual (end-user) demand. It can however lead to the inefficient use of scarce resources and the underutilization of new capabilities because the customers (police investigators) are unaware that they exist or in what way they could assist their inquiry. It may also pigeon-hole the available forensic expertise to only complete the task that has been initiated. It is possible that there were other applications of the forensic capabilities but there is a lack of authority to approach or explore them. This can be demotivating for a scientist and lead to a linear, production-line approach to service delivery that is not optimal, particularly in the face of complicated or complex problems. Moreover, innovation to explore or develop new capabilities in the first place, can be inhibited because of the lack of demand (be that true or perceived).

A FSP with a task- or service-based delivery model may focus on ensuring their capabilities are relevant and effective across all phases of the criminal investigation, including, ideally, its planning. But, in reality, this approach is typically applied after a crime had been suspected, or detected, and often after the inquiries are well-progressed. Culturally, the FSP may be peripheral to the core investigative machine and, as a result, not well integrated into the criminal justice system in which they operate. This loss of connection can lead to a limited ability to guide, influence and drive impact and change.

2.4.2 *Forensic Consultancy Model*

As discussed above, the task- or service-based delivery model can lead to the inefficient use of scarce resources and the underutilization of capabilities because investigators are unaware that they exist. The 'Forensic Consultancy Model' instead advocates for early engagement and an open, ongoing dialogue between investigators and forensic specialists regarding investigative questions, gaps and opportunities. The forensic scientist involved in this dialogue, known as the forensic capability advisor, forensic advisor or forensic coordinator, can then advise on the most appropriate forensic capabilities to meet those needs [19, 20]. Early engagement, consultation and real-time connections with specialist teams is fundamental to operational success. This model, now embedded in operational casework at the Australian Federal Police (AFP), enables problem solving and a holistic multi-disciplinary view to address investigative objectives. Here we outline AFP Forensics' experiences in developing and implementing the Forensic Consultancy Model in a complex and dynamic threat environment. The benefits and opportunities that have been realized in the prevention, detection, investigation and disruption of crime are also discussed.

The AFP Investigations Doctrine (similarly to the forensic doctrine) represents the philosophy for AFP investigations. It is a guide for all investigators and members when conducting an investigation. Specifically, when referencing the point at which an investigator requires the support of specialist capability areas, it says:

> Operations support capability owners should be consulted early during the planning stage to determine how each can be best utilized. Through the consultative process the investigator should nominate objectives required and operations support will determine the most suitable approaches for achieving those objectives.

Forensic science engages and responds flexibly using the consultancy model to work more closely with investigators, getting involved early at the planning stage of an operation or investigation to better define the forensic objectives. For investigators, this has the effect of simplifying engagement and removing the need to orientate themselves within the nest of forensic specializations and expertise. For forensic scientists, it allows them to adopt a problem-centered approach to operational work that is fully collaborative and agnostic to rank or discipline. The forensic consultancy model re-positions the value forensics can play as part of a collaborative, multi-disciplinary operational capability.

To consult is to ask advice or confer with someone. In the investigative context, consulting is more than simply giving advice. Forensic consultancy advocates for true collaboration. It is about getting a group of people to come together and contribute their expertise for the benefit of a shared objective, project, or mission.

Applying the consultancy model follows from a logical four-step approach to problem solving as outlined below:

1. *Articulate and Define the Problem*
   Approach this stage with the objective of identifying the issue at hand. The problem is brought to the center of the discussion and response.
2. *Identify All Viable Alternatives for Forensic Exploitation*
   Requires an openness to what is possible as well as the ability to compare the merits of the possible alternatives. Estimating the complexity, time, and resources necessary for each approach is important, as well as the return that could be expected from various strategies.
3. *Choose the Best Forensic Examination Plan/Strategy*
   Strong decision-making is essential at this stage. After carefully considering the available forensic options, the best strategy for the problem must be selected and explained. Confidence from forensic members in their knowledge of their specialized fields, and their reasoning in reaching their decision is important. Failing to identify and commit to a clear and effective plan undermines the overall process.
4. *Implement the Solution*
   Implementation is the critical point. Members draw up an examination plan, communicate it with the appropriate personnel, and follow it through. Monitoring, oversight, and ongoing communication are essential as success will typically depend upon a series of steps and participants (and operational circumstances will invariably change).

The forensic consultancy model is scalable. It can be applied for events or items within an investigation; for a complex investigation involving a series of crimes or offence elements; or at an operational level to, for example, identify linkages between multiple investigations. It can even be applied at a strategic level for identifying forensic solutions to address a particular crime phenomenon or explore innovative solutions to address a new or emerging threat.

The benefits of the consultancy model have been profound. We have seen increased forensics involvement across a full spectrum of crime priorities and that involvement includes a broader range of capabilities than was previously utilized. We have also witnessed a resurgence in the value of traditional disciplines, particularly in concert with the Forensic Intelligence model (Sect. 2.4.3). However, a decrease in the overall items/units of work is observed, that is, there is a net gain from triaging out unnecessary work. An increase in the adaptive problem-solving capacity of the AFP Forensics command has also been observed which has been reinforced operationally and through innovation on many occasions.

2.4.3 Forensic Intelligence

Historically, the primary focus of forensic laboratories has been in supporting criminal investigations and, usually, criminal prosecutions with the key output being the generation of appropriate court reports. This traditional forensic science model has formed around a 'traditional' approach to policing. Such investigations can of course be very complicated and highly iterative, but are largely reactive or responsive, linear 'prosecution-directed' means of controlling crime [21]. The typical traditional objective is to identify offenders and address their past criminal acts through the justice system [22]. Forensic science workflows and doctrine have mirrored this, reinforcing linear and often siloed uni-disciplinary approaches.

Many agencies have now recognized the broader value and impact that forensic science can play and also provide forensic intelligence services aimed at supporting a rapid response to crime, and crime prevention and disruption initiatives. As Raymond puts it:

> Forensic intelligence necessitates collaboration, cooperation and partnerships between forensic scientists and police; it moves away from a reactive, incident-driven strategy towards a proactive strategy that focuses on establishing links to achieve broad goals of crime reduction and crime prevention; and it necessitates the incorporation of forensic scientists (and other relevant agencies and practitioners) in the 'ownership' and management of crime issues [23].

There have been several proposed definitions for Forensic intelligence (FORINT), but one recently agreed by an Australian multi-jurisdictional specialist advisory group is '*Forensic intelligence is intelligence derived from technical and forensic information and expertise*' [21, 24]. Where intelligence as a process involves planning, information collection and collation, analysis and dissemination; as an output it is a product derived from adding value to information, to provide insight and influence decision making. FORINT, is generated through the analysis of forensic findings, often enhanced by combining other sources of intelligence, such as human intelligence and open-source intelligence [25]. Like other forms of intelligence, it is used to drive operations within a law enforcement agency to identify crime trends, assist with deployment and tactics, and enhance public safety. However, forensic intelligence should not stand on its own. It should become an integral part of the overall investigative and intelligence-led strategies [26].

Research has shown that there are some organizational and cultural barriers to the development and implementation of 'forensic intelligence' models in Australian jurisdictions [23]. Leadership was found to be a key factor in the successful uptake of intelligence-led policing models such as FORINT.

The Australian Federal Police (AFP) have a long history of building and adapting FORINT capability in response to shifts in our wider operating environment and to inform and influence operational decision-making. Here we outline the AFP experience with implementing reform to its forensic operating model including the establishment of a dedicated FORINT capability. As discussed earlier, support from others with influence such as operational police commands and their leadership is critical when implementing significant change to the forensic operating model. For example, embarking on the emergence of a forensic intelligence practice would only succeed if it operated in concert with the established criminal and security intelligence domains, in alignment with their doctrine and practice, and with output that was seen to add value to the broader intelligence picture.

Technical intelligence areas had existed within the AFP Forensics command for over twenty years before we commenced the FORINT reforms. Specifically, we had partnered and built capability in areas of forensic drug intelligence [27], and weapons technical intelligence (including chemical, biological, radiological, nuclear and explosives, or CBRNE). As a key component of reforming the AFP operating model, however, FORINT has been since established as a discipline or capability in its own right. The AFP FORINT unit applies an all-source fusion model providing intelligence derived from forensic information and other sources. The following objectives are achieved through this capability:

- Inform operations and planning strategies and identify new lines of inquiry.
- Identify convergences between cases or crime types and identify targetable vulnerabilities.
- Proactive generation of intelligence products and timely action that informs and influences operational decision-making.
- Identify trends or emergent technologies / methodologies from forensic data that have strategic or policy implications for Forensics and the AFP.

AFP FORINT personnel hold scientific subject matter expertise that is complemented by intelligence training and tradecraft. Integration with the forensic command alongside other forensic capabilities allows the FORINT unit to identify and exploit unique forensic opportunities for intelligence outcomes, and also to incorporate crime-domain expertise through their collaborative relationships with other intelligence and investigations teams.

As an established specialist intelligence area the FORINT unit now develops product at the Tactical, Operational and Strategic level. At the tactical level, FORINT assessments focus on specifics of targets and the identification of new leads. Outputs are generally produced in a short time scale in support of frontline policing or investigators undertaking case-specific actions. Two examples that are regularly produced include: (i) Flash Reports focusing on emerging methodologies or modus operandi (MO) and which increase situational awareness through science; (ii) Geographic Profiling assessing location of interest (LOI) alternatives and prioritising resources on focus areas (hot-spotting).

At the operational level, FORINT assessments illuminate criminal networks and pervasive problems, across crime types and jurisdictional borders, identifying opportunities and options for the leadership cohort. Recommendations may include re-prioritisation, resourcing, and greater crime reduction strategies, but not just proximate actions.

At the strategic level, FORINT assessments address matters such as the broader criminal environment, emerging trends, high-level policy, and so on. The audience is typically senior leadership, or decision-makers. Strategic intelligence findings often lead to change in legislation or regulation—thereby closing vulnerabilities and reducing the risk to the community. In a recent example a FORINT product led to law reform to prohibit the importation of previously unregulated commercially available electromagnetic weapons[28].

The FORINT model is embedded into every aspect of our forensic operating model. All data fields captured in our Forensic Management System (FMS) have been assessed and their formats structured so that there is a passive collection process occurring that builds our FORINT holdings. The schema has been built onto our own FORINT module (iForensic) which is now being explored as a possible national system. Members can also report observations or results that they believe to be of potential intelligence value as a notice to the FORINT team.

An operating model that fully embraces FORINT has the effect of enhancing integration and multi-disciplinary problem-solving, orientates forensic expertise toward different questions and outcomes, and assists to identify emerging capabilities of enduring forensic value and prove them through their contributions to FORINT. Our experiences lead us to strongly recommend this approach to any FSP as a means to expand relevance and impact and leverage additional value from forensic science capabilities.

2.5 Innovation

As previously discussed, traditional forensic operating models favor stringent science, deployed iteratively via highly specialized experts and institutions, primarily in support of judicial decision-making. More contemporary models uphold these traditional objectives but are also adopting increased integration and digitization and a greater contribution to crime disruption and prevention. Notwithstanding the forensic operating model at play, innovation has not been a core strength of the forensic sector. In our experience the burden of operational demand and the scarcity of available resources (particularly to enable a vibrant research and development culture or domain) have limited our evolution in this area. A culture of continuous improvement is common, and every case to some degree offers its own challenges to successful forensic examination, and these are hallmarks of a form of innovation that our field is well known for. However, as yet, innovation has not been a systemic feature of our environment or our operating models.

So, what needs to change to increase our innovative and adaptive potential? Firstly, forensic scientists must accept their responsibility and promote their capacity as complex problem solvers. The problem space we occupy should not be rigidly predetermined by our own bureaucracy, discipline-centric traditions or the impositions of an overbearing task-response model. By liberating our identity in this way, we can explore, potentially through research and innovation, how our contributions can be expanded and diversified. But we must believe in the value of this change and relentlessly pursue it. Our experience of driving such a reform is that it has led to increased capabilities, increased opportunities and consistent growth in resources and influence.

Secondly, innovation and change involve risk and a preparedness to step into a new space. It is our observation that forensic careers and contributions are expanding across a range of industries (for example finance and communications) and areas of government (for example anti-corruption and counter-fraud activities). Democratized technologies and our connected world also make available a range of tools and applications to allow our stakeholders, including frontline police and the community, to adopt forensic-like tools and applications cheaply and easily. It is common to hear complaints from our forensic expert community about the low fidelity or scientific rigor of such tools, in comparison to our established, validated methodologies. Those criticisms are well-founded. But, if the competitor approaches are rapid, accessible, and scalable, they offer some distinct benefits to stringent, time-consuming and expensive laboratory-based approaches. The key from our perspective is adaptation and influence and seeking to shape these external approaches not shut them out. There are benefits in terms of the information-gathering and operational reach of these expansionary technologies. Tethering these to the custodians of forensic best-practice creates the best of both worlds and there are numerous opportunities for FSPs to be more expeditionary and innovative in this regard.

Thirdly, FSPs need a renewed openness to partnership and a preparedness to partner differently. This openness needs to also be extended towards forensic science from our key vendor and academic collaborators. Frontier issues such as disruptive technology, future workforce, and the threat environment are coalescing in previously unseen ways and meeting these challenges will require new skills, perspectives, ideas and capabilities. Choreographing this effort, when needed, and under operational conditions, can only be achieved if we have pre-positioned the critical relationships and ways of working openly and collaboratively. Experimenting with new partnership approaches through innovation labs or "sandpit" environments can establish important foundations. Embedding new skills through partnership into forensic commands (such as technologists, data engineers, analysts) is another starting point for pioneering democratization models that are emerging from the technology sector. Forensic leaders must venture forth and create these intellectual and practical linkages for their commands and institutions. Failing to do so runs the risk of stagnating at a time of unprecedented change.

2.6 Conclusion

Through this chapter the authors have illustrated the diversity across the forensic science field, with a particular thematic focus on the external operating environment, the business models that exist in various jurisdictions, and the influence that this combination of features has on our collective capacity to innovate. The authors have highlighted also that, due to the pace of change, we can expect increased diversity in the future, and that diversity will bring both opportunity and risk for FSPs.

In this chapter it is acknowledged that for any single FSP, it is likely that only parts of this narrative will directly apply to them. It is also acknowledged that the external or organizational factors that exist can practically constrain the ability to adapt in the face of external change. But it is the authors' hope that through this description of the diverse approaches that exist, potential options or solutions are included within. Reflecting on the authors' experiences at AFP Forensics, two critical factors that have enabled growth of forensic capabilities and enhanced impact are (1) a stronger connection outside to the operational problem-space and (2) a stronger cultural identity inside that believes in the use specialist scientific and technological capability to help identify solutions. Our forensic specializations should not be seen as a box that only contains tasks and services that fit neatly within its walls but rather a box upon which we can stand to reach higher and further to help address new and emerging challenges in our criminal justice systems, and our communities.

References

1. Roux, C., Bucht, R., Crispino, F., De Forest, P., Lennard, C., Margot, P., Miranda, M. D., NicDaeid, N., Ribaux, O., & Ross, A. (2022). The Sydney declaration–Revisiting the essence of forensic science through its fundamental principles. *Forensic Science International, 332*, 111182.
2. Catoggio, D., & Pearman, C. (2018). Australasian forensic science summit 2016: Business models towards 2030. *Australian Journal of Forensic Sciences, 50*(3), 282–292.
3. Walsh, S. J. (2023). Forensic science in the criminal justice system: The good, the bad and the academy. *Australian Journal of Forensic Sciences, 55*(3), 285–294. https://doi.org/10.1080/00450618.2023.2200913
4. Bedford, K. (2011). Forensic science service provider models—Is there a 'best' option? *Australian Journal of Forensic Sciences, 43*(2–3), 147–156. https://doi.org/10.1080/00450618.2010.541498
5. Darroch, S., & Mazerolle, L. (2013). Intelligence-led policing: A comparative analysis of organizational factors influencing innovation uptake. *Police Quarterly, 16*(1), 3–37. https://doi.org/10.1177/1098611112467411
6. Allen, R. Y. (2002). Assessing the impediments to organizational change: A view of community policing. *Journal of Criminal Justice, 30*(6), 511–517.
7. Braga, A. A., & Weisburd, D. L. (2006). *Police innovation and crime prevention: Lessons learned from police research over the past 20 years*. This review draws upon material available in David L Weisburd and Anthony A Braga (Eds.).
8. Sofronoff, W. (2022). *Commission of inquiry into forensic DNA testing in Queensland*.
9. McAndrew, W. P. (2012). Are forensic science services club goods? An analysis of the optimal forensic science service delivery model. *Forensic Science Policy & Management, 3*(4), 151.

10. Maguire, C., Houck, M. M., Williams, R., & Speaker, P. J. (2012). Efficiency and the cost-effective delivery of forensic science services: Insourcing, outsourcing, and privatization. *Forensic Science Policy & Management, 3*(2), 62.
11. McAndrew, W. P. (2012). Is privatization inevitable for forensic science laboratories? *Forensic Science Policy & Management: An International Journal, 3*(1), 42–52. https://doi.org/10.1080/19409044.2012.720641
12. Speaker, P. J. (2013). Forensic science service provider models: Data-driven support for better delivery options. *The Australian Journal of Forensic Science, 45*(4), 398.
13. Speaker, P. J. (2021). An independent evaluation of laboratory staffing needs: Launching the forensic laboratory workforce calculator. *Forensic Science International: Synergy, 3*, 100137. https://doi.org/10.1016/j.fsisyn.2021.100137
14. Koppl, R. (2005). How to improve forensic science. *European Journal of Law and Economics, 20*, 255–286.
15. Centres of Specialisation Framework: A Concept Paper. (2016). *Australian New Zealand Policing Advisory Agency National Institute of Forensic Science.* https://www.anzpaa.org.au/ArticleDocuments/676/Centres%20of%20Specialisation%20Framework%20-%20A%20Concept%20Paper.pdf.aspx. Accessed June 17, 2023.
16. Amoako, E. N. (2020). *The regulation of forensic science in England and Wales.* Ph.D. Thesis, University of Northumbria at Newcastle (United Kingdom), England.
17. Gallop, A., & Brown, J. (2014). The market future for forensic science services in England and Wales. *Policing: A Journal of Policy and Practice, 8*(3):254–264.
18. Budowle, B., Kayser, M., & Sajantila, A. (2011). *The demise of the United Kingdom's forensic science service (FSS): Loss of world-leading engine of innovation and development in the forensic sciences* (Vol. 2). BioMed Central.
19. Bitzer, S. (2019). Forensic case coordination in Europe—Their role within 5 European institutes. *Forensic Science International (Online), 300*, 1–5. https://doi.org/10.1016/j.forsciint.2019.04.016
20. Bitzer, S., Miranda, M. D., & Bucht, R. E. (2022). Forensic advisors: The missing link. *Interdisciplinary Reviews Forensic Science, 4*(3). https://doi.org/10.1002/wfs2.1444
21. Taylor, M. L. (2023). Designing the future of forensic science: Mêtis and forensic intelligence. *Australian Journal of Forensic Sciences*, 1–20. https://doi.org/10.1080/00450618.2023.2218429
22. Innes, M., & Sheptycki, J. W. E. (2004). From detection to disruption. *International Criminal Justice Review, 14*(1), 1–24. https://doi.org/10.1177/105756770401400101
23. Raymond, T., & Julian, R. (2015). Forensic intelligence in policing: Organisational and cultural change. *The Australian Journal of Forensic Science, 47*(4), 371.
24. Forensic Intelligence Lexicon. (2022). *Australian New Zealand Policing Advisory Agency National Institute of Forensic Science.* https://www.anzpaa.org.au/ArticleDocuments/2304/Forensic%20Intelligence%20Lexicon%202022%20v1.PDF.aspx. Accessed July 8, 2023.
25. Garvey, T., LaBerge, G., & Wartell, J. (2023). *Forensic intelligence models: assessment of current practices in the United States and internationally.* National Institute of Justice.
26. Ross, A. (2015). Elements of a forensic intelligence model. *The Australian Journal of Forensic Science, 47*(1), 8.
27. Collins, M., Huttunen, J., Evans, I., & Robertson, J. (2007). Illicit drug profiling: The Australian experience. *Australian Journal of Forensic Sciences, 39*(1), 25–32.
28. Australian Customs Notice No. 2022/06: Electromagnetic Weapons. (2022). *Australian Border Force.* https://www.abf.gov.au/help-and-support-subsite/CustomsNotices/2022-06.pdf. Accessed July 8, 2023.

Chapter 3
Innovation Through the Liaison with Academia and End Users

Carolyn Lovell and Stephen Bleay

Abstract This chapter discusses the importance of establishing dialogue between academia (one of the innovation stakeholders) and the end-users (the beneficiaries of the research), and how governmental bodies have instigated and fostered these linkages. An overview is given of the main UK government organisations that have driven research in forensic science from the 1980s to the present day, together with government reviews of the forensic landscape impacting upon research and development. The interactions between government, academia and end-users to drive innovations in the fields the fields of fingerprints, DNA and digital forensics are described, and it is concluded that there are significant differences in the way the collective research community in each field has approached development and implementation of novel technology. Examples are reported where such three-way collaborations between academia, end-user and government have produced highly effective end products, but there is also scope for improving effectiveness of dialogue between these parties, particularly in the rapidly evolving digital forensics discipline.

3.1 Introduction

The use and application of forensic science can make a significant contribution to the needs of the criminal justice system (CJS) as a whole, delivering benefits across many key 'impact points', including generating lines of enquiry, exonerating and safeguarding the innocent and providing evidence in prosecutions. Forensic science is a complex interdisciplinary field, with multiple stakeholders' drivers and pressures. In principle, it could include any academic discipline that could serve the CJS whether directly (as in the case of technological developments) or indirectly (e.g. social science), shedding light on important trends in society and criminality

C. Lovell (✉)
Office of the Chief Scientific Adviser, National Police Chief's Council, London, UK
e-mail: carolyn.lovell@npcc.police.uk

S. Bleay
School of Applied Sciences, London South Bank University, London, UK

S. Francese and R. S. P. King (eds.), *Driving Forensic Innovation in the 21st Century*,
https://doi.org/10.1007/978-3-031-56556-4_3

that provide necessary context to interpret the meaning and significance of things. Research collaboration has wide-reaching benefits and is of particular importance in the field of criminal justice and forensic science. In both fields, the often-rapid changes in workplace skills and the evolving legal and societal challenges facing modern criminal justice systems, require a more problem-based learning approach which is essential to improving evidence-based practice [1]. There are many stages between the collection of traces at a crime scene and the use of the evidence within a courtroom; the journey starts with those who collect the traces that have the potential to become evidence, progressing through to those that analyse the traces and present the results and then to others who must decide on the usefulness as evidence. These users comprise of the police, other law enforcement agencies and the Crown Prosecution Service (CPS), who must ultimately decide whether to prosecute. Finally, the forensic science reaches the court, which comprises of lawyers, judges, and jurors who need to understand the forensic evidence in the context of the case presented [2]. Academic researchers must therefore have a clear understanding of the realities of the end-user needs and environment, which can only be gained through interaction with an end-user and ideally the wider stakeholder community in order to take a system-wide approach.

The forensic innovation ecosystem is complex and may provide challenges for businesses, industry and academia to engage with effectively. Historically, these engagements have often been borne out of external factors and have evolved in synergy with the needs of end-users and stakeholders, providing the driving force for innovation and funding. Requirements for new methods to answer forensic questions have also led to new fields of forensic science being developed [3] such as the emerging areas of microbial forensics, digital forensics and forensic medicine. These new fields have emerged from casework requirements and the associated need for dedicated forensically relevant evidence bases to underpin new methods that often originate from scientific disciplines [4]. Examples of specific drivers to innovation originating from end-user requirements include the Provisional Irish Republican Army (IRA) campaign in Northern Ireland and mainland Britain during the 1970s and 1980s. These events led to focused efforts to increase the recovery of fingerprint evidence from substrates encountered in explosive devices, such as plastic bags, electrical tape and fabrics. Consequently, several new fingermark visualisation processes emerged from research endeavors in that time period.

Further, changes in legislation banning the use of chlorinated fluorocarbons (CFCs), and other solvents producing greenhouse gases, in the 1990s resulted in significant efforts by industry to develop lower impact alternatives, and the importance of such solvents in fingermark visualisation reagent formulations resulted in government organisations taking active roles in the formulation and evaluation of novel alternatives.

The availability of funding is obviously a critical factor in determining whether a particular process (and associated equipment) proceeds from a laboratory concept to operational reality. This chapter will, using examples, outline the importance of establishing dialogue between academia (one of the innovation stakeholders) and the end users (the exploiters of the research) and how governmental bodies have instigated and fostered these connections to ensure that high priority and fit-for-purpose forensic science research is delivered.

3.2 Drivers for Collaboration: Government Agencies Involved in Research and Innovation

Scientific research and innovation can have a positive impact on society, especially in the arena of forensic science, as illustrated through the introduction of the National DNA Database, further fingerprint visualisation and identification capabilities, and, more recently, digital forensics, which play a significant role in the CJS. However, to fully achieve operational impact, scientists must engage with end-users and key stakeholders from the very beginning of the research process to build knowledge and confidence and integrate any new process into an organisation or workflow. This collaboration tends to be realised through the formation of practitioner or stakeholder engagement groups and includes dialogue between the research team and end-users, which can involve the exchange of ideas, identifying what works and more importantly what will not, providing knowledge for informed decision-making on the application of the science. This interaction creates active involvement of the stakeholders in the research process for the journey of the project, developing a level of commitment in the scientific process that all end users can understand and engage with. Of importance, Mason [5] states that research and innovation is a '*team sport*' and we all need to be on the same team. Any new idea or innovation requires buy-in from many people, all of whom are likely to have differing priorities, incentives and perspectives. As such, time, consultation and trust are important factors to success, setting priorities for the activities with a level of governance and senior level support is critical.

The desire to work with academia and across governmental agencies and policing has long been recognised when commissioning and evaluating research and development activities for policing and forensic science. There is a long history of UK governmental agencies with remits to carry out research and produce targeted innovation outputs for the forensic science sector. Although the history extends beyond this, those involved since the 1980s are shown in Fig. 3.1.

The Forensic Science Service (FSS) was a government-owned company (GovCo) in the United Kingdom which provided forensic science services to the police forces and government agencies of England and Wales, as well as other countries. It was established in the early 1980s, bringing together pre-existing regional forensic science laboratories and the Home Office Central Research Establishment at Aldermaston into a single organisation. Between the early 1990s and its closure in 2011, the FSS progressed from a public to a commercial organisation and, over the same time period, a commercial market developed for forensic services. The FSS became an Executive Agency of the Home Office in 1991. Prior to this, there was no monetary charging mechanism for forensic services and services were, in effect, free at the

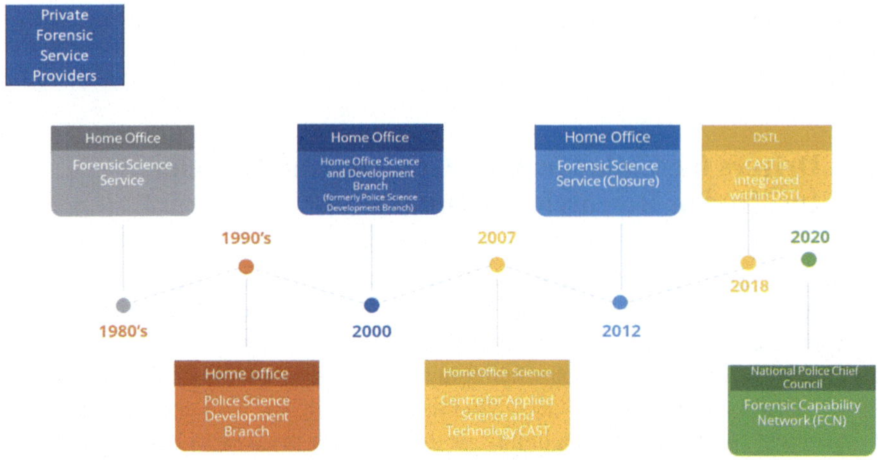

Fig. 3.1 Organisations engaged with forensic science end-users since the early 1980's

point of use. In 1996, the Metropolitan Police Forensic Science Laboratory became a part of the FSS, which then acquired Trading Fund status in 1999. These changes opened the possibility of a market in forensic science services and, as noted by the Association of Chief Police Officers (ACPO), "introduced financial discipline into forensic science provision and procurement" such that "costs and value added by forensic support became clearer to police forces".

During the mid-late 1990s the companies LGC and later Forensic Alliance started to penetrate the market. However, the FSS remained ACPO's "preferred supplier" until 2002, with many forces opting to extend "what was effectively a 'gentleman's agreement' with the FSS to provide services". The commercial environment necessitated formal contractual arrangements for provision of forensic services to become the norm rather than the exception [6] In the early 2000s the FSS competed with private forensic service providers and held around 60% of the market share in 2010 [7].

In 2010 a decision was made by the government to close the FSS, citing the shrinking forensic science market, increased police insourcing and operating losses as the reason. However, concerns were expressed at this time regarding reductions in research and development activity in the sector and the wider impact this could have on the criminal justice system and furthermore lack of consultation with the Home Office Chief Scientific Adviser. The Forensic Science Service was a leading world class organisation, with focused internal research and development which addressed current forensic challenges as they arose. A parliamentary review that focused on forensic science research and development in the UK was stood up in 2011 [7], and many were sceptical of the timing of this stating it would have been beneficial to have undertaken this before the announcement of the closure of the FSS.

There were no governmental ring-fenced finances for forensic science research and development during the time the FSS operated, however in comparison to other private forensic service providers at that time, a significant spend of £3–4 million on research and development by the FSS was detailed within the 2011 parliamentary review of forensic science. This is relevant as the FSS was the national focus for forensic R&D with established links with academia across many scientific disciplines which presented opportunities to address the complex interdisciplinary forensic assessments and analysis required during case work. It was unlikely that this could be achieved in any other forensic service provider at the time because they did not have the same breadth of expertise across all forensic disciplines as the FSS, given that there was more focus on areas offering commercial returns. The FSS engaged with end-users to support research and development when considering new processes and actively sought feedback. Other forensic service providers were mainly focussed on early developmental stages of research and development and not necessarily engaged with the end-user requirements until later on in the process.

Mennell [8] highlighted a challenge in developing a model that forensic service providers and others can interact with, which included the identification of end-user requirements and stakeholder engagement to aid forensic science research and innovation. It is recognised that advancements in applied sciences such as forensic science occur when innovative technologies and methodologies are implemented by end-users. The reality is that simply identifying or developing a new forensic technology or technique does not ensure that it will be successfully adopted and integrated by practitioners in the criminal justice community. Factors such as ease of use, affordability and availability from commercial sources have to be addressed for the new forensic science technologies to be put into practical use. A workshop held with senior forensic users during 2009 stipulated that there was a real need for the police service to identify its current and future strategic requirements [8]. This would assist the police service in fostering collaborations, developing a pipeline of innovation and investment and maintaining connections across the landscape with key end-users and partners which included the Home Office Science and Development Branch.

The Home Office Science and Development Branch (HOSDB) (formerly the Police Scientific Development Branch) was a branch of the Home Office which provided scientific research into new and emerging technologies that could be utilised to fight crime and support other police functions, and as such was also another government organisation influencing forensic science innovation. HOSDB was a team of scientists and engineers that established close engagement with end-users including the police and other law enforcement agencies, as well as a range of other government departments, and considered science and technology solutions for policing and the wider Home Office portfolio as a whole [9]. Activities focused specifically on areas such as counter terrorism, policy, law enforcement, offender management and immigration in addition to certain areas of forensic science. With an annual spend of approximately £25 million, the team provided technical advice, set technical standards and were internationally renowned. The HOSDB were the conduit between commercial manufacturers/academia and the end-user. However, HOSDB recognised that there were challenges in end-users expressing their requirements clearly in order to achieve real time benefits. Without this clarity, too much time could be spent in the research and development space without clear plans to progress technology to the implementation stage. Through engagement with the end-user communities, HOSDB aimed to understand the operational needs and the context of where new technologies could add real time benefits, moving away from focusing on solutions and also considering what technologies the end-user already had access to (Fig. 3.2). The scientists also ensured they had first-hand experience of the end-user requirements by attending crime scenes and live operations to maximise their experience and knowledge in order to advise and develop the most appropriate solutions for the job in hand.

A key forensic-related development that originated from the PSDB/HOSDB was the Manual of Fingerprint Development Techniques (now the Fingermark Visualisation Manual), first published in 1986, which since has been endorsed and used by every police force in the United Kingdom and several others worldwide.

A further rebrand of Home Office Science functions in 2007 led to the creation of the Centre for Applied Science and Technology (CAST) building on the previous functions of HOSDB. CAST had extensive networks within the UK and abroad with government, industry and academia and so were able to influence and develop the most cost-effective technologies to solve end user problems. CAST aimed to translate end-user needs into scientific and technological requirements to drive innovative and cost-effective solutions across the science and technology supply base. Through collaborations with academia, end users and industry, CAST were able to benefit from the European-funded Horizon research programme, where end-user engagement and impact are assessed as part of the funding process. CAST were established partners in over 13 projects, which included developing new techniques for the transfer of information from crime scenes, detection methods for hazardous crime scenes using

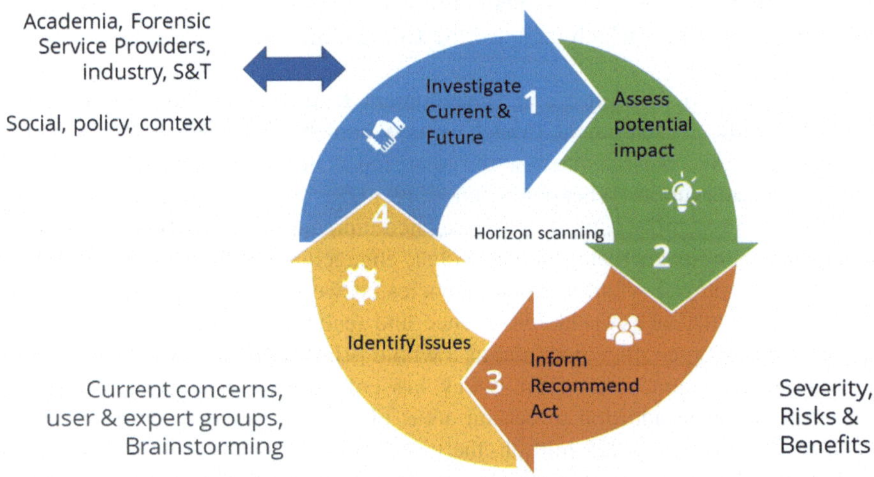

Fig. 3.2 Diagram illustrating the HOSDB model of engaging stakeholders to support end-user requirements in Science and Technology (adapted from [9], no permission needed as in open source)

advanced technology as well as developing new methods for analysing large volumes of data in digital forensic cases.

Following a review instigated in 2016 by the Home Office Permanent Secretary, CAST was officially integrated into the Defence Science and Technology Laboratory (Dstl) as part of the Ministry of Defence (MOD) on the 1st April 2018. Dstl became the primary delivery organisation for the provision of science and technology required by the Home Office, with funding for Home Office priorities being determined and funded by a Home Office Commissioning team. It was felt by the review panel, and particularly following the aftermath of the Salisbury poisoning in March 2018, that Dstl would provide continued resilience and expertise across a range of science and technology, being able to respond to the government at any time with the integrated organisation addressing both Home Office and MoD forensic science needs.

3.3 Governmental Reviews and Impact on Research and Innovation

The changes and developments since the late 1990's have been mirrored by a series of governmental reviews and reforms focussed specifically on the provision of forensic science services to the CJS. In some cases, these reviews have been a driver for change, and in other cases the review or report has been in response to a change in environment.

These include the Silverman review in 2011 [10], carried out soon after the closure of the FSS. The Home Office commissioned Professor Bernard Silverman, the then Home Office Chief Scientific Advisor, to review forensic science research. His report published in June 2011 concluded that the research landscape was fragmented and that improved coordination and communication with end-users was needed to drive innovation effectively. A Forensic Science Special Interest Group (SIG) was created at the recommendation of Silverman, in order to encourage collaboration and research opportunities across key stakeholders within the CJS. This was effectively a Knowledge Transfer Network (KTN) aimed to focus activity and accelerate innovation in cross-disciplinary topics of strategic importance. The specialist interest groups were time-bound activities that were intended to achieve their objectives over a small number of years and then be replaced by new, higher-priority areas of focus. A steering board was set up of representatives from academia, National Crime Agency, Dstl, Home Office CAST, the Forensic Science Regulator, the Chartered Society of Forensic Sciences and small and large forensic service providers. An innovation database was established which held a list of research requirements and also where new innovations were underway, the database comprised of three sections, challenges, contributors and stakeholders. A key activity of the SIG was a Forensic Science Technology Showcase that provided researchers and developers a chance to demonstrate their new technologies and techniques to end-user groups. The SIG also produced a series of reports, including 'Taking Forensic Research and Development to Market' [11]. A challenge for the SIG was ensuring that those that needed to be aware of the innovation database were kept informed and aware of it. Especially challenging for the SIG was accessing organisations within policing and the Home Office. Concerns were raised regarding duplication of effort by differing organisations [12]. The KTN assigned a forensic lead working in this domain 1 day a week in order to maintain the steering group and innovation database [13]. The funding for the SIG was ultimately withdrawn in line with the KTN policy in 2018. However, it was recognised that ongoing facilitation of communication across the forensic science sector was required based on the sensitivity, complexity and interdisciplinary nature of forensic science.

Some funding of forensic science innovation in the mid-2010s was also provided by the Police Innovation Fund, initiated in 2013 and replaced by the Police Transformation Fund in 2016. Each police force was allocated funding to be spent on innovative policing-focused projects, and some forces chose to use this in forensic areas. Table 3.1 gives a summary of forensic science-related projects funded over the period 2014–16.

Of these projects the custody footwear capture system was implemented within the MPS but not more widely, development of rapid DNA technology has continued for a range of applications, and MALDI-MSI has increased in maturity and could be considered for use on casework.

In 2015 the Government Chief Scientific Adviser Sir Mark Walport chose to focus his annual review on forensic science, and his document 'Forensic Science and Beyond' [2] outlined steps required to secure the UK's forensic science sector for the long term, placing specific emphasis on innovation and new market opportunities, applying forensic science principles to new areas and identifying technologies developed in other industries that could be adapted for the forensic sector.

However, some issues began to surface following the closure of the FSS. Reports by the BBC in 2013 highlighted higher costs associated with forensic science and further challenges were reported within the media linked to austerity and falling standards placing a higher risk on miscarriages of justice.

The Home Office published its Forensic Science Strategy in 2016 [14], with the aim of addressing some of these concerns. However, this was not universally seen as the solution, with one MP describing it as vague and incoherent [15].

Of more recent significance is the 2017–2019 report by the House of Lords Science and Technology Committee, 'Forensic Science and the CJS A Blue Print for change' [16], which heard evidence from a wide range of practitioners, academics and CJS stakeholders. They reported a lack of coordinated strategic thinking specific to research and development in forensic science, stating that there was no formal established process for legal or forensic practitioners (end-users) to engage and outline areas requiring research. Following the House of Lords review, the Forensic Capability Network (FCN) was established in 2020 with a specific focus to support several of the recommendations highlighted in the report, specifically the forensic marketplace, research and development and forensic science quality standards. The FCN strives to deliver a collective voice for the forensic community with a recognition of the challenges of understanding the diverse needs and circumstances of end-users and

Table 3.1 Forensic science-related projects funded by the Police Innovation Fund, 2014–16

Lead force	Other partners	Bid name/details	Award/ Year
Metropolitan Police Service	All forces England and Wales Home Office National DNA Database (NDNAD) Delivery Unit National Footwear Strategy Group Bluestar Software	Digitised capture of custody footwear impressions for integration with The National Footwear Database and real-time intelligence	£304,250 (2015/16)
West Yorkshire	South Yorkshire North Yorkshire Humberside Home Office Centre for Applied Science and Technology National Crime Agency Regional CTU University of Huddersfield (to support evaluation with CAST)	Live-Time Forensics (Forensic Intelligence Database)	£237,300 (2015/16)
Lancashire		Investigate/introduce rapid DNA profiling technology in criminal investigations	£339,990 (2014/15)
Nottinghamshire	Derbyshire Leicestershire Lincolnshire Northamptonshire	Investigate / introduce rapid DNA profiling technology in criminal investigations	£91,400 (2014/15)
Metropolitan Police Service	Kings College London	Forensic Biosensors—introducing innovative technologies to crime prevention	£113,340 (2014/15)
West Yorkshire	Sheffield Hallam University	Chemical Profiling of fingermarks—MALDI MSP and MALDI MSI method refinement for operational deployment in casework	£26,984 (2014/15)

aims to bridge the gap between scientific and law enforcement communities, and to disseminate detailed information to the field about new technologies and their effectiveness. The FCN wants to advance technology for policing by supporting the testing and evaluation of emerging technologies applicable to forensic science, providing a national reach, knowledge sharing and discussion panels through expert groups and bringing end-users together with academia and industry to remove barriers to implementation and acceptance ensuring that technologies and innovations showing promise are placed into the hands of forward thinking practitioners, stakeholders and policy makers.

Policing now has its first Chief Scientific Adviser, Professor Paul Taylor, with a recognition that science and technology has become integral to policing's ability to deliver an efficient and effective service and the complexity of opportunities and threats that new technologies bring and the exploitation of these by criminals has motivated policing to deliver the first Science and Technology Strategy [17].

The strategy commits to delivering a science system for policing, setting out the continued benefits from collaborations with industry and academia as well as a defined mission to engage widely, and be clear about the end-user needs and how best to work with policing in seeking new ideas, innovations and forms of delivery.

3.4 Innovation in Different Forensic Disciplines

The fact that 'forensic science' is a broad term encompassing multiple disciplines means that there is no 'one size fits all' approach that has been applied to driving innovation, and the interaction between governmental bodies, academia, the end-user (and industry) varies. Because there is no single approach to innovation, there is merit in reviewing how innovations in the two principal individualisation disciplines, Fingerprints and DNA, have been initiated, and also how the rapidly expanding discipline of Digital Forensics is being addressed.

3.4.1 Fingerprints

3.4.1.1 Background

The field of fingermark visualisation and imaging is not one that has been traditionally renowned for driving innovation. The first process widely used for fingermark visualisation was the simple application of powders [18], with effective combinations of brushes and powders being achieved through experimentation. The chemical processes adopted for fingermark visualisation have not, with the exception of 1,2-indandione [19] and more recently Lumicyano™ [20], used chemicals that have been synthesized specifically for fingermark enhancement. Those that are most widely used have mostly been adapted from chemicals already in use for other purposes, based on a knowledge of the substances most abundant within fingermarks. As a few examples, ninhydrin was already well-known as a colorimetric indicator for amines before it was utilised to react with amino acids in fingermarks; silver nitrate was selected because it was known to react with chlorides; Solvent Black 3 and Oil Red O were already used as histological fat stains before being adopted as reagents to stain the sebaceous constituents of fingermarks and any and fatty contaminants present.

Many of the processes used for fingermark visualisation are therefore simple, where the surface bearing the fingermark is exposed to a liquid chemical to produce a reaction or interaction which reveals the fingermark. The additional factor that has required a degree of innovation is where the optimum conditions required for fingermark visualization are not achieved at the standard laboratory conditions of temperature and humidity. In these circumstances, specialist equipment may be required to provide these conditions. In some cases, this may be an adaptation of existing commercial equipment, but there are several examples (e.g. cyanoacrylate fuming chambers, controlled humidity ninhydrin ovens) where equipment has been developed specifically for the purposes of fingermark visualisation.

If the range of fingermark visualisation processes is considered, in nearly all cases where specialist equipment is required to obtain optimum results, the original observation of the process was fortuitous, and it was lateral thinking by scientists in academia/industry and/or practitioners that raised awareness of the potential. An interesting exception to this is the electrostatic detection apparatus (ESDA), where initial government funding was provided to academia (the London College of Printing) to develop an electrostatic development method for visualising fingermarks on fabric and paper, but observations during testing resulted in the highly successful commercialisation of this system for the alternative application of revealing indented writing [21].

Examples of the fortuitous discovery of fingermark visualisation processes include the independent observation in at least three countries in the late 1970s that cyanoacrylate 'superglue' vapours could develop fingermarks on surfaces if contained within enclosed spaces [22, 23]. In 1964, Tolansky had noted that vacuum metal deposition developed unwanted fingermarks on glass articles being metallized for use as optical components [24], and in the mid-1970s Menzel observed that a high-powered laser revealed many fingermarks on surfaces within his laboratories at the Xerox Corporation [25].

In these cases, the observation that the process was capable of revealing fingermarks was a starting point, but taking the step from a concept, to provision of practical equipment providing optimum processing conditions that could be easily used in a laboratory, required a combination of a necessity for practitioners to change from current practices, and a willingness by organisations to fund the development needed. In the 1970s and 1980s such development was often initially funded by government departments who produced prototypes that were passed to industry for subsequent commercialisation, but more recently this role has been increasingly taken on by manufacturers. Many of the processes that have successfully progressed from an experimental environment to the fingerprint enhancement laboratory have relied on collaborations between government, industry and academia, examples being the 'Quaser' series of filtered high intensity light sources for fluorescence examination, and the 'Sandridge' and large 'MVC' cabinets for cyanoacrylate fuming. Engagement with practitioners, often involving direct involvement in the running of operational trials, has also been an important factor in ensuring uptake.

3.4.1.2 Innovation Case Study: Vacuum Metal Deposition

An historical example of how dialogue between academia and government organisations resulted in the introduction of a novel process for fingermark visualization is vacuum metal deposition. The origins of the vacuum metal deposition fingermark visualization process lie in academia and the recognition by an academic researcher of the significance of some apparently undesirable results.

In 1964 Professor Tolansky of Royal Holloway College London was using the vacuum metal deposition process to produce thin metal films on optical components, when he observed that unwanted fingermarks were developed in regions where the glass had been handled. He wrote to the Home Office to suggest that this method be investigated as a more sensitive alternative to powdering for fingermark enhancement. At that time, however, there was no perceived benefit in the method, no government research group investigating fingermark enhancement, and it was therefore not pursued further. However, after publication of similar observations by French researchers [26], the Home Office revived their interest in the process and funded academic research at the Royal Holloway College under the supervision of Professor Tolansky. The PhD research was conducted by David Hambley, who used a relatively small vacuum bell jar to deposit films of different metals (singly, and in combination) to develop fingermarks on paper and fabric substrates. The results demonstrated that the process had much promise of improved effectiveness over existing methods, but the small-scale equipment used in the project was impractical for use on the size of exhibits typically encountered in casework. Further investment was therefore required to produce equipment that could be used in fingerprint enhancement laboratories.

In the late 1960s and throughout the 1970s, the Home Office were actively funding research and development into novel methods for fingermark visualisation, with one driver being identification of individuals involved in the IRA terrorism activities at the time. Research into fingermark visualisation was then conducted by two groups, the Police Scientific Development Branch based at Sandridge (UK), who investigated physics-based techniques, and the Home Office Central Research Establishment (later part of the FSS) based at Aldermaston, who explored chemistry-based approaches. Vacuum metal deposition fell under the remit of the PSDB group at Sandridge.

The next stage was to scale up the process from a laboratory bell jar, as used by Hambley, to a system capable of holding larger items such as bags, bottles and fabrics. This was achieved by collaboration between government and industry, with contracts placed with industry to produce modified industrial equipment that could deposit a specific combination of metals (gold, followed by cadmium) that had been identified as giving optimum results in the academic studies (Fig. 3.3).

Further trials using these modified chambers showed that the results obtained using the bell jar could be replicated at a larger scale, and also demonstrated that VMD significantly outperformed all other techniques then available on polyethylene, which was being increasingly encountered as a substrate as the use of plastic bags increased [27]. Following the results of these studies, the process was adopted by a

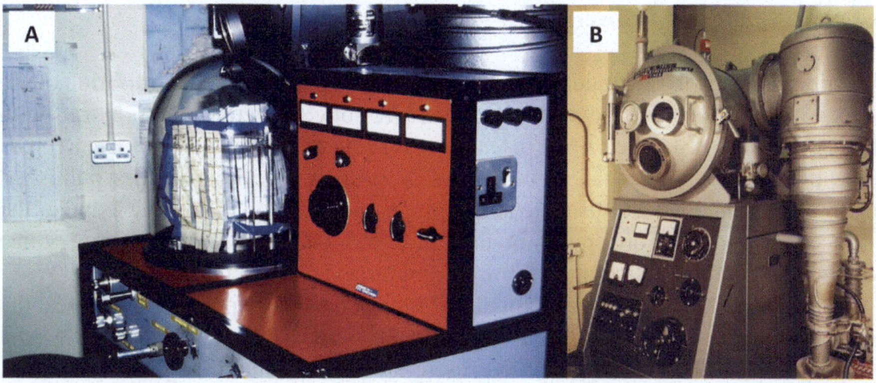

Fig. 3.3 Early stages in the development of the vacuum metal deposition process; **a**: small scale experiments using a bell jar vacuum chamber, and **b**: one of the first VMD chambers modified specifically for fingermark visualization. Reproduced by permission of Dstl, © Crown copyright—property of Dstl

number of police forces with operational requirements and funding for equipment, and operational trials showed that it was highly effective in developing fingermarks on a wide range of porous and semi-porous materials.

Commercial manufacturers, mainly Edwards and later West Technology, then produced equipment specifically designed for fingermark visualisation. For many years, the design of such equipment was relatively unchanged, with the major improvement being the production of larger chambers to accommodate items the size of a domestic refuse bag. There have been few refinements to the fundamental process, apart from a change to zinc as the second deposition metal to replace cadmium (due to its toxicity). A single stage VMD process using silver was introduced operationally in the late 2000s, but this was based on work previously conducted on single metals by Hambley during his PhD studies.

Recent innovation in this area has solely come from the manufacturers (e.g. West Technology) who have invested in new technologies such as touch screen control and integrated pumping systems to produce equipment that is more compact and potentially portable, and does not require additional infrastructure such as external pumps. Such innovation has been internally funded by manufacturers to increase the market for what has been regarded as specialist equipment, rather than being provided from central government funds. The development of cheaper, portable systems has had a positive impact by making the technology accessible to a range of end-users who would previously have found it unaffordable, and has revived interest in the technique.

3.4.1.3 Academia—Government—End-User Engagement

An important step in the fingermark visualisation field was the standardisation of the processes and processing sequences used in UK police fingerprint laboratories with the compilation of Home Office research results and knowledge (both from PSDB and the FSS) into the Manual of Fingerprint Development Techniques, first published in 1986. This enabled end-users to select processes based on their knowledge of the surface type and exposure environment of the exhibit and meant that different police forces were nominally using the same formulations and working procedures.

After the publication of the Manual of Fingerprint Development Techniques, the research conducted by the PSDB (later HOSDB and CAST) was overseen by a practitioner-based user group with representation from different regions of the UK, chaired by a Scientific Support Manager and with a membership of predominantly fingerprint enhancement laboratory staff with some crime scene investigator input. The group ultimately reported to the ACPO Fingerprint Board but operated at several levels below the main Board itself. The User group provided feedback on the results obtained from research and also some practitioner input on what research may be required in future. However, to a large extent, the Home Office research team acted as an intelligent customer, interacting with international researchers (both government organisations and academia) and reviewing enquiries received from practitioners to identify which areas of research were likely to have most operational benefit. The research itself was mainly conducted within Home Office laboratories at Sandridge, with very limited outsourcing of work to academia. Interaction with academia did take place, although this was predominantly via 1-year undergraduate and 3-month Master placement students carrying out research projects in the Home Office laboratories. This began to change in the mid-2000s with a growing recognition that academia was conducting research into fingermark visualisation and/or analysis using advanced equipment not available in government laboratories [28–31] and that greater interaction between government and academia was required. This had the advantages of providing the Home Office with early sight of techniques with operational potential, and also gave academia a better understanding of the research methodologies used in fingermark research and the level of rigour required to provide confidence that a new method gave advantages over existing published processes. This led to the Home Office part-funding a series of PhD projects with academic partners to explore some of these emerging technologies in greater depth.

Two other related influences emerged in the early 2010s that changed the relationship between government, academia and practitioners. The creation of the Forensic Science Regulator and the requirement for fingerprint laboratories to be accredited to the ISO 17025 standard meant that validation evidence was required for all fingermark visualisation processes in use in police laboratories. Around the same time, CAST commenced on a major revision of the Manual of Fingerprint Development Techniques (later re-titled the Fingermark Visualisation Manual (FVM)) [32]. Both endeavours required an extensive review of the experimental data collected on each process and publication of the relevant parts of that data. This process also highlighted that there were gaps in knowledge about the underlying theory and the performance of some of the processes which could not be covered by work at CAST in the timescales available, and, as a consequence, an extensive academic network was engaged with the project work required. This was successful in producing data that supported accreditation of all main processes in the FVM and publication of the underpinning data in the Fingerprint Source Book and Technique Validation Reports that were provided to UK law enforcement agencies. The FVM also presented a new approach in that it grouped the hundreds of processes that have been published in literature into a series of categories ranging from 'A' (highly effective processes for routine use) to 'F' (not to be used for health and safety reasons). The FVM also included a published methodology of the stages of research and development that a process should pass through before it becomes a Category A process accepted for widespread use. For the first time, the FVM also included innovative processes that were still under development within academia but that it was believed may have potential to give improved performance in future over the Category A processes in use at the time. The publication of the Home Office Fingerprint Research Methodology [33] and International Fingerprint Research Group Guidelines [34] as peer-reviewed papers also provided transparency on the types of test and validation data required to advance a process in maturity (or Technology Readiness Level) and take it from a theoretical concept to a regularly used operational method.

Following the publication of the FVM and rollout to practitioners via a series of training workshops, CAST instigated the Industry/Academia Working Group, designed to build on the relationships with academia developed during data collection and the existing relationships with practitioners. The group was intended as a discussion forum for government (CAST) and practitioners (police force laboratories) to directly raise the main operational issues or strategic requirements (e.g. knife crime, corrosive substances, carrying out more analysis at the scene) with academia (who may have the resources, equipment and students to address them). Because of the increasing move away from the model of government funding of the development of novel equipment for fingermark visualisation to development being funded by forensic equipment manufacturers, industry representatives were also invited to these meetings. These meetings continued until CAST was integrated into the Defence Science and Technology Laboratory (Dstl) and the funding model for government fingerprint research funding changed from being directly from the Home Office via CAST, to funding allocated to Dstl by the Home Office Commissioning team. Dstl are also a funder of forensic science research to address Ministry of Defence priorities, and one objective of the integration was to bring fingerprint research activities for the Home Office and Ministry of Defence under a single umbrella.

Another role played by Dstl is to host the Defence and Security Accelerator (DASA), part of the Ministry of Defence, who have a remit to fund innovative work that can be exploited in the defence or security fields. DASA have a network of innovation partners and seek bids from academia and business, often along focused themes but also Open calls. Similarly, the UKRI and Innovate UK run the Knowledge Transfer Partnership scheme which connects businesses with innovative ideas with academia and a graduate or postgraduate KTP Associate. Although neither scheme has a stream specifically for forensic science, both have recently funded projects related to innovation in fingermark visualisation and enhancement (and other forensic disciplines). There is no specific requirement to engage end-users in these projects, although this would be a desirable approach to increase the likelihood of subsequent uptake.

3.4.2 DNA

3.4.2.1 Background

In 1984, Alec Jeffreys introduced DNA profiling in the field of forensic genetics in a laboratory in the Department of Genetics at the University of Leicester and proved that some regions in the DNA chain have repetitive sequences, which vary among individuals. This led to the UK being the first country to take forward the so-called forensic DNA 'revolution' [35, 36] Due to this discovery DNA profiling was first applied in an immigration case in 1988 [37] and later the first forensic case was solved using DNA analysis [38]. It was quickly recognised the significant difference and use this technology could make to the Criminal Justice System with regards to the identification of suspects in police cases [35], particularly where the identify of participant(s) was unknown.

3.4.2.2 The National DNA Database (NDNAD)

Creation of the NDNAD

In 1993, following a number of high-profile miscarriages of justice (for example the Birmingham Six, who had been jailed for planting an IRA bomb, but whose convictions were subsequently quashed), the Royal Commission on Criminal Justice recommended that a forensic DNA database be established; the database was proposed as a more objective form of forensic identification, with as much potential to eliminate suspects as to secure convictions. Subsequently, the 1994 Criminal Justice and Public Order Act (CJPOA) enabled the NDNAD for England and Wales to be established. The UK's National DNA Database (NDNADB), created in 1995, is both one of the longest established, and biggest of such forensic science databases worldwide [39].

The use of DNA in such serious crimes has helped secure significant financial investment and political commitment to expand the forensic databases (Fig. 3.4). Prior to this, DNA technology and DNA profiling as an investigation tool was still fairly limited in its use.

In 2004, the Criminal Justice Act 2003 extended police powers to allow DNA samples to be taken without consent from anyone arrested in England or Wales on suspicion of any recordable offence, regardless of whether or not they were charged, and to retain the DNA information indefinitely.

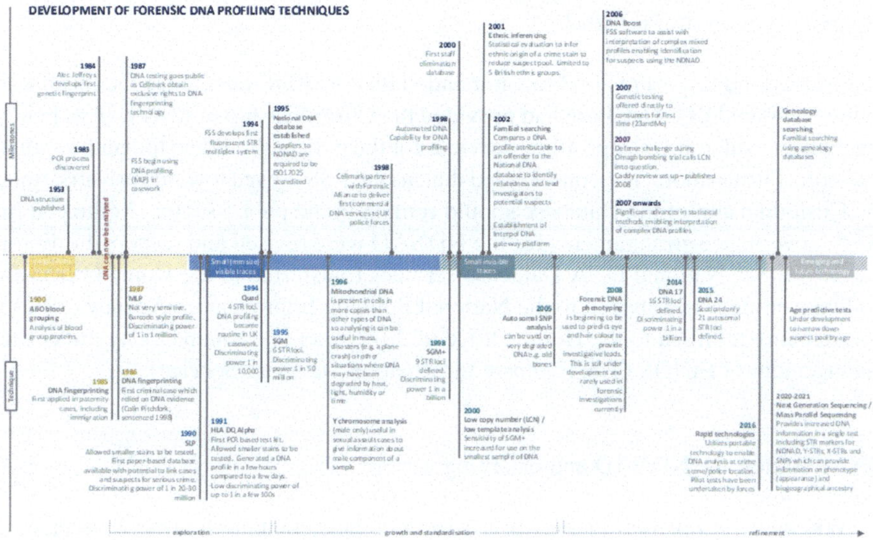

Fig. 3.4 Development of forensic DNA profiling techniques, Courtesy of the forensic capability network

At this time, it was apparent that no other State had greater freedom to obtain, use and store genetic information from its citizens raising concerns about the genetic privacy of non-convicted individuals. The compatibility of the retention regime with article 8 of the European Convention on Human Rights (right to privacy) was challenged (S and Marper v UK [2008]) resulting in the European Court of Human Rights (ECtHR) deciding that DNA from suspected but not convicted people should not be kept on the database. Changes in legislation were brought about by the Protection of Freedoms Act 2012 (PoFA) which is the statue under which the retention and use of DNA information is currently governed. Recognising the sensitivity of the information that could be obtained from a DNA sample, PoFA requires the destruction of DNA samples within 6 months of the sample being taken, unless it is retained under the Criminal Procedure and Investigations Act (1996). With regards the DNA profile, the Act permitted these to be retained indefinitely for convicted individuals (with specific exceptions) but their continued retention for those who are not charged or convicted was considered unlawful. In response to this, during 2012 and 2013 approximately 1.7 million DNA profiles taken from volunteers and non-convicted individuals, including children, were removed from the NDNAD and, through the Anti-Social Behaviour, Crime and Policing Act 2014 (ASBCPA), police are able to take a fresh sample when investigations are restarted after being discontinued. More recently, in the case of *Gaughran versus the United Kingdom (2020)* [40], the ECtHR ruled that the indefinite retention of DNA from all convicted adults is disproportionate. The Ministry of Justice responded to this judgement concluding that no change to legislation was required as it has now been addressed by the Data Protection Act 2018.

Custodianship of the NDNAD

The McFarland Report in 2003 recommended that the FSS, who, since the inception of the National DNA Database had provided the Custodianship of it, as well as being the main provider of DNA profiling services for the police, should no longer have that dual role. Furthermore, it recommended that, as the FSS moved towards privatisation, the Custodianship of the Database should remain in the public sector. At the end of 2005, governance arrangements for the NDNAD were revised and responsibility for the delivery of National DNA Database services transferred to the Home Office. In 2009 governance transferred to the National Policing Improvement Agency (NPIA) before being returned to the Home Office in 2012 where it remains today under the management of FINDS (The Forensic Information Database Service).

DNA Profiles, the NDNAD and Charging

In 2004 the CPS released Prosecution Team Guidance making it possible to charge a suspect on the basis of a DNA 'intelligence' match report rather than, as had previously been the case, an 'evidential' report. The guidance was clear, that a charge could not be based on a DNA match alone and that additional appropriate evidence was required. This shift in process was part of the newly implemented Staged Reporting process designed to drive efficient and effective case progression by encouraging early cooperation/defence identification of issues/guilty plea.

Transnational Exchange

Over the past two decades, the fight against cross-border crime and terrorism has increased interest in the transnational exchange of forensic DNA data. The first vehicle for exchanging DNA profiles between different countries was the INTERPOL DNA Gateway set up in 2002. In support of this, participating Member States can restrict their DNA profiles to specified countries and law enforcement agencies where appropriate. In addition to rules regarding data handling, there are also rules regarding sample handling; laboratories carrying out the analysis are required to have accreditation to ISO 17025 or an equivalent national standard.

In 2008, with a view to strengthening cooperation between EU member states in combatting terrorism and cross-border crime, the Prüm Decisions were incorporated into EU law making it mandatory for the DNA databases of member states to be accessible by other member countries. This data exchange system, commonly referred to as the Prüm system, allows for the automatic exchange of data on the basis of a decentralised database system and, as with the Interpol system, DNA data remains the property of the member state where it was collected. Adoption has proved difficult due several challenges associated with legal, political and technical difficulties encountered. However as of December 2020, although there are 26 Member States exchanging DNA data, the UK is currently exchanging with just 11 countries.

Governance of the NDNAD

There have been substantial social and ethical issues raised relating to the size, scope and governance of the NDNAD. Between 2000 and 2005 various independent review bodies called for more public accountability in the way the NDNAD was operated. Their recommendations consistently highlighted the need for an independent body with lay membership to oversee the workings of the Database and for the establishment of an ethics committee to which that oversight group could refer issues for advice. As a result, in 2003 the NDNAD User Board was expanded to include a member of the Human Genetics Commission. The Board continued to develop, becoming the NDNAD Strategy Board in 2005 and providing a structure to ensure independence of governance from users of the Database by 2008. Further, in 2007 an independent 'NDNAD Ethics Group' was established to provide advice to Ministers and the DNA Board on the ethical operation of the NDNAD. In July 2017, the Ethics Group was replaced by the Biometrics and Forensics Ethics Group (BFEG). The remit of the BFEG expands beyond that of the NDNAD Ethics Group with committee members from across academia and includes ethical issues associated with the retention and use of human samples and biometric identifiers (including DNA, fingerprints and facial recognition) used for differentiation between, or identification of, individuals.

Other significant changes to bring about increased public confidence in the operation of the National DNA Database include the establishment of the NDNAD Strategy Board and the Biometrics Commissioner as statutory bodies responsible for the oversight of the Database. The participation of independent Board members is influential in both strategic policy and decision making, as well as day-to-day operation of the National DNA Database—supporting the Board's ability to conduct its primary role to support criminal investigation in a way that is proportionate and transparent and encourages public confidence.

The general high level of sustainable demand has been possible due to advancements and developments in the technology and capabilities across a broad range of crime types. The forensic service providers have invested in automated technology and by 2005 the automation of DNA analysis and interpretation enabled the process to speed up from several weeks to just a few days.

3.4.2.3 Technological Aspects of DNA Analysis

The development of DNA analysis over the last 30 years or so can be broadly categorised into 3 phases. The first phase, between 1985 and 1995, can be considered the 'exploration phase' where different methodologies were developed. The first method used for forensic DNA identity testing was that of 'genetic fingerprinting' and in 1986 it was used to link the murder of two girls, whilst also eliminating a suspect. In 1987, Colin Pitchfork was found to match the sample and he was convicted in 1988.

Technology quickly moved on with the development of more rapid and sensitive PCR assays (HLA DQ alpha) and, subsequently combined with the more discriminating STR markers (Quad). The second phase, 'growth and standardisation' saw the launch of the NDNAD and the standardisation of DNA analysis to using multiplex STR systems (SGM). Over time more STR markers were included (SGM+) making the test more discriminating and reducing the chance of two people having the same set of markers enabling much larger populations of suspects to be analysed without the possibility of them having the same profile. Quality standards were set with the NDNAD Custodian requiring providers to the NDNAD to be UKAS accredited to ISO/IEC 17,025 and to participate in a specified proficiency-testing programme. Profiling systems became automated enabling a dramatic reduction in the time of sample processing. Despite these significant advances in DNA profiling technology, the potential for their investigative exploitation would not have been possible without the enabling legislative framework which was enacted between 1994 and 2001. Likewise, the rapid expansion of the NDNAD between 2000 and 2005 would not have been possible without the funding from the Home Office. It is apparent that developments in DNA profiling occurred in synergy with the State commitment to its application in forensic crime investigation and without this governmental commitment the technology would likely have remained limited in its development and applications. The third phase and the future beyond can be considered the refinement phase. Here laboratories have developed sophisticated software to assist with the interpretation of even more complex DNA results and in the future are developing ways to conduct more analyses with a single test and to make DNA testing more rapid and more mobile.

The sensitivity of DNA analysis has increased to such an extent that DNA profiles can be obtained from as little as a few cells and from traces that are invisible. As a result, the risk has also increased of detecting extraneous DNA in samples that may be unrelated to the crime itself. The extraneous DNA may have been present for entirely innocent reasons at the crime scene prior to the crime being committed (e.g. secondary or tertiary transfer), or it may have been deposited inadvertently after the incident such as contamination by police investigators attending the scene [41, 42], crime scene investigators collecting samples for laboratory examination, the laboratory staff who process the samples and contaminated materials used in the processing of the samples. As a result, a raft of measures has been developed to reduce the level of post-incident contamination and to improve the ability to detect it when it does occur. For example: anti-contamination measures (barrier clothing, restricted access, DNA-free consumables and cleaning regimes) have been introduced for scene and laboratory examinations; elimination databases contain DNA profiles of laboratory staff and visitors, police staff and consumable manufacturers to allow checks to be made to determine whether the DNA profile obtained could have originated from individuals involved in or in the environment of, the recovery and analysis of the sample; quality control measures and requirements are in place to check for systematic contamination of the consumables and reagents use in the recovery and analysis process.

The successful use of DNA for criminal cases led to a continued increase in cases submitted by the police to the forensic service providers. DNA technologies advanced increasing sensitivity. This rapid rise in cases led to a significant back log in DNA cases.

In response to this, the workforce was significantly increased under the DNA expansion Programme launched in April 2000 with an aim to accelerate the growth of the NDNAD. The total investment in this programme via the government to March 2005 was £240.8 million. This enabled policing to increase suspect sampling and the recruitment of 650 additional crime scene investigators to attend more crime scenes and recover more DNA samples [43].

Historically, the FSS provided training to policing, Crime Prosecution Service, and the judiciary regarding the use and application of forensic science. This was the case through the funding made available from the DNA Expansion Programme to ensure that every user was provided with an in-service programme with the same information across the UK regarding the use and capabilities of DNA profiling. Since this date however, whilst the technologies have continued to advance, training has predominantly been left to individual forces to procure or deliver. As recently observed with the introduction of the DNA 17 technology, police forces were provided with a general leaflet for forces to understand and disseminate. This, as well as a reduction in bespoke forensic science awareness training for student officer training, is likely to increase risks to investigations based on an inconsistent assessment of evidential value and, perhaps, missed forensic opportunities at a time when science and technology has been identified as integral to UK policing.

3.4.2.4 Academia—Government—End-User Engagement

In contrast to developments in fingermark visualisation and analysis technologies, the relationship between academia, government and the end-user has been very different in the DNA field in England and Wales. This is partly due to the different relationship between the police end-user and the laboratory conducting the analysis. In the case of fingermark visualisation and fingerprint identification, these are functions that are carried out internally by the police and, in comparison to large analytical laboratories, the investment requirements to equip fingerprint enhancement laboratories and identification bureaux are low. More specialist forensic functions such as DNA analysis are almost always carried out by a specialist laboratory (previously the FSS, now by one of the commercial FSPs), and exhibits are sent to those laboratories for analysis. Exhibits may be swabbed or taped for DNA within clean facilities at a police accredited laboratory, but those samples will subsequently be submitted to an FSP.

As a consequence, although the breakthrough that demonstrated DNA profiling could be applied to identifying individuals in a forensic context was developed in academia, subsequent innovations in the field over the next couple of decades were driven by researchers with the FSS laboratories who had an understanding of the types of forensic sample that could be recovered from crime scenes, the anti-contamination measures required, and the end-user requirements. Very few papers published on the forensic applications of DNA profiling by UK organisations after the initial publications by Jeffrey include academic co-authors.

Although, over time, some of the FSS staff began to move to academic institutions and to conduct independent research, the principal innovations in the analysis equipment, profiling methodologies and analysis software since the closure of the FSS have been mainly driven by the forensic service providers rather than academia, government or end-users.

There are few examples of liaison between end-users and academia in the UK in DNA analysis although one example of note is research into recovery and analysis of touch DNA, which was conducted as a collaboration between the Metropolitan Police Service (MPS) and Kings College London (KCL), with an MPS-funded member of staff embedded at KCL and coordinating research conducted there. This collaboration resulted in co-authored touch DNA-related publications [44, 45] but the embedding of MPS-funded staff at KCL has not been continued in recent years. KCL are one of very few academic institutions that have accredited DNA facilities and are also leaders in the use of the massively parallel sequencing approach used for forensic phenotyping. Some KCL research is conducted in partnership with Eurofins (one of the main forensic service providers for DNA analysis in the UK).

However, in general the cost of equipment and consumables associated with DNA analysis makes it difficult for academia to conduct extensive studies of novel methods on the scale possible for fingermark visualisation, which may partly explain the lower level of obvious academic involvement in advances in this field. The fact that there are multiple FSPs with their own analysis methodologies also makes it more difficult to develop innovations that are applicable to all end-users. In addition, because the laboratory conducting the analysis is often a separate entity from the police end-user, the collaborations that have been observed in the fingerprint field are more difficult to achieve. Many collaborations that do occur tend to be at a local rather than a national level, making it more difficult to implement innovative technology more broadly.

3.4.3 Digital Forensics

3.4.3.1 General Overview

The digital revolution has transformed the ways in which people commit crime. It has presented new opportunities for criminals to exploit long established forms of crime, such as child abuse and fraud, whilst also creating new methods, such as enhanced scams and county-line drug networks. The exponential growth of digital technology and the use of the internet as a way of life means almost any crime will now generate a trail of digital evidence [46]. Digital forensics is a branch of forensic science encompassing the recovery, investigation, examination and analysis of material found in digital devices. Digital evidence can be collected from an array of sources, such as computers, smartphones, remote storage, unmanned aerial systems, ship borne equipment and more. Digital forensics inevitably plays a vital role in nearly every criminal investigation in modern times as new technology develops more and more rapidly [46].

Historically, digital forensics was seen as a niche crime and was managed through policing's 'hi-tec' crime units. However, it has now become a core part of almost every criminal case and has emerged as a forensic discipline as the investigative questions and enquiries have continued to develop. The exponential growth of digital technology and the volume of data that is now available and relevant to criminal cases is at a stage that it threatens to overwhelm the police and the CJS. It is a current key challenge for the CJS specifically associated with the amount and the complexity of the data. The usefulness, relevance, and contribution of the data for investigations and the CJS needs to be fully explored. As an example, a single mobile phone is estimated to be able to contain one terabyte of data, which is equivalent to approximately 78 million pages of written documentation [14]. This presents a real challenge for policing in not only storing the data, but also analysing and interpreting it.

The technical challenge brings with it ethical issues to consider, mobile phones contain significant amounts of personal data, their behaviours and location all now available for policing and the courts to review and scrutinise. Citizens demand and expect more from those investigating and detecting crime. The notion of trust and legitimacy of the science and the ethical use of data within the CJS is significant. The introduction of evidence via non-traditional ways such as screen shots (message templates/generators) and other digital formats are increasing.

Historically, digital forensics has been delivered in a context marked by budgetary restrictions, financial uncertainty and short-term planning. Forces at different stages of preparedness, with variable resources and expertise have been dealing with an increase in demand for analysis as they try to keep up with the pace of change and adapt to new ways of criminal behaviour. This is now at odds with how policing procures services, which can be slow to respond, and over recent years there has been a lack of investment in policing information technology systems. Concerns were raised within policing and across government regarding the state of digital forensic capability in England and Wales, the House of Lords Science and Technology Committee [14] said:

> the rapid growth of digital forensic evidence presents challenges to the criminal justice system. We were not presented with evidence of any discernible strategy to deal with them.

Integral to this is a requirement for closer collaboration with law enforcement, vendors and academia and legal practitioners to reduce the gap between new technologies and their use in the investigation in alleged criminal activities. This includes the development of scientifically robust analytical tools to enable investigators to access and examine data from digital devices which will address the legitimate expectations of the Courts and the public. An inspection in December 2022 completed by His Majesty's Inspectorate of Constabulary and Fire and Rescue Services (HMICFRS) [47] made several recommendations for the direction of Digital Forensics within policing, one being that by November 2024 Chief Constables should integrate digital forensic services under their existing forensic science structures. This recognised the importance of the earlier developments in forensic science such as DNA and Fingerprints which are regulated, professional and trusted within the CJS and HMICFRS are keen to ensure that digital forensics follows the same framework. However, to do this collaboration is required across a broad range of stakeholders. Solutions are needed to generate the data and research required to scientifically underpin the approaches used for legal acceptance within the CJS and be able to know how to scientifically examine a technology before it reaches the market.

3.4.3.2 Academia—Government—End-User Engagement

Recent years has seen government and other partners such as the Forensic Science Regulator argue the need for a strategic approach to forensics [48–50]. Further to this the forensic science provision failed to align with the Policing Vision 2025 [51], and ultimately was fragmented and poorly equipped to address any future challenges, especially in digital forensics. Whilst there was no appetite to deliver a new national body, a more coordinated and collaborative approach was required. The National Police Chiefs Council established the Transforming Forensic Programme in 2018 with £30 million funding from the Police Transformation Fund. This was established to provide a strategic and sustainable response to the current challenges and risks for digital forensics and broader forensic domains [52]. Further to this is the NPCC Digital Forensic Portfolio board which sought to develop standardisation and has included national service level requirements, and the development of national models of validation and aimed to standardise digital forensic methods. The board is striving to reduce duplication across the 43 police forces.

The Forensic Capability Network was a product of the Transforming Forensics programme, with an area of focus specifically for digital forensics to develop a continued focus on future technical challenges and opportunities. The NPCC published the Digital Forensic Strategy in July 2020 [53] which laid out a roadmap for improving provision and use of digital forensics across law enforcement. This identified numerous areas for improvement which included improved operations, commercial practices, research and development, meeting the data challenge and developing the workforce. The strategy recognises that there has been limited strategic engagement with partners such as academia and industry in order to work on longer term solutions. Whilst some of the larger forces have engaged with academia/industry on an individual basis to develop and access new capabilities, this approach is generally inconsistent and risks being repetitive and inefficient with limited opportunities to share, which leads policing to be slow in responding to new capabilities that might already exist. Currently the field has had a more general focus on quicker wins over strategic opportunities for tomorrow's policing service, resulting in a patchwork of successes occurring at force level which are not therefore replicated nationally.

One national initiative of relevance to digital forensics is Operation Bluestone/Soteria which is a collaborative program of research between participating forces and UK universities, aimed at building a new national operating model for the investigation of rape and serious sexual offences. There are six workstreams underway of which one is specifically focussed on performance and digital forensics and it is anticipated to inform current and future policing operating models.

The academic landscape for digital forensics as opposed to the physical forensic domain is fragmented, this is due, in part, to the broad range of activities that sit within digital and data science and the fact that physical forensic science has developed over several decades. The FCN has introduced an academic digital research group aiming to bridge the gap and develop core areas for research and development and seek to share research and practice. Furthermore, UKRI in June 2023 held a research sandpit for funding research projects specifically focussed on Digital Forensics.

A new Digital Forensic programme was created in April 2022 to continue to support policing to meet the digital challenges and deliver against the 2020 NPCC Digital Forensic Strategy, this led to the completion of the Transforming Forensic programme in March 2023, where many of the services defined by the transforming forensic programme were incorporated into the Police Digital Service (PDS). The PDS aims to enhance digital services and capabilities and is the delivery vehicle for the National Police Digital Strategy 2020–2030. More is needed in terms of understanding the organisational challenges encountered in the delivery of digital forensic support; for example: "how does organisational change impact on this delivery? What is good practice in digital forensics? What is successful change and how is it implemented? How can we identify and disseminate 'what-works' in several key areas such as triage, accreditation, risk assessment, training, support and retention of workforce? A Digital Forensic Capability Group has been established to support and consider some of these challenges with end users and identify areas for continued research, with the Forensic Capability Network supporting coordination with key stakeholders.

The Home Office has instigated research specifically focussed on determining the value of digital forensics for investigations, three universities worked in collaboration with end users to interrogate policing systems and practices with focus on the application of digital forensics in sexual offence cases, child abuse cases and CCTV analysis for homicide investigation, this later developed into the Home Office Forensic Science Impact model and is accessible via www.gov.uk.

There remains an urgency to develop a future operating model for UK Digital Forensics, this is underway led by the Home Office and is due to conclude findings later in 2023. Other collaborations with end-users and academia have been progressed with policing through funding made available through the Chief Scientific Advisers Science, Technology Analysis and Research fund (STAR), which is an annual fund, focussed specifically at improving police service delivery, these are either proof of concept projects or those requiring operationalisation. There are an increasing number of digital forensic projects with academia and end-users presenting opportunities for successful projects to be considered for delivery at national scale.

Other governmental bodies, namely Dstl, support the delivery of digital forensics through commissions via the Home Office Commissioning hub, focussed on future science as well as hosting a digital crime scene group with end-users to address current technical investigation challenges as they arise.

The recruitment, retention and well-being of practitioners is crucial to the provision of forensic support services to forces. Several factors have been attributed to the challenges in the recruitment and retention of digital forensic practitioners and related personnel. For instance, the viewing of indecent images of children is often categorised as primary traumatisation and a traumatic stress factor. More is needed in terms of understanding how personnel are trained and retained nationally. 2023 will see the introduction of a digital forensic apprenticeship scheme developed in collaboration with the FCN academia and broader stakeholder; further to this, the College of Policing have developed front line officer training Operation Modify which supports new and serving officers to acquire the digital skills they need to undertake investigations effectively.

Understandably, Digital Forensics as a science and as applied to policing is facing significant challenges purely on the pace technology continues to develop, the landscape remains in a state of flux and we are likely to witness currently established models and practices obsolete in the future, as data grows and cloud services become the norm, more emphasis will be required for established relationships and dedicated funding in order to utilise the skills and expertise of broader data scientists and forensic science experts for the results to be present in a court of law.

3.5 Conclusions

Recognizably, it is not ideal for any one part of the academia—end-user—government tripartite to operate in isolation when developing innovative forensic science solutions. Academia need awareness of real-world issues from end-users to focus their research, end-users need awareness of what could be done to continually improve their service to police customers and the CJS, and government have a role to play in both providing funding and also impetus to collaborative activities. Developments in the fingerprints and DNA disciplines have occurred in very different ways with varying levels of engagement between these areas. In the past, government organisations such as the FSS and HOSDB/CAST have played an active role in driving innovation, acting as an intelligent customer on behalf of the end-user and also conducting a significant amount of research in-house. Although academia has initiated some of the most significant innovations in fields such as fingerprints and DNA, they have not always been closely engaged in the subsequent developments. The current forensic science landscape is different, there is significantly less internal forensic science-related research by government (with Dstl still carrying out some Home Office and MoD-funded activity) and the role of government has become more to facilitate dialogue between academia, industry and end-users, to articulate the current high priority challenges, and to focus collaborative efforts to address these. There have been previous initiatives such as the Police Innovation Fund and now the Police Chief Scientific Adviser's Science Technology Analysis and Research (STAR) Fund that have funded forensic innovations at an individual police force/end-user level, but there is greater long-term benefit in trying to produce solutions that can be implemented nationally. The formation of the Forensic Capability Network and the appointment of a National Policing Chief Scientific Adviser aim to address this issue, although it is too early to comment on what impact this has had.

References

1. Gilmour. (2023). Enhancing research collaboration within a large university department. *Innovations in Education and Teaching International*. https://doi.org/10.1080/.14703297.2023.2209064
2. Walport, M., Craig, C., & Surkovic, E. (2015). Forensic science and beyond: Authenticity, provenance and assurance. In: *Annual report of the government chief scientific adviser, Government Office for Science*. [https://assets.publishing.service.gov.uk/government/uploads/system/uploads/attachment_data/file/506461/gs-15-37a-forensic-science-beyond-report.pdf. Accessed July 22, 2023.
3. Madea, B., & Saukko, P. (2007). Future in forensic medicine as an academic discipline—Focussing on research. *Forensic Science International, 165*(2–3), 87–91. https://doi.org/10.1016/j.forsciint.2006.05.030
4. Carew, R., French, R., & Morgan, R. M. (2020). 3D forensic science: A new field integrating 3D imaging and 3D printing in crime reconstruction. *Forensic Science International: Synergy, 3*(4), 100205. https://doi.org/10.1016/j.fsisyn.2021.100205
5. Mason, L. (2022). *The modern malaise of innovation: Overwhelm, complexity, and herding cats*. https://thelivinglib.org/the-modern-malaise-of-innovation-overwhelm-complexity-and-herding-cats/. Accessed July 22, 2023.
6. House of Commons Science and Technology Committee. (2006). *Seventh report of session 2005–6*. House of Commons. https://publications.parliament.uk/pa/cm200506/cmselect/cmsctech/900/90002.htm. Accessed September 4, 2023.
7. House of Commons Science and Technology Committee. (2011). *The forensic science service. Seventh Report of Session 2010–12*. House of Commons, London. https://publications.parliament.uk/pa/cm201012/cmselect/cmsctech/855/855.pdf. Accessed July 22, 2023.
8. Mennell, J. (2010). Fostering forensic innovation. *Measurement and Control, 43*(8), 248–250. https://doi.org/10.1177/002029401004300805
9. Pratt, A. (2008). *Protecting the public using science and technology: A UK Perspective, presentation*. https://www.statewatch.org/media/documents/news/2008/oct/uk-ho-tech-presentation.pdf. Accessed July 22, 2023.
10. Silverman, B. (2011). *Research and development in forensic science: A review*. Home Office. https://assets.publishing.service.gov.uk/government/uploads/system/uploads/attachment_data/file/118916/forensic-science-review-report.pdf. Accessed July 22, 2023.
11. Forensic Science Special Interest Group. (2013). *Taking Forensic Science R&D to Market*. ESP KTN, Horsham.
12. Forensic Science Special Interest Group (FoSciSIG). (2016). FRS0024, written evidence to parliament. In: *FST0024—Evidence on forensic science strategy (parliament.uk)*. Accessed July 28, 2023.
13. Forensic Science Special Interest Group (FoSciSIG). (2018). FRS0040, written evidence to Parliament. In: *FRS0040—Evidence on forensic science (parliament.uk)*. Accessed July 28, 2023.
14. Home Office. (2016). *Forensic science strategy: A national approach to forensic science delivery in the criminal justice system*. https://assets.publishing.service.gov.uk/government/uploads/system/uploads/attachment_data/file/506652/54493_Cm_9217_Forensic_Science_Strategy_Accessible.pdf. Accessed July 22, 2023.
15. BBC. (2016). *Forensic science strategy vague and incoherent, MPs say*. September 17, 2016. https://www.bbc.com/news/uk-37390923. Accessed September 23, 2023.

16. House of Lords Science and Technology Committee Report. (2019). *Forensic science and the criminal justice system: A blueprint for change*. 1 May 2019, HL paper 333 of session 2017–19. https://publications.parliament.uk/pa/ld201719/ldselect/ldsctech/333/333.pdf. Accessed July 22, 2023.
17. NPCC Science and Technology Strategy. (2022). [https://science.police.uk/site/assets/files/1253/npcc_science_and_technology_strategy-1.pdf. Accessed July 28, 2023.
18. Faulds, H. (1905). *Guide to fingerprint identification*. Hanley.
19. Ramatowski, R., Cantu, A. A., Joullie, M. M., & Petrovskaia, O. (1997). 1,2-Indanediones: a preliminary evaluation of a new class of amino acid visualising reagents. *Fingerprint Whorld, 23*(90), 131–140.
20. Prete, C., Galmiche, L., Quenum-Possy-Berry, F.-G., Allain, C., Thiburce, N., & Colard, T. (2013). Lumicyano™: A new fluorescent cyanoacrylate for a one-step luminescent latent fingermark development. *Forensic Science International, 233*(1–3), 104–112.
21. Foster, D. J., & Morantz, D. J. (1979). An Electrostatic Imaging Technique for the Detection of Indented Impressions in Documents. *Forensic Science International, 13*, 51–54.
22. Haines, S. A. (1982). *Canadian Police News Magazine*, pp 22–3.
23. Wood, L. W. (1991). The discovery of super glue fuming. *Fingerprint Whorld, 16*(64), 117–118.
24. Hambley, D. S. (1972). *The physics of vacuum evaporation development of latent fingerprints*, PhD Thesis. The Royal Holloway College, University of London.
25. Dalrymple, B. E., Duff, J. M., & Menzel, E. R. (1977). Inherent fingerprint luminescence—Detection by laser. *Journal of Forensic Sciences, 22*(1), 106–115.
26. Theys, P., Lepareux, A., Chevet, G., & Ceccaldi, P. F. (1968). New technique for bringing out latent fingerprints on paper: Vacuum metallisation. *International Criminal Police Review, 217*, 106–108.
27. Kent, T., Thomas, G. L., Reynoldson, T. E., & East, H. W. (1976). A vacuum coating technique for the development of latent fingerprints on polythene. *Journal of the Forensic Science Society, 16*(2), 93–101.
28. Williams, G., McMurray, H. N., & Worsley, D. A. (2001). Latent fingerprint detection using a scanning kelvin microprobe. *Journal of Forensic Sciences, 46*(5), 1085–1092.
29. Archer, N. E., Charles, Y., Elliott, J. A., & Jickells, S. (2005). Changes in the lipid composition of latent fingerprint residue with time after deposition on a surface. *Forensic Science International, 154*, 224–239.
30. Ricci, C., Phiriyavityopas, P., Curum, N., Chan, K. L. A., Jickells, S., & Kazarian, S. G. (2007). Chemical imaging of latent fingerprint residues. *Applied Spectroscopy, 61*, 514–522.
31. Wolstenholme, R., Bradshaw, R., Clench, M. R., & Francese, S. (2009). Study of latent fingermarks by matrix-assisted laser desorption/ionisation mass spectrometry imaging of endogenous lipids. *Rapid Communications in Mass Spectrometry, 23*(19), 3031–3039.
32. Bandey, H. (ed.) (2014). *Fingermark visualisation manual* (1st ed.). Home Office.
33. Sears, V. G., Bleay, S. M., Bandey, H. L., & Bowman, V. J. (2012). A methodology for finger mark research. *Science & Justice, 52*(3), 145–160.
34. IFRG. (2014). Guidelines for the assessment of fingermark detection techniques. *Journal of Forensic Identification, 64*(2), 174–200.
35. Gill, P., Jeffreys, A., & Werrett, D. (1985). Forensic application of DNA 'fingerprints.' *Nature, 318*, 577–579. https://doi.org/10.1038/318577a0
36. Jeffreys, A., Wilson, V., & Thein, S. (1985). Individual-specific 'fingerprints' of human DNA. *Nature, 316*, 76–79. https://doi.org/10.1038/316076a0
37. Jeffreys, A., Brookfield, J., & Semeonoff, R. (1985). Positive identification of an immigration test-case using human DNA fingerprints. *Nature, 317*, 818–819. https://doi.org/10.1038/317818a0
38. Aronson, J. D. (2005). DNA fingerprinting on trial: The dramatic early history of a new forensic technique. *Endeavour, 29*(3), 126–131.
39. Amankwaa, A. O., & McCartney, C. (2019). The effectiveness of the UK national DNA database. *Forensic Science International: Synergy, 1*, 45–55. https://doi.org/10.1016/j.fsisyn.2019.03.004

40. European Court of Human Rights. (2020). Gaughran v. the United Kingdom—45245/15. Judgment 13.2.2020.
41. Lapointe, M., Rogic, A., Bourgoin, S., Jolicoeur, C., & Séguin, D. (2015). Leading-edge forensic DNA analyses and the necessity of including crime scene investigators, police officers and technicians in a DNA elimination database. *Forensic Science International: Genetics, 19*, 50–55.
42. Pickrahn, I., Kreindl, G., Müller, E., Dunkelmann, B., Zahrer, W., Cemper-Kiesslich, J., & Neuhuber, F. (2017). Contamination incidents in the pre-analytical phase of forensic DNA analysis in Austria—Statistics of 17 years. *Forensic Science International: Genetics, 31*, 12–18.
43. McCartney, C. (2006). The DNA expansion programme and criminal investigation. *The British Journal of Criminology, 46*(2), 175–192. https://doi.org/10.1093/bjc/azi094
44. Sewell, J., Quinones, I., Ames, C., Multaney, B., Curtis, S., Seeboruth, H., Moore, S., & Daniel, B. (2008). Recovery of DNA and fingerprints from touched documents. *Forensic Science International: Genetics, 2*(4), 281–285.
45. Quinones, I., & Daniel, B. (2012). Cell free DNA as a component of forensic evidence recovered from touched surfaces. *Forensic Science International: Genetics, 6*(1), 26–30.
46. Muir, R., & Walcott, S. (2021). *Unleashing the value of digital forensics*. The Police Foundation. https://www.police-foundation.org.uk/wp-content/uploads/2010/10/value_of_digital_forensics.pdf. Accessed July 22, 2023.
47. HMIFRS. (2022). *An inspection into how well the police and other agencies use digital forensics in their investigations*. https://www.justiceinspectorates.gov.uk/hmicfrs/publication-html/how-well-the-police-and-other-agencies-use-digital-forensics-in-their-investigations/. Accessed July 22, 2023.
48. Tully, G. (2017). *Forensic science regulator: Annual report*. November 2015–2016. https://assets.publishing.service.gov.uk/government/uploads/system/uploads/attachment_data/file/581653/FSR_Annual_Report_v1.0.pdf. Accessed July 22, 2023.
49. Tully, G. (2018). *Forensic science regulator: Annual report*. November 2016–2017. https://assets.publishing.service.gov.uk/government/uploads/system/uploads/attachment_data/file/674761/FSRAnnual_Report_2017_v1_01.pdf. Accessed July 22, 2023.
50. Tully, G. (2019). *Forensic science regulator: Annual report*. November 2017–2018. https://assets.publishing.service.gov.uk/government/uploads/system/uploads/attachment_data/file/918342/FSRAnnual_Report_2018.pdf. Accessed July 22, 2023.
51. APCC/NPCC. (2016). *Policing Vision 2025*. [https://npcc.police.uk/documents/policing%20vision.pdf. Accessed July 28, 2023.
52. Transforming Forensics/FCN/NPCC/APCC, Digital Forensic Science Strategy. (2020). https://www.npcc.police.uk/SysSiteAssets/media/downloads/publications/publications-log/2020/national-digital-forensic-science-strategy.pdf. Accessed July 22, 2023.
53. NPCC/APCC National Policing Digital Strategy. (2020). https://pds.police.uk/wp-content/uploads/2020/01/National-Policing-Digital-Strategy-2020-2030.pdf. Accessed July 22, 2023.

Chapter 4
Forensic Science Innovation in the UK: Roadblocks and Enablers

Ruth M. Morgan

Abstract Forensic science is an innovative discipline that seeks to address the challenges of crime reconstruction. Innovation has enhanced the accuracy, reliability and speed of detection across a broad range of materials from DNA to digital traces. There is also a growing body of work addressing the foundational science required to underpin the evaluative interpretation of traces in case specific contexts. However, as a discipline, forensic science faces notable challenges which, if left unaddressed, have the potential to impact future developments and capabilities to serve the justice system. This is a serious concern given the rapid pace of change, particularly with the growing relevance of digital evidence, and the accompanied growing demands on forensic science. The contested identity of forensic science (what it is considered to be, and who it is considered to be for), along with the fragmentation of forensic science from crime scene to court, are profound issues that impact how forensic science is valued and the level and strategy of investment made. Therefore, addressing these core issues is critical to identifying the current and potential future roadblocks and enablers of innovation. A sustainable and thriving innovation capability in forensic science is critical, especially given that new challenges are emerging at pace, and innovation achieved today may well not be fit for purpose in five years time. A hierarchical representation of key factors that can be considered as levers to identify roadblocks and enablers to innovation in forensic science presents the importance of context, values, culture, processes and methods. Ultimately, it is critical that innovation is facilitated by establishing "win–win" situations for all stakeholders so that forensic science is valued and innovation is enabled. Re-imagining the infrastructures that frame innovation activities will be important. Considering how to achieve appropriate regulation that also creates opportunity for innovative activities has the potential to remove barriers to innovation where it is possible to do so, and to foster enablers. It will also be important to reduce friction and create opportunities

R. M. Morgan (✉)
UCL Centre for the Forensic Sciences, 35 Tavistock Square, London WC1H 9EZ, UK
e-mail: ruth.morgan@ucl.ac.uk

Department of Security and Crime Science, UCL, 35 Tavistock Square, London WC1H 9EZ, UK

The Arista Institute, UCL Faculty of Engineering Sciences and UCL Faculty of Arts and Humanities, Torrington Place, London WC1E 7JE, UK

S. Francese and R. S. P. King (eds.), *Driving Forensic Innovation in the 21st Century*,
https://doi.org/10.1007/978-3-031-56556-4_4

for curiosity, creativity and exploration to achieve both innovation today, and ensure a pipeline of research and development for the innovations that will be needed in the future.

4.1 Introduction

A key challenge for innovation in forensic science lies in its position at a nexus between policing, science and law [1]. As a result, forensic science necessarily operates within a broad and dynamic multi-stakeholder context, which has arguably led to a diversity of understanding of what forensic science 'is' and what it is 'for' [2]. In addition, innovation in forensic science can be argued to fall into two broad categories of purpose; first addressing the need to ensure highly accurate, timely and cost effective analytical detection capabilities (to answer the 'what is it?' and 'who is it from?' questions pertinent to crime reconstructions); and second, addressing the need to establish foundational science to underpin the evaluative interpretation of materials in order to generate intelligence and evidence (answering the questions 'how did this happen?' and 'when did it happen?').

It may be argued that developing consensus on the identity of forensic science and on the requirements of research and development in forensic science, is core to the question of innovation. The issues of the identity of forensic science alongside the fragmentation of forensic science from crime scene to court, exacerbate the existing challenges to innovation by impacting the level of investment, and the priorities for that investment. As such, the first step to overcoming roadblocks and finding pathways to innovation is establishing forensic science as a distinct (albeit) interdisciplinary discipline.

This chapter considers the context of forensic science, and the issues that arise from multiple stakeholders and the resulting fragmentation of the forensic science process from crime scene to court. The impact of fragmentation is then outlined in terms of the oversight and leadership of forensic science, and the research and development landscape. Finally, a hierarchical visualisation of key factors for tackling challenges to innovation is presented which seeks to assist with identifying the existing roadblocks, and creating opportunities for establishing enablers of innovation that are appropriate for today and for the future.

4.2 The Forensic Science Context

Forensic science has undergone significant developments and technological transformation in the last twenty years. Not only have detection capabilities improved significantly in terms of accuracy, speed and resolution (for example in DNA [3–6]), but there has also been a growing recognition of the value that science can bring to matters of justice from both law and justice bodies (the police and the courts) [7, 8].

Alongside this, there has also been a broader public engagement with forensic science in mainstream media (print, film, documentary etc.) [9], and the growth of the crime genre in fictional drama, true crime and documentary productions that have raised the profile of science evidence and the potential value it brings to reconstructing crime events. Furthermore, there has been a marked transition from the focus on science evidence that physical traces can provide, to a growing engagement with the digital materials that make up the digital footprint of an individual and groups of individuals, and there is increasing recognition of the importance of digital materials for intelligence and crime reconstruction in physical crime investigations, as well as cyber-crime investigations [10].

Forensic science attracts the attention of this broad range of audiences because it sits at the intersection of policing, law and science. The intersectionality of forensic science makes it both compelling and, at the same time, a complex discipline. It has different capabilities and roles at different times and in different situations, and simultaneously navigates the different requirements that different individuals, communities and institutions expect and need from forensic science in those different contexts [11].

What forensic science is considered to be, and what it is considered to be for, varies for different stakeholders within the criminal justice system [2, 12]. Different expectations impact how forensic science is valued, who is considered accountable for how forensic science is applied in investigations and in court, and also how the resources dedicated to the growth and development of forensic science capabilities are deployed. Therefore, forensic science continues to face significant challenges that arguably stem from its fragmented and contested identity [13]. These challenges form the basis of many roadblocks to innovation that have been encountered to date and include the endeavours to ensure quality standards [14], the pipeline of innovation to meet the challenges of crime investigation now and in the future [10], and the scientific underpinning for the detection and interpretation of traces in a crime reconstruction context [15].

4.3 Key Challenges: Identity Issues

It has become increasingly recognised that one symptom of forensic science having multiple stakeholders, is that different terms are used to define it. 'Forensic Science' and 'the Forensic Sciences' are often used interchangeably [2], and whilst this may appear to be an inconsequential difference, the implications are highly significant to understanding the challenges of innovation [2] and are worthy of consideration here.

The term used to name a discipline will define what that discipline is, how it will evolve, and, ultimately, shapes how it is perceived by those within and outside of the discipline [16]. Forensic science is often considered to be a field that draws on a broad range of sciences that can be applied to forensic challenges [17]. As such, it is often referred to as the 'forensic sciences' which communicates that forensic science is a collection of applied 'core sciences' and therefore a 'field of interest', rather than a clearly defined discipline in its own right [2]. Taking this approach enables innovation in forensic science that addresses the operational needs of crime detection (answering questions in the genre of what is this particle made of?, or who left this DNA profile?). This often happens through technological advances that create capabilities to detect and classify materials more quickly and accurately (for example enabling rapid 3D scanning of a crime scene, or real time facial recognition or substance detection).

However, there are two issues if forensic science is considered as the application of a collection of other disciplines to forensic questions. First, technologies can be transposed in to a 'forensic' problem without sufficient modification for the specific forensic context [2]. Critical issues for the use of new capabilities in forensic science will be its cost, the length of time it takes to generate an insight, and the deployment of that capability in a crime reconstruction context where specialised skills may not be routinely available. If these issues are not addressed, the use and impact of a new capability will be unlikely (at least in the short term) [2].

Second, considering Forensic Science as the application of 'parent disciplines' is a challenge to innovation because it limits its scope to activities related to the crime scene and the analysis of specimens for forensic service delivery [17, 18]. This limits the opportunities to contribute more broadly across the criminal justice system [2]. If forensic science is considered to be a coherent discipline, it can address the whole process from crime scene to court (thereby addressing source attribution, activity level and offence level propositions), and bring together insights, needs and challenges from the multistakeholder community. This paves the way for innovation that has the potential to be impactful in specific challenge areas (such as a detection capability (answering the 'what' and 'who' questions), or foundational research areas (that can contribute to answering the 'how' and 'when' questions) and also fuel the development of new theory and lay foundations for the advances and innovations necessary to face the challenges currently on the horizon and those further into the future.

4.4 Key Challenges: Fragmentation

In 2019, the House of Lords Science and Technology Select Committee published the findings of their inquiry into forensic science [10]. The report highlighted the issues of the contested identity of forensic science and its fragmentation. The impact of fragmentation was particularly apparent in two areas; oversight, leadership and responsibility of forensic science, and research and development.

4.4.1 Oversight, Leadership and Responsibility

During the inquiry it became clear that there was no one department or body that had the overall oversight and responsibility for forensic science in its remit. The investigative aspect of forensic science was broadly in the policing sphere with accountability to the Home Office. The courts and legal aspects were under the auspices of the Ministry of Justice [10].

Within this multi-stakeholder system there are both institutions and individuals. Institutions, whether it is the police, the courts or the science domain, have different cultures and ways of producing and retaining knowledge. Institutions or collections of institutions operate within distinctive infrastructures [11]. Different infrastructures establish different processes for creating and retaining knowledge that can lead to different ways of communicating knowledge which can ultimately manifest in different lexicons and terminology, and within those, different meanings of common terms. Institutions also have different incentive structures and are being measured in different ways which tends to drive how things are done (infrastructure and processes), the types of knowledge that are produced and the way that knowledge is applied. Different institutions also operate within different time frames. Government departments are cognisant of political cycles, industry is often constrained by financial cycles and shareholder expectations, and research within university infrastructures is working in academic cycles which are often longer than two years [19].

Therefore, a key challenge for forensic science is being able to incorporate the different requirements, expectations, forms of knowledge production and time frames in ways that deliver science insights to key actors to support the broad justice system. There are multiple ways in which a multi-actor system, such as the one in which forensic science operates, can create roadblocks to innovation. One example of this is how forensic science being a fragmented system impacts what is valued. If different stakeholders are responsible for different parts of the justice system, whether that is investigating crime, or prosecuting or defending individuals in court, each stakeholder will naturally value certain parts of the system (the investigation or the trying of a case) over and above other parts. Therefore, there is a tendency for stakeholders to use what limited resources are available to invest in the specific parts of the system that are most relevant to them. However, in a fragmented system that incorporates the crime scene through to court, it becomes very challenging to quantify and track how the benefits of those investments diffuse throughout the whole system. For example, if the police invest in developing a new technological capability for real time analyses that will aid investigators to rule out suspects rapidly, the courts will benefit with potentially fewer cases coming to court. However, the burden of that investment falls on the police rather than being shared across the whole system and this can lead to understandable tensions and different understandings of what is considered to be 'valuable' and a "priority". In essence, investments in one place may benefit other parts of the system but a lack of connectivity between the different parts of the system can mean that the burden of that investment is not shared.

4.4.2 *Research and Development*

A key roadblock, when it comes to research and development in forensic science, has its roots in the multi-stakeholder context of forensic science, and the often divergent requirements that different stakeholders have from the discipline. Research and development as a term has a very specific remit within government departments and in forensic science, and this has tended to focus attention onto detection capabilities and addressing short term needs to support investigations. Within the research community (often within the university sector) research and development, as a term, has a broader remit. Within the research community, the remit of research and development addresses short term operational detection challenges and growing the analytical capabilities to detect traces and identify individuals, as well as medium to longer term challenges (such as addressing future crime, and horizon scanning research and development efforts). It also incorporates a consideration of the foundational science that is needed to underpin every part of the forensic science process to support evaluative interpretation and transparency of decision making, and the communication of those findings in specific contexts. One challenge for innovation in forensic science stems from these different understandings of the term 'research and development' and the different expectations that different stakeholders bring to innovation. For example, the drivers and needs of policing are not always compatible with time frames of research councils and their requirement for the proposed research to demonstrate 'novelty'.

Once the variation in what is meant by the terminology of 'research and development' and its scope is acknowledged, it is possible to have more effective and productive interactions and to find pathways for innovation. However, two core issues remain when it comes to existing roadblocks to research and development in forensic science that need to be addressed. The necessity for a) truly interdisciplinary ways of working and producing knowledge, and b) the amount of funding that is made available for forensic science research and development, who the funders are, and the strategy and vision of those funders that directs what is funded.

4.4.2.1 Interdisciplinarity

It is widely acknowledged that multidisciplinarity is core to effective forensic science given the relevance of multiple disciplinary perspectives and methods to forensic science research questions [11]. Interdisciplinarity is related to multidisciplinarity and yet incorporates methodology to go beyond disciplinary borders and synthesise and harmonise the connections between disciplines into a coherent whole, essentially becoming greater than the sum of its parts. Interdisciplinarity is a term often used, and it is championed as the way to tackle complex multifaceted challenges that sit at intersections with multiple stakeholders (such as the challenges faced in forensic science) and yet it remains fundamentally difficult to achieve.

Arguably, there are two fundamental aspects to why achieving interdisciplinary innovation is so challenging. First, there is a strong body of work in forensic science that seeks to take insights and capabilities from certain disciplines and apply them to particular challenges in forensic science. For example, the physics of fluids underpins core blood pattern analysis theory, and biological science underpins DNA analysis. In forensic science these capabilities are applied from the parent discipline into the forensic science context. This leads to a multidisciplinary situation in forensic science innovation, where there is a primary discipline (for example biology that enables us to quantify and generate DNA profiles) and then a secondary discipline is brought in to add a capability (for example statistics that can offer insight into the probabilities that are relevant). Imagine if the innovation process started at the end point, for example identifying the need to be able to establish the identity of an individual. It would be possible to start exploring that challenge in the specific context in which that capability is relevant. It might result in a biological solution based on genetic markers, but it might equally result in a different solution, perhaps even a solution that is different for different contexts.

The second aspect is the applied nature of forensic science as a discipline. Innovation in forensic science seeks to address the needs of particular stakeholders whether that is the police or the courts. To achieve an end result that is fit for purpose and truly problem solving, ground-breaking and innovative, it is crucial to have specific context relevant research questions that will generate results that actually address the specific challenge faced. This requires a systems view of forensic science. Insights from so-called parent disciplines will be generated from answering important question(s) relevant to that parent discipline. Directly applying those insights into a different context without sufficient modification is unlikely to achieve the level of sustainable and wide-reaching impact that can be achieved if solutions are designed for specific challenges in the first place. Further, specific discipline focussed research questions need to be derived from a holistic view of forensic science that incorporates a deep appreciation of stakeholder needs (and perceived needs), alongside a deep understanding of science, the type of questions it can and cannot answer, as well as a capacity to incorporate uncertainty and risk that is relevant to the context [19].

4.4.2.2 Funding

Historically, the approach to funding forensic science research in the UK has been derived from considering forensic science research as an applied multidisciplinary endeavour. This has taken the form of funders identifying important capabilities and insights from relevant disciplines such as chemistry or biology and applying them into forensic science with a varying degree of modification [20]. This has arguably resulted in a situation where the detection capabilities for forensic science have undergone significant development, and innovation has been possible [21, 22]. Innovation has therefore led to enhanced capabilities that can answer the identification and classification questions (what is this trace? whom does the trace belong to?). Yet, significant gaps continue to exist that were identified in 2009 [23] and have persisted [10, 24] in terms of the scientific foundations underpinning the evaluative interpretations of forensic materials and ensuring that findings from research within other disciplinary frameworks are applied with appropriate modification to address the specific forensic science context. Serious challenges remain when it comes to being able to interpret what the identification, classification or comparison of a trace, or mark, means in a specific forensic science context (answering the how did that trace get to where it has been found, and when did it get there?).

This may be illustrated by considering research council funding in the UK, between 2009 and 2018. During this time, UK Research and Innovation (UKRI) identified 150 research projects that had relevance to forensic science [10]. Only 69 of these projects (46% of the stated funding allocation) were primarily forensic science research projects with specific forensic science research questions (£17.2 million which was less than 0.03% of the total stated UKRI budget over this time frame) [24]. When considering the 150 projects initially identified, the funding allocated to research projects that have relevance to forensic science has decreased year on year since 2015 (when £13.3 million was awarded) to £11.2 million in 2016, £5.5 million in 2017 and £1.1 million in 2018. The dedicated forensic science research projects that were funded 2009–2018 were predominantly focussed on developing technological capabilities to assist with detection challenges (£15 million) with only £2.2 million being awarded to research that contributes to the foundational underpinning science that supports transparent and robust evaluative interpretation.

There are of course other ways of funding research and innovation that could include funding from industry stakeholders. The motivation for research and development in industry settings is clearly and understandably focussed on a particular set of challenges that are likely to impact quality, turnaround times, accuracy of classification and return on investment. In addition to a different set of strategic priorities, forensic service providers in the UK have been under immense pressure, as has been addressed in detail elsewhere [10, 25, 26]. The industry has maintained its research capability, and yet the stress and strain within a marketized system under severe pressure (the size of the forensic science services market was reduced from *ca.* £120 million pa in 2008 to *ca.* £50–55 million in 2018, and the spending on commercial providers fell even more sharply, by approximately 29% [10]) has reduced the scope and opportunity for research activities at the order that existed within the former Forensic Science Service, before 2012.

Looking forward, to overcome these challenges and to support vibrant and thriving innovation activity within forensic science, it is clear that it is going to be important to fund research and innovation activities, and that funding needs to be directed both strategically and effectively [20]. This means findings ways to bring interdisciplinarity where it is appropriate into multidisciplinary settings, responding to rapidly evolving criminal activities made possible with new tools and virtual spaces, and as a result arguably more inputs from different disciplines across the social sciences, arts and humanities than has traditionally been the case will be necessary. It is going to require a consideration of the whole ecosystem of forensic science in a way that not only acknowledges the value that different disciplinary perspectives can bring, and the increasing synergy between technological challenges and societal challenge, but also incorporate a broad range of stakeholders and the needs of the short, medium and longer term. It is also going to be important that both technological and foundational research are valued and supported.

4.5 Pathways Forward

When considering the roadblocks and enablers to innovation in forensic science, many of the roadblocks appear to be derivatives of a diversity of views regarding what forensic science is and what it is for (for example is forensic science a context to apply parent discipline capabilities into, or a discipline in its own right?), and the value assigned to technological innovation and foundational science, as well as organisational structures (including the fragmentation of forensic science across the activities of investigation, analysis, prosecution and trying of cases) and infrastructural challenges (the different modes of knowledge production in different stakeholder communities, the different time frames that institutions are working within, and the different types of value forensic science has within those different settings).

Looking forward, considering the current landscape and taking a broad perspective that accommodates the large-scale conditions as well as drilling down to reveal specific attributes at the smaller scale, may offer insights into how to overcome the existing roadblocks and to put enablers in place. To this end Fig. 4.1 outlines a hierarchical visualisation of key factors that can be considered when tackling challenges to innovation to assist with identifying roadblocks and finding enablers.

The broad context that forensic science innovation is operating within is the overarching large-scale consideration at the top of the hierarchy. Once the context has been identified, considering the values that are in place in that innovation environment and the culture that results, creates opportunities to examine where blockers are and where it might be possible to explore ways of finding pathways through. Engaging with the existing processes and methods in place and assessing where change is needed can then create opportunities to address more tangible blocks that can be neutralised or transformed into enablers. As such, it is hoped that this hierarchy of factors offers an opportunity to ask context-appropriate questions to identify roadblocks and use different levers to find enablers that unlock the potential of innovation in the interconnected system of forensic science, as well as situate forensic science in the broader research and innovation landscape.

4.5.1 Context

At the broad scale, understanding the context within which forensic science innovation is seeking to develop is a helpful exercise. Mapping the drivers and challenges of the economic, political and value systems of different societies is critical to being able to navigate and achieve innovation. The social contract for science is a pervading

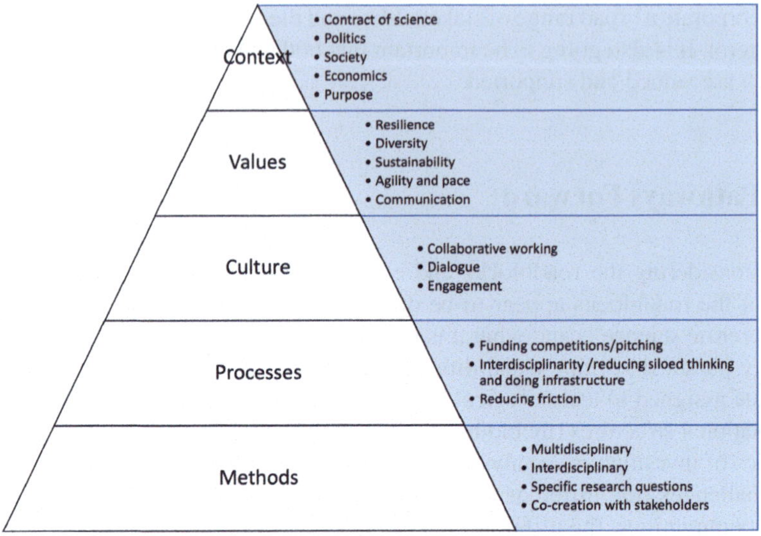

Fig. 4.1 A hierarchical visualisation of key factors that can be considered when tackling challenges to innovation to assist with identifying roadblocks and finding enablers

part of this context, even if it is not explicitly discussed or formalised. It is broadly agreed that a social contract for science was formalised after World War II from the work of Bush [27] and Steelman [28] with a partnership between government who financially supported universities to undertake 'basic' research that was not being addressed in industry. Scientists who undertook research funded through government did so with the expectation that the outputs from that research would bring benefit to society in some form. This initial contract has evolved over the last 70 years. It is now possible to frame research and innovation as an activity that is not only largely funded by the state but one that is assessed on its value in terms of productivity [29], and therefore incentivised for (financially measurable) outputs [30]. This creates a risk that the only form of output that is valued is one that contributes to measures of GDP rather than a broader range of value, some of which may not be financially exploitable.

In forensic science it is possible to identify the type of research that can thrive in such a context, especially where it is possible to produce patentable capabilities and marketable products. Other forms of research are arguably just as valuable in terms of their contribution to culture, society, wellbeing and trust, and may even contribute indirectly to greater productivity (such as improved wellbeing of analysts leading to increases in engagement, efficiency and productivity [31]), and yet the timelines that these 'results' materialise are longer than the time frames of financial years or political cycles which can minimise their visibility and thus their perceived value. It is also particularly relevant to note that when the contract for science was introduced, government funding for science research predominantly focussed on topics and questions that were not being addressed in industry (which was therefore often 'basic' or blue skies research). In recent times this has changed, and government spending on science research is much more closely aligned with industry priorities, creating a gap in funding for the more foundational 'basic' research. As such, forensic science research and innovation, especially where foundational research is concerned, has hit significant roadblocks in terms of access to funding, and ensuring a pipeline of basic research being in development for applications in the medium to long term.

4.5.2 Values

Having taken into account the broad context, it is possible to consider the roadblocks and enablers of innovation through the lens of values and the culture that those values create. Promoting and fostering resilience, sustainability and agility creates opportunities for innovation in a range of different contexts, whether that is in terms of making incremental progress over the longer term (such as developing and refining a detection capability), or responding to sudden shifts in the status quo in the relatively immediate term (such as creating new systems harness the power of emerging digital tools). Valuing sustainability also has a significant impact on the ecosystem within which innovation takes place. It is important to be able to value short term breakthroughs of high technological readiness levels, and the longer-term blue skies work that may (or may not) lead to innovation in the longer term. Sustainability of a research and innovation ecosystem will also be impacted by the diversity of teams and forms of data that are driving innovation forward. Bringing different perspectives together, whether that is differences from disciplinary, generational, regional or sector backgrounds, will offer greater opportunities for innovation [32], particularly in multidisciplinary settings such as forensic science.

4.5.3 Culture

Culture is closely connected to values and shaped by them. As such, culture clearly has a significant impact on the opportunities for innovation. The level of risk-taking that is normalised in different settings, the thresholds and tolerances of uncertainty, the approach to competition and collaborative working will all impact the way that innovation happens, and the level of impact that innovation can achieve. There is fluidity to a culture, it develops over time and in response to external factors. Yet it is possible to suggest that an enabler of innovation will be a supportive and dynamic culture that promotes diverse and critical thinking, collaborative working, avoids a 'winner takes all' model, and where it is possible to be curious and creative about challenges that have short- and long-term perspectives.

4.5.4 Processes

Considering innovation within this framework allows a focus at the broad global scale (context) regional scale (values and culture) and the local scale (processes and methods). Addressing the local scale can offer opportunities to scrutinise the existing processes and methods that are followed to achieve innovation activities and identify where there might be opportunities to re-imagine those approaches to enable and achieve innovation.

The processes in operation within institutions and disciplines frame 'how things are done', whether that is the processes which are followed to fund research projects, or how risk assessments are created and scrutinised. There is much discussion of the perils of siloed thinking and siloed working and the importance of creating opportunities to break down the boundaries between disciplines and key stakeholders in the forensic science ecosystem. It is evident that many of the processes that are currently in place reinforce disciplinary siloes in terms of how research calls are framed and how research proposals are pitched. It is promising that there are increasing mentions of interdisciplinary working in many research council calls, and more joint council calls being made available for research addressing complex challenge areas. However, it is possible to argue that there is still a need to create more funding opportunities for specific forensic science research questions to catalyse innovation opportunities. For forensic science innovation to thrive, investment is needed to enable interdisciplinary collaborative research in a sustainable way. Short-term (less than 18 months) projects are likely to favour research that builds on existing findings and lead to incremental developments. This is important work, and at the same time there is a clear need to ensure that alongside these types of projects there is sufficient opportunities for broad collaboration and research being undertaken to ensure that there is a pipeline of research activity that will ensure that forensic science is delivering the very best science for application in the justice system in five-, ten- and twenty-years time.

A specific example of a process that could be considered an enabler, but that is also a potential roadblock, is the manner in which research projects are proposed and funded. Submitting a research proposal is a lengthy process, that takes many hours of time over months and years from the lead researcher, the collaborators, partners, and administrative teams based in the institutions seeking funding and the funding institutions that oversee the competitive process. On top of the directly attributable time to writing and submitting the proposal, there is all the time that is spent building a network of collaborators and partners and building trust that can take many years of dedicated work. The success rate of funding applications is often cited to be in the region of 21% [33]. As such, winning funding for a research project can take years and when funding is awarded, it is often for relatively short periods of time (2–5 years). Given the length of the process, many recipients of funding start applying for the next grant as soon as they have been successful, to the point where success is celebrated at the point of winning the grant, rather than at the end of the grant when the breakthrough or innovation is achieved.

During the COVID-19 pandemic the power of human ingenuity and drive was very evident in terms of re-thinking the way research ideas were pitched and funded, to reduce the timelines and accommodate different ways of working. In many cases this created opportunities to build more diverse teams, and the sense of urgency instilled a focus and strong set of guiding principles on both the outcomes of the work and the ways in which those outcomes were communicated. This raises important questions; what if all the person's hours that it takes to win funding for research and innovation activities was directed less on the process of winning funding and more onto the challenges that need to be addressed? What if it was possible to change the processes to make the most of those person hours, reduce the friction of the existing system, and get brilliant diverse teams doing excellent research and creating innovative solutions more effectively?

4.5.5 Methods

The methods that are utilised for research and development are key to the degree in which innovation and impact are achieved, as well as the type of innovation that results. There have been many successes from using well established challenge-focussed innovation pathways that have codified processes and pathways to test, fail and iterate to achieve innovation and find solutions to existing challenges. The innovation of the dual-cyclone vacuum cleaner is often cited as an innovation success that ultimately revolutionised home cleaning products. However, it is also important to consider other approaches. For example, a solutions-driven approach where the solution to a challenge is imagined as a starting point (rather than an end point), can create an 'impeller' [34] that catalyses the creation of impactful solutions in a more step-wise change model [35].

In an applied discipline such as forensic science, the importance of research and development activities that address specific research questions relevant to forensic science challenges is critical (Sect. 4.4.2.1). While it is possible to take established approaches and methods from other disciplines, they must be modified to ensure they are appropriate for the forensic science context to have real world impact [36].

It is also important in a multi-stakeholder challenge area to be finding ways of designing and undertaking research that bring the different perspectives together from across the stakeholder communities throughout the entire research and development process. This will ensure that not only are the research questions relevant, but the methods are appropriate and the outputs that are produced are relevant and implementable, and, where appropriate, deployable. Excellent science does not always achieve the intended levels of innovation, yet there are a growing number of examples where carefully considered design and methods has resulted in real world impact [37].

4.6 Summary

The pace of change is gathering momentum, technological developments and capabilities are growing exponentially, which creates challenges and incredible opportunities. As we look forward and consider how best to address the existing roadblocks to innovation, we need to be cognisant that the innovations we seek will be realised in a world that will be different to what it is now. There is a need to regain critical systemic thinking to re-imagine what a thriving forensic science discipline could be and should be. The infrastructure that will be needed to support forensic science is likely to be different to the one that exists today and yet it will likely remain one that draws on the insights from a broad range of disciplines in a diversity of contexts. To achieve a thriving innovation capacity within forensic science it is possible to argue that key ingredients will be creating resilience within the system, reducing the frictions that currently exist and act as roadblocks to innovation, and articulating the value of forensic science more clearly and engagingly across society (from policy makers to the public).

Resilience is a key attribute in a rapidly changing system to withstand the incremental changes (such as the increasing sensitivity of detection capabilities which create new challenges for the evaluative interpretations of a trace) and the stepwise paradigm shifting changes (such as artificial intelligence tools, and sensitivity of data capture approaches which change the role of the human in reconstructing crime events). To build resilience it is important to foster diverse interactions that bring together disciplinary, generational, regional, global, cultural and neurodiverse perspectives. It will also be important to consider forensic science as an ecosystem where different approaches and skills are needed for a thriving community, rather than creating false dichotomies between methods or forms of knowledge [15].

Articulating the value of forensic science to different stakeholders in different contexts will also be critical for thriving innovation capacity in forensic science. Value is highly contingent on context, and developing how the value of forensic science is presented in ways that engage decision makers and policy makers will be an important way to create enablers of innovation. Communicating the value of forensic science is also critical to building trust between science and scientists with the public, policy makers, the media and industry. Trust is core to innovation in forensic science, given its application into the justice system and the foundational place a trustworthy justice system has in society.

Related to building trust, is the dialogue and collaboration that is nurtured within the forensic science community as well as between the science community and professional and industry communities and broader society. For forensic science innovation to be valued and enabled, it needs to be agreed what types of questions forensic science can answer, and what questions cannot be answered at the moment, (or perhaps from a philosophical point of view, will not ever be possible to answer). A key part of this ongoing conversation must also be developing the ways we understand and communicate the inherent uncertainty that is fundamental to scientific observation and interpretation.

Finally, to catalyse forensic science research and development that leads to innovation, it will be important to address the questions of how we enable collaborative working to create centres of excellence that have porous boundaries so that discovery and innovation are a joint endeavour (with and for people). Allied questions must be considered such as how we create long term sustainable programmes of research that can be flexible to emerging challenges, offer deep insights, and at the same time achieve both analytical detection capabilities and foundational research to ensure that there is innovation now and in the future.

References

1. Fraser, J., & Williams, R. (2009). *Handbook of forensic science.* Willan Cullompton.
2. Morgan, R. M. (2019). Forensic science. The importance of identity in theory and practice. *Forensic Science International: Synergy, 1*, 239–242.
3. Van Oorschot, R. A., Ballantyne, K. N., & Mitchell, R. J. (2010). Forensic trace DNA: A review. *Investigative Genetics, 1*(1), 1–17.
4. Børsting, C., & Morling, N. (2015). Next generation sequencing and its applications in forensic genetics. *Forensic Science International: Genetics, 18*, 78–89.
5. Gill, P., Haned, H., Bleka, O., Hansson, O., Dørum, G., & Egeland, T. (2015). Genotyping and interpretation of STR-DNA: Low-template, mixtures and database matches—Twenty years of research and development. *Forensic Science International: Genetics, 18*, 100–117.
6. van Oorschot, R. A., Szkuta, B., Meakin, G. E., Kokshoorn, B., & Goray, M. (2019). DNA transfer in forensic science: A review. *Forensic Science International: Genetics, 38*, 140–166.
7. Bitzer, S., Margot, P., & Delémont, O. (2019). Is forensic science worth it? *Policing: A Journal of Policy and Practice, 13*(1), 12–20.
8. Woodman, P. A., Spiranovic, C., Julian, R., Ballantyne, K. N., & Kelty, S. F. (2020). The impact of chemical trace evidence on justice outcomes: Exploring the additive value of forensic science disciplines. *Forensic science International, 307*, 110121.
9. Marsh, I., & Melville, G. (2019). *Crime, justice and the media.* Routledge.
10. House of Lords Science and Technology Select Committee. (2019). Forensic *9science and the criminal justice system: A blueprint for change. In 3rd Report of session 2017–2019 HL Paper 333. Available at: https://publications.parliament.uk/pa/ld201719/ldselect/ldsctech/333/333.pdf. Accessed July 1, 2023.
11. Morgan, R. M. (2017). Conceptualising forensic science and forensic reconstruction. Part II: The critical interaction between research, policy/law and practice. *Science and Justice, 57*(6), 460–467.
12. Roux, C., Bucht, R., Crispino, F., De Forest, P., Lennard, C., Margot, P., Miranda, M. D., NicDaeid, N., Ribaux, O., Ross, A., & Willis, S. (2022). The Sydney declaration–Revisiting the essence of forensic science through its fundamental principles. *Forensic Science International, 332*, 111182.
13. Morgan, R. M. (2022). Forensic science, revealing the unseen and the unknown. In R. M. Morgan, & P. Coldwell (Eds.), *Picturing the invisible: Exploring interdisciplinary synergies from the arts and the sciences* (pp. 11–24). UCL Press. http://www.jstor.org/stable/j.ctv1v090jc.8
14. Tully, G., Cohen, N., Compton, D., Davies, G., Isbell, R., & Watson, T. (2020). Quality standards for digital forensics: Learning from experience in England and Wales. *Forensic Science International: Digital Investigation, 32*, 200905.
15. Morgan, R. M. (2018). Forensic science needs both the 'hedgehog' and the 'fox.' *Forensic Science International, 292*, e10–e12.

16. Armstrong, C., & Fontaine, S. (1989). The power of naming: Names that create and define the discipline. *WPA: Writing Program Administration, 13*(1–2), 5–14.
17. Roux, C., Crispino, F., & Ribaux, O. (2012). From forensics to forensic science. *Current Issues in Criminal Justice, 24*(1), 7–24.
18. Morgan, R. M. (2017). Conceptualising forensic science and forensic reconstruction. Part I: A conceptual model. *Science and Justice, 57*(6), 455–459.
19. Earwaker, H., Nakhaeizadeh, S., Smit, N. M., & Morgan, R. M. (2020). A cultural change to enable improved decision-making in forensic science: A six phased approach. *Science and Justice, 60*(1), 9–19.
20. Morgan, R. M., & Levin, E. A. (2019). A crisis for the future of forensic science: Lessons from the UK of the importance of epistemology for funding research and development. *Forensic Science International: Synergy, 1*, 243–252.
21. Francese, S., Bradshaw, R., & Denison, N. (2017). An update on MALDI mass spectrometry based technology for the analysis of fingermarks–stepping into operational deployment. *The Analyst, 142*(14), 2518–2546.
22. Bailey, M. J., De Puit, M., & Romolo, F. S. (2022). Surface analysis techniques in forensic science: Successes, challenges, and opportunities for operational deployment. *Annual Review of Analytical Chemistry, 15*, 173–196.
23. The National Academy of Sciences (NAS). (2009). *Strengthening forensic science in the United States: A path forward*. https://www.ojp.gov/pdffiles1/nij/grants/228091.pdf
24. President Council of Advisors on Science and Technology (PCAST) Report to the President. (2016). *Forensic science and the criminal courts: Ensuring scientific validity of feature comparison methods*. See https://obamawhitehouse.archives.gov/sites/default/files/microsites/ostp/PCAST/pcast_forensic_science_report_final.pdf
25. Richmond, K. M. (2022). *Marketisation and forensic science provision in England and Wales*. Emerald Publishing Limited.
26. The Forensic Science Regulator. (2021). Annual Report 17th November 2019–16th November 2020. Available at: https://assets.publishing.service.gov.uk/government/uploads/system/uploads/attachment_data/file/950087/FSR_Annual_Report_2019-2020_Issue_1.pdf. Accessed July 1, 2023.
27. Bush, V. (1945). Science the endless frontier. A report to the President by Vannevar Bush, Director of the office of scientific research and development. United States Government Printing Office, Washington. See https://apo.org.au/node/62466
28. Steelman, J. R. (1948). Science and public policy. *The Bulletin of the Atomic Scientists, 4*, 23–31. https://doi.org/10.1080/00963402.1948.11460154
29. Guston, D. H. (2000). *Between politics and science: Assuring the integrity and productivity of research*. Cambridge University Press.
30. Morgan, R. M., Kneebone, R. L., Pyenson, N. D., Sholts, S. B., Houstoun, W., Butler, B., & Chesters, K. (2023). Regaining creativity in science: Insights from conversation. *Royal Society Open Science, 10*(5), 230134.
31. Almazrouei, M. A., Dror, I. E., & Morgan, R. M. (2020). Organizational and human factors affecting forensic decision-making: Workplace stress and feedback. *Journal of Forensic Sciences, 65*(6), 1968–1977.
32. Syed, M. (2019). *Rebel ideas: The power of diverse thinking*. Hachette UK.
33. UKRI. (2021). Competitive funding decisions. Available at https://www.ukri.org/what-we-do/what-we-have-funded/competitive-funding-decisions/
34. Watkins, A., & May, S. (2021). *Innovation sucks!: Time to think differently*. Routledge.
35. Morgan, R. M. (2022) *Why the 21st century needs more idealism in science and science policy*. Frontiers Policy Labs. https://doi.org/10.25453/plabs.22202965.v1
36. Morgan, R. M., & Bull, P. A. (2007). Forensic geoscience and crime detection. Identification, interpretation and presentation in forensic geoscience. *Minerva Medicolegale, 127*(2), 73–89.
37. Earwaker, H., Morgan, R. M., Harris, A., & Hall, L. (2015). Fingermark submission decision making within a UK fingerprint laboratory: Do experts get the marks they need? *Science and Justice, 55*(4), 239–247.

Chapter 5
On the Importance of Recognition and Mitigation of Bias in Forensic Science

Deborah Davis, Gage A. Miller, Demi J. Hart, and Alexis A. Hogan

Abstract This chapter reviews the causes of cognitive bias in forensic examinations and methods to enable mitigation. Causes relating to the nature of human cognition, the forensic task itself, emotion and motivation, contextual information (such as other case evidence), and individual differences, among others are considered. Where and how cognitive biases are afforded the opportunity to infect forensic judgment and decision-making are reviewed. Given that biases cannot be eliminated through awareness nor by attempts to control one's own biases, suggested reforms aimed primarily at preventing opportunities for biases to operate are reviewed. Though many such recommended reforms are aimed toward greater standardization and/or automation, we note that because standardized and automated systems are designed by humans subject to the many cognitive biases discussed herein they cannot be assumed to eliminate bias.

5.1 Introduction

The forensic sciences entered a new era of criticism and discontent in 2005 when the United States Congress authorized the National Academy of Sciences to conduct a review of the forensic sciences. Their comprehensive, and rather scathing report on the status of the forensic sciences (henceforth NAS Report) [1] was published in 2009. Though criticism and discontent had been brewing for some time, the NAS Report was comprehensive, well-documented, clearly and compellingly written, and authored and reviewed by a large group of indisputably qualified and distinguished scientists. It was based on reviews of extensive bodies of relevant scientific literature and testimony from both scientists and forensic practitioners and it highlighted realities concerning the forensic disciplines that could not be realistically denied. Although the NAS Report focused on forensic science in the United States, its findings clearly applied to forensic science as it is practiced in the United Kingdom and other countries.

D. Davis (✉) · G. A. Miller · D. J. Hart · A. A. Hogan
University of Nevada, Reno, US
e-mail: debdavis@unr.edu

S. Francese and R. S. P. King (eds.), *Driving Forensic Innovation in the 21st Century*,
https://doi.org/10.1007/978-3-031-56556-4_5

In part, the report focused on the accuracy of information provided by forensic examiners. That is, to what extent had the purported "science" underlying forensic examinations, been tested? How accurate were the findings in the various forensic disciplines? Were the rates of errors known? How were individual practitioners trained and tested? Among the central findings of the report were disturbing rates of errors, the lack of testing for accuracy and reliability within many forensic disciplines as a whole, as well as deficiencies in training and testing within individual labs and for individual examiners. These were attributed, amongst other reasons, to the lack of standardized principles and procedures for forensic examinations, and to the lack of certification and accreditation requirements for labs or persons, both within and between jurisdictions [1]. The Report provided extensive analyses of the various forensic disciplines and the existence and sources of errors within them.

Of central concern to this chapter, the NAS Report devoted considerable attention to the issue of bias as a source of error. It pointed to several general sources with the potential to bias forensic decision-making: (1) common features of human cognition or motivation, (2) specific features of forensic procedures, and (3) task-irrelevant contextual information present in individual examinations that might suggest conclusions (pp. 4–9).

To address these concerns, the NAS Report made three primary recommendations: (1) the removal of administrative control of forensic laboratories from law enforcement agencies or prosecutorial offices; (2) funding of research to test accuracy and establish error rates, and (3) the development and funding of research programs examining the role of human observer bias and human error in forensic examinations in order to promote the development of standard operating procedures "to minimize, to the greatest extent reasonably possible, potential bias and sources of human error in forensic practice," along with development of strict practice protocols designed to avoid bias ([1]: S-18; 4–9). The Report discussed a number of cognitive biases that should be addressed: most prominently "confirmation biases" (see 5.2.2.1).

Though the NAS Report seemed to have little impact at first, it was followed by a series of additional reports noting the same issues with the forensic sciences (including the problem of bias), elaborating upon them, and making similar recommendations. The National Commission on Forensic Science published a 2015 report on bias, offering recommendations for minimizing it [2]. This was followed in 2016 by an extensive report by the President's Council of Advisors on Science and Technology (henceforth PCAST Report) documenting little progress, offering more detailed analyses of some forensic disciplines, and further pointing to sources of biases and the need to mitigate them [3]. Meanwhile, academic publications steadily amassed, documenting instances of forensic errors across the US, the United Kingdom and other countries, and reporting experiments that demonstrated various forms of biasing effects on forensic judgments. An organization of academics called the Center for Statistics and Applications in Forensic Evidence (CSAFE) was formed to promote progress in forensic sciences through research, development of new methods, and consultation and guidance to forensic professionals.

Today, in accordance with the original recommendation of the NAS Report, an organization exists within the National Institute of Standards and Technology

(NIST) called the Organization of Scientific Area Committees for Forensic Sciences, or OSAC [4]. Formed in 2014, the organization includes over 475 members and consists of a Forensic Science Standards Board (OSAC's governing board), individual committees for each area of forensic sciences, and five resource committees (Human Factors; Legal; Quality; Statistics and Terminology). The purpose of the organization is to improve the accuracy and reliability of forensic sciences and to develop standard practices for communicating the results of forensic examinations. A significant concern of OSAC is the avoidance, or at least mitigation, of bias in forensic examinations. The Human Factors Committee (on which the corresponding author sits) is specifically tasked with this purpose and consists largely of psychologists and academics whose disciplines have long included relevant scientific literature on sources and control of bias. At this point in the history of the forensic sciences, recognition of the place of biases in forensic examinations and attempts to address them have begun to come of age.

In the following sections, the nature and bases of bias in forensic decision-making are addressed. First is consideration of the points at which bias must be considered within the processes of forensic examinations. Next, specific sources or types of bias involved are reviewed. Finally, strategies that have been suggested for mitigation of these biases are discussed.

5.2 Mitigating Bias: First Identify the Opportunities and Sources

5.2.1 Opportunities

Forensic examinations are often complex, including many points at which opportunities for bias can arise. To understand where and how this can occur, one must first understand the task facing the forensic examiner, the points at which decisions are made, the procedures used for examination, and the nature of biases with the opportunity to infect each point. Bias can begin to operate, for instance, even before a crime scene is examined: such as when a woman is dead, and suspicion of the husband is set in motion even before investigation begins. Such initial impressions or theories of the case can direct attention to and interpretation of what is seen and may affect decisions of which evidence to collect or send to examiners for testing. This early information can create a "bias cascade," [5], whereby information from the crime scene biases analytical work in the laboratory.

In some instances, bias might arise as the result of processes preceding the specific examiner's procedures. For instance, the International Automatic Fingerprint Identification System (IAFIS) will print out a set of prints possibly matching the inputted crime scene print that is rank ordered. The examiner will then compare the print with the highest ranking first. In addition to determining which print is used as the comparator to the crime scene print, this ranking itself can create a stronger expectation of match. Evidence has shown, for example, that fingerprint examiners are more likely to judge the same print to match if it is believed to have ranked higher in this output as compared to if it is believed to have ranked lower [6].

Once a forensic examination begins, there can be multiple activities or decision points with opportunities for bias at each: biases that may or may not be of the same type or source. If technology underpinned by Artificial Intelligence is used for the examination (such as facial identification systems), human bias may have affected the software and therefore be reflected in the output of the machine learning algorithm. If not, human examiners can be affected by bias in their decisions. In many cases, for example, the examiner must first decide whether the sample in question (fingerprint, DNA, document, footwear, tire impression, etc.) is suitable for testing. In some cases, the sample must then be characterized or described (such as when the fingerprint examiner must note important features of the crime scene and comparator prints). At this point, bias can infect such issues as the thoroughness of the inspection and documentation, and what kinds of features are focused on (e.g., common versus unique features). The examiner might choose between different tests for the same question: such as the choice between different DNA testing strategies. The procedure itself can also either directly cause or encourage bias, and cognitive biases of the examiner can also affect tests or interpretations. In some cases, such as handlers of detection dogs, the forensic professional can affect the operation of the testing agent: such as when subtle examiner cues can cause the dog to falsely alert.

To fully understand where opportunities exist for bias to infect processes and decisions, one must have, in effect, a flow chart describing the chain of activities and decisions of the forensic examiners. At each point, one must ask: "*Can* bias operate here?" (Is this evidence sufficiently ambiguous to leave room for interpretation? Is there opportunity for subjectivity or behavioral confirmation processes)? If so, "What causes of bias can operate?" And "What can be done to avoid or mitigate that source of bias?" Though such an analysis is crucial, it is not within our scope to provide this analysis for specific forensic disciplines. We do, however, provide illustrative examples in the following sections.

5.2.2 Sources of Bias

Many specific sources of bias have been identified by the NAS Report and the others that followed, as well as by scientists investigating forensic confirmation biases. These biases can lead different examiners, or even the same examiner, to interpret the same physical evidence in different ways, so that different conclusions are reached. Indeed, these inconsistencies have led some to suggest that "inconsistency is the most consistent finding in the forensic sciences" [7].

Sufficiently numerous sources of bias exist as to lead Dror to introduce a classification scheme to organize them [8]. This scheme categorizes biases into three broad groups, each encompassing several specific sources of biases. We summarize and discuss these classifications in the sections to come, along with some additions.

5.2.2.1 Nature and Cognition

Perhaps the most influential general source of bias is that of the nature of cognition. Cognition works such that incoming information is processed in the context of existing knowledge and expectations. This context allows us to recognize what we experience, to interpret information, and to react accordingly. Contextual effects on cognition are rational and needed to navigate the world. The correct interpretation of the same sound, shape, word, or sentence can indeed be quite different in different contexts. Because from infancy, we have learned to rely in part on context and the expectations it creates for interpretation, it is difficult, if not impossible, to ignore context even when necessary for objectivity. Confirmation biases in interpretation are thereby inherent to cognition and are not unique to forensic examinations.

Nevertheless, after reviewing the history and sources of confirmation biases in general, Kassin and colleagues defined "forensic confirmation bias" as "the class of effects through which an individual's pre-existing beliefs, expectations, motives, and situational context influence the collection, perception, and interpretation of evidence during the course of a criminal case" [9]. Though not explicitly mentioned in this definition, these authors also reviewed *behavioral* confirmation biases. These occur when one unknowingly creates evidence appearing to confirm the hypothesis, such as when one's own behavior influences the evidence to be interpreted (as when a forensic examiner creates or affects a sample for examination).

A number of additional inherent cognitive processes are also implicated in biasing forensic examinations. These include cognitive dissonance [10], "anchoring" [11], and "sunk costs" [12]: effects leading one to be invested in the justification of an initial decision, to place too much weight on initial information, or to be unwilling to discard or waste the effort thus far invested in an examination. Each makes it difficult to appropriately accommodate new (especially inconsistent) information or to overturn a decision. Additional contributors are "patternicity" (the tendency to see patterns that do not exist exist or are not meaningful [13]), the need for cognitive closure, underestimation of complexity, the tendency to read too much significance into coincidences and surprises, and misunderstanding of probability [1].

As the NAS 2009 report noted, "Such cognitive biases are not the result of character flaws; instead, they are common features of decision-making, and they cannot be willed away" [1]. Nevertheless, some triggers of confirmation biases are relatively specific to forensic contexts (see the following sections).

Although the general cognitive biases outlined here can be of importance to most forensic disciplines, the tendency to overperceive patterns, or "pareidolia" [14], can be of particular importance for the interpretation of poor vocal recordings, handwritten notes, and other degraded stimuli where the forensic task is interpretation of the evidence.

The most commonly documented form of pareidolia is face pareidolia, which causes people to perceive faces where they should not be (e.g., in a piece of toast, the clouds, on a tortilla, etc. [14]. Similarly, pareidolia can occur with sounds [13, 15, 16], and, as with any form of pareidolia, will be enhanced by expectations. Indeed, laboratory studies have shown how expectations can lead to perceptions of "ghost voices," criminality-related or other speech in random noise [15, 16], or degraded recordings [17].

In a 2006 TED Talk, Michael Shermer provided a clever illustration of what has been found in lab studies of the effects of expectations on speech perception [13]. He played a specific verse of Stairway to Heaven [18], running the recording in reverse: playing it once with no lyrics displayed and a second time with the alleged backward satanic lyrics displayed. Without the expectations of the displayed lyrics, virtually no one recognized any words, save a few who recognized "Satan." With lyrics displayed, however, most could "hear" the following:

> Oh here's to my sweet Satan. The one whose little path would make me sad whose power is Satan. He'll give you, give you 666. There was a little toolshed where he made us suffer, sad Satan.

The "hidden message" could suddenly be perceived from what was initially random sounds and noise. Such alleged (often Satanic) messages have been widely discussed in internet postings [19, 20]. One alleged backward message was the basis of a lawsuit filed by the parents of two young men against the rock band Judas Priest. The lawsuit alleged that embedded subliminal messages suggesting suicide in the song (when played backward) had provoked the two youths to form a suicide pact. Both shot themselves in the face after repeatedly listening to the song. One died and the other was profoundly disfigured [21].

Analogous to Schermer's demonstration, having a transcript (essentially another's interpretation) can influence what people think is heard in degraded voice recordings [13, 17]. Once a lawsuit is filed, expected backwards lyrics or other presumed wording will be common knowledge and would be expected to bias perceptions among all those tasked with judging whether they are indeed present.

5.2.2.2 Individual Differences

Dror points to a number of individual differences that impact forensic confirmation biases [8]. In our view, one of the most important is the criteria for judgment adopted by the individual examiners. For match judgments, for example, there are not always criteria for exactly how to determine a match. The footwear examiner might identify a given number of unique features (those acquired after manufacture, such as wear and tear marks) that are shared or unshared by the suspect shoe and those of the impression at the crime scene. However, standards are not in place to dictate how many shared marks or what degree of clarity and uniqueness must be found to justify a match judgment. Similar issues exist across other match examinations, including fingerprints. An individual examiner can, therefore, have a bias toward finding or eschewing matches, based on personal criteria for achieving sufficient certainty to justify the judgment. Generally, poorly articulated standards for judgments that are necessarily subjective in nature provide great opportunity for individual differences to create directional biases (or, indeed, inconsistency [1]).

5.2.2.3 Case-Specific Sources of Bias

Case-specific sources of bias refer to factors that can lead to bias for the specific case at hand, as opposed to leading to bias across multiple cases. They are provoked by the stimuli provided for analysis (such as the two fingerprints for comparison) or otherwise influenced by additional information presented or perceived as case-relevant (such as exposure to other case evidence or others' opinions).

Emotion and Inference in Reaction to the Stimuli to Be Examined

If the case information evokes emotion, the emotions can provoke motivations influencing the forensic judgments. This point has been illustrated when the emotion-provoking information is other case information. Two studies showed, for example, that fingerprint examiners were more likely to provide match judgments when exposed to gruesome photos of the murder victim [22, 23]. However, in some cases, the stimulus to be judged is emotion-provoking itself, as when a voice recording reveals screaming and evidence of pain and distress [8]. Medical examiners and odontologists are often exposed to serious injuries or death, with the potential to provoke emotion: and increased rates of distress and PTSD are observed in forensic professionals exposed to evidence of violence and death [24, 25]. Evidence might also provoke bias through expectations or motivations triggered by other aspects of its content, such as the content of voice recordings or handwriting samples, and so on [26].

The stimuli to be examined can also provoke inferences concerning likely interpretations through other sorts of cues. A number of cues incorporated in recordings can affect speech perception, for example. They can facilitate or mislead the interpretation of speech actually embedded in noise [27]. Implicit factors stereotypically associated with a speaker, such as gender [28], sexual orientation [29], age [30] and nationality [31], or cultural cues such as animals [32] have also influenced perception of speech. Such cues can impair interpretation when inconsistent with the speech itself. For example, when participants were shown a Caucasian person's face before listening to sentences spoken by a native-accented English speaker, they were more likely to understand the sentence's content than when shown a Chinese person's face [33]. However, when shown a Chinese person's face before listening to Mandarin-accented English sentences [34], people had an easier time understanding the sentence's content than those shown a Caucasian person's face. Similar effects are to be expected with the interpretation of degraded or unclear handwriting: for example, if the sample appears to be written in a feminine writing style. With any vocal or written sample, expectations can be evoked by features of the stimulus, with resulting biases in interpretation more likely with more degraded stimuli. Reflecting such effects, Gold and French pointed to the importance of the order in which speech samples should be examined, recommending that lower-quality samples should be examined first, in order to avoid bias in interpretation of the lower-quality samples due to the content of higher-quality samples [35]. The higher the quality or clearer the sample, the less opportunity for bias to operate (see [9] for review of enhanced confirmation bias effects for "elastic" or ambiguous evidence across forensic disciplines, even DNA).

Bias Due to Features of Procedures

Dror suggested that in the case of match judgments the examiner can be biased by knowledge of which sample came from the suspect [8]. In essence, the materials known to come from the suspect guide the interpretation of the case evidence, creating a bias toward the detection of similarities (and lack of attention to or disregard of inconsistencies). The biasing effects of using suspect materials as the referent for examination have been demonstrated across a number of match judgments (see [25] for review). A different referent effect was shown by Fraser-Mackenzie and colleagues, who found that fingerprint examiners' decisions concerning the adequacy of a latent print for examination depended upon whether and what comparison prints were shown with it [36].

A rather complex example is offered in some cases of footwear match judgments. For example, the first author heard the following account of the procedure from a footwear examiner: *if a suspect jumps off the roof onto the roof of a car and slides, leaving a streak instead of a clear print, the examiner may attempt to recreate the appearance of the streak in question with the shoe of the suspect.* Using such a procedure, the examiner is, in effect, asking, "*Can* this shoe be a match to the one that made this mark?" He can try multiple recreations of the jump to see if a comparable mark can be made. In this instance, the examiner is not only using the suspect sample shoe as the single comparator but is also actively trying to make that shoe create the same mark as that from the crime scene.

Many other examples of procedural sources of bias exist, including the previously discussed example of the biasing effects of IAFIS rankings of possible fingerprint matches [6], which can be mitigated in part by use of random ordering of potential matches. The length of candidate lists can also matter, as illustrated with regard to candidates for facial recognition [37]. Moreover, Dror reviewed other kinds of standards for comparison with the potential to bias interpretation of case evidence including and beyond match judgments: such as having a theory, chart, or pattern in mind that is used as a standard for evaluation or that creates an expectation for the result [8].

Contextual Information

Contextual information that is, or is perceived as, case-relevant, but that is not task-relevant provides great potential for bias. As a result, many have called for measures to isolate forensic examiners from potentially biasing contextual information. As early as 1894, Hagen recommended avoidance of contextual information: suggesting that the examiner "must depend wholly upon what is seen, leaving out of consideration all suggestions or hints from interested parties or knowledge of the moral evidence or aspects of the case". This recommendation was echoed by many others to come [1–3, 5, 9, 38, 39]. Such information can be case-relevant in that it might seem to suggest guilt or innocence. But it may not be task-relevant, in that the information is not needed and should not be used to do the task at hand (such as a match decision). Task-irrelevant contextual information can be information that provokes emotion, as noted above. However, among the most damaging contextual information is case-relevant evidence, theories, or discussions. This information might include evidence or expressed opinions directly relevant to guilt or identity, such as a suspect confession or eyewitness identification: or indirectly relevant, such as stereotypical fit to perpetrators of the crime in question, or to suicidality (e.g., financial or relationship troubles). Such task-irrelevant contextual information has been found to promote two standard manifestations of the confirmation bias: biases in information processing (attention to, search for, and interpretation of information) and behavioral confirmation processes.

As noted earlier, many forensic judgments are complex and offer multiple points at which bias might infect the examination process. Most forensic examinations offer opportunities for interpretative bias when they render their judgments, such as whether there is or is not a "match," whether a death was homicide, suicide, natural causes or undetermined, and others. However, there are many other decisions that precede the final forensic finding of interest. For example, for several forensic examinations, the first decision is whether or not the sample(s) in question are of sufficient quality for analysis, such as fingerprints or other impressions to be matched, or DNA samples [3]. Expectations or motivations (see subsection on motivations below) can bias these judgments: for example, if the examiner knows police have a suspect who is perceived as very likely guilty and confirming evidence is needed for prosecution. In such a case, the motivation to facilitate prosecution could lead the examiner to attempt an examination of an inappropriately poor sample.

The search for information can likewise be infected by bias: as when evidence collection at a crime scene is driven by existing or emerging theories of the case, or when a toxicologist's or medical examiner's choice of tests or specific examinations is affected by knowledge of a person's background, medical history, drug use, or of the investigators' theories of the case. For instance, forensic toxicology trainees who read an irrelevant case history prior to testing for opiates were shown to perform different tests than those who did not see the history [40]. The contextual knowledge can also cause a deviation from standard testing protocols such that additional tests are performed to test the hypothesis deriving from the contextual information, or when standards indicating follow-up testing to verify uncertain results are eschewed because the first test is consistent with expectation.

Interpretive biases can take many forms. The contextual information might directly affect the finding. The examiner might overweight, underweight, or neglect aspects of the available information in justification of the expected judgment. Likewise, the examiner might overlook or underweight the importance of the *absence* of certain data or findings supporting the expected result or fail to consider alternative hypotheses or conclusions [8].

Behavioral confirmation biases can be of particular importance in some forensic disciplines. For example, though dog detection judgments can suffer from an interpretive bias when the handler interprets whether there has or has not been an alert [41]; they may also suffer from a behavioral confirmation bias if the handler expecting the presence of a substance consciously or unconsciously cues the dog to alert [42–44].

The operation of contextual biases has been demonstrated across a broad range of forensic science domains. Kukucka and Dror recently provided a summary of empirical studies demonstrating contextual biases in forensic decisions, including fingerprints, handwriting, bloodstains, anthropology, firearms, shoeprints, pathology, crime scene investigation, hair analysis, DNA, dog handling, arson, toxicology, bitemarks, and digital forensics [45]. Most studies investigated bias due to exposure to case information such as a suspect confession, eyewitness identification, other forensic evidence, or features of the suspect associated with criminal stereotypes. However, other sources of bias included emotional context, peer opinion, adversarial allegiance, evidence lineup, base rate, historical context, and reference materials.

5.2.2.4 Environment, Culture, and Experience

In contrast to the above case-specific sources of bias, there are a number of biasing influences that can operate across cases. The first set of these concerns environment, culture, and experience.

Base-Rate Bias

The sum total of an examiner's experiences with cases, both their own and others they are aware of, can form the basis of expectations concerning the most likely result in a specific case. Based on their experience across cases, or within certain categories of cases, an examiner can have an expectation (even unconscious) of match or no match, of human or machine error, of a particular cause of death, and so on. If the examiner expects that a particular answer is most common, that expectation can bias findings in the same way that expectations based on any source can do so [8]; see [46] for an empirical demonstration of the effects of prevalence during training on judgments of novice fingerprint examiners). The higher the base rate of a particular finding in the examiner's practice for the type of case or circumstances at hand, the stronger will be the expectation of a particular finding for the case currently in question (see

[47, 48] for an example regarding workplace safety investigators). Relatedly, the low-prevalence effect refers to the tendency to miss objects or features that are rare and, therefore, unexpected [49]. Facial mismatches (on fake IDs), for example, are less likely to be detected in a context where their occurrence is infrequent [50]. As with any basis of expectations, the base-rate bias can promote biases in the collection and interpretation of information, as well as behavioral confirmation processes.

Explicit or implicit assumptions concerning base rates might be one reason for inconclusive decisions among forensic examiners. For example, studies of forensic cartridge case examinations have shown that inconclusive decisions are more common for cases that do not match than for those that do [51]. To the extent that examiners have learned through their history of examinations that matches are more common than non-matches, this can create an expectation of match that is violated when there is no match. Rather than accepting that there is no match, the examiner's confusion might be expressed through a finding of inconclusive. Such a process would be more likely in cases where an expectation of match is created by biasing contextual factors, and would be particularly detrimental where misleading evidence has led to that expectation. What could have been exonerating evidence (a no-match finding) is never produced, misleading the investigation and promoting the prosecution of the innocent.

A different source of bias relating to base rates was identified in the NAS Report [1]. That is, the tendency to overestimate the probative value of information because base rates are *not* considered (an instance of the "base-rate fallacy" identified by Kahneman and Tversky [52]. For instance, "suppose carpet fibers from a crime scene are found to match carpet fibers found in a suspect's home. The probative value of this information depends on the rate at which such fibers are found in homes in addition to that of the suspect. If the carpet fibers are extremely common, the presence of matching fibers in the suspect's home will be of little probative value" [1].

The issue of unknown base rates has been raised with regard to many forms of match decisions, where the base rates of particular patterns are unknown. For example, with regard to fingerprints, the commonality of particular ridge patterns in a population can affect the degree to which a match in those patterns suggests two prints come from a common source. If both prints share a rare feature, this is more suggestive of a match than sharing of common features [3]. This is most critical, as most countries do not have a set criteria of how many corresponding minutia are needed to declare a 'match.'Moreover, the *number* of matching minutia is not a sufficient criteria because different minutia carry different evidentiary power depending on their commonality.

Structural-Motivational Factors

As previously discussed, a primary recommendation of the many organizations and reports on the status of forensic sciences has been to separate forensic examiners from law enforcement. Currently, many forensic laboratories and examiners in the

United States are affiliated with Law Enforcement and, in some cases, operate within the prosecutor's office. As early as 2009, the National Academy of Sciences recommended the removal of all forensic laboratories and facilities from affiliation with and control by law enforcement organizations or prosecutors' offices [1]. This recommendation was designed to remove bias in forensic decisions resulting from allegiance, or the "my side" bias, the motivation to facilitate the needs of law enforcement for evidence supporting prosecution of favored suspects, or general pressures to solve the case [1, 53, 54]. Forensic practitioners report that they are personally motivated to catch criminals, particularly in high profile cases, and acknowledge that the need for closure (by providing an answer) and the joy of finding a match are also motivating factors [55]. Reflecting these are other processes, some research has revealed a tendency of forensic experts to produce findings favoring the side that retained them [54].

The Issue of Conflicts of Interests

A relatively unique feature of some forensic disciplines is the dual role that forensic examiners play as both treatment providers and objective examiners. This is true to some extent for odontologists with regard to some types of functions, such as mandated reporters of abuse. It is of constant concern, however, for forensic nurse sexual assault examiners. They must treat the patient (and many consequently view this as their primary role) but must also collect evidence to be used in court, including victim statements and accounts of the alleged incident. This dual role can create a conflict of interest for the nurse examiner, such that (s)he might believe the alleged victim and desire to facilitate prosecution of the accused, and yet be obligated to provide objective evidence. SANEs (Sexual Assault Nurse Examiners) are sometimes called to testify as to their interpretations of observed marks or injuries (e.g., is this the result of rape or can it be the result of normal intercourse) and concerning the nature of victims' statements, as well as to the collection and findings of other evidence and tests. Bias can exert effects on interpretation, decisions of what evidence to collect, and other processes comparable to those discussed earlier. However, given a presumption of the accused's guilt, there is also potential for bias in decisions of what to include of the alleged victim's statements or demeanor (or how to summarize or characterize them) in written reports or testimony. No requirements for audio or video recording of victim interviews, examinations, or statements currently exist. What might the SANE do, for example, if (s)he knows a statement the alleged victim makes might undermine prosecution? Might that statement be left out of the report? While some such decisions can be the result of unconscious biases, there is also potential for the motivation to help victims and prosecute their assailants to encourage deliberate omissions or mischaracterizations. Though not directly relevant to SANE examinations and reports, Martin and colleagues demonstrated biases in nurses' notes in a somewhat different context: showing a tendency of mental health nurses working with inpatients to write notes reflecting negative stereotypes of the mentally ill [56].

5.3 Proposed Solutions

5.3.1 Instill Humility

Efforts to mitigate cognitive biases will be most successful if practitioners "buy in" and acknowledge the existence and importance of cognitive bias and, of course, also buy in to the proposed procedures to mitigate them. Notwithstanding its importance, several barriers to this "buy in" exist. This problem was addressed even as early as the NAS Report [1]. It pointed to the unwillingness of many forensic examiners to acknowledge either error at all, or bias as a source of error, with some claiming perfect accuracy. Dror pointed to six "fallacies of bias" that lead to the minimization or dismissal of the existence of forensic confirmation biases [8]. These include (1) Ethical Misconceptions, or the belief that bias is the result of intentional dishonesty, discrimination, lack of care and so on; (2) "Bad Apples," or bad decisions happen for only incompetent individuals; (3) "Expert Immunity," suggesting that experts are impartial and immune to biases; (4) "Technological Protection," suggesting that use of automated technology such as machines, software, and so on can eliminate bias (notwithstanding that these are programmed and operated by humans); (5) "Bias Blind Spot" denying personal susceptibility while recognizing that others, even other experts, can be affected; and (6) "Illusion of Control" or awareness of the existence of bias, but belief that this awareness will allow one to control and eliminate it.

Unfortunately, after learning of the nature of cognitive biases, many forensic examiners nevertheless believe they are objective and immune to cognitive biases, even as they are clearly affected by them in practice [35–38, 48, 57–59]. Indeed, a survey of 403 forensic examiners [38] revealed very concerning rates of unrealistic beliefs. For example, a bare majority of 52% viewed cognitive bias as a problem within their own discipline, but only 26% believed it affects them personally. Perhaps most concerning for mitigation efforts, only 49% believed they should be shielded from potentially biasing information, whereas a strong majority (71%) believed they would prevent bias by deliberate avoidance of effects of their expectations. Partly for this reason, education on the existence, sources, and widespread nature (sparing none) of cognitive biases is fundamental to training programs that are recommended by some as a mechanism of mitigation of bias [60, 61].

Some have argued that task-irrelevant contextual information is beneficial, or even necessary, for their accuracy [59, 62, 63]. When the contextual information suggests the correct answer, this will be necessarily true. However, many forms of contextual information are not truly probative, though they may seem so, and hence bias examiners: for example, information priming stereotypes of those likely to commit the crime in question. Even if it is probative and leads the examiner to the correct decision, this decision is no longer the independent evidence it should be [25, 45, 64, 65]. Various terms have been posed for effects of this non-independence of evidence. "Corroboration inflation" [66], the "investigative echo chamber" [67], "coherence-based reasoning" [68], or "bias snowball effect" [8] all referring to inflated perceived probative value of non-independent evidence.

5.3.2 Context Management and the Prevention of Exposure to Task-Irrelevant Information

Given that one cannot simply will bias away, the best way to prevent its operation is to deny it the opportunity. Therefore, a necessary step in managing cognitive biases is to prevent exposure to potentially biasing information insofar as possible [3, 5, 38, 39, 69]. A first step in this regard is to distinguish between task-relevant information that is necessary for the completion of the task and task-irrelevant information that is unnecessary for that purpose.

In some cases, the determination of what is or is not task-relevant is simple. For example, to provide an analysis of whether two fingerprints come from the same source, one needs only the two fingerprints. For other forensic judgments, the issue is more complicated. Much controversy has surrounded what information is necessary for the determinations of medical examiners, for example [5, 70]. Some things that might bias judgments might yet be relevant to the determination of the cause or manner of death. Similarly, fire investigation protocols currently state that investigators working across forensic disciplines (including the fire scene investigators, medical examiners, chemists, pathologists and others) should freely share information between them: though some have begun to point out the impact of cognitive biases and the need for more strict context management procedures [69]. Such issues concerning the balance of task-relevance versus the potential for causing bias have inspired the development of sequential unmasking procedures described in sections to come.

Once the determination of task-relevance is made, context management procedures can be put into place to restrict examiner access to task-irrelevant information. In most cases, this will involve the prevention of exposure to information concerning the case, its investigation, opinions or theories of the case, the identity of suspects, the source of samples for comparison, and much more. To accomplish this, contact with law enforcement should be prevented or restricted, as reflected in the many previously referenced calls to separate forensics structurally and behaviorally from investigators and prosecutors.

Clearly, to carry out the full process of forensic examination and provide conclusions, someone involved must know potentially biasing information, such as the source of the samples given to the examiner. To handle this, many have recommended the use of case managers within the forensics unit that will possess the necessary information and control what information is given to the examiners and when. They will ensure that the examiner receives only task-relevant information, or, if some task-relevant information might also promote bias, the case manager can ensure that it is provided as late as possible in the process of the forensic examination.

5.3.2.1 Sequential Unmasking

As noted earlier, it is not always possible to remove access to all potentially biasing information. Accordingly, the issue of *when* such information should be introduced to the forensic examiner has received considerable attention. It is well recognized that the order in which information is introduced exerts important effects on decision making processes and outcomes across domains ranging from simple impressions of people [71] to persuasive presentations [72], to complex financial decisions [73], to those of forensic examiners [74] or juries, and many others. Since information introduced earlier has the potential to exert greater effects on the interpretation of information to come, the essential strategy of sequential unmasking procedures is to delay the introduction of potentially biasing information for as long as possible.

"Sequential Unmasking" was first described by Krane and colleagues [75]. "Linear Sequential Unmasking" (LSU) was then developed by Dror and colleagues [76]. In response to the discovery that fingerprint examiners identified fewer features in a specific fingerprint if it was presented with the suspect's fingerprint than if presented alone, the authors suggested Linear Sequential Unmaking (LSU). The examiner would first examine the crime scene evidence without a comparison sample and thoroughly document their observations and initial judgments before exposure to the suspect sample. This was expected to both prevent the use of the suspect sample as the referent for comparison (as described earlier) and lead the examiner to more thoroughly examine the features of the crime scene sample.

Most recently, Dror and Kukula proposed "Linear Sequential Unmasking-*Expanded*" (LSU-*E*) as a mechanism more broadly applicable across forensic sciences: to not only address bias, but also noise in forensic decision-making [74]. Examiners must first form an opinion only on the basis of the evidence itself before receiving additional relevant information. LSU-*E* further specifies that remaining evidence must be introduced in order according to the three criteria of objectivity, relevance, and potential to bias decisions. Such criteria can be of particular use for judgments for those such as medical examiners, who have a much larger set of examinations and tests to perform, and information to consider.

Variations of sequential unmasking procedures have been tested and shown feasible in forensic entomology [73], forensic document examination [77], DNA analysis [78], firearms examination [79], even in forensic chemistry [80], and others. Nevertheless, the procedure is novel and more complex than traditional procedures and can be more costly; and on these bases has generated resistance among some. Accordingly, it may be wise to use LSU-*E* in situations affording the greatest opportunity for bias [45].

5.3.3 Use of Evidence Lineups

When police present possible suspects to an eyewitness, they commonly either use a "show-up" or "cold-show" procedure, where one person is presented and the witness must indicate whether that person is the perpetrator or not; or a "line-up" procedure, where multiple persons (commonly 6–8) are presented, and the witness can indicate which, if any, of them is the perpetrator. The single suspect procedure is widely considered by both eye-witness scientists and legal scholars to be suggestive, leading to the expectation that the presented person is likely the perpetrator. Indeed, an innocent person presented in the context of a show-up procedure is more likely to be misidentified than the same person presented in the context of a lineup procedure [81], and best practice recommendations for identification procedures now suggest the use of show-ups only when necessary [82, 83].

In accordance with this reasoning, some have suggested that the common forensic procedure of comparing a sample of unknown origin from a crime scene to a single suspect's sample might create an expectation of a match. That is, examiners might infer that simply because the particular suspect fingerprint is presented to them, there must be evidence to implicate him. In contrast, a comparison of that crime scene sample to a "line-up" of comparison samples would, at minimum, diffuse that expectation such that it would not center uniquely on the suspect [1, 8, 26, 84–87]. Similar recommendations for blind testing and lineups have been made regarding reducing biases in dog detection [41, 44, 88].

Results of studies comparing the use of evidence lineups to evidence show-ups have, on balance, revealed similar findings to those of eyewitness identification studies. That is, evidence lineups reduce the number of correct matches, but in some studies, also reduce the rate of misidentifications (see [26] for review). However, Few studies have been conducted, results have been somewhat inconsistent, and more research is needed to more clearly document the differences between procedures.

It should be noted, however, that should the idea of evidence lineups be adopted, methodological challenges similar to those that have been faced for eyewitness lineups must be faced: such as how to choose fillers, how many fillers should be used, in what order samples should be examined, and so on.

5.3.4 Heavily Scripted and Standardized Procedures and Tech

One way to limit the opportunity for confirmation biases to operate is to standardize procedures and measures in ways that limit the choices of the forensic examiner: for what tests to perform, how to perform them, or how to interpret them. Measures should be as objective and unsusceptible to interpretation as possible. Detection dogs' manner of alert, for example, should be standardized, clear, and readily identifiable by both professional and lay observers [41]. Indeed, the original recommendations of the NAS Report included standardization of procedures across laboratories [1]. Nevertheless, as reflected in our previous discussions of procedural sources of bias, standardized procedures will not eliminate bias if they are structured in a way that promotes bias. Nor will automated measures or software protect if biases affect the programming or technology.

5.3.5 *Minimize Opportunity for Behavioral Confirmation Processes to Operate*

Where opportunity exists for the behavior of a forensic practitioner to affect a forensic finding, every effort should be taken to remove that opportunity where at all possible. In part, such opportunities can be minimized by the aforementioned strategies to standardize testing procedures. However, in other cases, the testing procedure itself must avoid the opportunity for behavioral confirmation processes to operate. For example, detection dogs can be taught "independent patterning," whereby they canvas target regions on their own without being led by the human handler [41]. This greatly reduces the opportunity for the expectations of the handlers to cause them to consciously or unconsciously cue the dogs to alert. More generally, some believe the opportunity for bias can be eliminated by technology. However, this is not always a good solution, as technologies are designed or programmed by humans and can incorporate their biases, as illustrated by documented racial biases in facial identification tech [89]. Moreover, technology such as the use of IAFIS can create error based on incidental similarity. The larger the database, the greater chance of producing non-matches that are highly similar to the suspect [90], thus inviting false positive matches.

5.3.6 *Use of Multiple Examiners*

Many have recommended that two or more examiners should do the same forensic examination, and some methods and some labs have incorporated such a step [91]. Fingerprint analysis, for example, has long used the ACE-V (Analysis, Comparison, Evaluation, Verification) method, with the V referring to the use of a second examiner to "verify" the conclusion of the first. For this to effectively mitigate bias, however, it is necessary to keep the two examiners separate, as examiners have been shown to change their opinions upon exposure to a different conclusion by another examiner [92]. They must not discuss the case, and the second examiner must not know of the conclusions of the first. The verifier should not know the identity of the original examiner, and that original examiner should not select the verifier. Cross-laboratory verifications are considered ideal, though not always feasible [9].

It is also important to note that if two examiners are exposed to the same biasing influences (such as the IAFIS ranking, or the use of the suspect sample as the sole comparator, or case evidence), the agreement between their findings will be much less meaningful [93]. Finally, some laboratories use verification only if the initial examiner finds a match. Among other reasons to avoid this restriction, the previously discussed "low prevalence" effect will be especially strong (in this case low prevalence of previous disagreements with other examiners), and the base rate expectation of match extraordinarily high for the second examiner. The request to make a second evaluation essentially explicitly informs the second examiner that the first examiner did find a match.

In a different vein, the same examiner should not be used for different forensic examinations. For example, the same examiner should not contribute to both crime scene examination and forensic comparison examinations. Though perhaps an uncommon occurrence for many forensic examinations, medical examiners are often present at crime scenes and then perform their autopsies and arrive at determinations of cause and manner of death that surely can be affected by what is observed at the scene.

5.3.7 Using a Differential Diagnosis Approach

Some have recommended the use of a "differential diagnosis" approach, whereby a list of all possible conclusions is actively considered and evaluated, and the examiner presents each along with their likelihood: as opposed to considering a restricted range of possibilities and presenting a single conclusion [8, 94]. Some forensic disciplines, such as fire investigation, currently do recommend such an approach [69, 95, 96]. Research on confirmatory hypothesis testing has shown that even focus on the *question* of whether a hypothesis is true biases information search and interpretation of information in favor of the hypothesis [97, 98]. Similar effects occur if one forms an initial hypothesis [99]. The differential diagnosis approach can prevent a "rush to judgment," minimize effects of expectations associated with focus on one hypothesis and encourage more thorough consideration of all relevant evidence. As Liden and colleagues noted "a given body of data can in fact be compatible with an infinite number of theories. Therefore, mere consistency between data and theory is insufficient. It is also required that the theory is better compatible with the data than other theories" [94].

5.3.8 Training Programs

Some organizations have recommended training programs to educate practitioners on the importance of cognitive bias and the pervasive susceptibility of humans to it [9, 60, 61]. Given that awareness of bias does not help one to will it away, education alone will not be sufficient. Training programs will only be effective to the extent that they inform and train participants on procedures such as those discussed above that prevent the opportunity for bias to operate.

5.4 Conclusions

Much has changed for forensic sciences in the last twenty years, as awareness of the role of bias in forensic decisions has steadily increased. Early reactions to calls for recognition and mitigation of biases infecting forensic examinations included primary denial and hostility; however, the many reports such as those of National Academy, the National Commission on Forensic Sciences, and PCAST, the rapidly expanding related scientific literature and empirical demonstrations of confirmation biases (even in studies using practicing professionals), and the formation and activities of the Organization of Scientific Area Committees for Forensic Sciences (centered in large part on mitigation of bias) have steadily eroded such negative reactions. Though much remains to be done, it has become increasingly clear to all that the future of forensic sciences must include recognition and mitigation of bias: both for human examinations and for human designed procedures and technology.

References

1. National Research Council. (2009). *Strengthening forensic science in the United States: A path forward*. National Academies Press.
2. National Commission on Forensic Science. (2015). *Ensuring that forensic analysis is based upon task-relevant information*. US Department of Justice. https://www.justice.gov/ncfs/file/818196/download
3. President's Council of Advisors on Science and Technology. (2016). Forensic science in criminal courts: Ensuring scientific validity of feature-comparison methods. Retrieved from https://www.whitehouse.gov/sites/default/files/microsites/ostp/PCAST/pcast_forensic_science_report_final.pdf
4. National Institute of Standards and Technology (n.d.). The Organization of Scientific Area Committees for Forensic Science. https://www.nist.gov/organization-scientific-area-committees-forensic-science
5. Dror, I. E. (2018). Biases in forensic experts. *Science, 360*, 243. https://doi.org/10.1126/science.aat8443
6. Dror, I. E., Wertheim, K., Fraser-Mackenzie, P., & Walajtys, J. (2012). The impact of human-technology cooperation and distributed cognition in forensic science: Biasing effects of AFIS contextual information on human experts. *Journal of Forensic Sciences, 57*, 343–352. https://doi-org.unr.idm.oclc.org/10.1111/j.1556-4029.2011.02013.x
7. Dror, I. E. (2023). The most consistent finding in forensic science is inconsistency. *Journal of Forensic Science, 68*, 1851–1855. https://doi-org.unr.idm.oclc.org/10.1111/1556-4029.15369
8. Dror, I. E. (2020). Cognitive and human factors in expert decision-making: Six fallacies and the eight sources of bias. *Analytical Chemistry, 92*, 7998–8004. https://pubs.acs.org/doi/10.1021/acs.analchem.0c00704
9. Kassin, S. M., Dror, I. E., & Kukucka, J. (2013). The forensic confirmation bias: Problems, perspectives, and proposed solutions. *Journal of Applied Research in Memory and Cognition, 2*(1), 42–52. https://doi.org/10.1016/j.jarmac.2013.01.001
10. Festinger, L. (1957). *A theory of cognitive dissonance*. Stanford University Press.
11. Nisbett, R., & Ross, L. (1980). *Human inference: Strategies and shortcomings of social judgement*. Prentice Hall.
12. Arkes, H. R., & Blumer, C. (1985). The psychology of sunk cost. *Organizational Behavior and Human Decision Processes, 35*(1), 124–140. https://doi.org/10.1016/07495978(85)90049-4

13. Shermer, M. (2006). *Why people believe weird things.* Michael Shermer: Why people Believe weird things|TED Talk. https://www.ted.com/talks/michael_shermer_why_people_believe_weird_things
14. Liu, J., Li, J., Feng, L., Li, L., Tian, J., & Lee, K. (2014). Seeing Jesus in toast: Neural and behavioral correlates of face pareidolia. *Cortex, 53*, 60–77. https://doi.org/10.1016/j.cortex.2014.01.013
15. Nees, M. (October 30, 2015). *Hearing ghost voices relies on pseudoscience and fallibility of human perception.* The conversation. https://theconversation.com/hearing-ghost-voices-relies-on-pseudoscience-and-fallibility-of-human-perception-48160
16. Nees, M. A., & Phillips, C. (2014). Auditory pareidolia: Effects of contextual priming on perceptions of purportedly paranormal and ambiguous auditory stimuli. *Applied Cognitive Psychology, 29*(1), 129–134. https://doi.org/10.1002/acp.3068
17. Lange, N. D., Thomas, R. P., Dana, J., & Dawes, R. M. (2011). Contextual biases in the interpretation of auditory evidence. *Law and Human Behavior, 35*, 178–187. https://doi.org/10.1007/s10979-010-9226-4
18. Zeppelin, L. (1971). Stairway to heaven [Song]. On *Led Zeppelin IV* [Album]. Atlantic records.
19. Steve Terreberry. (December 10, 2022). *These backwards messages in songs should be banned!* [Video]. YouTube. https://www.youtube.com/watch?v=nekIGUFfvD0
20. RoomieOfficial. (December 7, 2022). *Famous songs in reverse (SECRET MESSAGES!)* [Video]. YouTube. https://www.youtube.com/watch?v=h3C2xhvTJDo
21. Rolli, B. (2023). Why Judas priest was sued over better by you, better than me. *Ultimate classic rock*. https://ultimateclassicrock.com/judas-priest-better-by-you-better-than-me-lawsuit/
22. Dror, I. E., Peron, A. E., Hind, S.-L., & Charlton, D. (2005). When emotions get the better of us: The effect of contextual top-down processing on matching fingerprints. *Applied Cognitive Psychology, 19*, 799–809. https://doi-org.unr.idm.oclc.org/10.1002/acp.1130
23. Osborne, N. K. P., & Zajac, R. (2016). An imperfect match? Crime-related context influences fingerprint decisions. *Applied Cognitive Psychology, 30*, 126–134. https://doi.org/10.1002/acp.3180
24. Chiam, S., Louise, J., & Higgins, D. (2022). "Identified", "probable", "possible", or "exclude:" The influence of task-irrelevant information on forensic odontology identification opinion. *Science and Justice, 62*, 461–470. https://doi.org/10.1016/j.scijus.2022.06.002
25. Cooper, G. S., & Meterko, V. (2019). Cognitive bias research in forensic science: A systematic review. *Forensic Science International, 297*, 35–46. https://doi.org/10.1016/j.forsciint.2019.01.016
26. Kukucka, J., Dror, I. E., Yu, M., Hall, L., & Morgan, R. M. (2020). The impact of evidence lineups on fingerprint expert decisions. *Applied Cognitive Psychology, 34*(5), 1143–1153. https://doi-org.unr.idm.oclc.org/10.1002/acp.3703
27. Bruce, D. J. (1958). The effect of listeners anticipations on the intelligibility of heard speech. *Language and Speech, 1*(2), 79–97. https://doi.org/10.1177/002383095800100202
28. Strand, E. A., & Johnson, K. (1996). Gradient and visual speaker normalization in the perception of fricatives. *Natural Language Processing and Speech Technology*, 14–26. https://doi.org/10.1515/9783110821895-003
29. Munson, B., Jefferson, S. V., & McDonald, E. C. (2006). The influence of perceived sexual orientation on fricative identification. *The Journal of the Acoustical Society of America, 119*(4), 2427–2437. https://doi.org/10.1121/1.2173521
30. Drager, K. (2011). Speaker age and vowel perception. *Language and Speech, 54*(1), 99–121. https://doi.org/10.1177/0023830910388017
31. Hay, J., Nolan, A., & Drager, K. (2006). From fush to feesh: exemplar priming in speech perception. *The Linguistic Review, 23*(3). https://doi.org/10.1515/tlr.2006.014
32. Hay, J., & Drager, K. (2010). Stuffed toys and speech perception. *Linguistics, 48*(4). https://doi.org/10.1515/ling.2010.027
33. Kang, O., & Rubin, D. L. (2009). Reverse linguistic stereotyping: Measuring the effect of listener expectations on speech evaluation. *Journal of Language and Social Psychology, 28*(4), 441–456. https://doi.org/10.1177/0261927x09341950

34. McGowan, K. B. (2015). Social expectation improves speech perception in noise. *Language and Speech, 58*(4), 502–521. https://doi.org/10.1177/0023830914565191
35. Gold, E., & French, P. (2019). International practices in forensic speaker comparisons: Second survey. *International Journal of Speech, Language and the Law, 26*(1), 1–20. https://doi.org/10.1558/ijsll.38028
36. Fraser-Mackenzie, P. A. F., Bucht, R. E., & Dror, I. E. (2013). Forensic judgment and decision-making. In P. H. Crowley, & T. R. Zentall (Eds.), *Comparative decision-making* (pp. 385–415). Oxford University Press.
37. Heyer, R., & Semmler, C. (2013). Forensic confirmation bias: The case of facial image comparison. *Journal of Applied Research in Memory and Cognition, 2*(1), 68–70. https://doi.org/10.1016/j.jarmac.2013.01.008
38. Kukucka, J., Kassin, S. M., Zapf, P. A., & Dror, I. E. (2017). Cognitive bias and blindness: A global survey of forensic science examiners. *Journal of Applied Research in Memory and Cognition, 6*, 452–459. https://doi.org/10.1016/j.jarmac.2017.09.001
39. Thompson, W. C. (2011). What role should investigative facts play in the evaluation of scientific evidence*?. Australian Journal of Forensic Sciences, 43*, 123–134. https://doi.org/10.1080/00450618.2010.541499
40. Hamnett, H. J., & Dror, I. E. (2020). The effect of contextual information on decision-making in forensic toxicology. *Forensic Science International: Synergy, 2*, 339–348. https://doi.org/10.1016/j.fsisyn.2020.06.003
41. Minhinnick, S. (2016). Statistical reliability confounders and improvement in advanced dog training: Patterns, routines, targets, alerts, distractors, reinforcement, and other issues. In T. Jezierski, J. Ensminger, & L. E. Papet (Eds.), *Canine olfaction science and law: Advances in forensic science, medicine, conservation, and environmental remediation* (pp. 197–212). CRC Press.
42. Lit, L., Schweitzer, J. B., & Oberbauer, A. M. (2011). Handler beliefs affect scent detection dog outcomes. *Animal Cognition, 14*, 387–394. https://doi.org/10.1007/s10071-010-0373-2
43. Taslitz, A. E. (1990). Does the cold nose know—The unscientific myth of the dog scent lineup. *Hastings Law Journal, 42*(1), 15–134.
44. Taslitz, A. E. (2013). The cold nose might actually know: Science and scent lineups. *Criminal Justice, 28*, 4–8 & 55–56.
45. Kukucka, J., & Dror, I. E. (2023). Human factors in forensic science: Psychological causes of bias and error. In D. DeMatteo & K. C. Scherr (Eds.), *The Oxford handbook of psychology and law* (pp. 621–642). Oxford University.
46. Growns, B., & Kukucka, J. (2021). The prevalence effect in fingerprint identification: Match and non-match base rates impact misses and false alarms. *Applied Cognitive Psychology, 35*, 751–760. https://doi-org.unr.idm.oclc.org/10.1002/acp.3800
47. Dror, I. E., & Langenburg, G. (2019). Cannot Decide: The fine line between appropriate inconclusive determinations versus unjustifiably deciding not to decide. *Journal of Forensic Sciences, 64*(1), 10–15. https://doi-org.unr.idm.oclc.org/10.1111/1556-4029.13854
48. MacLean, C. L., & Dror, I. E. (2023). Measuring base-rate bias error in workplace safety investigators. *Journal of Safety Research, 84*, 108–116. https://doi.org/10.1016/j.jsr.2022.10.012
49. Horowitz, T. S. (2017). Prevalence in visual search: From the clinic to the lab and back again. *Japanese Psychological Research, 59*, 65–108. https://doi-org.unr.idm.oclc.org/10.1111/jpr.12153
50. Papesh, M. H., & Goldinger, S. D. (2014). Infrequent identity mismatches are frequently undetected. *Attention, Perception, and Psychophysics, 76*, 1335–1349. https://doi.org/10.3758/s13414-014-0630-6
51. Smith, A., & Wells, G. L. (2023). Telling us less than what they know: Expert inconclusive reports conceal exculpatory evidence in forensic cartridge-case comparisons. *Journal of Applied Research in Memory and Cognition*. https://doi.org/10.1037/mac0000138
52. Kahneman, D., & Tversky, A. (1979). Prospect theory: An analysis of decision under risk. *Econometrica, 47*(2). Prospect Theory: An Analysis of Decision under Risk (mit.edu).

53. Morgan, R. M. (2017). Conceptualising forensic science and forensic reconstruction. Part II: The critical interaction between research, policy/law and practice. *Science and Justice, 57*, 460–467. https://doi.org/10.1016/j.scijus.2017.06.003
54. Murrie, D. C., Boccaccini, M. T., Guarnera, L. A., & Rufino, K. A. (2013). Are forensic experts biased by the side that retained them? *Psychological Science, 24*, 1889–1897. https://doi.org/10.1177/0956797613481812
55. Charlton, D., Fraser-Mackenzie, P. A. F., & Dror, I. E. (2010). Emotional experiences and motivating factors associated with fingerprint analysis. *Journal of Forensic Sciences, 55*, 385–393. https://doi-org.unr.idm.oclc.org/10.1111/j.1556-4029.2009.01295.x
56. Martin, K., Ricciardelli, R., & Dror, I. E. (2020). How forensic mental health nurses' perspectives of their patients can bias healthcare. *Journal of Clinical Nursing, 29*, 2482–2494. https://doi.org/10.1111/jocn.15264
57. Buckelton, J., Evett, I., & Weir, B. (2014). Letter to editor in response to editorial by Risinger et al. *Science and Justice, 54*, 510. https://doi.org/10.1016/j.scijus.2014.07.003
58. Champod, C. (2014). Research focused mainly on bias will paralyse forensic science. *Science and Justice, 54*, 107–109. https://doi.org/10.1016/j.scijus.2014.02.004
59. Oliver, W. R. (2018). Comment on Dror, Kukucka, Kassin, and Zapf (2018), When expert decision-making goes wrong. *Journal of Applied Research in Memory and Cognition, 7*, 314–315. https://doi.org/10.1016/j.jarmac.2018.01.010
60. Rhodes, R. (2014). Cognitive bias in forensic speech science. *Proceedings of IAFPA*. https://www.pholab.uzh.ch/static/IAFPA/abstracts/RHODESrichard.pdf
61. Lit, L., & Crawford, C. A. (2006). Effects of training paradigms on search dog performance. *Applied Animal Behaviour Science, 98*(3–4), 277–292. https://doi.org/10.1016/j.applanim.2005.08.022
62. Curley, L. J., Munro, J., & Lages, M. (2020). An inconvenient truth: More rigorous and ecologically valid research is needed to properly understand cognitive bias in forensic decisions. *Forensic Science International: Synergy, 2*, 107–109. https://doi.org/10.1016/j.fsisyn.2020.01.004
63. Elaad, E. (2013). Psychological contamination in forensic decisions. *Journal of Applied Research in Memory and Cognition, 2*, 76–77. https://doi.org/10.1016/j.jarmac.2013.01.006
64. Despodova, N. M., Kukucka, J., & Hiley, A. (2020). Can defense attorneys detect forensic confirmation bias? Effects on evidentiary judgments and trial Strategies. *Research Spotlight, 228*(3), 216–220. https://doi.org/10.1027/2151-2604/a000414
65. Page, M., Taylor, J., & Blenkin, M. (2012). Context effects and observer bias-implications for forensic odontology. *Journal of Forensic Sciences, 57*(1), 108–112. https://doi.org/10.1111/j.1556-4029.2011.01903.x
66. Kassin, S. M. (2012). Why confessions trump innocence. *American Psychologist, 67*, 431–445.
67. Saks, M. J., Risinger, D. M., Rosenthal, R., & Thompson, W. C. (2003). Context effects in forensic science: A review and application of the science of science to crime laboratory practice in the United States. *Science and Justice, 43*, 77–90.
68. Simon, D. (2011). The limited diagnosticity of criminal trials. *Vanderbilt Law Review, 64*, 143–223.
69. Morling, N. R., & Henneberg, M. L. (2020). Contextual information and cognitive bias in the forensic investigation of fatal fires: Do these incidents present an increased risk of flawed decision-making? *International Journal of Law, Crime and Justice*. https://doi.org/10.1016/j.ijlcj.2020.100406
70. Dror, I. E. (2022). The use and abuse of the elusive construct of inconclusive decisions. *Law, Probability and Risk, 21*(1), 85–87. https://doi.org/10.1093/lpr/mgac008
71. Asch, S. E. (1964). Forming impressions of personality. *Journal of Abnormal and Social Psychology, 41*, 258–290.
72. Hovland, C. I. (Ed). *The order of presentation in persuasion*. Yale University Press.
73. Archer, M. S., & Wallman, J. F. (2016). Context effects in forensic entomology and use of sequential unmasking in casework. *Journal of Forensic Sciences, 61*, 1270–1277. https://doi.org/10.1111/1556-4029.13139

74. Dror, I. E., & Kukucka, J. (2021). Linear sequential unmasking–expanded (LSU-E): A general approach for improving decision-making as well as minimizing bias. *Forensic Science International: Synergy, 3*, 100–161. https://doi.org/10.1016/j.fsisyn.2021.100161
75. Krane, D., Ford, S., Gilder, J., Inman, K., Jamieson, A., & Koppl, R. (2008). Sequential unmasking: A means of minimizing observer effects in forensic DNA interpretation. *Journal of Forensic Sciences, 53*, 1006–1107.
76. Dror, I. E., Thompson, W. C., Meisner, C. A., Kornfield, I., Drane, D., & Saks, M. (2015). Context management toolbox: A linear sequential unmasking (LSU) approach in minimizing cognitive bias in forensic decision-making. *Journal of Forensic Sciences, 60*(4), 1111–1112. https://doi.org/10.1111/1556-4029.12805
77. Found, B., & Ganas, J. (2013). The management of domain irrelevant context information in forensic handwriting examination casework. *Science and Justice, 53*, 154–158. https://doi.org/10.1016/j.scijus.2012.10.004
78. Jeanguenat, A. M., Budowle, B., & Dror, I. E. (2017). Strengthening forensic DNA decision-making through a better understanding of the influence of cognitive bias. *Science and Justice, 57*, 415–420. https://doi.org/10.1016/j.scijus.2017.07.005
79. Mattijssen, E. J. A. T., Kerkhoff, W., Berger, C. E. H., Dror, I. E., & Stoel, R. D. (2016). Implementing context management in forensic casework: Minimizing contextual bias in firearms examination. *Science and Justice, 56*, 113–122. https://doi.org/10.1016/j.scijus.2015.11.004
80. Whitehead, F. A., Williams, M. R., & Sigman, M. E. (2022). Decision theory and linear sequential unmasking in forensic fire debris analysis: A proposed workflow. *Forensic Chemistry, 29*, 100426. https://doi.org/10.1016/j.forc.2022.100426
81. Neuschatz, J. S., Wetmore, S. A., Key, K. N., Cash, D. K., Gronlund, S. D., & Goodsell, C. A. (2016). A comprehensive evaluation of showups. In M. K. Miller & B. H. Bornstein (Eds.), *Advances in psychology and law* (pp. 43–69). Springer.
82. National Academy of Sciences. (2014). *Identifying the culprit: Assessing eyewitness identification*. National Academies Press.
83. Wells, G. L., Kovera, M. B., Douglass, A. B., Brewer, N., Meissner, C. A., & Wixted, J. T. (2020). Policy and procedure recommendations for the collection and preservation of eyewitness identification evidence. *Law and Human Behavior, 44*, 3–36. https://doi.org/10.1037/lhb0000359
84. Quigley-McBride, A., & Wells, G. L. (2018). Fillers can help control for contextual bias in forensic comparison tasks. *Law and Human Behavior, 42*, 295–305. https://doi.org/10.1037/lhb0000295
85. Risinger, D. M., Saks, M. J., Thompson, W. C., & Rosenthal, R. (2002). The Daubert/Kumho implications of observer effects in forensic science: Hidden problems of expectation and suggestion. *California Law Review, 90*, 1–56. https://doi.org/10.2307/3481305
86. Smith, A. M., Mackovichova, S., Jalava, S. T., & Pozzulo, J. (2020). Fair forensic-object lineups are superior to forensic-object showups. *Journal of Applied Research in Memory and Cognition, 9*, 68–82. https://doi.org/10.1016/j.jarmac.2019.11.001
87. Whitman, G., & Koppl, R. (2010). Rational bias in forensic science. *Law, Probability, and Risk, 9*, 69–90. https://doi.org/10.1093/lpr/mgp028
88. Johnen, D., Wolfgang, H., & Fischer-Tenhagen, C. (2017). An approach to identify bias in scent detection dog testing. *Applied Animal Behaviour Science, 189*, 1–12. https://doi.org/10.1016/j.applanim.2017.01.001
89. Lohr, S. (February 9, 2018). Facial recognition is accurate, if you're a white guy. *The New York Times*. https://www.nytimes.com/2018/02/09/technology/facial-recognition-race-artificial-intelligence.html
90. Dror, I. E., & Mnookin, J. (2010). The use of technology in human expert domains: In Challenges and risks arising from the use of automated fingerprint identification systems forensics. *Law, Probability and Risk, 9*(1), 47–67.
91. Ballantyne, K. N., Edmond, G., & Found, B. (2017). Peer review in forensic science. *Forensic Science International, 277*, 66–76. https://doi.org/10.1016/j.forsciint.2017.05.020

92. Merlino, M. L. (2015). *Validity, reliability, accuracy, and bias in forensic signature identification.* National Institute of Justice. https://www.ncjrs.gov/pd34iles1/nij/grants/248565.pdf
93. Langenburg, G., Champod, C., & Wertheim, P. (2009). Testing for potential contextual bias effects during the verification stage of the ACE-V methodology when conducting fingerprint comparisons. *Journal of Forensic Sciences, 54*, 571–582. https://doi-org.unr.idm.oclc.org/10.1111/j.1556-4029.2009.01025.x
94. Liden, M., Thiblin, I., & Dror, I. E. (2023). The role of alternative hypotheses in reducing bias in forensic experts' decision-making. *Science and Justice, 63*, 581–587. https://doi.org/10.1016/j.scijus.2023.07.005
95. DeHaan, J. D., & Icove, D. J. (2014). Kirk's Fire Investigation: Pearson, New International Edition. Pearson Education Ltd, Harlow.
96. National Fire Protection Association. (2017). NFPA 921: Guide for fire and explosion investigation. NFPA, Quincy.
97. Wason, P. C. (1960). On the failure to eliminate hypotheses in a conceptual task. *Quarterly Journal of Experimental Psychology, 12*, 129–140. https://doi.org/10.1080/17470216008416717
98. Snyder, M., & Swann, W. B., Jr. (1978). Hypothesis-testing processes in social interaction. *Journal of Personality and Social Psychology, 36*, 1202–1212. https://doi.org/10.1037/00223514.36.11.1202
99. O'Brien, B. (2009). Prime suspect: An examination of factors that aggravate and counteract confirmation bias in criminal investigations. *Psychology, Public Policy and Law, 15*, 315–334.

Chapter 6
Three Critical Elements of Start-Up Success

Zoltán Székely

Abstract Compared to the already complex and difficult pathway to market for innovative start-ups, innovators in forensic sciences face additional challenges when developing a technology or a service for the market. This chapter presents a(n) (self-) assessment method for founders and investors to estimate and monitor the success potential of a start-up based on three critical elements: time, team, and traction. Time refers to the temporal factors that influence a start-up's performance and profitability. Team relates to the people who work on the start-up and their characteristics. Traction refers to the evidence of customer demand for the start-up's product or service. The chapter also features the context for innovation through presenting the evolution of the "helix" models (triple, quadruple, quintuple), and the most popular tools to measure readiness level at increasing complexity, from the well known Technology Readiness Level to the KTH Innovation Readiness Level™. Finally, itt also provides examples from the forensic market and suggests some practical tips to balance and optimize these elements, aiming to help forensic science practitioners and researchers to bring their innovations to the market.

6.1 Introduction

This chapter presents the "three critical elements" approach, a self-assessment method recommended for founders and investors to estimate and monitor the success potential of a start-up. The three critical elements considered are time, team, and traction, ("3T").

While the method has a general applicability, this chapter provides examples relating to the forensic market where possible. Although the volume of investment into forensic science is growing, organisations investing into this discipline are usually state, governmental or international organisations (such as The Bureau

Z. Székely (✉)
Székely Family & Co. Nonprofit Kft., Fő Utca 11. 7/20., 1191 Budapest, Hungary
e-mail: zoltan@szekely.family

S. Francese and R. S. P. King (eds.), *Driving Forensic Innovation in the 21st Century*,
https://doi.org/10.1007/978-3-031-56556-4_6

of Democracy of the US Department of State, The Center for Human Identification at UNT, Health Science Center at Fort Worth, INTERPOL), with a few exceptions like PricewaterhouseCoopers (PwC) forensic services. This The PwC team provides technology-driven forensic intelligence and analytics to help businesses build resilient strategies to protect value, build trust, and create opportunities as one of the Big Four accounting firms (along with Deloitte, EY and KPMG). This scenario is similar in the EU where the key player in this field is The European Network of Forensic Science Institutes (ENFSI), receiving direct grants ("Monopoly Programmes", MP) from the European Commission. These grants and investments fund projects of scientific nature, like complex identification procedure (CIP), cooperation and information sharing among laboratories (JLS/D1/2007/025), but they do not bringing these results to market. Therefore, founders and fundraisers of forensic start-ups who are willing to transition technologies to the market will likely have to compete on the open investment market, where familiarity with such generic method like the three critical elements of start-up success can provide an advantage.

Besides describing the 3T considered critical for success, the chapter also provides context to their use to achieve readiness levels of different types. Finally, to support understanding the rational behind choosing different readiness level assessment or a more complex technology readiness level, development and structure of the quintuple helix, the concept behind research and innovation policy for sustainability will be described.

This chapter is written for practitioners and researchers in forensics with the aim to give an initial guide in bringing their innovations to the market, and not for economists or business development scholars; therefore some of the research and study results, approaches and structures are intentionally presented in a simplified manner. Several presumptions are used, for example that the activities take place in a European socio-economical context (EEA, EU and UK) and that Keynes' approach on active influencing of the economy with various tools including but not restricted to redistribution and regulation is adopted by governments instead of Hayek's liberal position [1].

6.2 The 3Ts and Their Main Characteristics

The 3Ts: Time, Team and Traction are used by Székely Family and Co. Nonprofit Kft (SFC) to assess the viability of an idea, scientific result or technology to reach the market by founding a start-up. SFC is a fully privately-owned non-profit company operating in the fields of aerospace, defence, security and sustainability. It is one of the leading SME in the private Hungarian innovation sector, being the fifth entity on the list of Hungarian SMEs receiving the most EU funds from the Horizon Europe programme for research and innovation actions out of a total of 90 thousand similar entities nationwide. Its current projects include CBRN protection (https://peers-project.eu/), disaster resilience (http://b-prepared-project.com/), bidirectional charging of EVs (https://drive2x.eu/) and just twin transformation of society.

It also functions as a start-up studio, providing support to start-ups across Europe such as 27G-T (HU), Edugamitec (LU), Friendbase (SE), General Mechatronics (HU) Pedivan Ltd. (UK), Horge Technologies (HU). During the COVID-19 pandemic crisis, SFC exhibited resilience by growing in spite of the all well known difficulties that businesses faced and has supported the market roll-out of products as:

- Memomoti (https://memomoti.com/),
- NaBi—The Long Life Tracker (https://www.nabitrack.com/page-select) or
- RadNano dosimeter (https://27g.space/)

6.2.1 Time

The most important of the three critical elements is time. It affects the efficiency of operations, customer satisfaction, and profitability. Business owners must manage time wisely to make sure their goals are met and that they maximize profits. Time provides an opportunity to prioritize tasks and focus on the most important projects. This allows for the efficient allocation of resources and helps ensure work is being done in the most productive way possible. Time is more important than money, as money can be recovered or funds raised again, but time lost is lost forever. Especially for a start-up, time is even more critical than in the case of another type of business model.

The following key aspects can be identified in the dimension of time:

- time the team can dedicate to the start-up
- time needed to deploy the product or service
- time until actual funds are used up
- time until competitors roll out their own products or services
- time window of the market opportunity
- time available for fundraising
- time remaining from the patent or other protection of intellectual property

6.2.2 Time the Team Can Dedicate to the Start-Up

When launching new start-ups, it is not always the case that everyone works in a full-time rôle. On the contrary, it is likely that start-ups can only afford part-time experts. Even founders and C-level officers may participate in multiple companies or have a full-time job besides building the start-up, which they develop as a part-time activity. However, as the start-up advances and reaches higher technology or business readiness levels, a part-time role may simply not be enough. Sooner or later, fulfilling orders, proceeding with product development, keeping the company in shape, and having the financial cash flow in hand, will all need undivided focus. Yet, perhaps the most time-consuming part still remains in satisfying existing clients' needs, as well as further client acquisition. Eventually, the founders and key employees must choose between having this start-up as a full-time job or exiting it. Even the best start-up can fail because its key employees are not able to allocate enough time to move it forward.

6.2.3 Time Needed to Deploy the Product

In most of the cases an innovation on which a start-up is built is not immediately ready to be sold into the market. Even if it is technically ready and fully functional—especially in narrow and well-regulated segments such as forensic science, Pharmacy, baby care—there are special standards and regulatory requirements to comply with before selling the product can actually commence. Those requirements must be met, and appropriate administrative steps taken before the product can be sold to the customers, even if those customers are not individual consumers, but agencies, authorities or other organisations. An example of this lies in the procurement of forensic tools, which is usually carried out by public bodies and, as such, through public procurement. In the case of incubations carried out by SFC, it can be considered as the very regular case that the start-up builds on a new idea or on a fresh patent which is technically feasible and needed by the market, but not yet developed as a full feature product. Therefore, there is a need to spend hours and hours in designing, engineering or developing software to make the product operational and fully functional and provide a high quality for the customers. However, it also has to be remarked that the product may have follow-up versions and can be further developed even after its market release and the start-up shall not wait with market deployment after the first "Minimum Viable Product" version is.

Minimum Viable Product (MVP): A minimum viable product (MVP) is a version of a product with just enough features to be usable by early customers who can then provide feedback for future product development [2].

It is important to point out, that MVP does not imply a hastily deployment yielding a partly operational product, especially in market fields as forensic science. Having enough features meeting minimum viability reflects compliance with relevant standards and having accreditation where the MVP is available and even more importantly, fulfils the quality requirements of end-users. For example, in case of a forensic product to be sold in the EU, the product must comply with ENFSI guidelines. If the same product is to be sold in the US, it has to be accredited by the American Society of Crime Laboratory Directors/Laboratory Accreditation Board (ASCLD/LAB).

However, if a start-up aims to achieve the best possible product and highest number of features before releasing the first product version, then, technically speaking, they will likely fail to be first on the market. By the time they achieve such product, developed to the appropriate quality, the competition will have had a good chance to catch up and go ahead of them. Therefore, timely release and development is a very important timing issue and risk can only partly be mitigated by the novelty of the technology or by a clever intellectual property rights strategy.

6.2.4 Time Until Actual Funds Are Used Up

Every activity costs money. Start-ups are types of companies that strive to achieve their goals and land on the market before their overall available funds are used up. This is a very difficult game of balance and speed. The start-up has to spend enough money so that the development, innovation, market acquisition and growth may proceed, ensuring work will not stall, and people (employees, natural persons under direct contract, volunteers, helpers, ambassadors and owners themselves) are kept motivated. This does not only mean remuneration like salaries or premiums, but spending on things which are important to people, from certain aspects of the development or a logo design to joining or organising events or running charities. In most instances, the focus is on the velocity of using up the available funds. It is worthwhile, at this point, mentioning an important indicator called "burn rate".

According to Kenton, the burn rate is the pace at which a new company not yet generating profits consumes its cash reserves [3].

Burn rate is usually expressed in currency/month (e.g. 231,500 €/month), however in some high-pace project frameworks the monthly rate is replaced by a daily rate. The burn rate and the available funds (cash reserves) define the runway or cash runway, which means the time available until actual funds are used up.

Burn rate and runway have to be estimated in every reasonable start-up's business plan. Those indicators will change during the lifecycle of the company: successfully closed funding rounds—including additional investments from third parties or bridge funding—will extend the runway, increase of company size will increase the burn rate and shorten the runway. If the start-up fails to start revenue generation that exceeds the operating costs before it comes to the end of the runway, with no further fundraising opportunities, it will likely go bankrupt and must be wrapped up.

Indeed, this is what differentiates a start-up from another freshly started company, that they are in a business model where they accept negative cash flow, burn rate, and a limited runway (time) available, in order to get their product to market.

6.2.5 Time Until Competitors Roll Out Their Own Products

Unless the start-up is operating within a niche technical field or is a ground-breaking pioneer in that particular technology, it is probable that at least one other company is developing a very similar product, in parallel. Additionally, it is likely that a third party may choose to copy the product as soon as the first information appears on the market. Sooner or later every start-up and every product will have a competitor, either a copycat or a different kind of technology and comparable innovation. The length of the time advantage depends on multiple factors, such as the breakthrough nature of the innovation, effectiveness of intellectual property protection, the size of the actual market and so on. As this advantage diminishes, one or more competitors will be present, and they will roll out their own product. The time that is available before competitors arrive and the effective use of that time are critical to the success of a start-up. The objective, therefore, is "to be there first", and generate revenue until competitors arrive with their own product. With good timings, the start-up can have a product which has a unique value proposition across the market sector.

Value proposition: a value proposition is a simple statement that summarizes why a customer would choose your product or service [4].

In the absence of competitors during critical time, the company has a good chance to obtain contracts, make the best bid and win procurements, sell the product to consumers, convert the start-up model into a business model with consolidated cash-flow or scale-up, build a strong brand and a widen distributor network, thus making it highly likely that the funds invested will return. These funds can be re-invested into research, development, and innovation again, giving opportunity to keep or increase the advantage, as well as deploying more direct tools to strengthen market positions, such as M&A[1] or SPACs[2] (not discussed in this chapter). Therefore, start-ups developing innovative products and services must know the competitors' standing in the field and estimate the time left from the initial advantage. They can use this advantage to rush to the market, redefine the product to avoid competition as much as possible, target a very specific customer segment and tailor the product towards them, focus on branding, increase fundraising activities or strengthen its Intellectual Property Rights related to the product.

6.2.6 Time Window of the Market Opportunity

Occasionally, one product or service is needed as a timely intervention within the market. Face masks, for example, are a fascinating illustration of this. Five to ten years ago, face masks were less needed by the general population, but their necessity surged during the COVID-19 pandemic. Since the end of this pandemic, their requirement has somewhat diminished again. The same may be said for entilators, vaccines, tests and so on. Almost every product has a so-called time window of market opportunity when there is a spike in the need for the product. This can come from the value provided by the product or from the hype generated through marketing or from a public or private procurement wave launched by a change in regulations, policies or recent events. And this need is high.

Hype in marketing is a strategy of using extreme publicity. Hype as a modern marketing strategy is closely associated with social media. Marketing through hype often uses artificial scarcity to induce demand. Consumers of hyped products often

---

[1] Mergers and acquisitions (M&A) is a general term that describes the consolidation of companies or assets through various types of financial transactions. These transactions include mergers, acquisitions, consolidations, tender offers, purchase of assets, and management acquisitions.

[2] A special purpose acquisition company (SPAC) is formed to raise money through an initial public offering (IPO) to buy another company.

participate as a form of conspicuous consumption to signify characteristics about themselves [5].

There is a difference in the length of the time-window needed to reach the market according to the type of the product (and the nature of the need it satisfies). Consumer technology products are designed for mass-market consumption and are typically developed with speed and capable of catching a shorter time-to-market window. These products are often driven by consumer demand and are designed to be user-friendly, intuitive, and easy to use. They are typically less complex than forensic technology products and are not designed to withstand the rigors of forensic analysis. Forensic technology products, on the other hand, are designed for use in legal and investigative contexts. They are typically more complex than consumer technology products and require a longer time-to-market window. Forensic technology products must be able to withstand rigorous testing and analysis, as they may be used as evidence in legal proceedings. They must also be able to handle large volumes of data and provide accurate results.

Start-ups must foresee this time window coming and be ready to launch the product before the time window closes. In case of forensic start-ups, as they need a longer window, foresight is more important than in case of start-ups with consumer products.

For example, in 1997, John Colbert and Peter Watkins founded the Guidance Software where Shawn H. McCreight (Chief Technical Officer of the company) created the Encase forensic tool. This tool was used in forensic science to recover evidence from seized hard drives and released it in 1998. In 2002, the company released Encase Enterprise which was among the first network-enabled forensic tools. The founders identified the coming need of digital forensics and released a product addressing that need, way ahead of competitors. If a time window for a product is already open on the market, usually it is already late to start developing a product to respond to this time window. The best solution to catch this time window is the so-called blue ocean approach, when we are opening a time window for ourselves by creating a new market and combine it with a hype. A good example of this is identification of persons using machine perception (defined as the capability of a computer system to interpret data in a manner that is similar to the way humans use their senses to relate to the world around them and ensuring that such records are not tampered with). A "blue ocean" situation, when the new technology creates a new market will be discussed in more detail later in this chapter ("traction"); however in case of forensic products, this opportunity is very rare and limited to technological breakthroughs, new rules on criminal procedures, precedent cases and evidences, as obviously the idea to create a new *modus operandi* to have a new forensic product sold on the market is strongly discouraged. To give a very futuristic example, let us assume that humanity develops technology on how to teleport humans and criminals start a new, hit-and-run type *modus operandi*: by teleporting into houses, snatch what they can and teleport away. Then, the first forensic company who will develop technology to track down a teleport process and identify the teleported person will be in a "blue ocean" situation as be the only provider on the market who is able to provide a solution.

6.2.7 Time Available for Fundraising

The availability of funds and applicable timeframes to acquire those funds are both limited. Sometimes investors inject a lot of money into the economy, mostly through the stock market (sometimes called a 'bull market'), and thus it is very easy to obtain a capital raise with an initial public offering (IPO) and get investors and/or acquire funding from various governmental programmes (other funding sources exist). In other so-called economical down cycle times (also called a 'bear market'), it is very hard to get an investor or get a project funded. These cycles have to be taken into account when planning the start-ups fund raising activities and timeline in general.

The Center of Financial Research and Analysis (CFRA), a global leader in financial intelligence solutions and insights, performed an analysis on the S&P 500, a stock market index that is viewed as a measure of how well the stock market is performing overall. It includes around 500 of the largest U.S. companies. They found that a bear market [on the stock market] has lasted an average of 14 months. A bull market has had an average lifespan of about 60 months. The shortest bull market lasted 98 days and ran from June 1, 1932, to September 7, 1932. A bear market has had an average decline of around − 33%. A bull market has historically had an average rise of 165%. The shortest bear markets lasted about three months in 1987 and 1990. The longest bear market lingered for three years, from 1946 to 1949. The shallowest bear market loss took place in 1990, when the S&P 500 lost around 20%. The deepest by far happened during the financial crisis between 2007 and 2009. We saw the S&P 500 lose approximately 59% of its value in about 27 months [6].

In context of a start-up, this means that there will be 60 months on average with good chances to secure funding through one or more fundraising rounds, followed by one and a half year when the company must likely survive on the funds already acquired. Those shall be taken into account when planning cashflow and presenting to investors.

6.2.8 Time Remaining from the Patent or Other Intellectual Property

The system of patents and protection of intellectual properties does not provide permanent protection, the maximum time is limited, and an increasing fee must be paid annually to maintain it. However, there is a calculated risk of adoption given that, if there are no patents or other protections present, competitors may roll out their own product offerings easier. Moreover, competitors may disrupt our market by filing a patent themselves, covering the technology area, and limiting competing product offerings. A carefully planned and executed branding and intellectual property management activity can maintain appropriate shielding for the start-up and its product for the first two decades spent in development, and in the marketplace.

Strategically, it is often prudent to guard some key elements of the technology in question, as know-how, thereby reducing the likelihood of copycat technology.

Intellectual property (IP) refers to creations of the mind, such as inventions; literary and artistic works; designs; and symbols, names and images used in commerce.

There are 6 types of IP:

patent
copyright
trademark
industrial design
geographical indication
trade secret

Detailed description of the IP types is provided in Annex 1.

6.3 The Team

To be successful, a start-up needs a dedicated and motivated team, with individuals willing and capable to build the company and perform much better than an employee in a large corporation is required to or willing, on a similar pay grade. Team members are committed to the start-up, their team-mates, the product, and the vision of the company. They have a sense of ownership (or are actual shareholders) and take pride in their work, their accomplishments and are always looking for ways to improve. Many investors are willing to invest in start-ups that have a successful team. Investors for pre-seed or seed rounds, especially business angels do not only put their money in, usually they also become member of the team. This group of people must be assembled carefully, considering the following factors:

- size
- competences
- network
- internal relationships
- leadership
- motivation
- availability
- cost

6.3.1 Size

According to Burns, a team of five to seven people is generally considered to be of optimal size. It is true that in a team of this size, the disjunction of labour is possible, but active conversation between team members remains an important advantage. Each team member has the opportunity to directly converse with other team members, but the team is big enough to enable effectiveness, productivity and happiness [7]. If the size of the starting team is too big, it will increase the burning rate and shorten our runway. A too small team may not cover the competences needed and slow down product development. Forensic science is a complex field that requires specialized knowledge and expertise. A larger team can provide more resources and expertise to help ensure that forensic science efforts are successful. However, a larger team can also be more difficult to manage and may require more resources to maintain. Smaller teams may be more agile and able to respond more quickly to changing circumstances, but they may not have the same level of expertise or resources as larger teams. The opportunity of scaling up our business is not or very hardly exploitable without growing the team. On the other hand, scaling prematurely burns cash, and it's hard to course correct when the start-up has hundreds of employees. In case of forensic start-ups, the initial team must be larger than usual, as the development is a more complex task than in case of a consumer product. When the MVP is ready, part of the team has to be disbanded to ensure efficient go-to-market and optimise runway, then it has to be grown again for scale-up, but this time a different team than the first, focused on customer success, production and shipment rather than developing. To cope with this phenomenon, forensic start-ups regularly join forces with universities or research institutions, or spin-off from them, lending development team and capacities from those organizations or acquiring their technology via technology transfer. This way the start-up can start with a smaller team without losing capacity. In many cases the founders of the start-ups are part-time founders working in universities or research institutions [8].

Scaling up means accelerating growth with confidence, meaning that the resources that you put in should yield great results that are predictable and measurable [9].

For most forensic companies, scaling up to satisfy customer needs is very likely. For example, the ABFO Scale No. 2 was introduced in 1987 and is sold since globally.

6.3.2 Competences

As presented in the section on "time", a start-up is under constant time pressure, which means that there is only little or no time to perform internal trainings, nor they can afford to send a team member away for months to study and acquire a new competence. Therefore, the team has to be assembled to cover all necessary competences for the start-up. Besides technical competences relevant to the field where the company operates, general skills such as effective communication, resilience and creativity are needed. Furthermore, the team shall have strong determination, integrity, tenacity and self-criticism, competent in collaboration or delegation, showing respect and accountability. At least one team member shall have business competencies like financial management, marketing and sales [10]. Demonstrating lack of competence can quickly lead to losing precious time or money (or both), which can put the start-up into difficult situations. Even the most motivated people who are really the fans of our start-up will do more damaged than good if not having the competences needed but willing to participate. Sometimes founders must make harsh decisions and replace team members who are very good team players but not competent enough for the next phase of the company. This also includes founders; at a certain growth stage they also have to consider whether they still are the best person to lead the company or they shall take one step back (or exit) and get a CEO with a different mindset, more competent in leading a company already scaled up. As the company grows, it can put more resources on internal competence development, longer onboarding of new team members and sending existing members to further develop their competences.

6.3.3 Network

Networking may seem like a buzzword, but it's a critical aspect of business success. It's all about building relationships and making connections with people who can help you grow your business. It can help the start-up connect with potential customers, investors, mentors, and other key stakeholders who can help them grow their business. An extensive and rightly positioned network, for example an ENFSI connection (or being incubated at/being a spin-off from an ENFSI member) can give start-ups access to resources, insights, and expertise in their respective market field, that can help them overcome challenges and reach new heights. It also provides a way to connect with customers and increase product and company visibility when and to what extent it is needed, without prematurely exposing the start-up to its competition. When a team member is joining a start-up, it does not only bring its competences, but also brings its network. The starting network of the start-up is the accumulated network of its team members. The velocity of building the network is dependent on the networking competence of the team.

Networking is the act of building and cultivation of productive relationships for business and making connections with people who can help you achieve your goals.

A good start-up and its team do networking by:

- be authentic, reachable and approachable.
- attending events or conferences (not only sectoral, but also where customers and investors can be found).
- joining professional organizations (communities, clusters, platforms etc.).
- use of professional and general social media.
- follow-up leads and cultivate existing contacts—do not let people forget you unless you want it so.
- offer help before asking for it.
- focus on quality of your network instead on its quality.

6.3.4 Internal Relationships

Every team is made out from individuals with preferences around which individuals they like to work with and those individuals they rather not. A start-up team is more sensitive to the status of internal relationships than employees at a workplace. Good internal relationships can improve communication, increase trust and cooperation and boost morale. When communication between team members is fluid, there is less chance of misunderstanding and wasted time [11]. The company shall focus equally on developing both networking and internal relationships. Highest productivity and efficiency come from a balance of internal and external relationships, and this is directly related to success. Founders shall be ready and willing to spend time and resources to cultivate internal relationships not only between leaders and team members, but also between team members. Even if the start-ups can operate by remote work/home office, there have to be occasions when team members get together for a lunch, dinner or for some other activity everyone likes, be it an airsoft match or watching football.

Just like in case of competences, this balance needs to be developed and maintained sometimes by hard decisions on replacing team members. If a toxic person joins the team, it will pose a great risk to the success of the team and the company by bringing out the worst from the rest of the team. Sometimes this is not obvious when hiring, therefore founders shall look for signs such as gaslighting, lying or inability to apologize while working together. The loss in competences and network will always be smaller than the risk mitigated by that hard decision.

6.3.5 Leadership and Management

It was already mentioned that the leadership of the start-up has to make hard decisions. But this is not the only requirement towards leadership. Every team has to have at least one leader. A real one, which can lead by example, motivate people, communicate well, clearly and pertinently. Leadership can only be successful if it is complemented by strong management skills. The manager shall be excellent in delegating tasks and time management, to make sure the momentum built by leadership is channelled towards success. The balance between leadership and management is crucial for start-ups and businesses. Their quality will likely determine whether or not the business really takes off, as start-ups do not have the financial means to hire and motivate (keep) employees only through competitive salaries. They can only keep their team if the team feels motivated and connected to the company. The team's spirit has to be created and kept alive by the team leader, if this is working well, it will be stronger than the drawing force of well-paying bigger companies or competitors. Research results in the field including scholars as Zaech and Baldegger argue on the importance of leadership for start-ups [12]. Today, leadership is neglected in favour of management skills by start-up founders while experience shows that those two are both necessary ingredients of start-up success.

> Leadership is an interaction between two or more members of a group that often involves a structuring or restructuring of the situation and the perceptions and expectations of members. Leadership occurs when one group member modifies the motivation or competencies of others in the group. Any member of the group can exhibit some amount of leadership. [13]
>
> Entrepreneurial leadership describes a person influencing and directing another person towards a certain action or way of thinking in the context of a start-up. [14]
>
> Management (or managing) is the administration of organizations, whether they are a business, a nonprofit organization, or a government body through business administration, non-profit management, or the political science sub-field of public administration respectively. It is the science of managing the resources of businesses, governments, and other organizations.[3]

Both leaders and manager must show respect to their followers and are genuinely concerned with their personal growth and development, by providing them with opportunities that challenge them to learn new skills and abilities and by encouraging them to think continually about situations differently than they might have previously [15]. Their social interactions with their followers are based on coaching or mentoring relationships in which the leader takes responsibility for facilitating the growth and development of the follower [16], while the manager provides the neccessary resources in terms of time and money not only to allow the performance of tasks allocate to the person but to allow personal development as well.

6.3.6 Motivation

Launching, landing, and scaling up a start-up is not a sprint, but a marathon (which has to be run fast like a sprint). Motivation of the team is a decisive factor on the long run. The best choice for the leadership is to assemble the team from competent and motivated people. However even if they manage to involve the most motivated individuals for the initial team, leadership of the team has to work on keeping the team motivated. The motivation of the team is one of the most important factors that can affect start-ups. A motivated team can help a start-up overcome challenges and achieve success. According to an article in Harvard Business Review, successful start-up teams have several characteristics in common. These include a shared vision, complementary skills, mutual trust and respect, and a willingness to learn and adapt [17].

Results from a study investigating academic incubator programs suggest that founding teams that driven by a self-oriented motivation, exhibit a significant positive relationship with start-up survival. Such tendency is not demonstrated for start-ups whose founders act out of another-oriented motivation. Compared to others, start-ups

[3] https://en.wikipedia.org/wiki/management.

whose founding teams reach high levels of both self- and other-oriented motivation demonstrate a positive association with survival [18].

A motivated team can also help attract investors and customers by demonstrating their commitment to the start-up's success. On the other hand, a demotivated team can lead to poor performance, missed deadlines, and even failure.

6.3.7 Availability

Every resource is as useful as it is available. This is also true for teams, as all the efforts invested into assembling, competence, internal relationships, motivation is in vain if the team is not or just partly available when an important task has to be undertaken. Nowadays, it is not any more surprising that a start-up is made out of digital nomads, or that the team works remotely or in permanent home offices. On the contrary, this approach is very much favourable because decreases the burn rate through less need for office space. This may also mean that some members of the team are working across different time zones. Regardless of whether everyone is sitting in the same office floor or spread across the globe, it is essential to have a firm and proportionate availability of the team. Otherwise, the start-up will lose its competitive edge by lagging behind response to opportunities and threats. If there are people in the team who are talented, brilliant, competent, have good network but they are not available in most of the time because they are doing something else, the company practically lacks those employees and expertise.

6.3.8 Cost

Most people have to earn their living. Even if they are motivated and connected to the start-up, the company still must provide some form of remuneration or reward, to avoid losing those employees. In addition, the bigger the team, the more additional costs come from mailbox or workspace subscriptions to working equipment and office spaces. Remuneration and rewarding can have multiple forms, including not only salary but equity (worker's share), reimbursement of costs, covering internet for remote workers, paying premiums and so on. Team costs are significantly increasing the burn rate and therefore the founders have to make decisions whether they hire more or more expensive employees and try to achieve their objectives faster or keep the costs low but sacrifice some of the time advantage in turn. When a founder creates its business plan, the cost of the team shall be one if not the largest budget category on a 5-year basis and fundraising shall target to cover team costs for at least 2 years in advance. Teams are made of people, most of them are having families, relatives or friends to look after, and this shall not be taken lightly.

6.4 Traction

Traction is probably the most important part of launching and running a business. It is not equal with profit, especially in case of start-ups, it is equal with evidence of a consistent opportunity for growth.

Traction means there are clear indicators that the business is viable, and some degree of product or market fit has been achieved [19].

Investors demand traction. It means that a business has paying customers who believe in the product and bringing it forward by spreading the word on the value it provides. However in the case of start-ups, this is usually not available at the start; investors understand traction with a wider perspective, also covering the capability of pulling the interest on the start-up and his products and services. A start-up can search for, build and present traction using the following sources:

- target available market
- customer base
- conversion rate
- sales activity
- branding
- external factors
- company business development

6.4.1 Target Available Market

Target available market (TAM) refers to the total revenue opportunity available for a product or service. It is the maximum amount of revenue a business can generate by selling its product or service to every potential customer in its target market.

Target Available Market (TAM) is an important metric for traction as it helps to understand the potential size of their market and to assess the viability of the business model. It is calculated by multiplying the total number of potential customers by the average revenue per customer. TAM can be used to estimate the potential growth of a business and to make strategic decisions about how to allocate resources and prioritize initiatives. Investors consult market reports from consulting firms if they are not familiar with the actual market, especially when a large fund or bank is about to invest into a forensic technology company. This can lead to an assumption about the start-up's traction.

For example, Straits Research published the following report on Forensic Technology Market Size, Share and Forecast including the following freely available sample:

> The global forensic technology market size was valued at USD 14.78 billion in 2021 and is projected to reach USD 41.92 billion by 2030, registering a compound annual growth rate of 12.28% from 2022 to 2030.

As every market segment, forensics market can also be defined as a TAM (as a whole). However, it is more advantageous to further segment it into more focused sub-segments, for example digital forensics or niche areas under sub-segments, such as digital forensics on blockchain networks. A well-defined target market helps product design, sales and fundraising. It is strongly suggested that start-ups who do not have a full view on the market procure, analyse such a report before making strategic business decisions. Even if the planned product looks capable to cover a whole market segment, it is a good choice to first target a well-selected, strong sub-segment or niche with our MVP, then extend the coverage to neighbouring parts.

Turning back to the already mentioned EnCase software, it expanded gradually; it was first released as digital evidence collection tool for hard drives, then the next release was already network-enabled, then evolved further by adding an agent for automated endpoint security. The software evolved together with the internet and connectivity.

The processing of forensic samples and evidence is essential to the investigation and prosecution of criminal cases. Scanner electron microscopy, DNA fingerprinting, alternative light photography, facial reconstruction, and Laser Ablation Inductively Coupled Plasma Mass Spectrometry (LA-ICP-MS) are some of the technologies that are utilised in the various subfields of forensic science in order to conduct investigations and analyse the evidence. The high prices connected with this technology are the primary factor that is preventing the market from expanding, particularly in the developing and emerging nations of Asia Pacific and Africa.

The primary aspect that is driving the expansion of the market is the recent uptick in the number of violent crimes perpetrated all over the world. This has been the case in recent times. In addition to that, homicide on a global scale, robbery and sexual assault crimes are the secondary reasons that are fuelling the market expansion by boosting the demand for forensic innovation. In addition, North and South America have been responsible for a sizeable portion of the increase in crime rates over the past few years. Africa and Asia have followed in this trend, which is anticipated to present an opportunity for expansion over the next period of time" [20].

6.4.2 Customer Basis

A customer base is the group of people or organisations who repeatedly buy a company's products or use its services.

This group frequently engages with the business and provides the most financial value to the company. Depending on the industry, a customer base can be a specific group, or a target audience based on a buyer persona. It's essential to identify a customer base because these customers are incredibly valuable to a business. They buy its products the most and rely on the company to help them achieve their goals. Recognizing these customers will help a company's marketing, sales, and customer service teams build a productive relationship with its customer base.

In case of start-ups operating in the forensic market, building a good customer base is a key objective in order to achieve traction, as the number of customers procuring on this market is limited. Most forensic products and services are not typical consumer products, are not purchased by people 'en masse', rather procured by law enforcement authorities or criminal investigation bureaus in public procurement. Therefore, traction from customer base comes from such organisations and not from individuals. In cases involving products or services under development, this traction can be produced by innovation procurement programmes, such as the PCP actions in Horizon Europe, where public buyers blend product orders with grant for development and finalisation in a multi-phase project.

6.4.3 Conversion Rate

Conversion rate is the percentage of visitors who land on a website or page and then take an action, such as purchasing a product or submitting a form [21].

The action a user takes can be anything deemed important for the business, even if it doesn't necessarily translate into sales or revenue, for example sharing a content, becoming a follower or subscribing for a newsletter. Conversion rate measures the number of users who converted as a percentage of the total number of users that visited the site. The higher the conversion rate, the more effective the content.

If a start-up has a strong website or social media presence with a good conversion rate on—for example—converting visitors to followers, it will likely convince investors that they are capable of generating traction and acquire paying customers.

For a forensic science-based product, it is useful to have a newsletter, be present on (professional) social media (such as LinkedIn), appear on relevant events, such as the Forensics Europe Expo, EU Security Research Event, International Association of Chiefs of Police Conference or World Border Security Congress. It would also be important to engage the organisations in which the targeted experts work and whose role is in sales as well as being able to influence/inform decisions. It would be even better if this stakeholder engagement is deployed at both organisational and individual expert level; crime scene investigators and forensic experts are the end-users of the product and only their support and acceptance can ensure a long-term business success. Learning materials, free samples, free trainings, on-site demos, live support are key tools to engage this target audience. For example, the Horizon Europe project PEERS led by KPMG (Klynveld Pear Marwick Goerdeler, another one of the Big Four consulting companies) seeks to develop a complex information platform including a dataset, a community and different visualisations for stakeholders in the field of CBRN-E protection and forensic work. The landscape mapping activities in the project—which is led by SFC—will enable KPMG and other partners to better understand the stakeholders and define a better engagement practice.

6.4.4 Sales Activity

Sales is the process of systematically generating revenue with the product (service) in the chosen market segment in the race for market leadership [22].

Sales professionals are responsible for developing and managing relationships with prospective customers, identifying their needs, and presenting solutions that meet those needs. Referring back to subsection on teams and importance of having team members with good network, this is especially true for sales professionals. Every start-up shall aim to hire a good sales professional in their field with an extensive network.

In the beginning, start-up sales are mostly about establishing a continuous feedback loop between the business model, product, and customer. Only later will sales be standardized and optimized. Some crucial elements of a sales strategy include targeting a niche market, constructing specific buyer personas, definition of metrics to track, consider what investors got promised when closing fundraising.

For forensic companies, the number of clients is relatively low, but usually they award large or long-term contracts, therefore every client has great importance, sales activities have to be planned and implemented with this 'luxury car dealer' or 'private banker' approach.

6.4.5 Branding

Branding is the process of giving meaning to a specific organization, company, product, or service by creating and shaping a brand in consumers' minds. It is especially useful when the genre (type) of the product is distinctive enough to be unique or stand out from other products. For example, two glasses of mineral water look the same when poured out from two different bottles. When companies started to commercialize it, for example, by selling in glass and plastic bottles, they had to distinguish the water they bottled from the water bottled by the other company. This can happen by branding, a process of pairing appearance with emotional load.

> A brand is a name, term, design, symbol, or any other feature that identifies one seller's good or service as distinct from those of other sellers.[4]

Branding relates to the emotions people feel when thinking about branded products or services of a company or an organisation; emotions are based on perception (e.g. "the shoe is lightweight") and distinct emotional way (e.g. "the shoe makes me feel powerful"). Therefore, a brand is a combination of design and feeling.

Besides distinguishing own product from similar products, successful branding strategies are also adding to a company's reputation. This asset can affect a range of people, from consumers to employees, investors, shareholders, providers, and

[4] https://www.thebrandingjournal.com/2015/10/what-is-branding-definition/.

distributors.[5] A good brand does not only motivate customers to buy the product but also motivates employees, shareholders and investors, raising support for the company [23]. Same is true for investors, if they feel connected to the brand or feel that their reputation increases by becoming investors of the brand, the fundraising will become easy.

In many cases, start-ups have brands before they have products. A start-up should start branding as early as possible. The branding process starts long before designing a logo or thinking of a name for the new business or product. Branding starts with knowing your customer. The start-up has to know its customers well enough to understand what purpose they have for the new offering and what role it will play in their lives [24].

6.4.6 External Factors

External factors are slightly different for the rest of the critical elements and their factors, as they cannot be influenced by the company itself. The effect of these factors can be positive (increase traction) or negative (decrease traction). In the classical SWOT analysis framework these are called opportunities (positive) and threats (negative). For example, the breakout of COVID-19 increased traction for medical supplies companies; the European Green Deal created traction for PV panel manufacturing and installation companies and the Russo-Ukrainian War created traction for defence companies. When the EU introduced GDPR, it decreased traction for EU-based data science companies and service providers. The Hungarian government's discussions with the EU decrease traction for Hungary-based research and innovation service providers and EU plastics regulation decrease traction for plastic bottle manufacturers.

Start-ups have to cope with the impact of external factors either by pushing their growth to exploit the increasing traction or transform in order to avoid impact of a decrease in traction. The latter is very dangerous to start-ups in their pre-seed and seed phase, when usually they put up everything on one product—if an external factor decreases the traction for that product, the start-up is likely to crash.

6.4.7 Company Business Development

To convert traction into actual success, the business must grow together with the traction, and this has to be clearly demonstrated for investors. If this is not clearly planned and balanced with rest of traction elements, it can lead to spectacular failures and do great damage. A very simple example is when a webshop or other web service receives so many visitors that it collapses, or a factory receives so many product

[5] Loc. cit. 4.

orders that they cannot deliver or only with significant delay. Both lead to a lot of disappointed customers and missed opportunities for an income. Same happens if customer service, helpdesk or product support become overburdened, call centers make people wait on the line for tens of minutes, chatbots run into loops with answers. On the other hand, this is the easiest way to acquire additional funding from investors, to show that additional funding is needed to keep pace with traction.

Business development entails tasks and processes to develop and implement growth opportunities within and between organizations. It is a subset of the fields of business, commerce, and organizational theory. Business development is the creation of long-term value for an organization from customers, markets, and relationships [25]. *Business development can include many objectives, such as sales growth, business expansion, the formation of strategic partnerships, and increased profitability* [26].

6.5 The Quintuple Helix Model of Innovation and Its Predecessors

The **quintuple helix** (5 × H) is a framework that describes university-industry-government-public-environment interactions within a knowledge economy. This model can be particularly important for start-ups as it provides a comprehensive framework for understanding the various actors and factors that can influence their success as well as to identify new opportunities for innovation and growth that are aligned with sustainable development goals. It was co-developed by Elias G. Carayannis and David F. J. Campbell and adds a fifth helix, the natural environment, to the quadruple helix model [27]. This model can be applied in an interdisciplinary and transdisciplinary way to sustainable development. It adds as fifth helix the natural environment, more specifically socio-ecological interactions, meaning it can be applied in an interdisciplinary and transdisciplinary way to sustainable development.

Socio-ecological interactions refer to the ways in which human society and the natural environment interact and affect one another. A social-ecological system consists of a bio-geo-physical unit and its associated social actors and institutions [28]. *These systems are complex and adaptive and are delimited by spatial or functional boundaries surrounding particular ecosystems and their context problems* [29]. *An example of a socio-ecological interaction is a city in a river valley, where water flows and exact location within the drainage basin affect urban architecture from green spaces to sewer system, flood risk, water supply and their aggregated biomass production and carbon sequestration.*

This approach stresses the necessary socio-ecological transition of society and economy in the twenty-first century; therefore, the quintuple helix is ecologically sensitive. Within this framework of, the natural environments of society and the economy also should be seen as drivers for knowledge production and innovation, therefore defining opportunities for the knowledge economy. Its predecessor was the **quadruple helix** model, which incorporates the public via the concept of a 'media-based democracy', which emphasizes that when the political system (government) is developing innovation policy to develop the economy, it must adequately communicate its innovation policy with the public and civil society via the media to obtain public support for new strategies or policies. This extended the triple helix model of innovation.

The **triple helix** model of innovation refers to a set of interactions between academia (the university), industry and government, to foster economic and social development. It was first theorized by Henry Etzkowitz and Loet Leydesdorff in the 1990s [30]. It has been widely adopted and has participated in the transformation of each sector. The initial role of universities is to provide education to individuals and basic research. The government plays an important role in regulating markets and fostering economic and social development [31]. The role of industry is to produce commercial goods and thus bringing innovation to the market. Industry builds upon the research provided by universities to produce these goods. Therefore, interactions between the three actors revolve initially around these elements. In a linear model of innovation, universities are supposed to provide the research which industry will build upon to produce commercial goods. The other interactions take place through the involvement of industry managers and university faculty in both sectors. According to Etzkowitz, the transfer of people between university and industry constitutes a very important transfer of knowledge. The framework describes the interactions between these three sectors and explains the emergence of new hybrid organizations such as technology transfer offices and science parks.

Technology Transfer Offices (TTOs), or Technology Licensing Offices (TLOs), are responsible for technology transfer and other aspects of the commercialization of research that takes place in a university [32]. *TTOs engage in a variety of commercial activities that are meant to facilitate the process of bringing research developments to market, often acting as a channel between academia and industry* [33]. *Most major research universities have established TTOs in the past decades in an effort to increase the impact of university research and provide opportunities for financial gain* [34].

A science park is a property-based development that accommodates and fosters the growth of tenant firms and that is affiliated with a university (or a government and private research bodies) based on proximity, ownership, and/or governance [35]. *Science parks provide locations that foster innovation and the development and commercialisation of technology and where governments, universities and private companies may collaborate* [36]. *They can offer a number of shared resources, such as incubators, programs and collaboration activities, uninterruptible power supply, telecommunications hubs, reception and security, management offices, bank offices, convention centre, parking, and internal transportation.*

Start-ups can benefit from the quintuple helix model in several ways. By understanding the interactions between university-industry-government-public-environment, start-ups can better navigate the complex landscape of innovation and entrepreneurship. It can help identify new opportunities for innovation and growth that are aligned with sustainable development goals, which became a key element in most of the accessible funding programs. By incorporating the natural environment as a fifth helix, start-ups can develop products and services that are ecologically sensitive and contribute to the socio-ecological transition of society and economy. Additionally, the quintuple helix model can help start-ups to build relationships and partnerships with key actors in the innovation ecosystem, such as universities, industry partners, government agencies, and civil society organizations. These relationships can provide start-ups with access to resources, knowledge, and networks that can support their growth and success, especially TTOs and science parks (incubators and accelerators).

For example, forensic start-ups focusing on crimes against natural environment (e.g. pollution, wild animal trafficking, poaching, indiscriminate logging, dumping in rivers) can benefit from uptake of the quintuple helix, as there is more societal pressure on policymakers, governments and industry to take more effective steps in protecting the environment.

6.6 Measurements of Readiness

Measurement of the (market) readiness of a start-up or a product is becoming increasingly complex as the environment has developed. In the traditional view the focus was solely on hardware development stages, nowadays technology can take many forms (software, hardware, process). Multiple models to measure readiness have been developed to follow the trends of the evolution of the helix, starting from pure technology-focused readiness measurements to complex, societal sensitive measurements. Detailed descriptions of stages for each type of readiness measurements are provided in Annex 2.

6.6.1 Technology Readiness Level (TRL)

The first of such model was originally developed by NASA and is called **Technology Readiness Level (TRL)**, while in parallel the software development industry introduced a parallel model to measure stages of software development. By using TRL, organisations can assess the maturity of their technology at each stage of development and make informed decisions about when it is ready for deployment. The TRL has nine stages from observation of basic principles to an actual system proven in operation.

Advantage: using the TRL is that it allows a simple identification of technical progress.

Disadvantage: it does not provide information on other important aspects, for example user validation (traction) or capability to reach the next stage on time (team, time), therefore it is only useful for investors or funding authorities with deep knowledge in the market context and the status of the company.

6.6.2 Software Development Lifecycle

The **software development lifecycle** is similar to TRL and consists of four to seven stages, depending on size of the development. It starts with (pre)alpha and ends with release candidate (also called gamma or delta) or with end-of-lifecycle stage. The software development lifecycle is useful when developing a pure software-based solution, for example a digital forensic tool. In case a software is combined with a hardware (for example Holozcan, the holographic microscopy using image processing[6] developed in a Horizon 2020 project with Grant ID 101021723), the use of TRL for the software too is preferable to software development lifecycle.

Advantages: mature and widely known, industry-standard measurement for software readiness.

Disadvantages: it is only useable for software readiness.

6.6.3 Business Readiness Level (BRL)

Experience showed that high TRL products sometimes also failed on the market or start-ups having unique and ground-breaking high TRL technologies wrapped up before making any profit. When investigating, these experts concluded that there was an issue with the readiness of the team to do business and the fitting of the product to the market needs. Inspired by TRL and the Business Readiness Rate (BRR), an initiative of the open-source software development community, the Business Readiness Levels (BRL) were defined [37].

Business Readiness Level (BRL) is a concept that refers to the maturity of the business considerations developed alongside the technical development of an innovation. It is a valuable assessment tool for innovators seeking to establish a technology that is both financially viable and commercially feasible. The BRL scale is composed of nine levels, ranging from initial concept to fully embedded in the market. At each level, the BRL helps a start-up team or investor to understand where an innovation currently lies on the journey to creating real customer value and reducing the risk for the team.

Advantages: By using BRL, innovators can assess the maturity of their business proposition and measure progress in an objective manner.

Disadvantages: Business readiness is about the maturity of efforts in several different commercial functions, which can be misleading in case of ground-breaking technologies or disruptive business models.

[6] https://www.holozcan.com/.

There are programs which observe both TRL and BRL as criteria, for example the Horizon Europe EIC Accelerator program where an applicant has to demonstrate achievement of certain stages in both TRL and BRL (e.g., at least TRL6 and at least BRL6).

Two examples from companies supported by Székely Family and Co. Nonprofit incubator and accelerator:

Example 1: a new Total Ionisation Dosimeter developed by the start-up 27G-T to measure radiation dose absorbed by satellites in orbit can successfully represent its readiness by using TRL only. The company is operating on a narrow market with well-known customers and a steady price.

Example 2: the Narrowband IoT asset tracking device and connected services developed by General Mechatronics is sold to cell network operators, logistics companies and asset managers with many but yet unknown and unconverted customers on a market where competitors are also developing or offering competing products with different capabilities. In this case TRL is not enough to understand the value of this start-up, use of BRL is also needed to assess its chances to stand out from competition.

6.6.4 Social Readiness Level (SRL)

For many sustainable innovations, the traditional business approach poses a problem instead of being the solution. This is because moving to a more sustainable, innovative solution (e.g., new feedstock, materials of biological origin or bioprocess) inevitably competes with business-as-usual on cost and therefore will fall behind other, more conventional consumer product developments, when assessed on the BRL scale. If the customer does not recognize the value or need for a biobased solution, then commercial success and transformation will be limited. To gain traction, a product or service does not only need to provide a new or increased value, but the society also must be ready for it and needing it. In order to enable assessment of this kind of readiness, Murray, Caulier-Grice and Mulgan developed the Six Stages of Social Innovation in 2010 [38]. Adopting the six stages in parallel with TRL, the Innovation Fund Denmark defined **Social Readiness Levels (SRL)** in 2018, while TNO in The Netherlands devised Societal Embeddedness Levels (SEL) in 2020. For innovative solutions in forensics, the SRL is a very useful tool for measurement, as it describes otherwise hardly explainable values of an innovation like the societal benefits of more effective investigations.

Advantages: Detailed measurement, future-proof in the way that it responds well to the shifting of investor (funding) priorities towards sustainability and social transformation.

Disadvantages: There is no standard, widely accepted measurement method yet, different versions exist in parallel, and it also lacks post-conditional validation results.

6.6.5 Innovation Readiness Level (IRL)

Technology Readiness Level helps assessment of technological progress but does not provide information on how the business aspects of bringing that product to the market are addressed. To close this gap, Innovation Readiness Level (IRL) scales have been developed [39]. The IRL is linked to a certain innovation to describe how it progresses towards the market with a similar 9-staged levelling set. The World Intellectual Property Organisation emphasises that this multi-dimensional approach is not universally agreed, integrating various business-related aspects to a TRL-similar simplified scale [40]. Each idea defines the nine stages differently and these stages are adopted to a different extent across sectors and funding programmes [41].

Advantages: Supports investors to determine the business maturity of an innovation.

Disadvantages: The IRL concept is not universally agreed, therefore it depends on the actual investors (funders) whether it is a good choice or not. Just as in the case of the helix model, the readiness measurement becomes more and more complex as new elements come into play for consideration. The need of models is dependent on the complexity of the product or service under development and its target market.

6.6.6 KTH Innovation Readiness Level™

The KTH Innovation Readiness Level™ is a complete framework for guiding idea development and assessing idea status across key dimensions. Developed by the KTH Royal Institute of Technology Stockholm, it provides structure and support for idea owners as well as coaches and managers in the development of an early-stage idea to an innovation on the market [24].

The KTH Innovation Readiness Level™ is based on a model originally developed by NASA called Technology Readiness Levels (TRL). The TRL model is a scale from one to nine, where one refers to a very early-stage idea or a research result that seems interesting, and nine means that the innovation is fully functioning and implemented on the market. KTH Innovation adapted this model to cover six areas that they identified as the most important to focus on for all types of new ideas: technology, customer, business, intellectual property, team and funding. This approach can be particularly valuable for start-ups, as it provides a structured way to guide their development from an early-stage idea to an innovation on the market. By assessing their status across key dimensions such as technology, customer, business, intellectual property, team and funding, start-ups can identify areas where they need to focus their efforts and resources to achieve success.

Overall, it provides start-ups with a clear overview of all six areas that are important for their success and help founders figure out what their next step is, breaking down an ongoing and complex journey into smaller steps and help in selecting the actual focus (or sprint objective).

For example, if a start-up is strong in technology but weak in customer development, the framework can help them to identify this gap and focus their efforts on building relationships with potential customers. Similarly, if a start-up has a strong team but lacks funding, the framework can help them to identify this gap and focus their efforts on securing the resources they need.

Using this framework to guide their development, start-ups can increase their chances of achieving success by balancing their opportunities coming from the three critical factors of success. It also supports assessment of the start-up or the product for both founders and investors, creating a benchmark across different sectors.

6.7 Conclusion

The chapter discusses the three critical elements of start-up success: time, team, and traction, referred as the 3Ts. These elements are essential for start-ups to achieve their goals and maximize their profits. As such, the chapter aims to help practitioners and researchers in forensic science with an initial guide to bring their innovations to the market. In particular, it provides examples and insights from the forensic science market, where start-ups face specific challenges and opportunities. The chapter also features the context to the use of the three elements by relating them to different types of readiness levels and the quintuple helix model of research and innovation policy for sustainability.

Start-ups should:

- Be aware of the time constraints and opportunities they face and plan accordingly.
- Build a strong and diverse team that covers all the necessary skills and competencies for their business.
- Demonstrate traction by showing evidence of customer demand and market potential for their product or service.
- Choose from different types of readiness levels to assess their progress and identify areas for improvement, according to the complexity of their technology and the customer segment.
- Adopt a quintuple helix approach to research and innovation policy for sustainability that involves collaboration among academia, industry, government, civil society, and natural environment.

By following these suggestions, start-ups in the forensic science market can increase their chances of success and create value for themselves and society.

Annex 1

Patent

A patent is an exclusive right granted for an invention, which is a product or a process that provides, in general, a new way of doing something, or offers a new technical solution to a problem. To get a patent, technical information about the invention must be disclosed to the public in a patent application.

One example of a forensic patent is a method for improved forensic analysis using multi-view digital imaging of forensic specimens at a plurality of reflected, scattered, emitted, transmitted or absorbed wavelengths. This device, invented by Patrick J. Treado, David L. Exline and Julianne Wolfe, assigned to ChemImage Corp and filed under patent number US20090092281A1 in 2003, provides new detailed information to distinguish and differentiate forensic materials and samples. The patent was used for 10 years and was abandoned in 2013.

Copyright

Copyright is a legal term used to describe the rights that creators have over their literary and artistic works. Works covered by copyright range from books, music, paintings, sculpture and films, to computer programs, databases, advertisements, maps and technical drawings.

For example, the already mentioned EnCase software is now a copyright of Open-Text Corporation, the company which has acquired Guidance Software (the developer of EnCase) in 2017.

Trademark

A trademark is a sign capable of distinguishing the goods or services of one enterprise from those of other enterprises. Trademarks date back to ancient times when artisans used to put their signature or "mark" on their products.

For example, Foster & Freeman Limited has the word "foster + freeman" as their registered trademark (Trademark number 006396791) since 21/11/2008, last renewed on 03/05/2017, next expiry date on 26/10/2027. This trademark is valid for Nice classifications 9, 11, 35, 37, 38, 42, 45, which corresponds to the following fields:

9—Apparatus and instruments for use in forensic examination; software and electronic databases for use in forensic examination, the collection of evidence, processing of evidence and police casework management; computer software,

hardware and equipment for use in relation to forensic science, computer hardware and software for use in relation to digital imaging and document verification; display screens, cameras, lenses; microprocessors, microscopes, video camera and microscope interfacing equipment and systems; monitors, screens.
11—Humidifiers for use in scientific instruments, forensic light sources, alternate light sources, filters for use with torches, lights and lighting apparatus.
35—Retail services in relation to apparatus and instruments, software, computers, databases, all for use in forensic examination.
37—Maintenance and repair services in respect of instruments for forensic examination; hardware maintenance.
38—Providing access to databases.
42—Technical consultancy services in relation to apparatus, instruments, and software all designed for use in forensic examination; analysis and comparison of documents, document verification, glass refractive index measurement; software and hardware technical support and software maintenance.
45—Forensic services; investigative services; crime scene investigations; collection, processing and management of evidence.

This means that no other individual or organisation may brand its products or services commercialised in the fields above with the same label (foster + freeman) without infringing the trademark.

Industrial Design

An industrial design constitutes the ornamental or aesthetic aspect of an article. A design may consist of three-dimensional features, such as the shape or surface of an article, or of two-dimensional features, such as patterns, lines or colour.

An example of a protected design is a Tech-Long Dual Band Forensic Laser System design filed by Tech-Long Industry Limited under number 002839415-0001 on 28/10/2015 and expired on 28/10/2020. The registration consisted of a set of photos of the system, arrangement of sensors, handles and control panel. Design protection was valid for class/subclass 16.06 (Optical articles), which means that, between 2015 and 2020, a design and commercialisation of a product with similar look in that particular class would have been an infringement of the protected design.

Geographical Indication

Geographical indications and appellations of origin are signs used on goods that have a specific geographical origin and possess qualities, a reputation or characteristics that are essentially attributable to that place of origin. Most commonly, a geographical indication includes the name of the place of origin of the goods.

To date, there is no evidence on the use of this type of protection for forensic tools; geographical indication is typically used for food, beverages or luxury items such as "Tokaj wine" or "Kalocsai paprika".

Trade Secrets

Trade secrets are IP rights on confidential information which may be sold or licensed. The unauthorized acquisition, use or disclosure of such secret information in a manner contrary to honest commercial practices by others is regarded as an unfair practice and a violation of the trade secret protection.

This kind of protection is focusing on concealment of relevant knowledge rather than filing an official claim on it. As such, it is in contrast with requirements regularly set in public grants, for example awarded byHorizon Europe or other Open Science practices. In early stages of product development, especially while several technical or design solutions are not yet fully developed, nor clear, and therefore cannot be patented or submitted as industrial design, start-ups must rely on it. Having discussion with investors, submitting proposals for grant or negotiations with subcontractors puts this protection at risk, which is usually mitigated by non-disclosure agreements and—in certain countries—by legislation on protection of trade secrets.

Source for definitions in the annex:

World Intellectual Property Organization. Patents. *wipo.int.* [Online] https://www.wipo.int/patents/en/.

Annex 2

Detailed List of Readiness Measurements and Their Stages

Technology Readiness Levels (TRL)

The nine levels of TRL are:

1. Basic principles observed and reported: At this stage, scientific research begins to be translated into applied research and development.
2. Technology concept and/or application formulated: At this stage, the practical applications of the technology are identified and the concept is formulated.
3. Analytical and experimental critical function and/or characteristic proof of concept: At this stage, active research and development is initiated to establish proof of concept.
4. Component and/or breadboard validation in laboratory environment: At this stage, basic technological components are integrated to establish that they will work together.

5. Component and/or breadboard validation in relevant environment: At this stage, the basic technological components are tested in a simulated or somewhat realistic environment.
6. System/subsystem model or prototype demonstration in a relevant environment: At this stage, a representative model or prototype system is tested in a relevant environment.
7. System prototype demonstration in an operational environment: At this stage, a prototype system is demonstrated in an operational environment.
8. Actual system completed and qualified through test and demonstration: At this stage, the technology has been proven to work in its final form and under expected conditions.
9. Actual system proven through successful mission operations: At this final stage, the technology has been successfully applied in its final form and under mission conditions.

Software Development Stages

1. Pre-alpha refers to all activities performed during the software project before formal testing. These activities can include requirements analysis, software design, software development, and unit testing.
2. Alpha is the first phase of formal testing, during which the software is tested internally using white-box techniques. Alpha software may contain serious errors and may not contain all of the features that are planned for the final version.
3. Beta is the next phase, in which the software is tested by a larger group of users, typically outside of the organization that developed it. The beta phase is focused on reducing impacts on users and may include usability testing. This can be further divided into two sub-stages:
   a. closed beta with a recruited team of users and
   b. open beta with public access to the beta version (in case this stage is prolonged it is called perpetual beta)—usually this is the MVP stage for a software
4. Release Candidate (aka gamma or delta) is a phase in which the software is refined and tested further before the final version is released. This stage can be further divided into a Release Candidate and a Stable Release stage, where the latter means that the software passed all stages of verification and tests.
5. End-of-Life is the phase when the software is no longer sold or supported (updated), there are no new features, fixes or security updates, but it is still functional 'as-is'. However in some cases the developer releases the source code or abandons its IPR allowing reverse engineering of the software which then can be maintained further by volunteers (typical example are old MS-DOS games).

Please note that there are different adaptations of the model, number of stages can reach from four to seven.

Business Readiness Levels (BRL)

1. Initial concept: At this stage, the idea for the business is still in its early stages and may not be fully formed.

2. Problem–Solution Fit: At this stage, the focus is on identifying a problem that the business can solve and developing a solution that fits the needs of potential customers.
3. Build team and plan: At this stage, the focus is on building a team to execute the business plan and developing a detailed plan for bringing the business to market.
4. Customer definition: At this stage, the focus is on defining the target customer for the business and understanding their needs and desires.
5. Hypothesis Testing: At this stage, the focus is on testing key assumptions about the business and its potential customers to validate the business model.
6. Minimum Viable Product: At this stage, the focus is on developing a minimum viable product (MVP) that can be used to test the market and gather feedback from potential customers.
7. Feedback loop: At this stage, the focus is on gathering feedback from customers and using it to improve the product and business model.
8. Scale: At this stage, the focus is on scaling the business to reach a larger market and achieve growth.
9. Fully embedded in market: At this final stage, the business is fully established in the market and has achieved a stable position.

Social Readiness Levels (SRL)

1. Identifying problem and identifying societal readiness.
2. Formulation of problem, proposed solution(s) and potential impact, expected societal readiness; identifying relevant stakeholders for the project.
3. Initial testing of proposed solution(s) together with relevant stakeholders.
4. Problem validated through pilot testing in relevant environment to substantiate proposed impact and societal readiness.
5. Proposed solution(s) validated, now by relevant stakeholders in the area.
6. Solution(s) demonstrated in relevant environment and in co-operation with relevant stakeholders to gain initial feedback on potential impact.
7. Refinement of project and/or solution and, if needed, retesting in relevant environment with relevant stakeholders.
8. Proposed solution(s) as well as a plan for societal adaptation complete and qualified
9. Actual project solution(s) proven in relevant environment.

The Innovation Readiness Levels (IRL)

1. A new idea.
2. The business concept.
3. Idea/business proposal.
4. Create an actionable plan.
5. Scaled testing.
6. Design and testing of support systems.
7. Full testing of systems and products.
8. Ready for full scale operation.

References

1. Andersson, E., Haase, D., Anderson, P., Cortinovis, C., Goodness, J., Kendal, D., Lausch, A., McPhearson, T., Sikorska, D., & Wellmann, T. (2021). What are the traits of a social-ecological system: towards a framework in support of urban sustainability. *Nature*. https://doi.org/10.1038/s42949-020-00008-4
2. Ayman, R., Korabik, K., & Morris, S. (2009). Is transformational leadership always perceived as effective? Male subordinates' devaluation of female transformational leaders. *Journal of Applied Social Psychology*, 852–879.
3. Baskin, K. (2016. 10 3). *How to scale a startup*. MIT Management: https://mitsloan.mit.edu/ideas-made-to-matter/how-to-scale-a-startup
4. Bass, B. M., & Avolio, B. J. (1993). Transformational leadership and organizational culture. *Public Administration Quarterly*, 112–121.
5. Bass, B. M., & Bass, R. (2008). *The bass handbook of leadership: Theory, research, and application*. Simon & Schuster.
6. Bass, B. M., & Stogdil, R. M. (1990). *Bass & Stogdill's handbook of leadership: theory, research, and managerial applications*. Simon & Schuster.
7. Blank, T. H. (2023). Do founding team motivation types matter for student startups' survival? Self-oriented, other-oriented, and diverse motivations in academic incubators. *The Journal of Technology Transfer*. https://doi.org/10.1007/s10961-023-10004-2
8. Bolzani, D., Munari, F., Rasmussen, E., & Toschi, L. (2021). Technology transfer offices as providers of science and technology entrepreneurship education. *The Journal of Technology Transfer*, 335–365.
9. Brescia, F., Colombo, G., & Landoni, P. (2016). Organizational structures of Knowledge Transfer Offices: an analysis of the world's top-ranked universities. *The Journal of Technology Transfer*, 132–151.
10. Burns, S. (2020. 11 18). *How to build a startup team that's equipped to scale*. Forbes.com: https://www.forbes.com/sites/stephanieburns/2020/11/18/how-to-build-a-startup-team-thats-equipped-to-scale/
11. Carayannis, E., Barth, T., & Campbell, D. (2012). The Quintuple Helix innovation model: global warming as a challenge and driver for innovation. *Journal of Innovation and Entrepreneurship*, 1–12. https://doi.org/10.1186/2192-5372-1-2
12. Cassidy, N. G. (2018). *The effect of scarcity types on consumer preference in the high-end sneaker market*. Appalachian State University.
13. Dvir, N., & Gafni, R. (2018). When less is more: empirical study of the relation between consumer behavior and information provision on commercial landing pages. *Informing Science: The International Journal of an Emerging Transdiscipline*, 019–039.
14. Etzkowitz, H., & Leydersdorf, L. (1995). The Triple Helix—University-industry-government relations: A laboratory for knowledge based economic development. *EASST Review*, 14–19.
15. Evans, J. D., & Johnson, R. O. (2013). Tools for Managing early-stage business model innovation. *Research-Technology Management*, 52–56.
16. Gans, J., Scott, E. L., & Stern, S. (2018). Strategy for start-ups. *Harward Business Review*.
17. Glaser, M., Krause, G., Ratter, B., & Welp, M. (2008). Human-nature-interaction in the anthropocene. Potential of social-ecological systems analysis. *GAIA-Ecological Perspectives for Science and Society*, 77–80.
18. Hillenbrand, P. (2020. 4 13). *What start-ups need to scale and succeed-interview with James Bilefield*. McKinsey Digital: https://www.mckinsey.com/capabilities/mckinsey-digital/our-insights/what-start-ups-need-to-scale-and-succeed
19. Hilpert, M., & Giese, M. (2021. 5 4). *The top 10 mistakes in B2B sales*. Techstars: https://www.techstars.com/the-line/advice/the-top-10-mistakes-in-b2b-startup-sales
20. Holden, N. M. (2022). A readiness level framework for sustainable circular bioeconomy. *EFB Bioeconomy Journal*. https://doi.org/10.1016/j.bioeco.2022.100031

21. Houterman, J., Blok, V., & Omta, O. (2014). Venture capital financing of techno-entrepreneurial start-ups: drivers and barriers for investments in research-based spin-offs in the Dutch medical life sciences industry. In F. Therin (Ed), *Handbook of research on techno-entrepreneurship: how technology and entrepreneurship are shaping the development of industries and companies* (old.: 169). Edward Elgar Publishing.
22. Johnson, J. (2020. 12 15). *Gaining customer traction: 5 steps to customer growth.* US Chamber of Commerce: https://www.uschamber.com/co/grow/customers/customer-traction-guide
23. Kenton, W. (2023. 1 18). *Burn rate: What it is, 2 types, formula, and examples.* Investopedia: https://www.investopedia.com/terms/b/burnrate.asp
24. KTH. (2021). *kthinnovationreadinesslevel.com/.* Forrás: kthinnovationreadinesslevel.com/: https://kthinnovationreadinesslevel.com/
25. Leydersdorf, L. (2010). The knowledge-based economy and the triple helix model. *Annual Review of Information Science and Technology*, 367–417.
26. Luger, M. I., & Goldstein, H. A. (1991). *Technology in the garden: Research parks and regional economic development.* Chapel Hill: University of North Carolina Press.
27. Marion. (2023. 05 24). *What is branding?* The Branding Journal: https://www.thebrandingjournal.com/2015/10/what-is-branding-definition/
28. McCarthy, I. P., Silvestre, B. S., von Nordenflycht, A., & Breznitz, S. M. (2018). A typology of university research park strategies: What parks do and why it matters. *Journal of Engineering and Technology Management*, 110–122.
29. McGill, J. (2021. 12 1). *The power of internal relationships in the workplace.* LeadFuze: https://www.leadfuze.com/internal-relationship/
30. Murray, R., Caulier-Grice, J., & Mulgan, G. (2010). *The open book of social innovation.* The Young Foundation & NESTA.
31. Osterwalder, A. (2020). *The strategizer box set.* Wiley.
32. Ries, E. (2011). *The lean startup: how constant innovation creates radically successful businesses.* Portfolio Penguin.
33. Rothaermel, F. T., Agung, S. D., & Jiang, L. (2007). University entrepreneurship: a taxonomy of the literature. *Industrial and Corporate Change*, 692–791.
34. Schwab, C. (2023. 2 23). *How to invest in a bear market.* schwab.com: https://www.schwab.com/learn/story/how-to-invest-bear-market
35. Seth, S. (2022. 10 16). *Business Basics Guide.* Forrás: Investopedia: https://www.investopedia.com/articles/personal-finance/090815/basics-business-development.asp
36. Smith, S. W. (2017. 10 26). *Innovation readiness level.* The Entrepreneur's Advisor(TM): https://blog.theentrepreneursadvisor.com/2017/10/innovation-readiness-level/
37. Stan, A. (2022. 9 7). *Start branding your business as early as possible.* Forbes: https://www.forbes.com/sites/theyec/2022/09/07/start-branding-your-business-as-early-as-possible/
38. Straits Research. (2021). *Forensic technology market size, share and forecast to 2030.* Straits Research.
39. Wapshott, N. (2012). *Keynes Hayek: The Clash that defined modern economics.* WW Norton & Co.
40. World Intellectual Property Organization. (dátum nélk.). *Patents.* wipo.int: https://www.wipo.int/patents/en/
41. Zaech, S., & Baldegger, U. (2017). Leadership in start-ups. *International Small Business Journal*, 157–177. https://doi.org/10.1177/0266242616676883

Chapter 7
Use of AI Tools for Forensic Purposes: Ethical and Legal Considerations from an EU Perspective

Iñigo de Miguel Beriain and Luis Ignacio Arrechea de Miguel

Abstract Artificial Intelligence (AI) may be a useful tool for enhancing the work of forensic scientists, but it also raises crucial ethical and legal concerns, which are the focus of this chapter. Our view is that, firstly, AI should never be considered a substitute for "human-based forensics". This is because it is often necessary for a court to ask questions around the nature and the methods undertaken to carry out forensic examinations and when the subject matter is technically complex. This is especially true when we consider the lack of transparency of these tools, which can make it challenging to understand the reasoning behind the conclusions they lead to reach. This is a significant obstacle in a judicial debate. Therefore, it is necessary to include a human element in the process, a forensic expert capable of answering any questions that may arise from the use of these AI tools. If this requirement cannot be met, the use of AI would be illegitimate, as it would violate the defendant's right to defense. Secondly, the fact that AI tools will inevitably contain biases is cause of concern. The decisive factor is whether or not these biases are admissible. A bias that belongs to an unimportant category differs from a bias that belongs to a relevant category. An AI bias that is similar to that which is common in human-performed forensic science may be permissible, unless sensible arguments are put forward as to why an increased demand should be placed on the machines. Indeed, in modern times, the comparison to the human standard should indicate the acceptable range of bias. On the other hand, it is important to remember that AI can also be used to reduce bias in traditional forensic science by acknowledging, to begin with, that human decisions are influenced by cognitive bias.

I. de Miguel Beriain (✉) · L. I. A. de Miguel
University of the Basque Country, UPV/EHU, Leioa, Spain
e-mail: inigo.demiguelb@ehu.eus

I. de Miguel Beriain
Ikerbasque, Basque Foundation for Science, Bilbao, Spain

S. Francese and R. S. P. King (eds.), *Driving Forensic Innovation in the 21st Century*,
https://doi.org/10.1007/978-3-031-56556-4_7

7.1 Introduction

In a report published in 2009 by the National Academy of Sciences of the United States [1], it was mentioned that the field of digital forensics (DF) had undergone a process of rapid maturity. This process will likely speed up over the course of the next few years, because of the foreseeable exponential growth in the use of Artificial Intelligence (AI) models [2]. According to the OECD, AI can be defined as "a machine-based system that can, for a given set of human defined objectives, make predictions, recommendations, or decisions influencing real or virtual environments" [3]. It is precisely this capacity to develop these tasks that makes easy to foresee that the impressive advancement of AI will influence many human activities in the future. Today, the use of AI technology has deeply penetrated society, from advising us about movies or television shows that may be of interest, to our ability to meet financial obligations after taking out a loan [4].

In the specific field of forensic science, on the other hand, it is already quite clear that the advent of AI will bring about significant changes in the manner in which we have historically carried out forensic science investigations [4]. To give some examples, DNA evidence, pattern recognition, crime scene reconstruction, digital forensics, image processing, psycho/narco-analysis, ballistics, and satellite tracking are some of the areas where artificial intelligence can be used [5]. As Kamshad Moshin stated, "(AI) may save forensic investigators a significant amount of time while also ensuring that they have sufficient time and motivation to focus on other vital duties" [6].

However, the use of artificial intelligence in forensic practice is also associated to a number of ethical and legal issues that cannot be ignored. These concerns primarily relate to three applications: (i), the potential for AI to automate decision-making processes; (ii) the ethical and legal implications of the lack of transparency and the need to provide accurate explanations for the operating methods and the resulting data/conclusions the field of forensics; (iii) the ethical and legal implications related to the biases involved in the use of AI tools, as well as the application of AI to reveal these biases.

These areas will be broken down into a number of basic concerns throughout this chapter, in order to present their scope. At the same time, the authors will endeavor to propose an appropriate course of action aimed at reducing the likelihood of inflicting damage to the human interests and rights at stake. To this end, before entering a discussion on the ethical and legal implications it would be beneficial to start by discussing the applications of AI in forensics that have or will have the largest practical influence in the near future, as illustrated in the next section.

7.2 AI in Forensics: Present and Foreseeable Applications

What are the present and most foreseeable uses of AI in forensic science? This is a relatively difficult question to answer because collectively, we do not always apply the same definition to what forensic science is and what is not. Here, the authors will focus on a wide range of techniques and areas of application, from fingerprint to DNA analysis, for instance, as well as the replication of human intellectual processes by machines, particularly computer systems. The assistance that AI provides to forensic specialists in appropriately managing data and doing meta-analysis at multiple levels will also be considered in this chapter. However, our views may be at times quite general and some of them may not be applicable to all types of forensic science disciplines due to the constraints imposed by this chapter's word count.

With this in mind, the authors will start with the analysis of some examples of how AI can help Forensic Science as a whole. For this purpose, the classification scheme designed by Prof. Eman A. A. El-Din [5] will be used.

- *Crime scene reconstruction.* Bloodstains, fingerprints, and shell casings, among other types of evidence, can be automatically detected and classified using AI algorithms applied to crime scene photographs and 3D animation [7]. This not only saves investigators' time, but it also ensures that no crucial evidence is overlooked.
- *DNA evidence*: Health data and samples contained in biobanks have important forensic applications [8]. During the perpetration of a crime, biological material such as blood, saliva, semen and skin cells can be transferred through contact with people and objects. As DNA technology has advanced, so has the sensitivity of DNA analysis, allowing forensic scientists to detect and process previously undetected low-level, degraded, or otherwise ineffective DNA evidence [5]. Algorithms based on artificial intelligence can be used to analyze DNA samples with greater precision than conventional methods. This not only helps to ensure that the correct perpetrator of a crime is identified, but it also helps to prevent wrongful convictions, which can have devastating consequences for both the accused and the victims. There are currently two emerging forensic genetic technologies associated with AI that are proving to be very fruitful: forensic DNA phenotyping (FDP), which focuses on externally visible characteristics and biogeographical ancestry, and Next Generation Sequencing (NGS), which focuses on providing comprehensive DNA analysis [9]. AI also might help in separating DNA profiles and attempting to work out whether a DNA test came straight from the person of interest or is in the crime scene by chance [10].
- Odontology. Forensic odontology aids in the identification of individuals by evaluating the oral cavity structures. It is primarily often deployed for the identification of individuals after mass disasters or violent crimes that hinder recognition of a human being [11]. The identification of bite-marks, the prediction of mandibular morphology, the determination of gender, and the estimation of age have all been widespread applications of AI technology in forensic odontology. The majority of these AI models are based on artificial neural networks or convolutional neural networks. The findings of the studies are encouraging. According to studies, these

models exhibit accuracy and precision comparable to that of trained examiners [12].

- *Facial Reconstruction.* Facial reconstruction is the recreation of a face from the cranial remains of an unknown individual (i.e. unknown identity). In forensic anthropology, AI is used for craniofacial superimposition, particularly during the skull-face overlay stage, where skull models are superimposed on photographs of a person's face in order to identify the individual [5]. Indeed, the "*prediction of soft tissues based on the hard tissues of the skull and* vice versa *can be significantly improved upon big-data training of 3D CNN with additional metadata about age, sex, BMI or ethnicity. New algorithms to perform facial reconstruction from a given skull have forensic applications in helping to identify skeletal remains when additional information is unavailable*" [13].
- *Fingerprints.* A fingerprint is an impression left by the friction ridges of a human fingertip. In establishing evidence to support conviction or acquittal, fingerprints are often a decisive factor. However, criminals are increasingly altering their fingerprints in a variety of ways, such as burning, abrasion, application of strong chemicals and skin transplant, to alter the morphology of the surface of the fingertips in the effort of rendering their fingermarks not comparable against their fingerprint record (in terms of yielding a match). This makes it difficult for technicians and automatic sensors to recognize them. In this regard, deep learning emerges as a leading tool for the recognition of damaged fingerprints [14].
- *Post-Mortem interval.* Post-Mortem interval refers to the time that has elapsed since death [15]. Knowing this information enables proving/disproving of the defendant's testimony and/or witnesses. AI could aid forensic scientists in estimating the time since death. The quantitative level of Lactate dehydrogenase and aspartate aminotransferase as proteins, and cholesterol as lipids, in blood, as well as the blood pH, can be fed to the AI model which then provide an estimation of PMI.
- *Toxicology.* In forensic science, toxicological screening is a valuable source of information. Traditional methods, however, have limitations that AI could help us overcome. In the field of toxicology, there is currently a vast opportunity for the application of AI to the analysis of biological samples. As Wankhade et al. state, "AI has also potential uses in the following areas: (i) Disease Diagnosis, where AI can help with the diagnosis of diseases using medical images, such as CT, MRI, and PET scans [16], (ii) Disease Surveillance, where AI can be used to track unusual disease outbreaks. This includes monitoring the spread and evolution of pathogens, such as bacteria, viruses, fungi, and other infectious diseases [17], (iii) Forensic Autopsy and Pathology, where AI can help determine pathological causes of death. Autopsy and pathology reports are often long, tedious documents. AI can help shorten these documents by flagging key findings and conclusions [6], (iv) Toxicology Analysis and Forensics, where AI can be used to investigate the presence of drugs and poisons in biological samples, such as blood, urine, hair, saliva, and skin, (v) Drug Abuse, where using drug testing software, AI can identify trends in the drug abuse landscape. AI can also be used to flag abnormal and unusual usage patterns" [18].

7.3 Main Ethical and Legal Issues: Background

It is clear that the implementation of AI opens up a wide range of opportunities for the improvement of forensic science practice. This, however, does not mean that AI should be employed in every case and without constraints, nor does it indicate that it can. Unfortunately, some of the applications of artificial intelligence raise significant ethical and legal challenges, while for others, the manner in which the tools are designed, trained, or deployed may return inaccurate or even biased results that must be avoided. In other cases, it is necessary to combine AI tools and human based-decision making to reach an optimal outcome (that is, the type of outcome that serves well for the purposes of providing reliable evidence). As a consequence, the ethics of using AI, as a discipline, has become increasingly prominent in recent years, and the scientific literature offers many papers on the issue. Unfortunately, only a few of them are devoted to analyzing the ethical and legal issues related to their application in forensic science.

Similarly, evidence already exists about the way in which different legal frameworks could address these issues [14]. Clearly, there are a variety of approaches that nations or institutions take in order to face the challenges posed by AI tools, and each one is different. In this chapter the authors focus, in particular on the EU perspective. The USA and the UK remain important countries in the evaluation of the legal and ethical issues on the use of AI and insights into their perspectives in this matter can be gathered from other sources [17, 20, 21].

On 27th January 2017, a report was published by the European Parliament Committee on Legal Affairs (JURI) in relation to Civil Law Rules on Robotics with recommendations to the European Commission (Report-A8-0005/2017, (2015/2103(INL)). This document focused more on robotics than on AI, drawing immediate attention to autonomous vehicles, drones, and medical-care robots, and suggesting that specific rules might be required in these areas, proposing the approval of a Directive on this topic. The same year, the European Council stated that the EU should urgently address emerging trends such as AI, "while at the same time ensuring a high level of data protection, digital rights and ethical standards" and invited "the Commission to put together a European approach to artificial intelligence" [22]. Later, in April 2018, the EU Commission approved a Communication called "Artificial Intelligence for Europe" [23] which aimed to "ensure an appropriate ethical and legal framework, based on the Union's values and in line with the Charter of Fundamental Rights of the EU".

To obtain this objective, a working group, named the High-Level Expert Group on AI was created. On 8 April 2019, they presented their Ethics Guidelines for Trustworthy Artificial Intelligence [19], which constitute a key milestone in the regulation of AI in the EU arena. This first normative document was immediately followed by the White Paper on Artificial Intelligence: an European approach to excellence and trust, published on 19 February 2019 (COM (2020) 65 final), which was aimed at presenting policy options to enable a trustworthy and secure development of AI in Europe, respecting the values and rights of EU citizens.

This regulatory compendium has made it clear that some fundamental considerations must be taken into account when developing and/or employing AI processes in any human activity, including forensic science, and that several requirements must be fulfilled. These requirements are [19]:

1. Human agency and oversight, including fundamental rights, human agency and human oversight.
2. Technical robustness and safety, including resilience to attack and security, fall back plan and general safety, accuracy, reliability and reproducibility.
3. Privacy and data governance, including respect for privacy, quality and integrity of data, and access to data.
4. Transparency, including traceability, explicability and communication.
5. Diversity, non-discrimination and fairness, including the avoidance of unfair bias, accessibility and universal design, and stakeholder participation.
6. Societal and environmental wellbeing, including sustainability and environmental friendliness, social impact, society and democracy.
7. Accountability, including auditability, minimization and reporting of negative impact, trade-offs and redress.

Of all these requirements, there are three that seem particularly relevant when referring to the use of AI in forensic sciences: human agency, transparency and explanation and fairness. Each of them will be discussed in detail in the subsequent sections.

7.4 Automatisation and the Need to Have a Human Being Involved in the Decision-Making Process

An extreme use of AI in forensic science would be to directly replace the human professionals working in this field by performing their work. Of course, someone must feed the system with data, but, this aspect aside, humans would no longer be needed: the AI mechanisms alone could directly reconstruct crime scenes, determine the circumstances surrounding a death, proceed to identify certain bodies, and so on, provided, of course, that a human agent feeds them with the necessary data or samples and train the models.

Given the anticipated superiority of these technologies, both now or in a few years' time, this has been regarded as something that will constitute a breakthrough by a few enthusiasts of technology. On the other hand, there are a number of significant reasons why the authors do not believe that replacement is a viable option, either now or in the foreseeable future, for technical, social, ethical and legal reasons. Two case studies will be discussed to contextualise the authors' thoughts. The first case study will concern automation as a means of avoiding the perverse effects of economic incentives. The second case study concerns automation as a means of avoiding inequalities in the proceedings due to the competency levels and qualifications (or lack thereof) of expert witness.

7.4.1 AI as a Means to Preserve Integrity

One of the main weaknesses of forensic science is the ever-increasing prevalence of private consultant practices, which poses a significant threat to the integrity of the profession. It is possible for some private forensic examiners to have their integrity compromised because the majority of their income is contingent on their capacity to produce reports that meet the requirements of their customers. Although some ISO standards are applicable to laboratory based forensic or crime scene examination/investigation and comparison disciplines [24], there is no disciplinary standard that can be applied to some types of private consultants. Furthermore, there is no evidence that the standards developed by the ISO work well in practice. Thus, a recent survey shows *"evidence of a lack of fitness for purpose of ISO17025 as a standard for the forensic science continuum, a lack of agreement on what forensic science is and poor levels of recognition of crime scene investigation, many competences, particularly cognitive competences, are not identified, monitored or assessed and the incentive to gain accreditation and maintain continuous improvement is intrinsic rather than customer driven"* [25].

Thus, private consultancy poses the greatest potential threat of unethical behavior, since there is less oversight, fewer opportunities for peer review, and greater financial incentive. As Siegal convincingly explained, *"in many types of civil cases, the attorneys working for the plaintiff in a lawsuit often have a contingency fee arrangement with their client. This means that in a favorable judgment, they often collect a considerable percentage (often 33–50%) of what their client receives (…) This type of arrangement is fraught with problems. It exposes the scientist to more obvious charges of bias in the analysis of the plaintiff's evidence, thereby increasing the chances of a favorable verdict and a larger payoff."* [26].

Could replacing this type of private service with one produced by AI serve to avoid this kind of perverse incentive? In the authors' view, this is far from clear. Indeed, the introduction of AI-based technologies into evidence generation is strongly conditioned by the degree of reliability achievable in the design of such systems [16], as well as by our capacity to ensure that they do not include some kind of bias related to their owners' interests (or offering mitigating measures). After all, the developers of such a mechanism will also always have their own interests at heart, which may be very similar to those of forensic consultants. Therefore, unless we guarantee their neutrality, it is difficult to arrive at such a conclusion.

Furthermore, integrity does not seem to be the major issue, if forensic experts are subject to the most stringent form of quality control in the form of cross-examination in courts, where any malpractice, omissions, or fudging is very likely to be exposed.

Thus, the problem of maintaining a member's professional integrity in the field of forensic science may be less of an issue than it is in other professions. If the above is a true reflection of reality, replacing "human-based forensics" by AI tools would not make sense, at least on the basis of the reasons the authors have discussed.

7.4.2 AI as a Means to Avoid Mis-representations

A different argument for the replacement of practitioners by AI tools is the one that relates to insufficient technical skills by the "human-based forensics". It has often been pointed out that the presentation of credentials that do not closely match the actual skills of the person writing a forensic report can seriously affect the prosecution or the defence. As Yadav [27]wrote, *"Misrepresentations include educational degree attainment (e.g. claiming that an unearned PhD or a degree was awarded by a particular institution when, in fact, it was not), professional licensures or certifications (e.g. falsely claiming certification as a forensic Pathologist from the American Board of Pathology or a common tactic of equating having attained actual certification with being board "eligible"), employment history and data about previous testimonies such as number of times, locations,* etc. *Often, this is done to impress the client, the judge or jury in order to ward off challenges such as cross-examination by exaggerating the qualifications. Due to a lack of resources and fact-checking methods, such exaggerations are seldom detected and said acts are unethical and must be discouraged."*

It may be argued that the use of AI instead of a human agent could be of great assistance in ensuring a base level of quality in forensic analysis and thus resolve the issue of a lack of qualifications of some forensic analysts and/or a lack of quality of the reports or testimonies they provide. As Mesejo et al. stated, *"the use of AI in forensics "can also reduce human subjectivity and errors; and can contribute to provide a greater scientific basis that favors the admissibility of expert evidence, given that courtroom forensic testimony is often criticized by defense lawyers as lacking a scientific basis."* [28]. Thus, this replacement could be considered an ideal solution to reduce the range of incertitude of scientific forensics.

Furthermore, it would make the system more equitable, since it would distribute its successes and errors uniformly. The element of *luck* that comes with having one forensic analyst who is more skilled than another would disappear in the face of the uniformity that is imposed by the machine. This, of course, could be catastrophic if the mechanism is ineffective, since it would put everyone on the same level of risk. However, if it had an efficiency rating comparable to that of an intermediately skilled forensic scientist, then it might be considered an effective substitute for the current system.

Thus, it is clear that it may be extremely challenging to ascertain precisely when an AI mechanism can flawlessly replace human intervention. In fact, this appears to be more of a pipe dream than anything else, especially when we consider the fact that the operation of our legal systems often requires the presence of an intermediary between the technology and the court. There must be a forensic scientist who communicates to the decision-maker the contributions that the specific evidence-based and driven forensic discipline/technique can make to the facts at hand. It is entirely possible that, in some instances, the work of the forensic scientist will consist solely of re-stating what an AI mechanism suggests; however, in other circumstances, they will be required to go further, introducing nuances or, at the very least, explaining why what the AI suggests that a certain scenario is the most plausible explanation. This, of course, brings us to the terrain of transparency and explicability, which is what will be analyzed in the following section.

Thus, it seems quite clear that human intervention seems to be irreplaceable in forensic science, at least for a few more years. Furthermore, it is necessary to highlight that this kind of intervention is currently required by a significant number of the rules that govern the application of various decision-making mechanisms. This is particularly true if personal data are involved in the decision, which is often the case in forensic science. For instance, Article 22 of the General Data Protection Regulation (GDPR), which regulates the use of personal data in the EU, prohibits decisions that are solely based on automated processing but still produce a legal or meaningful effect, that is, the general prohibition can be translated into a right for humans to be included in the process. The General Data Protection Regulation ensures that decisions will continue to involve human reasoning alongside automated processing; as a result, automated processing will no longer serve as the only basis for decisions.

In addition, it is important to keep in mind that the mere formal inclusion of human intervention is sufficient to consider that a decision is not based solely on automated processing, as the Article 29 Working Party (WP29) has pointed out [29]. Thus, according to what Mendoza and Bygrave have indicated [30], even if a decision is formally attributed to a person, it will be based solely on automated processing if a person does not actively assess the outcome of the processing prior to it being formalized as a decision. This is the case even if the decision is formally attributed to the person in question. In addition, for human participation to have any value, it must be carried out by an individual who is authorized and qualified to make changes to the decision, and the analysis that they perform must account for all of the pertinent data. To summarize, it appears that, at this juncture, the involvement of the coroner is unavoidable, at least within the framework of the EU.

7.5 Transparency

7.5.1 Understanding Transparency

Artificial intelligence encompasses several methodologies, all of which are quite different from one another. There are some that are fairly easy to understand, making the delivery of all the data and conclusions convenient for the controller. Others, like deep learning (as per Oxford Languages Dictionary, "a type of machine learning based on artificial neural networks in which multiple layers of processing are used to extract progressively higher level features from data"), face substantial challenges due to a lack of transparency, which they must overcome. One of the variables that contributes to the difficulty of achieving transparency in artificial intelligence is the so-called "black box" issue [31], which is directly linked to opacity, a major problem in the context of AI. It is true that it is not always necessary to avoid the "black box" effect in order to reach useful conclusions. Several years ago, for instance, the FBI conducted a study to determine the reliability and accuracy of latent print examiners' decisions, a challenging and intricate problem in forensic science. To achieve this objective, researchers adopted a black box approach, evaluating the examiners' accuracy and consensus in decision-making rather than attempting to determine or dictate the decision-making process [32]. Despite this limitation, the study aimed to provide useful reference estimates that informed decision-making and guided future research by identifying the various types of errors made by experts in this field, additionally proposing countermeasures. However, subsequent research has revealed the flaws and shortcomings of such approaches, making the discussion more open than ever [33].

Thus, opacity is an issue that needs an adequate response, especially if AI tools are involved. As a matter of fact, "opacity" is one of the key threats that "fair" AI encounters, since it is in direct contrast with the necessity for transparency, which is key in terms of the ethical and legal use of these tools. Without transparency one can hardly provide an explanation of how evidence has been reached.

It is difficult to deal with opacity. At the very least, there are no less than three distinct types of opacity that are intrinsically present in AI, and each one manifests itself in a different way: (i) as intentional corporate or state secrecy; (ii) as technical illiteracy; and (iii) as epistemic opacity [34].

- *Opacity in the sense of deliberate state or corporate secrecy*

At the outset, it is necessary to think of a type of deliberate opacity, which has to do with the goal of any company to protect its trade secrets, so that its competitive advantage over its competitors is safeguarded. In other words, it is necessary to think of a form of deliberate opacity that has to do with the desire of any company to "have an edge" over its competitors. Naturally, this is an extremely important incentive, and the goal here is not so much to make the mechanisms more complicated, but to make it more difficult for a third party to comprehend how they operate.

If the legislation that governs industrial secrets were to provide the necessary level of protection for this type of secrecy, then perhaps it would be permissible to keep it a secret. Such regulation shall also be able to respond to legitimate interests, such as the protection of a company's competitive advantages, the upkeep of the system's security, or to prevent dishonest users from abusing the system for their own benefit. These are all examples of legitimate interests that people have. Nevertheless, it should be compatible with the incorporation of independent certification systems that are able to vouch for the fact that the mechanism in question complies with the requirements set out in the General Data Protection Regulation (GDPR). It should not be difficult, in the vast majority of cases, to provide the data along with the information they require to protect their interests, without concurrently releasing any commercially sensitive information. This is because it is not necessary for subjects to have an in-depth understanding of how the system operates; rather, they only need to be aware of the ways in which it may threaten their interests, rights, and liberties.

- *Technical ignorance in the form of "opacity".*

This form of opacity is caused by the unique abilities that are necessary to create and implement the algorithms, as well as the capacity to read and write the code. We may state that the codes employed in AI are a mystery for the vast majority of the public since they lack this specific knowledge; nonetheless, this should not be an impediment to the fulfillment of the obligation of information stipulated by the GDPR. A barrier that prevents an acceptable explanation of the objective of an AI system from being provided should not be the ability to grasp computer language. This applies not only to the stakeholders who are subject to profiling or automated decision making, but to everyone else as well.

- *Epistemic opacity*

This type of opacity is a result of the properties of machine learning algorithms and the required scale for their practical application. This is connected to the fact that humans are unable to interpret some computational models. In other words, the transition from the inputs that the model takes into the outputs that it generates is unfathomable from a human point of view. There is no prohibition on the use of this type of model at the regulatory level; however, it is recommended to follow the precautionary principle when using it. This is because the lack of interpretability may make it more difficult to identify biases in the model, which may, in turn, lead to discriminatory results or false or spurious correlations. Obviously, not all machine-learning models can be characterized in this manner as being opaque.

7.5.2 The Need for a Human Explanation

Thus, opacity is a serious ethical and legal issue that prevents transparency. Could opacity problems prevent AI from being useful in the field of forensic science? To answer this question, there are an additional two fundamental questions that need to be addressed. The first one is directly related to the tasks that will be performed by these mechanisms. It is difficult to deny the usefulness of computer simulations if, for example, we use them to reconstruct a crime scene or to suggest possibilities in ballistics that may initially seem less obvious to a human mind but later prove to be very consistent with the evidence. To bolster the credibility of the hypothesis, it is not necessary to demonstrate that a plausible explanation has not been conjured up out of one's own imagination. As a matter of fact, for the hypothesis to be used for its intended purpose, that is, to provide a consistent explanation to the court, it is sufficient for the human forensic scientist to acknowledge that the explanation provided by a machine is correct and be able to reproduce the arguments because they believe it to be true. Keeping this in mind, one can state that AI can be a very useful addition to the work of a forensic scientist.

It is a completely different matter to consider whether AI will ever be self-explanatory. From the authors' point of view, this is extremely unlikely to occur. Thus, at the end of the day, it will always be necessary for there to be an intermediary who is able to explain what the mechanism proposes and why it is plausible [35]. This is the absolute minimum requirement needed to make its use employable in a court of law: otherwise, the opacity of the AI tool could cause great harm to criminal proceedings [36]. Thus, regardless of the circumstances, it seems important to include a forensic scientist in the process from the start, at the very least so that they can evaluate the information that the tool provides and answer the questions that might be raised in the courts. As Lefevre stated, "*legal reasoning and the sentences handed down must be individualized too. AI can be used to support decision-making for doctors in forensic medicine, and it can also be used to structure the research necessary for the evolution of scientific knowledge in forensic medicine. To date, the AIs used to support decision-making remain fairly immature*" [37].

Thus, we must conclude that the problems of opacity associated with AI mechanisms are not insurmountable if a forensic scientist can adequately explain an AI-generated hypothesis. In this sense, a thorough understanding of how the mechanism operates is unnecessary. Even less important is revealing the algorithm's secret. What is important is that its results can be rationally justified by humans, but this intervention is, on the other hand, mandatory: "If we do not act upon the paths of a human-centered perspective, we will not be able to take advantage from the application of AI-based systems" [16].

It is however necessary to wonder if it is possible that, in some instances, we may utilize an AI tool without being able to provide such an explanation The authors believe that this needs an in-depth discussion. The acceptability of the use of an AI tools that are opaque will depend on the intended utility of the tool and our ability to check the plausibility of its results on a factual level. Imagine that we successfully employ an AI mechanism to determine the location of a victim's body or a crime weapon. Would it be a problem if we were unable to comprehend how the AI deduced its precise location from the algorithm's opacity? In the authors' opinion the answer is obviously no, as the finding itself would provide evidence of its accuracy. It would be absurd to sacrifice the instrument's utility for these purposes simply because we do not comprehend how it operates. However, this kind of use will be linked to a criminal investigation and not a part of the criminal procedure as such. In a trial, expert witness should be able to provide an explanation of the facts at stake. Stating that someone is supposed to have died at a certain time because an AI tool states so could hardly be acceptable.

Lastly, it is necessary to highlight that in some kind of concrete applications of AI tools, such as those related to digital forensics [38] there will always be a margin of error that needs to be appreciated and catered for. This is no easy task if how the tools work is not understood. Indeed, some experts have convincingly held that "the margin-of-error question becomes a matter of constitutionality, as the decision-making process must provide comprehensive and coherent reasoning from a legal and logical point of view. The need to reconstruct the logical path in a way that justifies and accounts for the results presented by the instrument clashes with the technical difficulties encountered in the process" [16]. If we are not able to fill this gap by using complementary tools, it will be impossible to base a judicial decision on the information provided by an AI mechanism related to digital forensics.

7.6 Bias

An additional consideration for the application and exploitation of AI comes in the form of bias. At the present time, there is a general consensus that bias is a serious ethical and legal problem in the field of AI. However, defining what exactly biases are and whether all of them should be combated is much more complex. In the first place, it is difficult because the idea of bias can be interpreted in a variety of ways [39]. For instance, one could use a purely technical definition. Indeed, "the degree to which a reference value deviates from the truth" is how the International Organization for Standardization (ISO) defines bias from a statistical point of view [40]. This deviation can contribute to undesirable or discriminating effects (such as an amplified sense of prejudice and stigmatization), but it also has the potential to be useful in certain settings (e.g., affirmative action policies and precision medicine practices) [41].

However, there are alternative approaches to the concept of bias [42]. From a sociological point of view, bias is almost always deemed to have a negative or discriminatory effect: the continuation of such biases could lead to unintended (in)direct discrimination against certain groups or people, potentially exacerbating prejudice and marginalization. This sociological concept of bias is directly linked to a fundamental principle that we call "fairness": bias is unacceptable since it is contrary to fairness [43]. Yet, fairness is another abstract notion that can be understood in a variety of ways, depending on the context. For example, the precise significance of what it means in the context of the GDPR has not yet been established [44]. However, it is quite clear that in order to achieve fairness in a system that is based on AI, we need to understand how the system can be biased, as well as where and how bias is formed. This is true regardless of the criteria that we choose to adhere to. This will always be the sole method available to reduce its impact or exert some degree of control over it. However, the regulations that we currently have in place do not provide us with a clear and exact definition of fairness.

To these preliminary concerns, we should add the difficulties associated with a legal framework that is currently experiencing a time of significant transformation, such as the EU legal framework. Presently, there are multiple regulatory tools that target data and/or artificial intelligence, such as the Network and Information Security Directive (NIS2 Directive), the Cyber Resiliency Act, the Data Act, the Data Governance Act, the Digital Markets Act, the Digital Services Act, or the Artificial

Intelligence Act. Some of these tools have already been enacted, while others are still at the planning stages (most of them are expected to be approved within the next few years).

One of the most direct references to bias in AI has been introduced in Article 10 of the AI Act, as its numbers (3) and (4) state that:

3. *Training, validation and testing data sets shall be relevant, representative, free of errors and complete. They shall have the appropriate statistical properties, including, where applicable, as regards the persons or groups of persons on which the high-risk AI system is intended to be used. These characteristics of the data sets may be met at the level of individual data sets or a combination thereof.*
4. *Training, validation and testing data sets shall take into account, to the extent required by the intended purpose, the characteristics or elements that are particular to the specific geographical, behavioral or functional setting within which the high-risk AI system is intended to be used.*

If adequately implemented, this legal framework should serve to reduce bias in the application of AI. Yet, it is impossible to create an AI devoid of all bias. As human beings, we are incapable of achieving this objective. The requirement, therefore, should not be that only AI tools devoid of bias are acceptable, but rather the parameters of AI use in forensic practice that incorporate bias; in other words, the level of bias that could be acceptable in a concrete context. This may be achieved in several ways. From our perspective, the most realistic comparison would be between the bias produced by an AI process after incorporating all the essential mechanisms to mitigate it and the bias introduced by standard forensic practice. It is important to realize, in this sense, that traditional forensic practice also contains many biases. We have sufficient evidence that extraneous information can result in cognitive bias in forensic pathology decision-making. For instance, in the case of forensic analysis, we know that although some laboratories have implemented bias mitigating strategies, with a varying impact on operational efficiency, there has been no systematic assessment of the risk posed by cognitive bias and, in practice, it is hard to imagine how to avoid this type of bias [45].

Research also suggests that forensic science practitioners are susceptible to various types of confirmation bias; in many cases, procedures have been put in place to reduce access to unnecessary information and control the order of providing relevant information. These procedures also mandate the use of multiple comparison samples instead of a single suspect exemplar; replication of results by analysts blinded to previous results may be beneficial [46]. For instance, a recent paper has shown a bias related to ethnicity: forensic pathologists are more likely to rule "homicide" rather than "accident" in deaths of black children compared to white children. This may arise because the base-rate expectation creates an a priori cognitive bias to rule that black children died as a result of homicide, which then perpetuates itself [47].

What does this mean in terms of the debate about the use of AI for forensic purposes? At this juncture, there are two very fascinating issues that need to be addressed. The first is that it does not make sense to disregard the use of AI because of the biases it includes, particularly if those biases are no more severe than those inherent in the traditional practice of forensic medicine. The decision as to what "more severe" means is bound to be difficult because the answer will be contingent on the definition of prejudice that is selected. Nevertheless, if we use the categories that European rules deem to be linked to discrimination (such as gender, race, sexual orientation, and so on), it will be much simpler for us to reach a consensus.

Conversely, it is also true that we could use AI tools as a way to reduce the bias that exists in the practice of forensic medicine. For example, algorithms could be used to alert forensic scientists to possible biases, thanks to an alternative interpretation of the data that excludes biased interpretations. This would help reduce the amount of bias that is present in the practice of forensic medicine. Indeed, the use of intelligent software is already making forensic investigations much simpler, providing an explanation for the reasoning process that differs from algorithm to algorithm, and significantly reducing errors caused by cognitive bias. This has the potential to result in significant time and effort savings as well as a major improvement in the quality of forensic analysis.

7.7 Conclusions

It is important to remember that AI can be an excellent tool for enhancing the work of forensic scientists, but it should never be viewed as a replacement for them. This is technically complicated to begin with, at least for the time being. And, because it is often necessary for a court to be able to ask questions about the forensic analyses conducted, leading to a certain conclusion, the role of the human intermediary is essential. In addition, it should be kept in mind that the regulations governing the use of personal data make it impossible to make automated decisions using such data. In practice, this rules out the possibility of eliminating the human element when the processing of personal data cannot be avoided, as is often the case in forensic science.

On the other hand, it is clear that the use of AI for forensic purposes creates numerous difficulties associated with the need to provide reasonable explanations for the facts. The opacity of these tools can make it difficult to comprehend the reasoning behind their conclusions. In a criminal investigation, this may not be a significant obstacle, but it certainly is in court. Consequently, it is necessary to again recommend the inclusion of a human element in the process, a forensic expert who can address any questions that may arise from the use of these capabilities. If this requirement cannot be met, the use of AI would be illegitimate, given that it would violate the right of the defendant to their defense. Therefore, the only sustainable solution is to face all the ethical problems relating to AI by applying a human-based vision. In this path forward, we must create a strong background in order to achieve a truly trustworthy AI ecosystem, also with the help of the EU ethics guidelines for more reliable AI, which are focused on the development of AI-based tools that permit compliance with all laws and regulations and with ethical principles, providing a more robust and reliable solution from both a technical and a social perspective [16].

Finally, we should bear in mind that AI mechanisms will inevitably contain biases. The crucial question is whether they are admissible. A bias that relates to an unimportant category does not appear to be the same as a bias that relates to an important category. And a bias comparable to that of a human forensic scientist is different from one that is manifestly superior. Indeed, the comparison to the human standard should indicate the limits of acceptable bias. On the other hand, we should remember that AI can be used to reduce bias in traditional forensic science by revealing patterns of discrimination that are not readily apparent.

References

1. Committee on Identifying the Needs of the Forensic Sciences Community, National Research Council (US). Committee on Science, Law Policy, Global Affairs, Committee on Science, Law, ... & Theoretical Statistics. (2009). *Strengthening forensic science in the United States: a path forward*. National Academy Press.
2. Walsh, T. (2018). *2062: The world that AI made*. Black Inc.
3. OECD. (2023). Recommendation of the Council on Artificial Intelligence. Accessed July 19, 2023 https://legalinstruments.oecd.org/en/instruments/OECD-LEGAL-0449
4. Véliz, C. (2021). *Privacy is power*. Melville House.
5. El-Din, A. A. (2022). Artificial intelligence in forensic science: Invasion or revolution? *Egyptian Society of Clinical Toxicology Journal, 10*(2), 20–32.
6. Mohsin, K. (January 31, 2023). Artificial intelligence in forensic science. *International Journal of Forensic Research, Artificial Intelligence in Forensic Science*, *4*(1), 172–173.
7. Ma, M., Zheng, H., & Lallie, H. (2010). Virtual reality and 3D animation in forensic visualization. *Journal of Forensic Sciences, 55*, 1227–1231.
8. O'Doherty, K. C., Christofides, E., Yen, J., Bentzen, H. B., Burke, W., Hallowell, N., Koenig, B. A., & Willison, D. J. (2016). If you build it, they will come: Unintended future uses of organised health data collections. *BMC Med Ethics*, *17*(1), 54. https://doi.org/10.1186/s12910-016-0137-x
9. Machado, H., & Granja, R. (2022). *Genetic surveillance and crime control: Social, cultural and political perspectives* (p. 212). Taylor & Francis.
10. Marciano, M. A., & Adelman, J. D. (2017). PACE: probabilistic assessment for contributor estimation—A machine learning-based assessment of the number of contributors in DNA mixtures. *Forensic Science International: Genetics, 27*, 82–91.
11. Smitha, T. (2021). Artificial intelligence in forensic odontology. *Journal of Forensic Dental Sciences* 01–02.
12. Khanagar, S. B., Al-Ehaideb, A., Maganur, P. C., Vishwanathaiah, S., Patil, S., Baeshen, H. A., & Bhandi, S. (2021). Developments, application, and performance of artificial intelligence in dentistry–A systematic review. *Journal of dental sciences, 16*(1), 508–522.
13. Thurzo, A., Kosnáčová, H. S., Kurilová, V., Kosmeľ, S., Beňuš, R., Moravanský, N., ... & Varga, I. (2021, November). Use of advanced artificial intelligence in forensic medicine, forensic anthropology and clinical anatomy. In *Healthcare* (Vol. 9, No. 11, p. 1545). MDPI.
14. Fattahi, J., & Mejri, M. (2021, January). Damaged fingerprint recognition by convolutional long short-term memory networks for forensic purposes. In 5th International Conference on Cryptography, Security and Privacy (CSP) (pp. 193–199). IEEE.
15. Khakare, M. R., & Fatangare, S. (2020). *Survey on Prediction of Post-Mortem Interval using Artificial Intelligence in Forensic Examination, 7*(5), 5760–5764.

16. Raffaella, B., Ferrazzano, M., & Summa, L. (2020). Legal issues in AI forensics: understanding the importance of humanware. In *Proceedings of the International Workshop on Applications of AI to Forensics 2020 (AI2Forensics 2020)*, pp. 13–20.
17. Cath, C., Wachter, S., Mittelstadt, B., Taddeo, M., & Floridi, L. (2018). Artificial intelligence and the 'good society': The US, EU, and UK approach. *Science and engineering ethics, 24*, 505–528.
18. Wankhade, T. D., Ingale, S. W., Mohite, P. M., Bankar, N. J., Wankhade, T., Ingale, S., & Mohite, P. (2022). Artificial intelligence in forensic medicine and toxicology: The future of forensic medicine. *Cureus, 14*(8).
19. AI, H. (2019). High-level expert group on artificial intelligence. *Ethics guidelines for trustworthy AI*. Accessed July 19, 2023 from https://www.aepd.es/sites/default/files/2019-12/ai-ethics-guidelines.pdf
20. Executive Office of the President National Science and Technology Council Committee on Technology. (2016). Preparing for the future of artificial intelligence. Washington, DC, USA. Accessed July 19, 2023 from https://obamawhitehouse.archives.gov/sites/default/files/whitehouse_files/microsites/ostp/NSTC/preparing_for_the_future_of_ai.pdf
21. House of Commons Science and Technology Committee. (2016a). Robotics and artificial intelligence (No. Fifth Report of Session 2016–17). London, UK. At: https://publications.parliament.uk/pa/cm201617/cmselect/cmsctech/145/145.pdf.
22. parliament.uk/pa/cm201617/cmselect/cmsctech/145/145.pdf.European Council meeting (19th October 2017). Accessed July 19, 2023 from http://data.consilium.europa.eu/doc/document/ST-14-2017-INIT/en/pdf
23. Communication from the Commission to the European Parliament, the European Council, the Council, the European Economic and Social Committee and the Committee of the Regions on Artificial Intelligence for Europe. COM/2018/237 https://eur-lex.europa.eu/legal-content/EN/TXT/PDF/?uri=CELEX:52018DC0237
24. Doyle, S. (2020). A review of the current quality standards framework supporting forensic science: Risks and opportunities. *Wiley Interdisciplinary Reviews: Forensic Science, 2*(3), e1365.
25. Neuteboom, W., Ross, A., Bugeja, L., Willis, S., Roux, C., & Lothridge, K. (2023). Management in forensic science: a closer inspection. *Forensic Science International*, 111779.
26. Siegal, J. A. (2012). Ethics in Forensic Science (Downs JCU, Swienton AR eds). Elsevier Ireland Ltd., pp. 59–79. https://doi.org/10.1016/B978-0-12-385019-5.00003-8
27. Yadav, P. K. (2017). Ethical issues across different fields of forensic science. *Egyptian journal of forensic sciences*, *7*, 1–6. https://doi.org/10.1186/s41935-017-0010-1
28. Mesejo, P., Martos, R., Ibáñez, Ó., Novo, J., & Ortega, M. (2020). A survey on artificial intelligence techniques for biomedical image analysis in skeleton-based forensic human identification. *Applied Sciences, 10*(14), 4703.
29. Lazcoz, G., & De Hert, P. (2022). Humans in the GDPR and AIA governance of automated and algorithmic systems. Essential pre-requisites against abdicating responsibilities. In *Essential pre-requisites against abdicating responsibilities*
30. Mendoza, I., & Bygrave, L. A. (2017). The right not to be subject to automated decisions based on profiling. *EU internet law: Regulation and enforcement*, 77–98.
31. Carabantes, M. (2020). Black-box artificial intelligence: An epistemological and critical analysis. *AI & Society, 35*(2), 309–317.
32. Ulery, B. T., Hicklin, R. A., Buscaglia, J., & Roberts, M. A. (2011). Accuracy and reliability of forensic latent fingerprint decisions. *Proceedings of the National Academy of Sciences, 108*(19), 7733–7738.
33. Khan, K., & Carriquiry, A. L. (2023). Shining a light on forensic black-box studies. Statistics and Public Policy, (just-accepted), 1–21.
34. Burrell, J. (2016). How the machine 'thinks': understanding opacity in machine learning algorithms. *Big Data Soc, 3*, 1–12. https://doi.org/10.1177/2053951715622512
35. Krivchenkov, A., Misnevs, B., & Pavlyuk, D. (2019). Intelligent methods in digital forensics: state of the art. In *Reliability and Statistics in Transportation and Communication: Selected*

Papers from the 18th International Conference on Reliability and Statistics in Transportation and Communication, RelStat'18, 17–20 October 2018, Riga, Latvia 18 (pp. 274–284). Springer International Publishing.

36. Palmiotto, F. (2021). The black box on trial: the impact of algorithmic opacity on fair trial rights in criminal proceedings. *Algorithmic Governance and Governance of Algorithms: Legal and Ethical Challenges*, 49–70.
37. Lefèvre, T. (2021). Artificial intelligence in forensic medicine. In *Artificial intelligence in medicine* (pp. 1–9). Cham: Springer International Publishing.
38. Horsman, G. (2019). Tool testing and reliability issues in the field of digital forensics. *Digital Investigation, 28*, 163–175.
39. Schwartz, R., Vassilev, A., Greene, K., Perine, L., Burt, A., & Hall, P. (2022). Towards a standard for identifying and managing bias in artificial intelligence. *NIST Special Publication, 1270*, 1–77.
40. ISO. (2021). General statistical terms and terms used in probability. Accessed July 19, 2023 from https://www.iso.org/standard/40145.html
41. Cirillo, D., Catuara-Solarz, S., Morey, C., Guney, E., Subirats, L., Mellino, S., & Mavridis, N. (2020). Sex and gender differences and biases in artificial intelligence for biomedicine and healthcare. *NPJ Digital Medicine, 3*(1), 81.
42. Cirillo, D., & Rementeria, M. J. (2022). Bias and fairness in machine learning and artificial intelligence. In *Sex and gender bias in technology and artificial intelligence* (pp. 57–75), Academic Press.
43. Varona, D., & Suárez, J. L. (2022). Discrimination, bias, fairness, and trustworthy AI. *Applied Sciences, 12*(12), 5826.
44. Malgieri, G. (2020, January). The concept of fairness in the GDPR: a linguistic and contextual interpretation. In *Proceedings of the 2020 Conference on fairness, accountability, and transparency* (pp. 154–166).
45. Camilleri, A., Abarno, D., Bird, C., Coxon, A., Mitchell, N., Redman, K., & Lindsay, H. (2019). A risk-based approach to cognitive bias in forensic science. *Science & Justice, 59*(5), 533–543.
46. Cooper, G. S., & Meterko, V. (2019). Cognitive bias research in forensic science: A systematic review. *Forensic Science International, 297*, 35–46.
47. Dror, I., Melinek, J., Arden, J. L., Kukucka, J., Hawkins, S., Carter, J., & Atherton, D. S. (2021). Cognitive bias in forensic pathology decisions. *Journal of Forensic Sciences, 66*(5), 1751–1757.

Chapter 8
Forensic Biometrics: Challenges, Innovation and Opportunities

Seth Nixon, Pietro Ruiu, Claudia Trignano, and Massimo Tistarelli

Abstract Forensic science has always benefited from the adoption and exploitation of novel technologies to perform and analyze measurements at a crime scene and in the laboratory. Modern information technologies boosted many forensic procedures, such as accelerating and automating the comparison of fingerprints and fingermarks, and, recently, the analysis and comparison of images from human faces. Moreover, the recent advent of fast and performant Machine Learning (often dubbed *AI*) models, greatly improved the applicability of automatic face recognition to operational scenarios. However, even though technology has enabled the development of such systems, there are several hindering factors which must be taken into account. In this chapter the technological, legal and societal factors potentially enabling and fostering the development and application of automatic face recognition in forensic procedures are described and discussed. Also, the current issues and main concerns, restricting the mass-adoption of automatic face recognition technologies in forensic cases are presented. This chapter attempts not only to document both enablers and roadblockers of forensic face recognition, but also provides some promising research avenues and suggestions for a better application of these technologies in today's society.

8.1 Introduction

In order to establish the truth about any law enforcement case, from the assessment of a claimed identity at a border crossing checkpoint to determining the culprit of a crime from biological traces recovered in the crime scene, an accurate forensic analysis is always required.

Forensic analysis can be often described as a three-step process. The first step is the *acquisition* of the data related to the event. Examples include a facial picture taken at a border crossing, fingermarks lifted at a crime scene or sensory data collected

S. Nixon · P. Ruiu · C. Trignano · M. Tistarelli (✉)
Department of Biomedical Sciences, University of Sassari, Viale San Pietro 47/A, 07100 Sassari, Italy
e-mail: tista@uniss.it

S. Francese and R. S. P. King (eds.), *Driving Forensic Innovation in the 21st Century*,
https://doi.org/10.1007/978-3-031-56556-4_8

from a vehicle control unit after a car crash. The second step is the *analysis* of the collected data which allows examiners to draw some conclusions about the event which produced the data. The last step, the *presentation*, reports the results of the analysis, in a way that is understandable by the key players in a court of law.

To appropriately address all three steps, it is mandatory to distinguish forensic *intelligence* from forensic *investigation*. Forensic intelligence is the process of gathering information to assist with the investigative process. The classic example is matching fingermarks lifted from two different, possibly geographically and time separated crime scenes. In this process, the identity of the suspect(s) is unknown, as well as if the traces come from a single or multiple subjects and whether they even committed the crime. If the fingermarks match, it is only possible to assign a probability for the same person to be present in both places. On the other hand, forensic investigation allows building strong, interpretable conclusions to contribute to a body of evidence in court. For example, in forensic face recognition, the forensic expert will produce an analysis on the similarity between a reference picture of the subject and the image of an unknown individual captured at the crime scene. The evidence stemming from this analysis must be produced in a probabilistic form, leaving the interpretation to a judge or a jury, contributing to the body of evidence for the prosecution or defense thesis.

In the framework of biometric technologies, depending on the modality and technique used, either one or both forensic intelligence and investigation can be gathered/ conducted. The earliest examples of forensic biometric investigation can be dated back to the Bertillonage system developed in the nineteenth century by French criminologist Alphonse Bertillon [1]. In this system, various soft and morphological characteristics of (a) convicted criminals or (b) suspects were stored on paper. Such characteristic measurements, including ear length, finger length, skin color, among a large number of others, were used to match descriptions between individuals. Fingerprint matching is likely the most widely used, trusted and accepted biometric form of intelligence-gathering in modern police investigations to be brought to court cases. While there is evidence to suggest fingerprints were used as proof of identity as far back as 300BC in China [2], modern fingerprint recognition has its genesis in the late nineteenth century in Great Britain with the work of Sir Francis Galton [3]. The features (*minutiae*) defined by Galton are still in use today. Fingerprints have been used extensively in law enforcement for identification or exclusion from further investigation of suspects, in both forensic intelligence and investigation. Examples include fingerprint traces found on lego blocks in a house in Arizona, associating John Sansing to a murder, for which he was later convicted [4].

While a picture of the convicted criminal was included in Bertillion's records, a rigorous and objective procedure for the forensic face analysis process has been developed only recently. Currently implemented procedures for forensic face analysis rely on two approaches: Human-based Face Analysis (HFA) and Automatic Face Recognition (AFR). The former requires the manual gathering of measurements of a face image, which are generally based on a standard procedure, such as the Facial Identification Scientific Working Group (FISWG) measurements [5], within the

Analyse, Comparison, Evaluation and Verification (ACE-V) framework [6]. Examples of these measurements are shown in Fig. 8.1. Forensic experts performing this task are generally well trained [7, 8]. Further, the UK MET police has a branch of *Super-Recognisers*, who are individuals *naturally gifted* in recognising individuality in faces [9]. The recognisers will calculate the strength of a match between two images, for instance a mugshot and a CCTV video frame, and present their results in a report. This can be used as a forensic investigation tool, as the results are presented in a comprehensible, evidential standard form. Some examples of the FISWG measurements are shown in Fig. 8.1.

Today's AFR systems are powerful tools, with the capacity of generating matches many orders of magnitude faster than humans. Additionally, with modern Deep Learning systems, accuracy has, from an empirical standpoint, surpassed that of humans. However, it is currently limited in its capacity to explain its decisions. This limits its utility in forensic investigation scenarios. AFR has been used in court as evidence in a few cases in the USA. However we believe these cases fall under the category of *misuse* rather than valid use cases. Generally AFR is used as a forensic intelligence tool, where a forensic examiner is often supported by the AFR generating a *shortlist* of the top *n* matches between a known gallery and a trace image. A *Human in the Loop* approach is followed, where a human expert performs the final forensic analysis and reporting.

As a result, any progress in AFR can be directly applied to support investigations in forensic cases whenever a strong, evidential reasoning is required. The aim of this chapter is to describe the main challenges and enablers for Forensic Biometrics, particularly for the analysis of human faces, and to discuss the most relevant techniques as well as the most likely future research directions. In Sect. 8.2 the main factors facilitating the implementation of automatic face recognition systems, both related to technological as well as legal and social issues, are described. Among them, Machine Learning, or AI-based models are discussed in subsection 8.2.1, while regulatory and social factors are considered in subsection 8.2.2.

The main challenges and roadblockers for the development and application of biometrics and computer-based face recognition in forensic cases are considered and analyzed in Sect. 8.3. They include technological limitations, such as the quality, bias and scarcity of real data, discussed in subsections 8.3.1, 8.3.2 and 8.3.3, as well as social acceptance, often driven by the media, and related to the misuse of automatic face recognition systems, discussed in subsection 8.3.5. The last Sects. (8.4 and 8.5) are devoted to the discussion around potential research avenues and conclusions relating to the current and future exploitation of automatic face recognition in forensic biometrics.

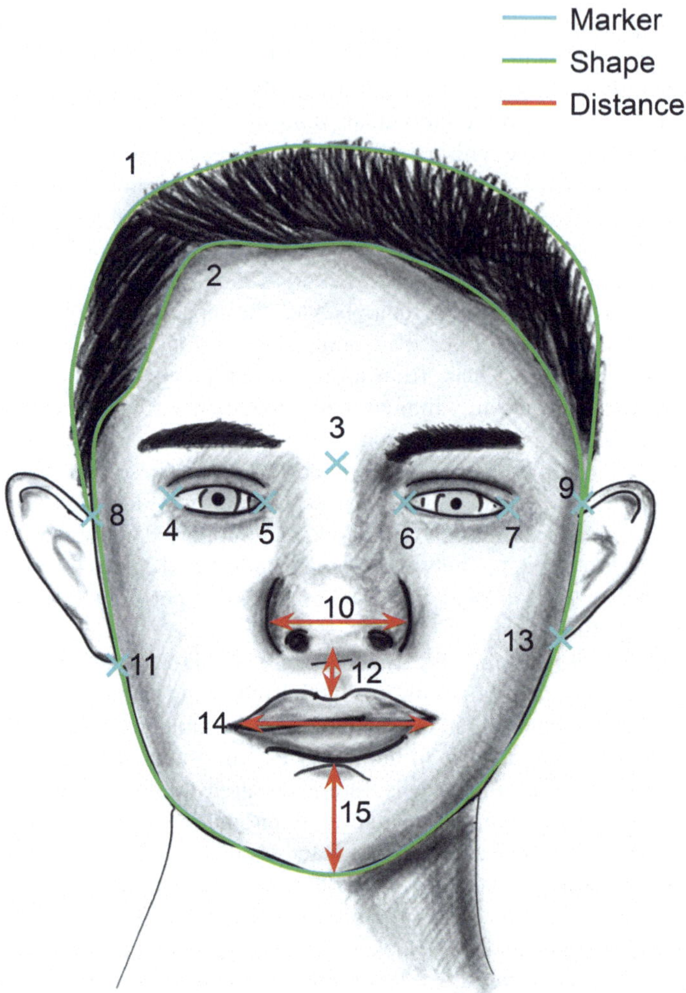

Fig. 8.1 Subset of the Holistic FISWG characteristic measurements. Marker positions in blue, shape cues in green, distances in red. 1: Cranial Vault shape/availability, 2: Facial Shape, 3: Nasal root position, 4–7: Eye corner positions 8–9: Ear tops, 10: Nasal width, 11 + 13: Ear bottoms, 12: Nose-mouth distance, 14: Mouth width, 15: Mouth-chin distance

8.2 Enablers of Forensic Biometrics

Two kinds of enablers for the deployment of biometrics and AFR in forensic cases are presented. Firstly, **AI technologies** are described, also discussing how speed and accuracy have improved biometric matching performance. Additionally, in Sect. 8.2.1.1, 8.2.1.2 and 8.2.1.3, also the relevance of eccentric techniques, such as **heterogeneous face recognition**, **3D face reconstruction** and **AI explainability**, is discussed. In Sects. 8.2.1.4 and 8.2.1.5 the impact of **data sprawl** and **novel applications** on new forensic applications of face recognition are analysed.

Secondly, **non-technical enablers** are considered. Finally, in Sects. 8.2.2.1 and 8.2.2.2, the **education** and **regulation** of biometric technologies and how the appropriate understanding and control of FFR technology are discussed in terms of enabling progress and crossing the valley of death for implementation.

8.2.1 AI Technologies for Face Recognition

The research conducted by Bledsoe, Wolf and Bisson in 1964, where facial measurements were manually taken and fed into a computer for classification, is widely considered to be the earliest work on automatic face recognition [10, 11]. However, because the research funding was provided by an unnamed intelligence agency, little of the work was published, not even on widely recognized scientific forums. The doctoral dissertation by Takeo Kanade was the next notable attempt to design a computer-based automatic system to recognize human faces from digital pictures [12]. Later, in 1987, the Karhunen-Loe've expansion was firstly proposed by Michael Kirby and Lawrence Sirovich, to linearly encode a dataset of facial images [13, 14]. This research was further extended by Matthew Turk and Alex Pentland who presented the first fully automatic system based on the Singular Value Decomposition of face images into a set of orthonormal "Eigenfaces" [15]. The same technique was also applied to detect a face within a given image. Other methods based on the classification of different image features, such as the Scale Invariant Feature Transform [16], Local Binary Patterns [17], Gabor Wavelets [18, 19], or even vectorized raw images [20], among others, were addressed. These methods, often described as *handcrafted* or classical techniques, design the image encoding and classification process based on well defined mathematical derivations.

Computer-based face recognition performance shifted significantly with the advent of Convolutional Neural Networks (CNNs). A first hardware implementation of Artificial Neural Networks, based on basic electrical circuits, has been jointly developed in 1943 by the neurophysiologist Warren McCulloch and the mathematicians Walter Pitts [21]. Subsequently, over the past 70 years, a full theory of data processing for simple, shallow networks, also with hidden layers, has been developed through the efforts of many researchers, including Frank Rosenblatt and Stephen Grossberg, among others [22–24]. However, the development of cost effective, powerful computing platforms, mainly based on GPUs, and the developments in the theory of Machine Learning, allowed to design and implement very complex architectures, including several hidden layers [25].

As the name suggests, similar to image processing techniques for feature extraction, such as Gabor band-pass filtering [26] and SIFT pyramidal filtering [27], the output of almost each layer within a CNN can be compared to the convolution of an image with a bank of *learned* filters. CNNs obviate the need for the hand-crafted filter design by automatically learning the filter weights from the input data. As the filter weights correspond to the activation parameters of each node connection in the network. Given a medium-sized CNN includes several layers, each with thousands of nodes, its representational capacity is significantly greater than any conventional handcrafted filtering method. Deep network models are generally designed with a fine-to-coarse structure, progressively reducing the scale of the input through the use of *pooling* operations to aggregate neighboring information. In order for non-linear functions to be learned by the model, non-linearity operators are also embedded.

To deploy any given deep learning model architecture for recognition, a training process is required to produce highly descriptive *embeddings* at the final layer. Training can be performed in many ways; the simplest is to append a classification layer after the last pooling layer of the network and adjust the connection weights by progressively back-propagating the error through the network. The size of the classification layer is (x,c), where x is the length of the embedding vector and c is the number of identities in the training dataset.. The classification error is computed with a suitable loss function, such as Cross Entropy Loss. After reaching a given error margin, the classification layer can be removed, retaining the *embeddings* as output layer. In principle, the descriptive ability, or the generalization power, of the *embeddings* is determined by the variability of the data in the training set. The similarity of two given images, or match score, is determined by computing the distance, according to some similarity metrics, between their two corresponding embeddings.

CNNs led to a step-change in facial recognition performance. Accuracy on benchmark datasets, considered extremely challenging at the time, swiftly reached the fabled 99.99% mark creating a need for newer, more challenging datasets. As the power of the machine learning techniques increased, by necessity, datasets with more face images of increasing low quality, and including additional variations in pose, lighting and expression, are required.

VGG-Face [28], among the best known and deployed CNNs, is possibly one of the first CNNs to be designed specifically for face recognition. The authors semi-automatically collected a dataset of 2.6 M images of 2.6 k different identities. The data was manually checked to identify and discard some of the wrongly labeled entries.

From this experiment, it resulted that the performance achieved training the network with a noisy, but larger dataset, including a few wrong labeled and poor quality samples, are better than using a smaller, clean dataset. Initially the model training was performed back-propagating the softmax log-loss and subsequently, to improve the model performance in terms of classification accuracy, triplet-loss was applied.

The Deep hidden IDentity features network model (DeepFace) [29] is an hybrid, 8 layer convolutional network, including both fully connected and locally connected layers, designed to exploit a large set of small models extracted from image patches at different scales. The output of the models was aggregated to build the final embedding. This was one of the first research papers suggesting AFR could outperform HFA. DeepID [30] and its variants (DeepID2, DeepID2 + , DeepID3) exploited fusion of multiple networks.

Specifically, the images of different facial regions and scales are separately fed into networks with the same architecture. The features learned from different networks are concatenated to form a powerful face representation, implicitly capturing the spatial information of face parts.

Softmax, the most commonly used training loss function, performs well in *closed-set* classification tasks, such as the Imagenet Large Scale Visual Recognition Challenge (ILSVRC) [31], where all the samples in the training and testing datasets are equally labeled. However, in real applications, face recognition is an *open-set* task, requiring the deployed network model to generalise well outside the training set. As an attempt to overcome these limitations, ArcFace [32] and the former error loss functions Sphereface and Cosface, projects the feature vectors onto a hypersphere such that they all have unit length. In this manner the geodesic distance (the distance across the surface of the hypersphere) between samples of the same class is minimised, while enforcing a larger margin between samples from different classes. This approach significantly improved the network capability to generalise classification across unknown identities and it is currently the best performing loss function for training face recognition models. As ArcFace requires a reasonably good initial state for the embeddings, often models are first trained with Cross Entropy Loss and then fine tuned with ArcFace.

CNNs are often exploited as a *backbone* for distilling a high level representation of the image features to be deployed by other task-dependent processes. Originally designed for Natural Language Processing [33], Vision Transformers (ViTs) can be also used as feature extraction backbones. ViTs split an input image into a set of primitives which are recursively compared one another, by means of a so called *self-attention* mechanism [34, 35]. Lacking the inductive biases of CNNs the ViT required a large amount of data and training to perform comparably. However, when presented with even larger amounts of data the ViT began to outperform. The inductive biases of the CNN, while beneficial with smaller amounts of data, became a constraint when data became very large; the ViT proved more general and scalable with the capacity for distant information, within an input, to communicate. In the modern world where data are progressively becoming more numerous, it is plausible that Vision Transformers will become the pre-eminent Vision model. The basic architectures of the CNN and the ViT are shown in Fig. 8.2.

The high performance of visual transformers naturally lead to an increased research interest and efforts. Notable works include the Shifted Window Transformer [36], Data Efficient Image Transformer [37] and the Longformer [38].

The superior classification accuracy and matching speed of AI based methods is a significant enabler of FFR. While the amount of time for a human to form a final match for evidence presentation will likely always remain the same or even increase (should new standards or requirements for face match evidence be introduced), decreasing the time for the generation of a suspects shortlist and increasing the matching accuracy are significant advantages that AI models can provide.

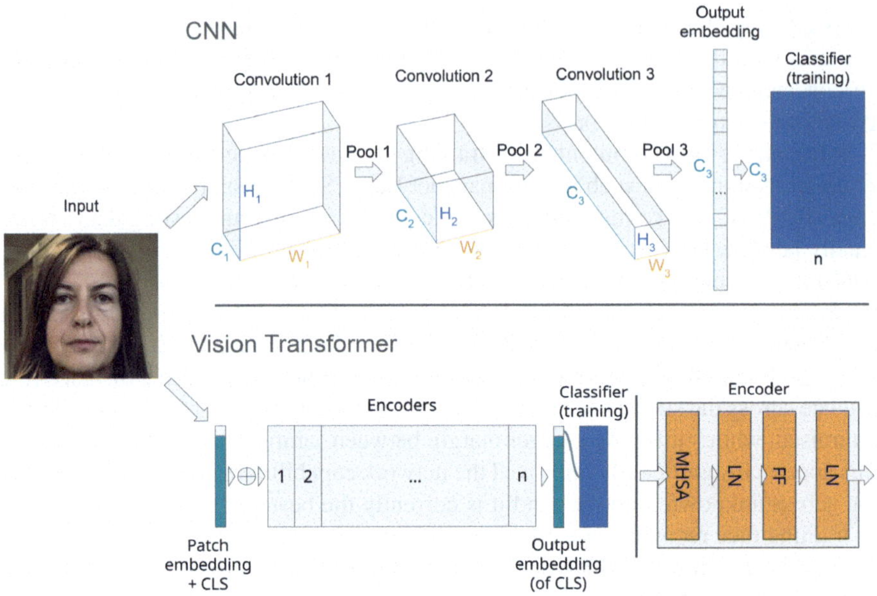

Fig. 8.2 Basic architectures of the CNN (above) and the ViT (below)

8.2.1.1 Heterogeneous Face Recognition

In several forensics cases, it is necessary to compare face images captured with different devices and from different environments. For example, if a face image captured from a CCTV camera on the crime scene is not available, a face sketch can be drawn by a *Forensic Sketch Artist* from the description given by eyewitnesses.

Matching sketches with digital pictures is a challenging task. Firstly, the sketch is based upon the memory of the eyewitness. Memory recall ability varies among people, as well as the capability to accurately describe their memory, leading to inaccurate or even wrong descriptions of the face. Secondly, the ability of the sketch artist to accurately understand the eyewitness description of the suspect varies. This is also compounded by their drawing ability. Additionally, other factors, such as the use of color, choice of artistic equipment and the background, increase the complexity of the task and may induce additional errors in the final sketch. The result is a sketched face image which may significantly differ from the actual suspect's face appearance, thus severely challenging any automatic face recognition system.

Several approaches to Heterogeneous Face Recognition have been proposed in the literature. In [39] two classical face matching techniques, based on holistic and component-based features, are successfully applied to a new face sketch database. Tang and Wang [40] compute the mapping from a dataset of facial pictures to the corresponding sketches. The computed mapping function is then applied to convert a reference digital picture into a synthetic sketch, to be matched against the hand-drawn face sketch of the suspect. More recently, deep learning-based approaches have been proposed, but the scarcity of data strongly hinders the research endeavors. Wan et al. and Fang et al. [41, 42] use a specially designed Generative Adversarial Network (GAN) (residual dense U-Net) to both generate a dataset of synthetic face sketches and to perform matching. With the data being synthesized as part of the process a large training dataset is not required. In Fig. 8.3 examples of generated synthetic face sketches are shown.

Other approaches [44, 45] apply transfer learning from pre-trained networks, both reducing the difference between face sketch and picture features and the number of images required for training.

Another example of heterogeneous face recognition is the comparison of images captured at different wavelengths. For instance, infrared (IR) cameras can capture

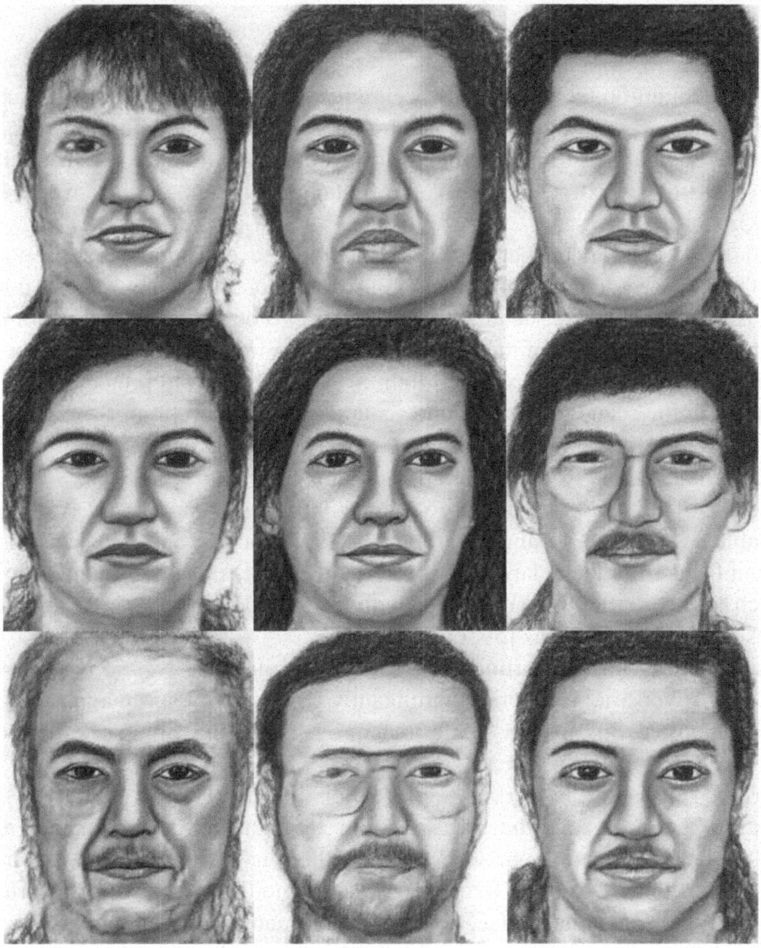

Fig. 8.3 Examples of sketches generated by a composition-aided GAN [43]

face images under low ambient illumination levels, to be matched against pictures acquired under daylight conditions [46, 47]. Another example is 3D to 2D face recognition. In [48] a pair of 2D and 3D face images are matched by projecting the 3D data to the estimated pose in the 2D image. The proposed method is applied to match electronic Identity Documents (eID) data to access data stored in the cloud [49].

Matching 3D to 2D face representations can be useful whenever the facial pose in a picture taken, for example, from a CCTV camera in the crime scene varies significantly from a mugshot of a suspect. The same procedure can be applied to improve the matching performance of an automatic face identification system at a border crossings checkpoint.

8.2.1.2 3D Face Reconstruction

3D facial recognition techniques has been a research subject for several years [50, 51], yet 3D data is not as easy to acquire as 2D data. That said, however, a 3D model may be obtained from 2D images in several ways, for example from either a sequence of images extracted from video footage, or two images, or even a single image [52–54].

Until the advent of deep learning-based methods, several approaches proposed in the past were based on the **triangulation** of two or more images, where the distance of all visible points in the scene, observed from two or more sensors, is computed by comparing the position of their projections on the image planes [55]. To perform an **active triangulation,** a structured light projector is used to project a pattern on the objects in the scene to improve the accuracy in the detection of surface points. **Shape from Shading** allows to estimate the 3D shape of an object by computing the surface normal vectors from the variations in image brightness [56].

In [57, 58] **3D Face Priors** are computed from 3D models (also called 3D Morphable Models) to parametrize both the 3D structure and facial expressions of human faces from facial keypoints extracted from 2D images. Recently the same approach has been seamlessly integrated with CNN models to better learn and capture changes in facial expressions [59, 60].

Deep learning-based methods, including Convolutional Neural Networks and Generative Adversarial Networks, significantly advanced the speed and accuracy of 3D face reconstruction from a single image, by leveraging large-scale face image datasets [61, 62].

In [63, 64] a neural network is trained to distill a feature representation jointly embedding 2D images and the corresponding 3D data. In this approach, synthetic data is exploited to train the network to learn the relationship between 2D images and the underlying 3D shapes. Recently diffusion models were applied as priors, to compute a highly accurate 3D face reconstruction (named Bidirectional Reflectance Distribution Function) from a single input image [65, 66].

The **Neural Radiance Field** (NeRF), which has gained considerable attention recently [67], enables the creation of highly detailed and realistic renderings from different viewpoints. NeRF represents 3D scenes as a radiance field, which is effectively approximated by a neural network. The radiance field provides a comprehensive description of both color and volume density for every point within the scene, allowing the synthesis of 2D images from any viewpoint. NeRF-based techniques have been successfully applied to face reconstruction [68, 69].

Despite the remarkable progress and potential of 3D reconstruction methods, when applied to face image data, the computed 3D data is likely to contain some errors, which can induce matching errors and restrict its usefulness as conclusive evidence. Therefore, precautions must be taken to prevent errors in the reconstruction from leading to gross mistakes in the matching process.

8.2.1.3 Explainability

Most forensic processes require a detailed description of the procedures followed to reach a decision, also reporting the choices made during the process. This is important to allow a forensic expert to clearly explain to a judge or a jury the process followed to build the body of evidence and the reliability of the conclusions reached. If any of the steps followed cannot be explained the entire reporting may be invalid. However, providing an explanation of the underpinning computational process is almost impossible for current deep learning models. In fact, despite of the unsurpassed performance of deep network models, a theory of deep learning is still missing [70]. For this reason, deep networks performance is rated in terms of accuracy, repeatability, robustness or other empirical metrics, but without any means for explaining how and why these results are obtained. AI explainability techniques attempt to provide information on the internal processes of deep models and address the lack of a theoretical background.

Dimensionality reduction (DR) techniques, including Principle Components Analysis (PCA), Multidimensional Scaling (MDS), Sammon mapping and Twisted Stochastic Neighborhood Embeddings (T-SNE), are often applied to visually represent high dimensional data. Among them, T-SNE allows the random projection of points from the original, high-dimensional space to the desired lower dimension. The projection is optimised to preserve as much as possible the inter-point distances in the low dimensional space. In [71] the *face space* generated by a CNN is visualized with T-SNE plots. By observing the plots, it is possible to derive some properties of the face representation distilled by the CNN. For example, the image quality increases from the center toward the periphery of the space, while other features such as the head pose are encoded by angular proximity within single identities.

Among the available deep learning models, Vision Transformers are intrinsically easier to be explained. In fact, the self-attention mechanism, with the class tokens attending the whole image and insisting on the most informative features, allows to provide an overall description of the underlying classification process by displaying the face image areas of higher attention. In Fig. 8.4 the attention maps computed from a visual transformer trained on face images are shown.

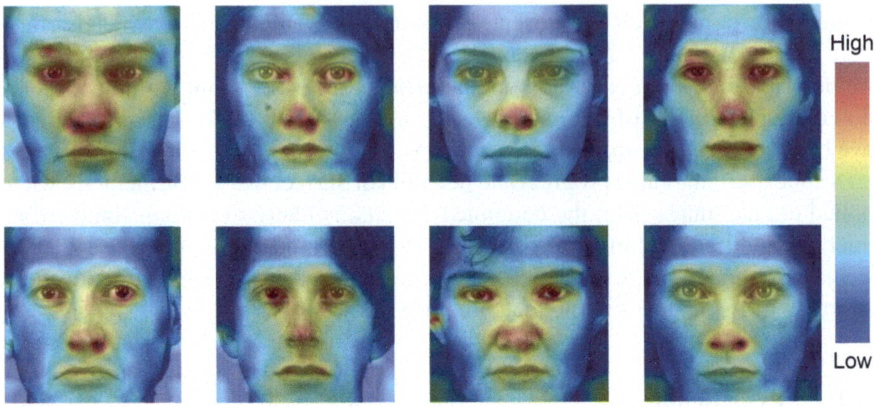

Fig. 8.4 Attention maps computed from a visual transformer trained on face images from the KDEF dataset [72]. The color encodes the intensity of the attention, as the number of times a point is taken into account during the self-attention process

As can be seen, the model is focusing on, or looking at, the most salient features of the face such as the eyes, nose and mouth. Interestingly, the attention mechanism embedded in vision transformers, as well as also the activation maps extracted from the hidden layers of CNNs, are marginally aligned with the quick and repeated changes in gaze directions observed in human vision while observing human faces [73–75].

8.2.1.4 Data Sprawl

In the earliest days of face recognition (~1960s), data was almost always proprietary. Some of the first work was conducted by Bledsoe, Wolf and Bisson, where their data were not images, but in fact measurements of the face [76]. If a researcher wanted to investigate this field, they had to collect their own data, be that images or measurements. The first large-scale public face database was the FacE REcognition Technology (FERET) database, developed by the National Institute of Standards in Technology (NIST) in the USA. This database contained 14,126 images of 1199 different subjects. The Face Recognition Vendor Tests (FRVT) came next as a mechanism for public evaluation of FR systems. Later NIST released the largest available dataset at the time, the Face Recognition Grand Challenge (FRGC) as a public test of available state of the art FR systems.

There are currently (as of October 2023) some large datasets available in the public domain. One commonly used dataset for training deep models is CASIA-WebFace with 500,000 images of 11,000 identities. Others for testing, with smaller sample counts but still large identity counts, include Labelled Faces in the Wild and Celeb-A. The largest dataset we have found is WebFace260M which in its largest (noisy) form has 260 M images of 4 M identities. This dataset is very big; in raw form it occupies around 50 TB of storage, and is at least an order of magnitude higher in sample and identity count than anything that came before publicly. The authors also offer an automatically cleaned smaller version called WebFace42M, with 42 M images of 2 M identities [77].

Most law enforcement agencies employ their own proprietary or national datasets for training AI models. The US Federal Bureau of Investigation deploys a database made of 640 M face images, including driving license mugshots from people residing in 21 out of 50 states [78]. Recently, the UK government announced plans to allow the police force to access the UK passport database to improve the performance of automatic face recognition technologies applied to catch criminals [79].

8.2.1.5 Novel Applications

New and emerging applications, such as novel applications of data classification or advanced adversarial approaches for evading recognition, may facilitate the introduction of biometric technologies to support forensic analysis.

Kinship verification [80], to determine if two subjects are related based on their picture, may contribute to the body of evidence in forensic intelligence or also in criminal investigations.

Biometric technologies can also be applied to cadaver segments for corpse identification. However, due to *postmortem* body deformations, including facial features, matching data from live and dead body parts. In [80] the authors report high error rates in the comparison of dead faces from pictures of the same living person, but samples captured within 48 h *postmortem* are still found to be useful for identification. The 3D-face reconstruction of the deceased can be either performed by forensic reconstruction specialists, or automatically. Kahler et al. [82] reconstruct human faces automatically from a 3D model of the skull. Even though errors may be induced by the lack of knowledge of the real muscle and skin structure of the face, the speed and accuracy achieved by the computer-based reconstruction make it useful for identification in forensic cases.

The automatic recognition of facial marks and tattoos, may also contribute to a body of evidence or assist in shortlist generation. Skin marks such as scars, moles, freckles, tattoos or deformities cannot uniquely characterize a subject, but they can significantly reduce the potential set of matches, or even allow to eliminate erroneous matches. As facial marks are always included in the list of facial features analysed by a forensic examiner [5], the automatic face mark identification and recognition can allow the forensic expert to accelerate the matching process. In [83] a Laplacian of Gaussian operator is applied on a normalised face image to detect marks. An improvement in Rank-1 matching accuracy, on the FERET and Mugshot databases, is reported by fusing the scores from recognition of facial marks with the scores from the FaceVACs commercial face recognition system.

Face recognition technology can be applied to detect adversarial behaviors, including facial alterations such as make-up, surgery or deliberate occlusion. The recent mass-usage of surgical masks during the COVID-19 pandemic led to increased research efforts in *periocular* recognition, to better exploit the image area around the eyes region for recognition [84]. Making the recognition process robust to face aging is also very important in matching pictures of the same individual captured at different times [85]. However, the lack of large longitudinal datasets, including face images of the same subjects taken far apart in time, somehow hindered the development of high performing deep learning models for age-independent face recognition.

8.2.2 Non Technological Enablers

Two main non-technological enablers to FFR can be identified. Firstly, national **regulations** and how appropriate control structures to discipline the use of AFR can enable its practical use in society. Secondly, **education** may lead to a better understanding of the strengths and limits of AFR techniques, thus avoiding their misuse in police investigations and other forensic processes.

8.2.2.1 Regulation

The lack of standards, codes of practice or guidelines is a peculiar inhibitor of AFR for producing evidence in forensic cases. Rather than acting as a blocker, proper regulations may enable and facilitate the deployment of AFR by providing the correct feeling to citizens, and avoiding the current hostile climate observed in some states and city councils.

In April 2021, drafting the AI act, the European Commission introduced the first regulatory framework for AI within the EU [86]. The proposed legislation is anticipated to undergo final approval by the beginning of 2024, paving the way for implementation during 2024 and 2025. This initiative scrutinizes AI systems, across various applications, evaluating and categorizing the risk posed to users. Each identified risk level involves a different regulation level. The outlined rules establish specific obligations for both providers and users contingent on the level of risk associated with the AI model in question. For instance, real-time and remote biometric identification systems, such as facial recognition technology, fall under this regulatory scope. AI systems deemed to carry an unacceptable risk, posing a significant threat to individuals, will be prohibited under the AI act.

Until AI-based systems, such as forensic biometric technologies, are accurate, unequivocally unbiased, and their potential misuse impaired, their acceptance and wide deployment will be hindered. Appropriate regulations can be a viable avenue to circumvent the current situation. With standards requiring interracial equity in performance, only recognition systems with proven unbiased performance can be used in civil applications. Minimum accuracy requirements and a comprehensive evaluation procedure could enforce performance constraints not only ensuring accurate matching but also boosting public trust. On the other hand, regulations on the practical use, limits of use and limits on interpretation of results could limit the potential for misuse.

8.2.2.2 Education

In forensic applications, the use of biometric recognition systems should be always supervised by a human operator and coupled with the support of a forensic expert. It is essential for anyone utilizing such systems to thoroughly grasp its abilities, restrictions, and appropriate use. As AFR can be an extremely powerful tool for personal identification, testing and licensing of practitioners is required. However, as discussed in Sect. 2.1.3, as it is not always straightforward to discern the reasoning behind a decision, explainability still remains one of the main AI challenges. Nevertheless, a fundamental understanding of the system's operational principles can notably assist human operators in making accurate investigative decisions and ethical choices.

As demonstrated by recent data related to the Federal Beaureu of Investigation (FBI) operational use of AFR, many operators lack the necessary training to use them accurately and responsibly. Between October 2019 and March 2022, seven law enforcement agencies within the Departments of Homeland Security and Justice used four facial recognition services from commercial and nonprofit entities to support criminal investigations. According to the Government Accountability Office (GAO), across the FBI, only 10 people out of 196 staff that accessed the service, completed the facial recognition training [87]. Education is fundamental, both for the users of AFR technology and for the general public. If public understanding of a technique, how and what it can be used for, and why it is useful, increases, so does their trust. Education should be differentiated on the basis of the usage and knowledge of the users. For example, biometric evidence should be described to a jury differently than to a judge. This is a matter of serious consideration as fingerprint evidence has been extensively presented in court for a long time [88].

8.3 Roadblockers of Forensic Biometrics

The adoption of biometrics in general and face recognition in particular, within the context of forensic science is a complex subject, involving several challenges. The decisions made by face recognition systems or forensic experts may have far reaching consequences, both at an individual level and in the larger social schema. We identify five major blockers to current FFR. The first two are related to the data automatic systems and humans are presented, specifically **data quality** (Sect. 8.3.1) and **data retraction** (Sect. 8.3.2). Next is **unfairness and bias**, i.e. how certain groups of individuals can be treated differently to others by an automatic system (Sect. 8.3.3). FFR has received significant media attention due to the **misuse of the technology**, and this is considered in Sect. 8.3.5. Finally, as discussed in Sect. 8.3.4, despite the high performance and power of modern automatic systems, they are not easily accepted to build **evidence** to be presented in court.

8.3.1 Data Quality

Biometric data quality encompasses most of the potential variations in the data captured in forensic scenario. Such variations may include the subject's pose, facial expression and age, or related to the image capturing device, such as illumination, resolution, motion blur, lens distortion and color depth.

Gallery images, such as custody pictures, are generally taken in very well controlled conditions. The head pose is fixed, neutral expression and without unnecessary adornments, such as eyeglasses. On the contrary, trace images, such as CCTV video images, may include any sort of variability. A forensic examiner, matching a trace image with a gallery image, needs to mentally remove all variabilities to focus the attention on the most descriptive and stable facial features. However, if the noise in the data is very high, it may surpass the amount of discriminative information making it impossible to produce a reliable match.

As it can be observed in Fig. 8.5, to enforce the generalization capability of the computational model, the data used for training face recognition systems often contain large variations. The largest and most useful datasets for training face recognition models are *scraped* from the internet. To build such datasets, large volumes of digital pictures, in this case containing human faces, are taken unscrupulously anywhere they can be found on the web, regardless of their quality. However, the quality of trace samples can simply be too low to be matched.

The matching accuracy reported in Fig. 8.5 is computed from a Vision Transformer trained with CASIA-Webface, a dataset of approximately 500 k images and 11 k

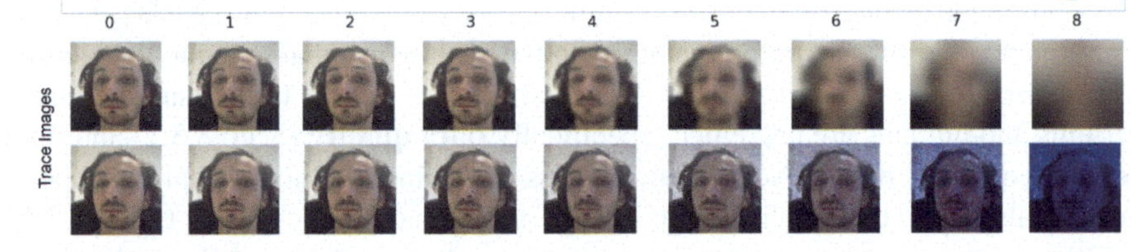

Fig. 8.5 Plot of the computed matching performance with increasing degradation of the face image quality due to image noise and decrease in resolution

identities. The embeddings for the gallery image and each of the degraded traces were extracted from the final hidden state of the class token and compared with a cosine similarity metric. As it can be noticed, the degradation of the trace image quality can be directly correlated with matching performance.

While imaging technologies, such as CCTV, are continuously improving, data quality is still an open issue in forensic face recognition. One reason is that traces are captured in a non-cooperative scenario, where the subjects in the crime scene, being aware of the capturing device, hide themselves to prevent being recognized. *Non-cooperative* refers to the subject being captured during normal behavior, and no other action is required, as opposed to **cooperative** where imaging conditions are well controlled and the subject is expected to cooperate to capture a high quality sample. To avoid being recognized, facial adornments such as a hat, mask, make-up, sun-glasses, facial hair and even aesthetic surgery, can be used to *obfuscate* the identity [89].

8.3.2 Data Retraction

The advent of deep learning models, on one hand allowed to quickly build very efficient automatic system to analyze and classify large amounts of data. On the other hand, these systems are progressively becoming more data hungry, requiring large datasets for training. Over time, several biometric datasets have been publicly released for scientific purposes, but sometimes they are suddenly retracted within a few years. However, retracting datasets produce the effect of both hindering the research endeavor, and lowering the scientific value of the experimental results published, as they can no longer be reproduced for fair comparison with the most recent research outcomes. Some well known examples of retracted face image datasets include: MegaFace with 6 M images from about 700 k identities, MS-Celeb [90] with 10 M images from 100 k identities, UMDFaces with 400 k images and 3.7 M video frames, from approximately 11 k identities. Other datasets such as VGG-Face2, with 3 M images from 9,000 identities, were made available as a set of web-links to the images, but never properly maintained. Probably because of the recently emerged privacy concerns for large face image datasets being collected from unaware people, the links to the images have been removed. Some of the links survived and are still connected to images sets, but only 800 k out of the original 3 M images are available.

The only solution to this problem is to establish a clear ethical and legal framework for the collection and storage of face image datasets. The European GDPR paved the way for reaching such standard and the AI act somehow extended its scope to the usage of datasets with deep learning models. However, the implementation of these regulations is not always an easy task and it may significantly vary from one country to another.

8.3.3 *Unfairness and Bias*

Computer programs are expected to be inherently impartial in the way data is processed, making no difference in their functionality regardless of the user. However, dealing with biometric identification, where the system is expected to perceive individual differences, this is even more true. Fairness in biometric identification entails impartiality, where no bias or preference is shown for any individual or group, based on inherent or acquired characteristics. Consequently, the performance of unfair biometric systems may change for different groups of individuals. More often in deep learning models, as the performance is determined by characteristics of the training data, unfairness is due to bias. Primarily due to the lower performance, sometimes demonstrated in matching ethnic minorities, bias in forensic biometrics is subject to much scrutiny, especially by the media.

Bias in deep learning models is observed as measurable partiality or discrimination in the predictions. Bias can be introduced into the system by unbalanced training data, the model architecture or even through the user feedback [91]. Two main sources of bias may be identified:

- **Data bias** primarily arises from some form of partiality in the collection of the training dataset. This may occur for several reasons: when aggregation metrics fail to consider subgroups, when the dataset's composition does not correspond to real-world proportions, when specific features are inaccurately measured, or when subgroups are not randomly sampled. Another source of bias arises from the user feedback, which can be influenced by prior biased machine learning decisions. For instance, feedback from users on previously biased deep learning decisions, such as the display of the most popular social posts, can be incorporated into training datasets, propagating the bias back in the system.
- **Model bias** is due to intrinsic characteristics of the model or inappropriate evaluation methods. For instance, it can arise when performance evaluation methods or benchmarks are unsuitable for the model in use. Additionally, specific algorithmic design choices, such as optimization, regularization, or the application of statistically biased estimators, can influence the final decision introducing bias.

As fair, transparent, and accountable AI technologies for socially impactful facial analysis applications are required, bias demands specific attention. Currently, considerable research efforts are devoted to explore new methodologies to measure and alleviate bias in the data as well in the computational models [92–94].

An effective technique to determine the bias level in a face image dataset is to feed the data to an attribute classifier to compute the age, ethnicity and gender distributions. In Fig. 8.6 the results of attribute classification for the CASIA-WebFace [95] obtained with the DeepFace library [96] are shown.

It is worth noting that the distributions presented in Fig. 8.6 are also obtained by a deep-learning model, which may be also biased. As such, the computed distributions can be only diagnostic of the data unbalance, but cannot provide an exact measurement. As it can be noticed, the CASIA-WebFace is strongly biased towards

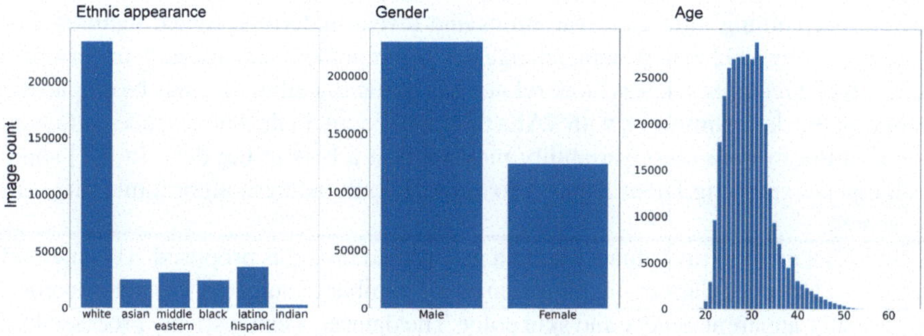

Fig. 8.6 Ethnicity, gender and age distributions of the CASIA-WebFace dataset [95]. Distributions were computed automatically with a pre-trained DeepFace model. Ethnicity and gender labels are also produced by DeepFace [96]

ethnically white, male subjects. The age distribution shows a peak over the age range 20–35, with no children and very few subjects over 50. Moreover, the labels produced by the DeepFace library approximately cover the spectrum of visually recognizable human facial features. However, as the taxonomy of apparent human characteristics such as age and gender is a matter of debate, it is difficult to attribute a well defined set of labels. The lack of a clear understanding on how to categorize sub-groups of human appearance, hinders the accurate evaluation of the data and model bias level. In order to mitigate bias in the data, more data can be added [97–99]. Towards this end, samples belonging to unbalanced classes can be added to the dataset, thus equalizing the data distributions among different categories. The added data can be either real or synthetic, for example produced by a generative model [100]. Another approach is to assign weights to the data, measuring the representativeness of each class and sample additional data points from underrepresented classes. Similarly, the loss weights assigned to the deep network nodes can be adjusted, increasing the weights of under-represented classes. Finally, the data batches can be balanced by randomly selecting data from each class. However, in this way individual members of under-represented classes might be over-represented, with respect to members of over-represented classes, leading to over-fitting.

In [93] an approach to assess bias in phenotypic subgroups for both face datasets and models is proposed. Data for each subject is firstly labeled based on the apparent gender and skin type. Gender is annotated using a binary sex label, which is a common practice among companies providing gender classification systems. The skin type is annotated using the six-point Fitzpatrick phenotype classification system, the gold standard for skin classification by dermatologists [101], ranging from lighter to darker. Data bias is determined simply by counting the number of subjects for each class label.

Another approach to assess bias within a dataset involves the use of AI generative models, which can reveal hidden features within a dataset. Generative models, such as Generative Adversarial Networks (GANs) and Variational Autoencoders (VAEs) proved to be effective in measuring data bias [92]. Such models can harness latent features explaining inter-class variations and reveal underrepresented features. For example, using a GAN to generate images of different faces, consistently underrepresented facial features, such as those related to a particular ethnicity, may be diagnostic of bias in the data. Similarly, with VAEs the small count, in the latent space, of factors contributing to intra-class variability may suggest a bias in the data. In [92] some techniques exploiting latent features to automatically address algorithmic bias, are presented.

In [93] a method to evaluate bias in a pre-trained model is proposed. This method requires a balanced dataset, including an equal number of subjects for each category, specifically apparent gender and skin color. The dataset is exhaustively processed by the pre-trained model, and the misclassification rates across the pre-defined classes indicates the bias level of the model. There is an abundance of tools and guidelines for assessing the fairness of AI models, including those listed below.

- Capsa© [102] is a tool, designed by Themis AI©, to quantify the risk and providing risk metrics for machine learning models.
- Aequitas© [103] is a tool to identify discrimination and bias in deep learning models, and providing guidance for the implementation to implement of fair predictive models.
- AI Fairness 360 (AIF360) [104] is an open-source library including techniques for identifying and alleviating bias in machine learning models at various stages of their lifecycle.
- Google©, Microsoft© and Meta© are releasing principles and practices concerning the ethical development and deployment of AI technologies [105–107], with the aim to offer insights into the company's strategy concerning AI ethics, fairness, transparency, privacy, and accountability in AI applications.

8.3.4 Proof of Evidence

Producing a body of evidence is the main goal of forensic investigation, but exploiting technological solutions to automatically infer biometric evaluations may be challenging. For human face analysis a set of measurements and observations, such as FISWG, are manually taken by a forensic examiner from a trace sample. These measurements are then used to perform a comparison with to a set of reference face images, often custody pictures, and the results reported in a document. This process must be rigorous, well detailed and, as a consequence, time consuming. An automatic system could potentially allow to maintain the rigor and detail but significantly reducing the time required, thus limiting the burden on courts and police forces, and minimising, or even avoiding, the time under custody of wrongly convicted individuals.

How can automatic systems produce forensic evidence? The most common practice in forensic science is to produce evidence as a *likelihood ratio*. This is the ratio between the probability of a match, given the prosecution hypothesis (when two samples match) and the probability of a match given the defense hypothesis (when the two samples do not match), as reported in Eq. 8.1:

$$LLR = \frac{P(m|Hp|)}{P(m|Hd|)} \tag{8.1}$$

where m is the match score, Hp and Hd are the prosecution and defense hypothesis respectively. The likelihood ratio represents the strength of a match when the typicality of the trait is taken into account.

The complexity of facial traits makes it difficult to produce evidence from an automatic system. Other complex biometric traits have been used in court, such as gait, or the way people walk. In [108] a set of hand-crafted features are exploited to measure human gait. From the genuine and impostor scores distributions a confidence measure for the matching scores is computed. According to a survey on the admissibility of forensic gait analysis [109], a stronger collaboration between legal and biometric experts is required to push automatic gait analysis forward, while evidence should be treated with caution, without a clear code of practice. The same conclusions can be drawn for automatic forensic face recognition. Moreover, as reported in [110], progress in automatic forensic face recognition is also limited by the lack of well grounded and *forensically relevant* datasets, collected from forensic use cases.

Uniqueness of biometric traits is also a matter of concern for the adoption of automatic systems in forensic investigations. All measurable biometric traits are developed in human embryos from the combination of both genetically and phenotypically driven, not fully stochastic, processes. Therefore, as human population increases, the probability for two individuals to present similar or even identical biometric traits increases. The Aadhar system, deployed by the Indian government, refused to register a new citizen because his fingerprints partially matched with 7 other individuals already present in the 1.3 billion people dataset [111]. The uniqueness of fingerprints was challenged under *Daubert's ruling* in the case of USA vs Byron Mitchell, as the defense claimed: "*the error rate is not known and the fundamental premise that 'Fingerprints are distinctive or unique' has not been put to test.*"[112]. Nowadays error rates are mandatory to present biometric evidence in court, and may hinder the jury's confidence in the evidence being presented. However, a cross-examination which brings to light the errors of the presented evidence, claimed to be incontrovertible, is even more harmful [88].

The estimation of AI model uncertainty may provide a more objective and understandable metric for the jury on the reliability of the presented evidence. Evidential Deep Learning [113, 114] has been proposed as an effective method to learn both data and model uncertainty in the computed predictions. In practical terms, taking into account both random factors and the absence of knowledge, the training process not only allows the network model learning to make predictions but also to assess their confidence or uncertainty. This can be extremely valuable in applications, such as forensic intelligence or investigations, where understanding and managing classification uncertainty is crucial.

For several social, ethical and legal reasons, regardless of the performance of automatic biometric recognition systems in terms of processing time and accuracy, it is important to maintain a human in the loop while producing a body of evidence. However, to improve legal outcomes and increase efficiency, it is also imperative to progressively increase the adoption of computer-based recognition systems in the procedures followed by forensic examiners.

8.3.5 Technological Misuse

The misuse of forensic face recognition technologies, often due to the lack of proper training or misapplication of regulations and good practices, coupled with public and media scrutiny, hampered the way towards their wider adoption in forensic cases.

Many documented cases reported the police misuse of FR technology to be generally associated with misidentification of minority groups. Particularly, there has been significant media scrutiny on a large number of cases involving black people. This underscores the clear link to biases, possibly stemming from human prejudices and the flawed training of deep neural networks.

In February 2019, Nijeer Parks was put under custody for 10 days, following which he was positively identified through off-the-shelves facial recognition software, in an accusation involving shoplifting candy and an attempt to hit a police officer with a car at an Hampton Inn. However, as it was later proved, at the time of the incident Parks was physically located 30 miles away from the crime scene. In November 2019 the case was dismissed for lack of evidence [115].

Despite he never visited Georgia State, Randal Quran Reed, a black male, was wrongly imprisoned for 3 days after he was misidentified in a crime scene occurred in Atlanta, by off-the-shelves facial recognition software. As of October 2023, he was filing a legal action against the Atlanta police force.

More recently, Porcha Woodruff, a black pregnant woman, was arrested in Detroit for robbery and car theft, after being identified by a witness among the faces of the individuals top ranked by a facial recognition system analysing the video footage, from a security camera in the crime scene [116].

A commonality among all reported misidentification cases is the improper handling of automatic recognition systems, and non-compliance to established investigative procedures. The rush to expedite processes, relying solely on fast technological outputs, often overcomes the requirement of critical human analysis and oversight. In turn, police officers overlook the nuances and complexities involved in accurately assessing situations, resulting in a flawed interpretation of the data provided by facial recognition systems. Moreover, the outcome of an automatic face search should never be used alone as evidence of guilt. For this reason, a proper procedure involves a forensic expert carefully analysing the list of suspects produced by the automatic face recognition software. Whenever a positive matching subject is found, the data should be used as investigative lead and not to automatically perform an arrest. In several cases, the procedures have been purposively trimmed or changed, aiming to speed up the decision-making process. This hasty approach often sacrifices thorough investigations, leading to misinterpretations and, consequently, misidentifications having detrimental impacts on individuals and even on the judicial system.

8.4 Future Directions of Forensic Face Recognition

Four key opportunities to advance forensic face recognition can be identified:

- **Evidence**: any understandable, explainable and provable algorithmic principle, including error rates, is fundamental for AI systems to produce evidence.
- **Bias**: impartiality of decisions is needed to ensure public trust.
- **Performance**: improved recognition accuracy leads to a more reliable matching.
- **Regulation**: appropriate regulation may facilitate the adoption of automatic face recognition systems to complement current investigative and legal practices in a transparent, accountable manner, reducing the potential for misuse.

One of the central issues regarding the deployment of deep learning-based face recognition is how forensic *evidence* is produced.

However, the progress in techniques for AI explainability is paving the way towards a better integration of contributions from automatic processes for human forensic experts to build a body of evidence. Most if not all current models are based on single image embeddings, limiting explanability to the formation of the embeddings alone. On the contrary, future dual input deep models, performing the embedding and matching simultaneously, may naturally lead to explanations involving both the formation of image embeddings and matching.

Ensuring equitable outcomes across human subgroups is of paramount importance in legal processes. For reaching the same acceptance in court of common biometric traits, such as fingerprints, as support to forensic investigation, unbiased and provably fair forensic face recognition systems are required. As discussed in Sect. 8.3.3, techniques for measuring and mitigating bias should be further developed. Additionally, biometric datasets containing fair and proportionally distributed data, should be also collected.

Even though a limited literature on Vision Transformers is currently available [35, 117], due to both the high performance and with larger datasets such as WebFace260m becoming available, growing research efforts are expected. On the other hand, the current scarcity of publicly available data, due to ongoing privacy regulations, such as the AI act, requires to design shallower, more understandable models which can be trained on a limited amount of data.

To enable adoption and use of new technologies in forensic procedures, appropriate regulations for automatic face recognition are envisaged. Scientists should closely work with forensic experts, legal professionals and policy makers pushing regulations to re-enable and control the use of automatic face recognition systems. A better understanding of the social impact of face recognition must be developed. This way several benefits will be attained, including lower policing costs, reducing false convictions as well the time required to identify the real culprit of a crime.

8.5 Conclusions

This chapter provided an overview of the potential of modern biometric recognition systems for forensic investigations and intelligence. The fast development of high performing, data-driven deep learning (often dubbed *AI*) models, attracted the attention of the media, depicting a catastrophic scenario of a near future society where these technologies are massively exploited and even misused for the control, or even replacement of humans. Often, current AI models are even considered "too clever" to be safely used in public environments. On the other hand, some "technology enthusiasts" pushed the local application of automatic recognition systems without a complete knowledge and control, thus sometimes exceeding the border of its fair usage.

Surely, this general outlook cannot facilitate the development and proper adoption of forensic biometrics technologies. Therefore an appropriate balance among the main actors and driving forces need to be achieved.

On one hand, scientific research must be facilitated to provide a basis for next generation technologies in the service of forensic science. This requires the availability of more data from real (possibly cold) cases to model and train more effective and secure automatic recognition systems. In turn, data can be only made available through a closer, open collaboration between academic institutions, forensic institutes, police forces and legal entities. In turn, policy makers and national authorities are required to objectively, but quickly analyze the state of the art and provide a sufficiently large and open framework to safely perform data collection and testing. On the other hand, training and education is of paramount importance to both diffuse a fair knowledge of the real potential and risks of current AI technologies, but also to allow all players involved in processing forensic cases to fully understand the "who", "what", "when" and "how" of current and future automatic biometric recognition systems.

Certainly, forensic science can greatly benefit from the adoption of todays' and tomorrow's technologies for automatic face recognition. The increasing scientific production in forensic biometrics of the last ten years and the growing interest of industry constitute a significant proof of its potential. However, further efforts, in several directions, are required to design, develop and deploy automatic face recognition systems in forensic procedures which are widely accepted and properly regulated, improving safety for a better lifestyle.

Acknowledgements This research has been conducted within the "Bando Fondazione di Sardegna 2022-2023" grant, the *Secure Passwordless Authentication for Digital Identities* (SPADA) project funded by the Italian Ministry of Education, University and Research (project code: ARS01 00785) and the PNRR M4C2 project Ecosystem of Innovation for Next Generation Sardinia (e.INS)—Spoke 06 "Digital Transformation".

References

1. Bertillon, A., McClaughry, R., & McClaughry, R. (1988). Signaletic Instructions Including the Theory and Practice of Anthropometrical Identification. *The Werner Company* (1896).
2. Xiang-Xin, Z., & Chun-Ge, L. (1988). The historical application of hand prints in Chinese litigation. *Journal of Forensic Identification, 38*(6), 277–284.
3. Galton, F. (1892). Fingerprints. Macmillan and Co.
4. Casetext (2003). State v. sansing. Supreme Court of Arizona, 409 Ariz. Adv. Rep. 23 206 Ariz. 232(77 P.3d 30). https://casetext.com/case/state-v-cons
5. Forensic Investigation Scientific Working Group. (2018). Facial image comparison feature list for morphological analysis. Retrieved January 20, 2020.
6. Reznicek, M., Ruth, R. M., & Schilens, D. M. (2010). Ace-v and the scientific method. *Journal of Forensic Identification, 60*(1), 87–103.
7. Forensic Investigation Scientific Working Group. (2020). Guide for role-based training in facial comparison. Psychon. Bull. Rev. https://www.fiswg.org/fiswg guide for rolebased training in facial comparison v1.0 20200717.pdf
8. Moreton, R., Havard, C., Strathie, A., & Pike, G. (2021). An international survey of applied facematching training courses. *Forensic Science International, 327*(110947), 1–32.
9. Russell, R., Duchaine, B., & Nakayama, K. (2009). Super-recognizers: People with extraordinary face recognition ability. *Psychonomic Bulletin and Review, 16*, 252–257.
10. Bledsoe, W. W. (1964). The model method in facial recognition. Tech. Rep. PRI 15, Panoramic Research, Inc.
11. Bledsoe, W. W., & Chan, H. (1965). A man-machine facial recognition system-some preliminary results. Tech. Rep. PRI 19A, Panoramic Research, Inc.
12. Kanade, T. (1973). Picture processing system by computer complex and recognition of human faces.
13. Kirby, M., & Sirovich, L. (1990). Application of the karhunen–loeve procedure for the characterisation of human faces. *IEEE Transaction Pattern Analysis and Machine Intelligence, 12*, 831–835.
14. Sirovich, L., & Kirby, M. (1987). Low-dimensional procedure for the characterization of human faces. *Journal of the Optical Society of America. A, Optics and Image Science, 4*(3), 519–524.
15. Turk, M., & Pentland, A. (1991). Eigenfaces for recognition. *Journal of Cognitive Neuroscience, 3*(1), 71–86.
16. Bicego, M., Lagorio, A., Grosso, E., & Tistarelli, M. (2006). On the use of sift features for face authentication. In 2006 Conference on Computer Vision and Pattern Recognition Workshop (CVPRW'06) (pp. 35–35). IEEE
17. Ahonen, T., Hadid, A., & Pietikainen, M. (2006). Face description with local binary patterns: Application to face recognition. *IEEE Transactions on Pattern Analysis and Machine Intelligence, 28*(12), 2037–2041.
18. Khellat-Kihel, S., Lagorio, A., & Tistarelli, M. (2018). Face recognition "on the move" combining incomplete information. In 2018 International Workshop on Biometrics and Forensics (IWBF) (pp. 1–6). IEEE.
19. Shen, L., & Bai, L. (2006). A review on Gabor wavelets for face recognition. *Pattern Analysis and Applications, 9*, 273–292.
20. Bicego, M., Grosso, E., & Tistarelli, M. (2005). Face authentication using one-class support vector machines. In Advances in Biometric Person Authentication: International Wokshop on Biometric Recognition Systems, IWBRS 2005, Beijing, China, October 22–23, 2005. Proceedings (pp. 15–22). Springer.
21. McCulloch, W., & Pitts, W. (1943). A logical calculus of ideas immanent in nervous activity. *Bulletin of Mathematical Biophysics, 5*, 115–133.
22. Carpenter, G., & Grossberg, S. (1987). A massively parallel architecture for a self-organizing neural pattern recognition machine. *Computer Vision, Graphics, and Image Processing, 37*, 54–115.

23. Grossberg, S., & Mingolla, E. (1986). Computer simulation of neural networks for perceptual psychology. *Behavior Research Methods, Instruments, and Computers, 18*, 601–607.
24. Rosenblatt, F. (1962). Principles of Neurodynamics: Perceptrons and the Theory of Brain Mechanisms. Spartan books.
25. LeCun, Y., Bengio, Y., & Hinton, G. (2015). Deep learning. *Nature, 521*(7553), 436–444.
26. Gabor, D. (1946). Theory of communication. part 1: The analysis of information. *Journal of the Institution of Electrical Engineers-part III: Radio and Communication Engineering, 93*(26), 429–441.
27. Lowe, D. G. (2004). Distinctive image features from scale-invariant keypoints. *International Journal of Computer Vision, 60*, 91–110.
28. Parkhi, O., Vedaldi, A., & Zisserman, A. (2015). Deep face recognition. In BMVC 2015-Proceedings of the British Machine Vision Conference 2015. British Machine Vision Association.
29. Taigman, Y., Yang, M., Ranzato, M., & Wolf, L. (2014). Deepface: Closing the gap to human-level performance in face verification. In Proceedings of the IEEE Conference on Computer Vision and Pattern Recognition (pp. 1701–1708).
30. Sun, Y., Wang, X., & Tang, X. (2014). Deep learning face representation from predicting 10,000 classes. In 2014 IEEE Conference on Computer Vision and Pattern Recognition (pp. 1891–1898).
31. Russakovsky, O., Deng, J., Su, H., Krause, J., Satheesh, S., Ma, S., Huang, Z., Karpathy, A., Khosla, A., Bernstein, M., Berg, A. C., & Fei-Fei, L. (2015). ImageNet large scale visual recognition challenge. *International Journal of Computer Vision (IJCV), 115*(3), 211–252.
32. Deng, J., Guo, J., Xue, N., & Zafeiriou, S. (2019). Arcface: Additive angular margin loss for deep face recognition. In Proceedings of the IEEE/CVF Conference on Computer Vision and Pattern Recognition (pp. 4690–4699).
33. Vaswani, A., Shazeer, N., Parmar, N., Uszkoreit, J., Jones, L., Gomez, A. N., Kaiser, L., & Polosukhin, I. (2017). Attention is all you need. In Advances in neural information processing systems (Vol. 30).
34. Dosovitskiy, A., Beyer, L., Kolesnikov, A., Weissenborn, D., Zhai, X., Unterthiner, T., Dehghani, M., Minderer, M., Heigold, G., Gelly, S., Uszkoreit, J., & Houlsby, N. (2021). An image is worth 16×16 words: Transformers for image recognition at scale.
35. Zhong, Y., & Deng, W. (2021). Face transformer for recognition. arXiv preprint arXiv:2103.14803
36. Liu, Z., Lin, Y., Cao, Y., Hu, H., Wei, Y., Zhang, Z., Lin, S., & Guo, B. (2021). Swin transformer: Hierarchical vision transformer using shifted windows. In Proceedings of the IEEE/CVF International Conference on Computer Vision (pp. 10012–10022).
37. Touvron, H., Cord, M., Douze, M., Massa, F., Sablayrolles, A., & Jegou, H. (2021). Training data- ´efficient image transformers and distillation through attention. In International Conference on Machine Learning (pp. 10347–10357). PMLR.
38. Zhang, P., Dai, X., Yang, J., Xiao, B., Yuan, L., Zhang, L., & Gao, J. (2021). Multi-scale vision longformer: A new vision transformer for high-resolution image encoding. In Proceedings of the IEEE/CVF International Conference on Computer Vision (pp. 2998–3008).
39. Klum, S., Han, H., Jain, A. K., & Klare, B. (2013). Sketch based face recognition: Forensic versus composite sketches. In 2013 International Conference on Biometrics (ICB) (pp. 1–8). IEEE.
40. Tang, X., & Wang, X. (2004). Face sketch recognition. *IEEE Transactions on Circuits and Systems for video Technology, 14*(1), 50–57.
41. Wan, W., & Lee, H. J. (2019). Generative adversarial multi-task learning for face sketch synthesis and recognition. In 2019 IEEE International Conference on Image Processing (ICIP) (pp. 4065–4069). IEEE.
42. Fang, Y., Deng, W., Du, J., & Hu, J. (2020). Identity-aware cyclegan for face photo-sketch synthesis and recognition. *Pattern Recognition, 102*, 107249.
43. Wan, W., Gao, Y., & Lee, H. J. (2019). Transfer deep feature learning for face sketch recognition. *Neural Computing and Applications, 31*, 9175–9184.

44. Yu, J., Xu, X., Gao, F., Shi, S., Wang, M., Tao, D., & Huang, Q. (2020). Toward realistic face photo–sketch synthesis via composition-aided GANs. *IEEE Transactions on Cybernetics, 51*(9), 4350–4362.
45. Sert, M., & Boyacı, E. (2019). Sketch recognition using transfer learning. *Multimedia Tools and Applications, 78*, 17095–17112.
46. Wilder, J., Phillips, P. J., Jiang, C., & Wiener, S. (1996). Comparison of visible and infrared imagery for face recognition. In Proceedings of the second international conference on automatic face and gesture recognition (pp. 182–187). IEEE.
47. Ouyang, S., Hospedales, T., Song, Y. Z., Li, X., Loy, C. C., & Wang, X. (2016). A survey on heterogeneous face recognition: Sketch, infra-red, 3d and low-resolution. *Image and Vision Computing, 56*, 28–48.
48. Ruiu, P., Lagorio, A., Cadoni, M., & Grosso, E. (2023). Enhancing eid card mobile-based authentication through 3d facial reconstruction. *Journal of Information Security and Applications, 77*, 103577.
49. Masala, G. L., Ruiu, P., & Grosso, E. (2018). Biometric authentication and data security in cloud computing. In *Computer and network security essentials* (pp. 337–353).
50. Lagorio, A., Cadoni, M., Grosso, E., & Tistarelli, M. (2015). A 3d algorithm for unsupervised face identification. In 3rd International Workshop on Biometrics and Forensics (IWBF 2015) (pp. 1–7). IEEE.
51. Tistarelli, M., Cadoni, M., Lagorio, A., & Grosso, E. (2016). Blending 2d and 3d face recognition. In Face recognition across the imaging spectrum (pp. 305–331).
52. Zollhofer, M., Thies, J., Garrido, P., Bradley, D., Beeler, T., Perez, P., Stamminger, M., ´ Nießner, M., & Theobalt, C. (2018). State of the art on monocular 3D face reconstruction, tracking, and applications. Computer Graphics Forum (Eurographics State of the Art Reports 2018), (Vol. 37(2)).
53. Tistarelli, M., & Sandini, G. (1990). Estimation of depth from motion using an anthropomorphic visual sensor. *Image and Vision Computing, 8*(4), 271–278.
54. Grosso, E., & Tistarelli, M. (1995). Active/dynamic stereo vision. *IEEE Transactions on Pattern Analysis and Machine Intelligence, 17*(9), 868–879.
55. Moons, T., Van Gool, L., & Vergauwen, M., et al. (2010). 3d reconstruction from multiple images part 1: Principles. *Foundations and Trends® in Computer Graphics and Vision 4*(4), 287–404.
56. Barron, J. T., & Malik, J. (2014). Shape, illumination, and reflectance from shading. *IEEE Transactions on Pattern Analysis and Machine Intelligence, 37*(8), 1670–1687.
57. Blanz, V., & Vetter, T. (1999). A morphable model for the synthesis of 3d faces. In Proceedings of the 26th Annual Conference on Computer Graphics and Interactive Techniques (pp. 187–194).
58. Egger, B., Smith, W. A., Tewari, A., Wuhrer, S., Zollhoefer, M., Beeler, T., Bernard, F., Bolkart, T., Kortylewski, A., Romdhani, S., et al. (2020). 3d morphable face models—Past, present, and future. *ACM Transactions on Graphics (ToG), 39*(5), 1–38.
59. Jourabloo, A., & Liu, X. (2016). Large-pose face alignment via cnn-based dense 3d model fitting. In Proceedings of the IEEE Conference on Computer Vision and Pattern Recognition (pp. 4188–4196).
60. Zhu, X., Lei, Z., Liu, X., Shi, H., & Li, S. Z. (2016). Face alignment across large poses: A 3d solution. In Proceedings of the IEEE Conference on Computer Vision and Pattern Recognition (pp. 146–155).
61. Gecer, B., Ploumpis, S., Kotsia, I., & Zafeiriou, S. (2019). Ganfit: Generative adversarial network fitting for high fidelity 3d face reconstruction. In Proceedings of the IEEE/CVF Conference on Computer Vision and Pattern Recognition (pp. 1155–1164).
62. Dou, P., Shah, S. K., & Kakadiaris, I. A. (2017). End-to-end 3d face reconstruction with deep neural networks. In Proceedings of the IEEE Conference on Computer Vision and Pattern Recognition (pp. 5908–5917).
63. Richardson, E., Sela, M., & Kimmel, R. (2016). 3d face reconstruction by learning from synthetic data. In 2016 Fourth International Conference on 3D Vision (3DV) (pp. 460–469). IEEE.

64. Li, Y., Su, H., Qi, C. R., Fish, N., Cohen-Or, D., & Guibas, L. J. (2015). Joint embeddings of shapes and images via cnn image purification. *ACM Transactions on Graphics (TOG), 34*(6), 1–12.
65. Papantoniou, F. P., Lattas, A., Moschoglou, S., & Zafeiriou, S. (2023). Relightify: Relightable 3d faces from a single image via diffusion models. arXiv preprint arXiv:2305. 06077.
66. Luo, H., Nagano, K., Kung, H. W., Xu, Q., Wang, Z., Wei, L., Hu, L., & Li, H. (2021). Normalized avatar synthesis using stylegan and perceptual refinement. In Proceedings of the IEEE/CVF Conference on Computer Vision and Pattern Recognition (pp. 11662–11672).
67. Mildenhall, B., Srinivasan, P. P., Tancik, M., Barron, J. T., Ramamoorthi, R., & Ng, R. (2021). Nerf: Representing scenes as neural radiance fields for view synthesis. *Communications of the ACM, 65*(1), 99–106.
68. Zhang, H., Xu, Y., Dai, T., |& Tang, T. C. K., et al. (2023). Fdnerf: Semantics-driven face reconstruction, prompt editing and relighting with diffusion models. arXiv preprint arXiv: 2306.00783.
69. Zhang, J., Li, X., Wan, Z., Wang, C., & Liao, J. (2022). Fdnerf: Few-shot dynamic neural radiance fields for face reconstruction and expression editing. In SIGGRAPH Asia 2022 Conference Papers (pp. 1–9).
70. Poggio, T., Banburski, A., & Liao, Q. (2020). Theoretical issues in deep networks. *PNAS, 117*(48), 30039–30045.
71. O'Toole, A. J., Castillo, C. D., Parde, C. J., Hill, M. Q., & Chellappa, R. (2018). Face space representations in deep convolutional neural networks. *Trends in Cognitive Sciences, 22*(9), 794–809.
72. Lundqvist, D., Flykt, A., & Öhman, A. (1998). Karolinska directed emotional faces. *PsycTESTS Dataset, 91*, 630.
73. Cadoni, M., Lagorio, A., & Grosso, E. (2020). Do cnn's features correlate with human fixations? In Proceedings of the 3rd International Conference on Applications of Intelligent Systems (pp. 1–6).
74. Cadoni, M., Lagorio, A., Khellat-Kihel, S., & Grosso, E. (2021). On the correlation between human fixations, handcrafted and cnn features. *Neural Computing and Applications, 33*, 11905–11922.
75. Cadoni, M., Nixon, S., Lagorio, A., & Fadda, M. (2022). Exploring attention on faces: similarities between humans and transformers. In 2022 18th IEEE International Conference on Advanced Video and Signal Based Surveillance (AVSS) (pp. 1–8). IEEE.
76. de Leeuw, K. M. M., & Bergstra, J. (2007). *The history of information security: A comprehensive handbook*. Elsevier.
77. Zhu, Z., Huang, G., Deng, J., Ye, Y., Huang, J., Chen, X., Zhu, J., Yang, T., Lu, J., Du, D., & Zhou, J. (2021). Webface260m: A benchmark unveiling the power of million-scale deep face recognition. In 2021 IEEE/CVF Conference on Computer Vision and Pattern Recognition (CVPR) (pp. 10487–10497). IEEE Computer Society.
78. Guliani, N. S. (2019). The fbi has access to over 640 million photos of us through its facial recognition database. ACLU. https://www.aclu.org/news/privacy-technology/fbi-hasaccess-over-640-million-photos-us-through
79. Singleton, T. (2023). Police access to passport photos 'risks public trust'. BBC. https://www.bbc.com/news/technology-67004576
80. Wu, X., Feng, X., Cao, X., Xu, X., Hu, D., Lopez, M. B., & Liu, L. (2022). Facial kinship verification: ´ A comprehensive review and outlook. *International Journal of Computer Vision, 130*(6), 1494–1525.
81. Khoo, L. S., & Mahmood, M. S. (2020). Application of facial recognition technology on identification of the dead during large scale disasters. *Forensic Science International: Synergy, 2*, 238.
82. Kahler, K., Haber, J., & Seidel, H. P. (2003). Reanimating the dead: Reconstruction of expressive faces ¨ from skull data. *ACM Transactions on Graphics (TOG), 22*(3), 554–561.

83. Jain, A. K., & Park, U. (2009). Facial marks: Soft biometric for face recognition. In 2009 16th IEEE International Conference on Image Processing (ICIP) (pp. 37–40). IEEE.
84. Sharma, R., & Ross, A. (2023). Periocular biometrics and its relevance to partially masked faces: A survey. *Computer Vision and Image Understanding, 226*, 103583.
85. Sawant, M. M., & Bhurchandi, K. M. (2019). Age invariant face recognition: A survey on facial aging databases, techniques and effect of aging. *Artificial Intelligence Review, 52*, 981–1008.
86. European Parliament. (2023). Eu AI Act: First Regulation on Artificial Intelligence. News European Parliament. https://www.europarl.europa.eu/news/en/headlines/society/20230601STO93804/eu-aiact-first-regulation-on-artificial-intelligence
87. Goodwin, G. (2023). Facial Recognition Services: Federal Law Enforcement Agencies Should Take Actions to Implement Training, and Policies for Civil Liberties. U.S. Government Accountability Office. https://www.gao.gov/products/gao-23-105607
88. Garrett, B., & Mitchell, G. (2013). How jurors evaluate fingerprint evidence: The relative importance of match language, method information, and error acknowledgment. *Journal of Empirical Legal Studies, 10*(3), 484–511.
89. Nappi, M., Ricciardi, S., & Tistarelli, M. (2016). Deceiving faces: When plastic surgery challenges face recognition. *Image and Vision Computing, 54*, 71–82.
90. Musil, S. (2023). Microsoft quietly pulls massive facial-recognition database from internet. CNET. https://www.cnet.com/tech/tech-industry/microsoft-quietly-pulls-facialrecognition-database-from-internet/
91. Mehrabi, N., Morstatter, F., Saxena, N., Lerman, K., & Galstyan, A. (2021). A survey on bias and fairness in machine learning. *ACM Computing Surveys (CSUR), 54*(6), 1–35.
92. Amini, A., Soleimany, A. P., Schwarting, W., Bhatia, S. N., & Rus, D. (2019). Uncovering and mitigating algorithmic bias through learned latent structure. In Proceedings of the 2019 AAAI/ACM Conference on AI, Ethics, and Society (pp. 289–295).
93. Buolamwini, J., & Gebru, T. (2018). Gender shades: Intersectional accuracy disparities in commercial gender classification. In Conference on Fairness, Accountability and Transparency (pp. 77–91). PMLR.
94. Hardt, M., Price, E., |& Srebro, N. (2016). Equality of opportunity in supervised learning. Advances in Neural Information Processing Systems (Vol. 29).
95. Yi, D., Lei, Z., Liao, S., & Li, S. Z. (2014). Learning face representation from scratch. arXiv preprint arXiv:1411.7923.
96. Serengil, S. I., & Ozpinar, A. (2021). Hyperextended lightface: A facial attribute analysis framework. In 2021 International Conference on Engineering and Emerging Technologies (ICEET) (pp. 1–4). IEEE.
97. Lu, Y., Guo, H., & Feldkamp, L. (1998). Robust neural learning from unbalanced data samples. In 1998 IEEE International Joint Conference on Neural Networks Proceedings. IEEE World Congress on Computational Intelligence (Cat. No. 98CH36227) (Vol. 3, pp. 1816–1821). IEEE.
98. More, A. (2016). Survey of resampling techniques for improving classification performance in unbalanced datasets. arXiv preprint arXiv:1608.06048
99. Zhou, Z. H., & Liu, X. Y. (2005). Training cost-sensitive neural networks with methods addressing the class imbalance problem. *IEEE Transactions on Knowledge and Data Engineering, 18*(1), 63–77.
100. Sattigeri, P., Hoffman, S. C., Chenthamarakshan, V., & Varshney, K. R. (2018). Fairness gan. arXiv preprint arXiv:1805.09910
101. Fitzpatrick, T. B. (1988). The validity and practicality of sun-reactive skin types i through vi. *Archives of dermatology, 124*(6), 869–871.
102. Lolla, S., Elistratov, I., Perez, A., Ahmadi, E., Rus, D., & Amini, A. (2023). Capsa: A Unified Framework For Quantifying Risk in Deep Neural Networks. arXiv preprint arXiv:2308.00231.
103. Saleiro, P., Kuester, B., Hinkson, L., London, J., Stevens, A., Anisfeld, A., Rodolfa, K.T., & Ghani, R. (2018). Aequitas: A bias and fairness audit toolkit. arXiv preprint arXiv:1811.05577
104. Bellamy, R.K., Dey, K., Hind, M., Hoffman, S.C., Houde, S., Kannan, K., Lohia, P., Martino, J., Mehta, S., & Mojsilovic, A., et al. (2018). AI Fairness 360: An Extensible Toolkit for

Detecting, Understanding, and Mitigating Unwanted Algorithmic Bias. arXiv preprint arXiv: 1810.01943
105. Google. (2022). RESPONSIBILITY: Responsible AI practices. Google. https://ai.google/responsibility/responsible-ai-practices/
106. Kloumann, I., & Tannen, J. (2021). ML Applications—How we're using Fairness Flow to help build AI that works better for everyone. Meta. https://ai.meta.com/blog/how-were-using-fairness-flow-to-help-build-ai-that-works-better-for-everyone/
107. Microsoft. (2023). Empowering Responsible AI Practises. Microsoft. https://www.microsoft.com/en-us/ai/responsible-ai
108. Bouchrika, I., Goffredo, M., Carter, J., & Nixon, M. (2011). On using gait in forensic biometrics. *Journal of Forensic Sciences, 56*(4), 882–889.
109. Macoveciuc, I., Rando, C. J., & Borrion, H. (2019). Forensic gait analysis and recognition: Standards of evidence admissibility. *Journal of forensic sciences, 64*(5), 1294–1303.
110. Zeinstra, C. G., Meuwly, D., Ruifrok, A. C., Veldhuis, R. N., & Spreeuwers, L. J. (2018). Forensic face recognition as a means to determine strength of evidence: A survey. *Forensic Science Review, 30*(1), 21–32.
111. Srivatsa, S. (2023). Uidai and the curious case of the man whose fingerprints match seven others. The Hindu. https://www.thehindu.com/news/national/karnataka/uidai-and-the curious-case-of-the-man-whose-fingerprints-match-seven-others/article22466491.ece
112. Court of Appeals for the Third Circuit 365 F.3d 215 (3d Cir. 2004), U.C.: United States of America v. Byron Mitchell Appellant, 365 F.3d 215 (3d Cir. 2004). Justia US Law. URL https://law.justia.com/cases/federal/appellate-courts/F3/365/215/608883/
113. Amini, A., Schwarting, W., Soleimany, A., & Rus, D. (2020). Deep evidential regression. *Advances in Neural Information Processing Systems, 33*, 14927–14937.
114. Oh, D., & Shin, B. (2022). Improving evidential deep learning via multi-task learning. *Proceedings of the AAAI Conference on Artificial Intelligence, 36*, 7895–7903.
115. Thanawala, S. (2023). Facial recognition technology jailed a man for days. his lawsuit joins others from black plaintiffs. The New York Times. https://www.nytimes.com/2020/12/29/technology/facial-recognition-misidentify-jail.html
116. Hill, K. (2023). Eight months pregnant and arrested after false facial recognition match. APNews. https://www.nytimes.com/2023/08/06/business/facial-recognition-falsearrest.html
117. Nixon, S., Ruiu, P., Cadoni, M., Lagorio, A., Tistarelli, M. (2023). Exploiting face recognizability with early exit vision transformers. In 2023 International Conference of the Biometrics Special Interest Group (BIOSIG) (pp. 1–7). IEEE.

Chapter 9
Algorithmic Enforcement Tools: Governing Opacity with Due Process

Giancarlo Frosio

Abstract This chapter explores the complex interplay between Artificial Intelligence (AI), algorithmic enforcement tools and digital forensics in the context of online content moderation. As AI-driven algorithms increasingly perform roles traditionally reserved for human experts, questions of transparency, accountability and due process take centre stage. The allure of automated efficiency often clashes with the imperative for transparency, particularly when algorithms function as opaque 'black boxes,' unamenable to public scrutiny or legal review. Instead, algorithmic enforcement tools for online moderation need to meet both technical and legal standards, akin to DNA tools in forensics. These algorithms require transparent decision-making logs and must withstand scrutiny for accuracy and bias. Failure to do so may lead to inability to lawfully implement algorithmic enforcement tools. This chapter critically analyses the rising phenomenon of 'private ordering,' where online intermediaries take on roles akin to law enforcement agencies, embedding policy decisions into algorithms and affecting online behaviour beyond mere legal compliance. Shifting the liability to online intermediaries has sparked a new form of private law enforcement but also raises concerns about 'machine-made justice', thereby necessitating a careful examination under frameworks such as the European Convention of Human Rights. The chapter also critically evaluates the ethical and legal challenges this presents, including the potential for over-enforcement and the erosion of fundamental human rights like due process, privacy, freedom of speech, and freedom to conduct a business. It interrogates existing and emerging regulatory frameworks such as the Digital Services Act (DSA). The DSA, with its emphasis on algorithmic transparency, accountability, and risk assessment, offers a potential pathway to balance technological advancements with fundamental human rights.

G. Frosio (✉)
School of Law, Queen's University, Belfast, Ireland
e-mail: g.frosio@qub.ac.uk

S. Francese and R. S. P. King (eds.), *Driving Forensic Innovation in the 21st Century*,
https://doi.org/10.1007/978-3-031-56556-4_9

9.1 Introduction

In an era marked by digital transformation, Artificial Intelligence (AI) and algorithmic mechanisms have not only become subjects of societal discourse but have also evolved into crucial tools for enforcement in the online arena (this Chapter develops and updates, within the context of digital forensic, previous works, including [1–3]). These advancements reflect the evolving landscape of the swiftly burgeoning field of digital forensics. Digital forensics seeks to collect, analyze, and leverage digital evidence across various legal spectrums, increasingly intersecting with the sphere of AI-driven algorithmic enforcement. One common and salient tension pervades both these areas: the friction between automated processes and the indispensable need for transparency and accountability. In the world of algorithmic content moderation, automated tools offer the allure of efficiency, swiftly sifting through vast swaths of data. However, these mechanisms often function as opaque 'black boxes,' rendering their decision-making processes impenetrable and thereby evading public scrutiny. A similar tension manifests in the field of digital forensics, where automated algorithms can analyze extensive datasets but may lack the transparency required for the integrity of legal procedures [4, 5].

Regulatory frameworks are evolving, and legislative imperatives push online intermediaries to engineer 'forensically sound' algorithms aimed at content sanitization. Driven by the high costs associated with manual content moderation and monitoring, these online entities are increasingly resorting to algorithmic solutions. By deploying such algorithmic tools for surveillance and content filtration, online intermediaries aim to mitigate their legal liabilities. Like the genetic fingerprinting or DNA sequencing tools used in traditional forensic science, algorithmic enforcement tools must be rigorously developed to satisfy both technological and legal requirements. Just as forensic tools must come with a 'chain of custody' and detailed procedural documentation, so too must algorithmic solutions. There must be a log of how decisions were made, why certain content was flagged, and what datasets were used for training. This can prove essential during judicial reviews or legislative inquiries. Courts and regulatory bodies must scrutinize the algorithms' accuracy, reliability, and potential biases. The coming years will likely see an intense focus on developing algorithmic models that not only are effective and efficient but also can withstand rigorous legal testing.

This interplay also leads to an intriguing paradigm: the privatization of digital forensic capabilities, alongside enforcement. Online platforms make policy decisions that get embedded into algorithmic tools, which are then responsible for 'policing' the digital space. This promotes new forms of 'private ordering' in law enforcement, effectively augmented by an extra layer of automated decision-making [6].

In this context, online intermediaries are compelled to make structural modifications for content sanitization. The architecture of the internet is being coded to become the law of cyberspace, as noted by theorists such as Lessig [7, pp. 3–60; 8, p. 111], transforming algorithms into implicit enforcers and digital 'evidence gatherers' [9]. In practice, automated filtering influences online behaviour to a far greater extent than merely ensuring compliance with the law. A legal system that shifts the liability equilibrium towards online intermediaries, who wield unparalleled influence over Internet architecture, can lead to profound architectural changes designed to mitigate liability. However, this transformation may inadvertently give rise to pervasive over-enforcement, concealed from view, ultimately conditioning users to a heavily censored online environment.

Foremost in this discussion are concerns about fundamental human rights. Algorithmic enforcement tools must also be designed to protect these rights. Existing tensions between algorithmic measures and established conventions, such as the European Convention of Human Rights (ECHR) and the Charter of Fundamental Rights of the European Union [10], need thorough examination, especially concerning filtering and monitoring measures, which would fail to strike a 'fair balance' between competing fundamental rights [11, 12; see also 13–15, § 36–38; 16, pp. 791–794].

This dynamic sets the stage for a host of critical issues, including ethical considerations, questions of due process, protection of freedom of expression, privacy, freedom to conduct a business, and the balance between technological innovation and legal fidelity. It is against this backdrop that recent developments in algorithmic enforcement online acquire significant importance. These have been characterized by legislative moves, such as Article 17 of the Copyright in the Digital Single Market Directive (C-DSM Directive) and the Digital Services Act (DSA), technological innovations, and evolving judicial interpretations, all of which aim to address the complexities arising from this tension between automation and accountability.

This chapter delves further into these intricate dynamics, examining how law, technology, and ethics coalesce in the era of algorithmic enforcement and digital forensics. It will commence by defining what algorithmic enforcement entails and then explore the voluntary, judicial, and legislative forces that shape this evolving landscape. Further, the chapter will critically analyse the tug-of-war between algorithmic enforcement and human rights, covering aspects like due process, freedom of information, and freedom of business. The concluding section will propose viable solutions aimed at safeguarding human rights while capitalizing on the advantages of algorithmic enforcement.

9.2 Algorithmic Enforcement Tools

AI is defined as the capability of computer systems to perform tasks typically requiring human intellect, such as visual perception, speech recognition, and decision-making [17]. The essence of AI's transformative promise lies in semi or fully independent decision-making, which fundamentally revolutionizes the landscape of enforcement [18, pp. 505–523; 19]. In the digital realm, these advancements bear a striking resemblance to elements of forensic innovation, such as the automation of evidence gathering and analysis.

Three key attributes—authority shift, automation, and centralization—characterize algorithmic decision-making and enforcement. Firstly, enforcement responsibility is increasingly moving from public institutions to private entities. Secondly, the enforcement process becomes automated, akin to forensic tools that automatically gather and analyse digital evidence. Thirdly, centralized enforcement allows a single algorithmic action to produce legal outcomes affecting multiple individuals simultaneously. On the other hand, the automation of law enforcement undeniably confers tangible advantages, particularly in enhancing efficiency and reducing operational costs [20, pp. 1764–1765].21, Article 22]. Elaborating on this, the Article 29 Working Party interprets "legal effects" as any processing activities that significantly influence an individual's legal entitlements or freedoms—such as the rights to association, electoral participation, or judicial recourse [see 22, p. 10]. This definition is expansive enough to likely encompass the impact on freedoms related to the receipt and dissemination of information, a topic that will be discussed in further detail subsequently.23

Algorithmic enforcement is rooted in the comprehensive gathering of data, which is subsequently processed by automated algorithms for decision-making purposes. The EU's General Data Protection Regulation (GDPR) stands as a pioneering legislative framework that offers a formal definition of such algorithmic enforcement. Specifically, the GDPR identifies "automated individual decision-making" as decisions rendered purely through automated data processing activities, including profiling, that have legal or similar substantive impacts on individuals [see

Automated Content Recognition (ACR) technologies like Google Content ID and Vimeo Copyright Match have become widespread, operating on principles comparable to digital fingerprinting in forensics. These technologies utilize digital fingerprinting techniques to cross-reference uploaded files against a repository of copyrighted works submitted by rights holders. Google's Content ID system, for instance, employs a four-pronged approach: (1) muting the audio of a matching uploaded video, (2) entirely blocking access to a video found to match copyrighted material, (3) monetizing the matched video on behalf of the copyright owner by inserting ads, and (4) analyzing viewer statistics for the matched video [see]. Vimeo's Copyright Match operates in a similar fashion. Furthermore, the Content ID system offers a level of customization, enabling rights holders to selectively block or monetize content based on the extent of copyrighted material present in a contested upload. It also incorporates a dispute resolution mechanism that allows end-users to challenge any claims made by copyright owners [see 24].

In addition to content identification, search manipulation through AI algorithms aims at sanitizing online activities considered potentially illicit. Although copyright enforcement has been traditionally a primary goal of search manipulation, it spans multiple online allegedly illicit activities. Search manipulation, demotion and delisting have been used to fight child-pornography [25]. Again, these techniques have been deployed against revenge porn [26, 27]. More recently, demotion has been applied to curb extremism and radicalization [28]. For several years, Google has been actively demoting websites suspected of hosting pirated content. In 2012, the company modified its PageRank search algorithm to incorporate the number of Digital Millennium Copyright Act (DMCA) notices received against each website [29, p. 200]. Subsequently, in 2014, Google further adjusted its algorithm to downgrade autocomplete predictions that would lead to search results featuring sites already demoted under DMCA stipulations [29, p. 200]. Commonly referred to as Google's "Pirate algorithm", this computational adjustment relegates or removes purported pirate and other allegedly illicit websites to lower positions in search results, effectively diminishing their visibility.29, p. 200]. In this context, every day Alibaba identifies up to 600 million product images with an accuracy rate of 98% [29, p. 200].

On the e-commerce front, platforms like Alibaba and eBay employ intricate AI technologies to combat counterfeiting and piracy. These technologies go beyond mere enforcement to collect an enormous amount of data with high accuracy rates, almost serving as 'digital forensic units' within these platforms. Alibaba's Intellectual Property Rights Protection system, for example, employs a plethora of advanced techniques ranging from semantic recognition algorithms to real-time interception systems to take down and sanitise allegedly infringing content [see

9.3 The Emergence of Algorithmic Content Moderation

As the narrative around Online Service Providers (OSPs) transitions from one of liability to one of "enhanced responsibility" [30], it has become increasingly imperative for OSPs to engage in proactive filtering and monitoring across a range of intermediary liability issues [31]. This paradigm shift is driven by the realization that OSPs hold an unprecedented influence over the informational ecosystem and the interactions taking place within it. Various factors, including voluntary agreements, judicial verdicts, and legislative reforms such as the European Union's recent overhaul of copyright laws, have contributed to this evolving landscape.

In this context, the advent of automated filtering and online algorithmic enforcement technologies emerges as an unavoidable trajectory. For OSPs, these tools offer the only scalable way to enforce regulations, manage infringement risks, and maintain cost-efficiency. The widespread deployment of such tools reflects an era where human oversight alone can no longer bear the sheer volume and complexity of online interactions.

9.3.1 The Rise of Private Ordering: Shifting from Intermediary Liability to Enhanced Responsibility

Private ordering is increasingly taking centre stage as a favoured mechanism for online enforcement, particularly in the realm of intellectual property. The trend toward voluntary self-enforcement through algorithmic measures, as well as the more generalized cleaning-up of online content, signifies a notable shift from focusing on intermediary liability to fostering a sense of "enhanced responsibility" [3, 1–33; 32, pp. 613–630; 33, p. 13]. In this evolving landscape, policy makers, along with stakeholders such as intellectual property owners, are intensifying efforts to persuade online intermediaries to adopt self-regulatory enforcement strategies. These are implemented alongside the legally required enforcement mechanisms, amplifying the intermediary's role in maintaining the integrity of online spaces.34; see also 35, 36, pp 315–323]. In their introductory remarks to

The shift from intermediary liability to platform responsibility is initially observed on a theoretical plane, with particular emphasis on the corporate social obligations of intermediaries and their role in upholding and advancing human rights [e.g., *The Responsibilities of Online Service Providers*, Mariarosaria Taddeo and Luciano Floridi underscore the growing societal expectation for OSPs to align their operations with prevailing social and cultural norms. This elevates the discourse to ponder what responsibilities OSPs should shoulder and what ethical frameworks should govern their conduct [37, p. 1].

Taddeo and Floridi pinpoint three major ethical quandaries: the orchestration and management of access to information, issues surrounding censorship and free speech, and concerns related to user privacy [38]. Firstly, the crux of the matter, according to these scholars, is not necessarily whether OSPs should be morally accountable for the actions of their users, but rather if they bear any ethical obligations for the distribution of third-party content that could be damaging [38, p. 10]. In line with this view, some theorists advocate for assigning moral responsibilities to OSPs concerning the dissemination of harmful or contentious material [39, p. 465; 40, pp. 67–74; 41, pp. 123–132].

Once more, theories of corporate social responsibility have been adapted to the digital realm to apply principles of human rights to entities that largely function outside the jurisdiction of conventional human rights law [35]. There are arguments suggesting that responsibilities usually ascribed to States—like those acknowledged by the UN Human Rights Council's declaration asserting internet freedom as a human right—should be extended to online platforms [42, pp. 37–61; 43, pp. 523–536; but see 44, pp. 453–478]. Specifically, the preamble of the Universal Declaration of Human Rights seems to endorse corporate duties to safeguard human rights, stating that "every individual and every organ of society" should work to advance these freedoms [45, Preamble]. Additional global frameworks supporting this notion include the Declaration of Human Duties and Responsibilities [46], the preamble of the UN Norms on the Responsibilities of Transnational Corporations and Other Business Enterprises [47], and the UN Guiding Principles on Business and Human Rights [48]. In a noteworthy development, the United Nations Human Rights Council has recently passed a resolution focused on the promotion, protection, and fulfilment of human rights on the internet. This resolution also tackles the issue of creating legally enforceable guidelines concerning corporate responsibilities in upholding human rights [34].

Responses from international institutions and organizations exhibit palpable ambivalence when grappling with intricate dilemmas surrounding private algorithmic enforcement. This ambiguity may contribute to the growing advocacy for private algorithmic solutions as perhaps the only sustainable policy route, despite its potential adverse implications for fundamental rights. On one hand, the 2016 Report by the UN Special Rapporteur for Free Expression includes assertive statements cautioning against state coercion of private entities into content removal. The report explicitly states that in the realm of information and communication technology, "States must not coerce or otherwise pressure the private sector into measures that needlessly or disproportionately impede freedom of expression, be it through legislation, policies, or informal methods" [49]. Furthermore, it advises that any action to remove digital content or access customer information should conform to duly enacted law, be subject to independent scrutiny, and be a necessary and proportionate means to achieve specific goals outlined under Article 19(3) of the International Covenant on Civil and Political Rights [49]. On the other hand, a Joint Declaration by the Three Special Rapporteurs for Freedom of Expression advocates self-regulatory approaches to managing online rights. However, they note that such approaches must be balanced with adequate safeguards for individual freedoms [50]. Similarly, the OCSE contends that while enhancing the transparency and accountability of private intermediaries is a valid objective, it should not result in undue governmental control over online content [51, p. 2].

Within this emerging framework, OSPs are increasingly employing algorithmic monitoring and filtering as a self-regulatory measure to cleanse the Internet of potential infringements and illicit speech, while also shielding themselves from legal actions related to third-party content. For instance, Google introduced its Content ID system in 2008 as an automated content vetting mechanism, following a significant lawsuit by Viacom over unauthorized uploads and views of copyrighted material on the YouTube platform [52]. Similarly, in 2014, Vimeo implemented a comparable filtering system, Copyright Match, after facing a copyright lawsuit from Capitol Records and EMI for user-uploaded music videos on its Vimeo platform [53].

Governments are increasingly encouraging OSPs to voluntarily implement algorithmic filtering and monitoring as a form of self-regulation. The EU Commission's *Communication on Online Platforms and the Digital Single Market* underscores the concept that 'the responsibility of online platforms is a key and cross-cutting issue' [54, p. 9]. Essentially, the Commission advocates for imposing a proactive duty on platforms to swiftly eliminate illegal content, rather than merely responding to complaints [54, p. 8]. A subsequent 2017 Communication from the Commission advances the notion of 'enhanced responsibility', urging OSPs to adopt voluntary but effective measures for automated content moderation through the use of automatic detection and filtering technologies [30, s 3.3.1-2].

Major tech companies like Facebook, Twitter, YouTube, and Microsoft have agreed to a code of conduct with the European Commission to combat the spread of illegal hate speech online [55]. In addition, these companies have committed to sharing digital fingerprints, or "hashes", to help identify terrorist content [56, 57]. Each platform, however, will maintain autonomy in setting its own removal policies [58]. The European Commission aims to formalize these initiatives through a regulatory framework, focusing particularly on countering online terrorism. A recent recommendation from the Commission advocates for the use of automated filtering as the most effective policy tool for hosting service providers to promptly identify and remove terrorist content [59]. Similar principles are included in a recent regulation for preventing dissemination of terrorist content online that is under review by the European Parliament [60].

9.3.2 Article 17 of the C-DSM Directive

Emerging legislation, such as the EU's C-DSM Directive, suggests a pivot towards obligating OSPs to implement algorithmic enforcement for filtering and monitoring content [61; see also 62, pp. 709–750; 63, pp. 101–138]. Specifically, Article 17 of this Directive represents a departure from the EU's existing 'negligence-based', 'no-monitoring obligations' model of intermediary liability [64, Articles 14–15]. It advocates for proactive content monitoring and filtering, likely accelerating the adoption of automated systems for copyright enforcement.

To bridge the perceived 'value gap'—an alleged unfair distribution of revenues generated from the online use of copyright-protected works among industry actors along the value chain—in the EU's digital landscape [65, Explanatory Memorandum, Part 1], the C-DSM reform obliges certain Online Content Sharing Service Providers (OCSSPs) to actively prevent copyright infringement [61, recital 61]. They are required to secure fair licensing agreements with rights holders [61, Article 17(1)], covering liability for user-uploaded content [61, Article 17(1)]. In the absence of such authorization, OCSSPs must make 'best efforts' to block infringing works or face liability [61, Article 17(1) and Recital 39; see also 62, 714–722]. Additionally, they must offer dispute resolution mechanisms for unwarranted content removal [61, Article 17(2)].

While the initial draft of the C-DSM Directive explicitly mentioned the use of effective technologies for blocking copyrighted material [63, 66–71], its finalized version, particularly Article 17, doesn't explicitly mandate automated filtering. Nonetheless, the practical implications are clear: the increased liability risks are likely to push OCSSPs towards automated content recognition and blocking systems. Manually monitoring user-uploaded content would be financially and logistically infeasible, threatening the viability of OCSSPs' business models. Automation emerges as the most efficient and cost-effective solution. Moreover, the criteria for 'best efforts' in accordance with 'high industry standards' are likely to create a de facto requirement for OCSSPs to adopt algorithmic monitoring systems for two key reasons. First, they could be deemed the most effective way to prevent unauthorized content. Second, they align with prevailing industry standards, especially as leading companies like Google are already utilizing such systems. In this context, for the purpose of assessing whether 'best' efforts have been made and high industry standards' have been met, it should also be considered 'the evolving state of the art as regards existing means, including potential future developments, to avoid the availability of different types of content and the cost of such means for the services'

[61, recital 66 para 2–3].72; see also 73–76, pp. 161–197]. The decision underscores the tension between automated enforcement and fundamental rights, particularly transparency and due process [77

In shaping OCSSPs liability, the new legislation brought about widespread concerns regarding fair balancing of the new provisions with fundamental rights of users to the extent that Poland challenged the new OCSSPs' obligations before the Court of Justice of the European Union (CJEU) on this very basis, with the CJEU rejecting the request of annulment, but making important clarifications to preserve users' rights [see]. Effective platform governance should prioritize preserving users' rights. Increased online enforcement, particularly over-enforcement, restricts access to information and limits free speech, compromising democratic dialogue. The CJEU aims to protect these rights against overly aggressive algorithmic enforcement, as evident in the *Republic of Poland* decision, which suggests that users have a fundamental right to share content online without undue algorithmic moderation [78, pp. 1145–1148; 79, p. 197]. In this landscape, how can online intermediaries, the internet's gatekeepers and algorithmic architects, strike a fair balance? How can independent oversight prevent these private entities from unilaterally determining online content? What role can regulation play to avert a dystopian 'black box society' for users [80]?

9.4 Algorithmic Enforcement and Human Rights

Algorithmic enforcement by OSPs presents a conundrum for human rights. While OSPs aim to act responsibly, their automated filtering systems can inadvertently compromise key human rights. Private companies like OSPs may be fundamentally ill-suited to make balanced legal decisions on rights issues, given their lack of constitutional standing.

The 'least-cost avoiders' principle suggests that liability should be assigned to the party that can prevent or mitigate harm at the lowest cost [see 81, 82]. In the context of content moderation OSPs are 'least-cost avoiders' due to their gatekeeping functions, economies of scale, and proprietary content moderation technologies. This often leads them to implement measures to minimize liability costs related to content moderation, especially by employing automated systems prone to overblocking. The issue then becomes tri-fold. Algorithmic actions by OSPs can severely impact users' rights, such as due process, freedom of speech, information access, and data privacy. OSPs will make choices to block or filter potentially illegal online content, affecting the rights of any parties impacted by such content. Imposing rigorous obligations on OSPs could also infringe upon their freedom to conduct business.

9.4.1 Due Process, Transparency, and Black Boxes

The rise of algorithmic decision-making challenges traditional due process, which ensures fairness in laws and legal proceedings [83]. Due process encompasses fair trials and just administrative actions, supported by impartial tribunals and protected by human rights conventions [45, Article 10; 84, Article 6; 10, Article 47–50]. After the CJEU's Costeja ruling on the right to be forgotten, Google's European Communications Director, Peter Barron, admitted they never anticipated making complex decisions typically reserved for courts. Increasingly, these decisions are made by algorithms and automated systems, not just by Google's legal team.

Perel and Elkin-Koren contend that OSPs wielding algorithmic enforcement signify a fundamental change in governance. Unlike traditional law enforcement, which separates duties like detection, prosecution, and adjudication among various public entities, OSPs handle these roles collectively, emphasizing mainly detection and prevention [85, p. 481]. This centralization in the hands of a few profit-driven, potentially biased platforms undermines due process [85, p. 481] and erodes inherent trust and accountability in established legal systems [85, p. 473].

Algorithmic enforcement poses three key due process challenges closely tied to the technical intricacies of neural networks: transparency, accountability, and contestability. Transparency involves disclosing the methods used in decision-making [86, 6–7; 87, pp. 4–8; 88, pp. 23–28], accountability entails being able to take responsibility for those decisions [85, pp. 481–484; 89], and contestability allows for challenging the results [86, pp. 6–7]. A fair judicial process can't exist without satisfying these criteria. However, both accountability and contestability hinge on transparency. Without transparency, it's nearly impossible to achieve genuine accountability or contestability. Several barriers hinder a transparent algorithmic process. This includes issues like trade secrets and confidential information [90, 91, pp. 1343–1429; 92]. It also involves governmental secrecy in automated decision-making, exemplified by tax authorities not disclosing the algorithms for selecting tax audits and customs authorities keeping secret the systems for selecting companies for IP infringement checks [see 91, p. 1367; 93, p. 658]. Additionally, it covers the technical complexity of rapidly evolving algorithms, including problems related to black boxes. In particular, black box problems arise when the inner workings of algorithms are so complex or opaque that even their developers can't easily explain how decisions are made, further complicating efforts at transparency, accountability, and contestability [80, 94, pp. 56–62; 95, pp. 671–732; 96]. The term implies that while you can see what goes into the "box" (input) and what comes out of it (output), the internal decision-making process remains hidden or incomprehensible [97].

9.4.2 Freedom of Information and Internet Access

Algorithmic enforcement can limit not just freedom of information but also internet access. Freedom of expression [10, Article 11; 84, Article 10] now covers both sharing and receiving information [98, § 27; 99, § 50; 100, § 36; 101, § 56; see also 102, p. 24] and has evolved into what many consider a fundamental right to internet access [103, 104]. This viewpoint stems from the internet's role in enhancing free speech and citizen engagement [105].

In Europe, various legal bodies affirm the importance of unhindered internet access as a human right. The European Court of Human Rights (ECtHR) has suggested that existing freedoms of expression should extend to include this right [99, para 31]. The Council of Europe also opposed 'three-strike' laws by declaring internet access as a 'fundamental right' [106, 107]. Similarly, France's Constitutional Council confirmed the democratic necessity of online access, stating that freedom of expression inherently includes the freedom to access the internet [108, § 12]. The European Commission has emphasized that restricting internet access impacts users' freedom of expression [109, § 3.4]. Various international and national entities, like the UN Human Rights Council, the Costa Rican Constitutional Court or the Finnish government, have further emphasized the fundamental nature of internet access [34, 110–112].

Measures that affect internet accessibility, like automated enforcement tools, could make States liable for infringing on freedom of expression rights. For instance, under Article 10 of the ECHR and its EU Charter counterpart, Article 11, courts have stated that the impact of website blocking must be carefully assessed. This includes evaluating its effect on legitimate communication and public interest, as well as considering alternative means of access [13, para 28]. The ECtHR has further clarified that while States have more latitude in regulating commercial speech, their discretion narrows when the speech involves public debates on matters of general interest [13, para 28]. The court also emphasized that public interest in information extends beyond just political contexts to include areas like sports, culture and religion [113, § 25; 114, § 28; 115, § 116; 116, § 34; 117, § 76].

Algorithmic delisting, particularly in relation to the right to be forgotten, presents human rights challenges, including tensions with access to information online. The CJEU ruled in 2014 that search engine operators are responsible for processing personal data found on third-party web pages [118]. As a result, search engines may be required to delete links leading to webpages that include such personal data under specific conditions. This ruling has sparked debate over its impact on freedom of expression [119–122]. The balance between privacy and free speech varies by jurisdiction; in Europe, privacy often takes precedence, while in the U.S., free speech is generally favored [38, pp. 18–19]. The CJEU has ruled that privacy usually outweighs both the search engine's economic interest and the public's interest in accessing the information, except in specific cases involving public figures [118, § 81; see also 123]. While Google states that delisting requests are not automated [66], the rising costs of manual enforcement make it likely that AI could be employed for this task in the future. Whether currently in practice or a future development, this poses a conundrum: AI may efficiently manage rising costs but is ill-suited to make nuanced decisions involving the balancing of human rights.

9.4.3 Freedom of Expression

The tension between human rights and algorithmic enforcement is notably evident in the area of freedom of expression, specifically the freedom to share information. Algorithmic tools like proactive filtering can significantly restrict this freedom by acting preemptively, unlike traditional notice-and-take-down methods that operate reactively. This shift in enforcement practices has relevant consequences on users' right.

In the case of *Google v. Louis Vuitton*, the CJEU Advocate General highlighted the superiority of civil liability rules rooted in negligence over strict intellectual property liability for online content governance. In this context, trademark owners would not wield overarching control over online uses of their marks, 'including [...] many lawful and even desirable uses' [67, § 123]. Instead, they would need to identify specific instances where Google's actions cause illegal harm to their trademarks [67, § 123]. This approach allows for a more balanced treatment of intellectual property rights, freedom of expression, and information access, balance that proactive algorithmic enforcement could disrupt. Reactive mechanisms like notice-and-take-down offer stronger protections for freedom of expression, requiring online intermediaries to assess the legality of content before removing it. As Van Eecke pointed out, this mechanism serves as a key balancing tool among the rights of content owners, online platforms, and users [68, pp. 1479–1480].

Ex-ante filtering systems employed by online platforms could disproportionately tip the scale in favour of property and personality rights at the expense of other fundamental freedoms. Such algorithmic enforcement can yield false positives, chilling free speech and affecting users' right to express themselves. The European Court of Justice has acknowledged that these measures can compromise freedom of information [15, § 50]. These systems may not adequately distinguish between lawful and unlawful content, leading to unintended blocking. These automated systems lack the nuance of human judgment, which is essential for distinguishing between lawful and unlawful content, assessing fair use or recognizing exceptions and limitations [15, § 50]. Furthermore, these algorithms often fail to account for complexities like the public domain status of certain works [15, § 50].

The adoption of Article 17 of the C-DSM Directive intensifies these concerns. It raises questions about the implications of increased content monitoring by OCSSPs and the growing use of automated systems, especially regarding the preservation of users' fundamental rights to expression and information.

9.4.4 Right to Privacy and Data Protection

The use of algorithmic enforcement technologies raises questions about balancing privacy and freedom of expression [10, Articles 8 and 11]. Courts have emphasized the need for OSPs to employ such tools, citing the internet's capacity to amplify privacy violations and the rapid, global spread of harmful content [e.g., 69, § 110]. By highlighting the internet's role in enabling defamation, hate speech, and speech inciting violence, courts bolster the argument for prioritizing privacy protections over freedom of expression by noting, for example, that '[d]defamatory and other types of clearly unlawful speech, including hate speech and speech inciting violence, can be disseminated like never before, worldwide, in a matter of seconds, and sometimes remain persistently available online' [70].

Courts have also cautioned, however, that unregulated use of monitoring and filtering technology could violate users' data protection rights. The CJEU has stressed that such systems could disproportionately affect user privacy, as monitoring requires identifying and processing personal data: 'requiring installation of the contested filtering system would involve the identification, systematic analysis and processing of information connected with the profiles created on the social network by its users. The information connected with those profiles is protected personal data because, in principle, it allows those users to be identified' [15, § 49)]. In cases like *Scarlet* and *Netlog*, the CJEU recognized for the first time a fundamental right to data protection, which may not be adequately balanced against copyright protections 'when a mechanism requiring the systematic processing of personal data is imposed in the name of the protection of intellectual property' [71, p. 34]. The European Court of Human Rights has also expressed concerns that these technologies could undermine the confidentiality of communications and individuals' privacy [10, Article 7], particularly when the systems scrutinize the content of communications [16, pp. 793–794].

9.4.5 Platforms, Freedom of Business and Innovation

Article 16 of the EU Charter also introduces the freedom to conduct business as another right that needs to be balanced when imposing automated enforcement systems on OSPs [10, Article 16]. Unlike freedom of expression, freedom to conduct a business is not recognized in other international human rights instruments, although some national constitutions provide for the protection of this right, as in the case of Article 41 of the Italian Constitution, Article 38 of the Spanish Constitution, Article 49 of the Croatian Constitution, and Article 74 of the Slovenian Constitution. Thus, it remains loosely defined in case law [124, para 49], affording states significant leeway to interfere [125, para 46; 126]. This relatively weaker nature of the right [127, pp. 326–344; 128, para 107] has led the CJEU to often favor rightsholders and parties seeking the removal of online content [14, para 49].

Imposing new enforcement obligations on OSPs raises the costs for platforms to enter and compete in the market, thereby diminishing innovation incentives. Under the new Article 17 of the C-DSM Directive, for example, OSPs, especially OCSSPs, may need to invest in expensive technology to meet legal requirements. The CJEU has highlighted the financial burden this places on OSPs, noting that unlimited monitoring would severely restrict hosting providers' business freedom [15, § 46]. This would necessitate the adoption of complex and expensive filtering systems [15, § 46], conflicting with both freedom to conduct a business and Article 3 of the Enforcement Directive, which stipulates that IP enforcement should not be overly complicated or costly, nor create trade barriers [129, Article 3].

9.5 Protecting Human Rights: Recent Developments in the Digital Services Act

Crucial social decisions online are increasingly made through automated enforcement by opaque algorithms, leading to a 'black box' society [80; see also 130, 131]. The main weakness in algorithmic enforcement lies in its lack of transparency and accountability, posing challenges to effective and democratic online regulation [93, 132, 133]. While concerns about algorithms replacing human decision-making exist [134, pp. 1–29; 135, 136], immediate regulatory action could focus on enhancing algorithmic transparency and accountability, guided by various academic proposals.

In the early phase of human-AI interaction, the question of algorithmic accountability is still unsettled, particularly in terms of 'to whom' algorithms should be held accountable and why [137, pp. 679–688]. While there's broad agreement that at a minimum, users should be the ones to hold algorithms accountable [96, 137, pp. 679–688; 138, 139], others advocate for extending this accountability to decision subjects [140, pp. 1–6] or even regulatory bodies [141]. Accountability isn't just a matter of code transparency [96]; it is also about making the algorithm's actions comprehensible to users and other stakeholders [137]. Tackling this issue requires overcoming various technical, organizational, and regulatory barriers to access relevant data [137]. Elkin-Koren and Perel offer a solution by suggesting grassroots oversight through 'tinkering' [142, p. 193]. This approach would allow individuals to systematically scrutinize how online platforms respond to representatives, like-real content submissions, thereby enhancing our understanding and oversight of these black box algorithms [143, pp. 669–678].

Some proposals advocate linking reduced liability for online intermediaries to enhanced algorithmic accountability to better align with human rights [137]. Measures for such accountability could encompass transparent automated decision-making, third-party audits, an independent complaints body, complete system transparency, permanent decision records, understandable explanations of automated decisions, and the option for human review [137, 144, 145]. Frederick Mostert emphasizes the need for regulators to establish a lasting online framework based on 'digital due process' [146, pp. 378–389]. This should involve transparent, globally accepted principles that address the challenges posed by online algorithmic enforcement [146, pp. 378–389], particularly its effects on free speech and data protection. Numerous attempts have been made to build such a 'constitutional' framework [147, pp. 302–319], such as the Manila Principles on Intermediary Liability, which aim to safeguard user rights like freedom of expression and privacy [148, Intro]. These principles should also align with the UN's 'Protect, Respect, and Remedy' Framework and its Guiding Principles on Business and Human Rights [48]. Once established, 'digital due process' principles could integrate with existing initiatives like Ranking Digital Rights, which grades online platforms based on their commitment to user rights such as privacy and free speech [149]. Platforms that score highly in algorithmic due process and accountability could be eligible for lighter liability standards. The modern system should operate on a principles-compliance-ranking-exemption basis to encourage due process and algorithmic accountability online.

In this vein, the recent DSA aims to bolster transparency, non-discrimination, and adherence to fundamental rights [150] in platform-driven algorithmic decisions.

First, platforms are required to disclose the use of automated tools in content moderation across three main touchpoints: Terms of Service [151, Article 14(1)], notifications to content flaggers [151, Recital 54, Article 16(6)], and rationales for content removal in statement of reasons [151, Recital 54, Article 17(3)(c)]. The DSA could be more effective if it specified when algorithms are used in the decision process [152]. Additionally, platforms should disclose the data sets used for training these algorithms, as suggested in the proposed AI Act, which advocates for more safeguards in this context [153]. Also, they should offer a clear explanation of the logic behind automated decisions. This obligation should be broader than what is required by Article 40(3) of [151], which only allows the Digital Service Coordinator of the Member State of establishment or the Commission to request Very Large Online Platforms and Very Large Online Search Engines to clarify the design, logic, functioning, and testing of their algorithmic systems, including recommender systems. Lastly, platforms should provide guidelines that allow users to contest these automated decisions [152].

Second, when using automated systems for internal complaint-handling, a human review mechanism should exist to ensure fair and accurate outcomes [151, Recital 58]. The DSA should adopt a 'human-in-command' approach, mandating not just the ability to monitor the AI system's overall activities and impacts, but also the flexibility to determine the conditions under which the AI is deployed [154, p. 15]. Ideally, an independent legal expert should conduct the human review, especially for complex issues like copyright law that require nuanced understanding. The DSA currently lacks explicit obligations requiring specialised expertise for human reviewers, a gap that should be filled either during its implementation or in subsequent amendments. Given the impracticality of having a large team of legal experts for every type of content, specialized legal expertise could be most effectively utilised in out-of-court dispute settlements, as specified in Article 21 of the DSA. This would ensure complex legal issues are addressed, safeguarding both the review process and the fundamental rights of all involved parties.

Third, the DSA requires Very Large Online Platforms (VLOPs) and Very large Online Search Engines (VLOSEs) to conduct extensive risk assessments for their algorithmic systems, focusing on potential impacts on fundamental rights [151, Recital 81]. They must also implement measures to mitigate these risks, including adjustments to service design, features or functioning, including their online interfaces [151, Article 35], content moderation processes, and decision-making resources.

Fourth, DSPs are required to publish annual transparency reports in a public database [151, Articles 15 and 24]. These reports must outline their use of automation in content moderation, providing details like purpose, accuracy indicators, error rates, and any applied safeguards [151, Article 15].

Fifth, to enhance accountability, VLOPs and VLOSEs must undergo independent audits to assess compliance with the DSA [151, Article 37]. These audits should rigorously examine algorithmic systems and require full cooperation from the providers, including access to relevant data and premises [151, Article 91].

On a final note, it is worth mentioning that the DSA lacks a detailed framework for accountability and redress concerning AI and automated decision-making. Future reform should focus on defining specific responsibilities for service providers and creating clear avenues for individuals to seek redress for harm caused by automated systems [153].

9.6 Conclusions

The tension between automated processes and the need for transparency and accountability is a common thread that runs through both algorithmic content moderation and digital forensics. In the realm of algorithmic content moderation, automated tools are employed to swiftly filter and moderate vast volumes of online content. While these tools significantly reduce manual labor and enable platforms to function at scale, they also operate in ways that can be opaque, limiting public scrutiny and understanding. As a result, questions arise regarding how these algorithms make decisions, particularly in ambiguous cases that require nuanced understanding and judgment. Similarly, in digital forensics, automated processes are increasingly being employed to sift through extensive data sets for digital evidence. Like content moderation tools, these forensic algorithms can function rapidly and at scale but can also be highly complex and opaque. Given that the results of digital forensics can have significant legal implications, the lack of transparency and accountability in these automated processes can become especially problematic. Moreover, as forensic algorithms evolve to incorporate machine learning and AI, their decision-making processes could become even less transparent, making third-party audits and scrutiny even more challenging.

Automated content moderation is shaping our digital social sphere in unprecedented ways, affecting billions of users every day. These AI-driven processes have a significant societal impact, especially as machine learning and data analytics empower platforms to pre-emptively flag or remove content. This phenomenon raises multiple challenges that intersect with the broader discourse on digital forensics and forensic innovation. Firstly, entrusting online content moderation to private entities removes the process from public scrutiny, raising questions of transparency and accountability. This shift towards 'machine-made justice' [155, p. 139]. Secondly, the delegation of legal decisions to automated systems also exacerbates existing tensions around the preservation of users' and OSPs' fundamental rights, including but not limited to due process, privacy, freedom of speech, and freedom to conduct a business.

Despite these complexities, legislators have frequently prioritized the roll-out of automated filtering and monitoring technologies—evidenced by provisions such as Article 17 of the C-DSM Directive—over establishing a resilient framework that also respects human rights. This trend could endanger the integrity of digital forensics, making the field heavily reliant on opaque and unsupervised algorithms. Consequently, this approach risks eroding human rights norms in the digital sphere, subtly diminishing them in ways that escape public scrutiny and oversight.

In contrast, emerging legislative initiatives offer a more balanced pathway. The evolving principles of algorithmic due process and the progressive 'constitutionalization' of algorithmic governance are gaining legal traction, most notably in groundbreaking legislations like the DSA. These developments offer an optimistic trajectory for remedying the unsustainable path that automated content moderation currently treads. The DSA is a pivotal instrument in this evolution, introducing mandatory provisions that seek to bolster algorithmic transparency, accountability, and risk assessment. These legal innovations serve as a regulatory tool to align algorithmic governance with fundamental human rights and ethical standards. For instance, the DSA mandates comprehensive risk assessments for platforms, rigorous transparency reports, and independent audits, which together lay the groundwork for implementing algorithmic due process principles. By institutionalizing these principles, the DSA can serve as a blueprint for algorithmic governance, one that enshrines a fair balance between technological advancement and the preservation of fundamental rights.

In navigating this transformative landscape, the essence of our challenge lies in operationalizing the nascent 'constitutionalization' of algorithmic governance. This is not a task for lawmakers or technologists alone; it calls for a synergetic alliance among forensic experts, legislators, and technologists. The aim is not merely to make digital forensics an adjudicatory instrument but to elevate it as a cornerstone of digital governance itself. By achieving this collaborative integration, we can imbue the very infrastructure of our digital world with enduring principles of transparency, accountability, and due process. In this way, we not only reconcile technological innovation with fundamental human rights but also architect a future where the digital and the democratic coexist in harmony. This synthesis, if successfully orchestrated, can stand as the capstone of our era, anchoring digital evolution in ethical bedrock.

References

1. Frosio, G. (2022). Regulatory shift in state intervention: From intermediary liability to responsibility. In E. Celeste, A. Heldt, & C. Iglesias Keller (Eds.), *Constitutionalising social media* (pp. 151–175). Hart Publishing.
2. Frosio, G. (2020). Algorithmic enforcement online. In P. Torremans (Ed.), *Intellectual property law and human rights* (4th edn, pp. 709–744). Wolters Kluwer.
3. Frosio, G. (2018). Why keep a dog and bark yourself? From intermediary liability to responsibility. *Oxford Journal of International Law & Information Technology, 25*, 1–33.
4. Hall, S. W., Sakzad, A., & Choo, K. K. (2022). Explainable artificial intelligence for digital forensics. *Forensic Science, 4*(2), e1434.
5. Solanke, A. A. (2022). Explainable digital forensics AI: Towards mitigating distrust in AI-based digital forensics analysis using interpretable models. *Forensic Science International: Digital Investigation, 42*, 301403.
6. Sag, M. (2017). Internet safe harbors and the transformation of copyright law. *Notre Dame L Review, 93*, 1.
7. Lessig, L. (1999). *The code and other laws of cyberspace*. Basic Books.
8. Mitchell, W. (1995). *City of bits: Space, place, and the Infobahn*. MIT Press.
9. Reidenberg, J. (1998). Lex informatica: The formulation of information policy rules through technology. *Texas L Review, 76*, 553.
10. EU Charter. (2012). Charter of fundamental rights of the European Union 2012 OJ (C 326) 391.
11. Frosio, G, & Geiger, C. (2023). Taking fundamental rights seriously in the digital services act's platform liability regime. Eur. Law J.
12. Barata, J, & Bassini, M. (2016). Freedom of expression in the Internet: Main trends of the case law of the European Court of Human Rights. In O. Pollicino, & G. Romeo (Eds.), *The internet and constitutional law: The protection of fundamental rights and constitutional adjudication in Europe*. Routledge.
13. *Akdeniz v Turkey*, ECtHR, App no. 20877/10, 11 March 2014
14. C-314/12, *UPC Telekabel Wien* (2014). EU:C:2014:192.
15. C-360/10, *Belgische Vereniging van Auteurs, Componisten en Uitgevers CVBA (SABAM) v. Netlog NV* (2012). ECLI:EU:C:2012:85, § 36–38.
16. Kulk, S., & Zuiderveen Borgesius, F. (2012). Filtering for copyright enforcement in Europe after the Sabam cases. *EIPR, 34*, 791–794.
17. Dictionary, Artificial Intelligence. https://www.dictionary.com/browse/artificial-intelligence
18. Yeung, K. (2017). Algorithmic regulation: A critical interrogation. *Regulation and Governance, 12*(4), 505–523.
19. Andrews, L. et al. (2017). *Algorithmic regulation*. LSE discussion paper no 85. https://www.kcl.ac.uk/law/research/centres/telos/assets/DP85-Algorithmic-Regulation-Sep-2017.pdf
20. Hartzog, W., Conti, G., Nelson, J., & Shay, L. (2015). Inefficiently automated law enforcement. *Michigan State Law Review, 2015*, 1763.
21. Regulation 2016/679/EU of the European Parliament and the Council of 27 April 2016 on the protection of natural persons with regard to the processing of personal data and on the free movement of such data, and repealing Directive 95/46/EC (2016) OJ L 119/1.
22. Article 29 Data Protection Working Party. (2017). *Guidelines on automated individual decision-making and profiling for the purposes of Regulation 2016/679. 17/EN WP 251.*
23. YouTube. (n.d.). *How content ID works.* https://support.google.com/youtube/answer/2797370?hl=en
24. YouTube. (n.d.). *Dispute a content ID claim.* https://support.google.com/youtube/answer/2797454?hl=en
25. Anjali, A., & Mattamana, A. (2010). Intermediary liability and child pornography a comparative analysis. *Journal of International Commercial Law and Technology, 5*, 48.
26. Suzor, N., Seignior, B., & Singleton, J. (2017). Non-consensual porn and the responsibility of online intermediaries. *Melbourne University Law Review, 40*(3), 1057–1097.

27. Walters, J. (2015, June 21). Google to exclude revenge porn from internet searches. *The Guardian.* https://www.theguardian.com/technology/2015/jun/20/google-excludes-revenge-porn-internet-searches
28. Quinn, B. (2016, February 2). Google to point extremist searches towards anti-radicalization websites. *The Guardian.* http://buff.ly/20J3pFi
29. Bridy, A. (2016). Copyright's digital deputies: DMCA-plus enforcement by internet intermediaries. In J. A. Rothchild (Ed.), *Research handbook on electronic commerce law* (p. 200). Edward Elgar Publishing.
30. European Commission. (2017). *Tackling illegal content online. Towards an enhanced responsibility of online platforms.* COM(2017) 555 final.
31. Frosio, G. (2017). The death of "no monitoring obligations": A story of untameable monsters. *JIPITEC, 8*, 199.
32. Frosio, G., & Husovec, M. (2020). Intermediary accountability and responsibility. In G. Frosio (Ed.), *The Oxford handbook of intermediary liability online* (pp. 613–630). Oxford University Press.
33. Husovec, M. (2017). *Injunctions against intermediaries in the European Union: Accountable but not liable?* Cambridge University Press.
34. United Nations Human Rights Council. (2014, June 20). *The promotion, protection and enjoyment of human rights on the internet*, A/HRC/RES/26/13.
35. Laidlaw, E. (2015). *Regulating speech in cyberspace: Gatekeepers.* Cambridge University Press.
36. Broeders, D. et al. (2017). Does great power come with great responsibility? The need to talk about corporate responsibility. In M. Taddeo, & L. Floridi (Eds.), *The responsibilities of online service providers* (pp. 315–323). Springer.
37. Taddeo, M., & Floridi, L. (Eds.). (2017). New civic responsibilities for online service providers. In *The responsibilities of online service providers.* Springer.
38. Taddeo, M., & Floridi, L. (2015). The debate on the moral responsibility of online service providers. *Science and Engineering Ethics, 1*, 5.
39. Cerf, V. (2011). First, do no harm. *Philosophy & Technology, 24*(4), 463, 465.
40. Vedder, A. (2001). Accountability of internet access and service providers—Strict liability entering ethics? *Ethics and Information Technology, 3*(1), 67–74.
41. Tavani, H., & Grodzinsky, F. (2002). Cyberstalking, personal privacy, and moral responsibility. *Ethics and Information Technology, 4*(2), 123–132.
42. Wettstein, F. (2012). Silence as complicity: Elements of a corporate duty to speak out against the violation of human rights. *Business Ethics Quarterly, 22*(01), 37–61.
43. Chen, S. (2009). Corporate responsibilities in internet-enabled social networks. *Journal of Business Ethics, 90*(4), 523–536.
44. Brenkert, G. (2009). Google, human rights, and moral compromise. *Journal of Business Ethics, 85*(4), 453–478.
45. Universal Declaration of Human Rights. (1948). G.A. Res. 217A (III), U.N. Doc. A/810.
46. UNESCO Declaration of Human Duties and Responsibilities. (1998). (Valencia Declaration).
47. United Nations. (2003, August 13). *Norms on the responsibilities of transnational corporations and other business enterprises.*
48. United Nations Human Rights, *Office of the High Commissioner. (2011). Guiding principles on business human rights: Implementing the United Nations "protect, respect, and remedy" framework.* A/HRC/RES/17/4.
49. United Nations Special Rapporteur. (2016, November 5). *Report of the Special Rapporteur on the promotion and protection of the right to freedom of opinion and expression.* A/HRC/32/38.
50. United Nations (UN) Special Rapporteur on Freedom of Opinion and Expression, the Organization for Security and Co-operation in Europe (OSCE) Representative on Freedom of the Media, the Organization of American States (OAS) Special Rapporteur on Freedom of Expression and the African Commission on Human and Peoples' Rights (ACHPR) Special Rapporteur on Freedom of Expression and Access to Information, International Mechanism

for Promoting Freedom of Expression (2011) Joint Declaration on Freedom of Expression and the Internet, 2b.
51. Organization for Security and Co-operation in Europe. (2016, 29 January). The representative on freedom of the media, Dunja Mijatovic, Communiqué No.1/2016, 3rd Communiqué on Open Journalism 2. https://www.osce.org/fom/219391?download=true
52. *Viacom Int'l v YouTube* Inc 676 F3d 19 (2nd Cir 2012).
53. *Capitol Records LLC v Vimeo* 972 F Supp 2d 500 (SDNY 2013) (US).
54. European Commission. (2016). *Online platforms and the digital single market: Opportunities and challenges for Europe*. COM (2016) 288 final.
55. European Commission. (2016). *European Commission and IT Companies announce code of conduct on illegal online hate speech*. Press Release (31 May 2016). http://europa.eu/rapid/press-release_IP-16-1937_en.htm
56. Google. (2016). Partnering to help curb the spread of terrorist content online. *Google Blog*. https://blog.google/topics/google-europe/partnering-help-curb-spread-terrorist-content-online
57. Solon, O. (2016). Facebook, Twitter, Google and Microsoft Team up to tackle extremist content. *The Guardian*. www.theguardian.com/technology/2016/dec/05/facebook-twitter-google-microsoft-terrorist-extremist-content
58. Facebook. (2016). Partnering to help curb spread of online terrorist content. *Facebook Newsroom*. https://newsroom.fb.com/news/2016/12/partnering-to-help-curb-spread-of-online-terrorist-content
59. European Commission. (2018). *Recommendation on measures to effectively tackle illegal content online*. C (2018) 1177 final.
60. Regulation 2021/784/EU of the European Parliament and of the Council of 29 April 2021 on addressing the dissemination of terrorist content online [2021] OJ L172/79.
61. Directive 2019/790/EU of the European Parliament and of the Council of 17 April 2019 on copyright and related rights in the Digital Single Market and amending Directives 96/9/EC and 2001/29/EC (2019) OJ L130/92.
62. Frosio, G. (2020). Reforming the C-DSM reform: A user-based copyright theory for commonplace creativity. *IIC, 52*(6), 709–750.
63. Frosio, G. (2018). To filter or not to filter? That is the question in EU copyright reform. *Cardozo Arts & Entertainment Law Journal, 36*(2), 101–138.
64. Directive 2000/31/EC of the European Parliament and the Council of 8 June 2000 on certain legal aspects of information society services, in particular electronic commerce, in the Internal Market [2000] OJ L 178/1.
65. European Commission. (2016). *Proposal for a directive of the European Parliament and of the Council on copyright in the Digital Single Market*. COM (2016) 593 final.
66. Corfield, G. (2018, March 19). Here is how Google handles Right To Be Forgotten requests. *The Register*. https://www.theregister.co.uk/2018/03/19/google_right_to_be_forgotten_request_process
67. C-236, 237 and 238/08, Joined Cases, Opinion of Advocate General, *Google France, S.A.R.L. & Google Inc. v Louis Vuitton Malletier SA, Viaticum S.A., Luteciel S.A.R.L., v. Centre Bational de Recherche en Relations Humaines (CNRRH) S.A.R.L., Pierre-Alexis Thonet, Bruno Raboin, Tiger, a franchisee of Unicis*, ECLI:EU:C:2009:569.
68. Van Eecke, P. (2011). Online service providers and liability: A plea for a balanced approach. *Common Market Law Review, 1455*, 1479–1480.
69. *Delfi AS v Estonia*, ECtHR, App no 64569/09, 2015.
70. *Google Brazil v Dafra*, Special Appeal no 1306157/SP, Superior Court of Justice, 24 March 2014). https://cyberlaw.stanford.edu/page/wilmap-brazil
71. González Fuster, G. (2012). Balancing intellectual property against data protection: A new right's wavering weight. *IDP, 14*, 34–37.
72. C-401/19, *Republic of Poland v European Parliament and Council of the European Union* (2022) ECLI:EU:C:2022:297.

73. Geiger, C., & Jütte, B. J. (2022, May 31). Constitutional safeguards in the "freedom of expression triangle"—Online content moderation and user rights after the CJEU's judgement on Article 17 Copyright DSM directive. *The Digital Constitutionalist*. https://digi-con.org/constitutional-safeguards-in-the-freedom-of-expression-triangle
74. Reda, J., Sellinger, J., & Servatius, M. (2020). Article 17 of the directive on copyright in the digital single market: A fundamental rights assessment. Study for the Gesellschaft für Freiheitsrechte. https://freiheitsrechte.org/home/wp-content/uploads/2020/11/GFF_Article17_Fundamental_Rights.pdf.
75. Husovec, M. (2020). Over-blocking: When is the EU legislator responsible? SSRN Research Paper no. 3784149. https://papers.ssrn.com/abstract_id=3784149
76. Cloutier, M. (2020). Poland's challenge to EU Directive 2019/790: Standing up to the destruction of European freedom of expression. *Dickinson Law Review, 125*, 161–197.
77. Geiger, C., & Jütte, B. J. (2021). Platform liability under Article 17 of the copyright in the digital single market directive, automated filtering and fundamental rights: An impossible match. *GRUR International, 70*(6), 517.
78. Frosio, G. (2022). Freedom to share. *IIC—International Review of Intellectual Property and Competition Law, 53*, 1145–1148.
79. Quintais, J. P., & Schwemmer, S. F. (2022). The interplay between the digital services act and sector regulation: How special is copyright? *European Journal of Risk Regulation, 13*(2), 191.
80. Pasquale, F. (2015). *The black box society: The secret algorithms that control money and information*. Harvard University Press.
81. Calabresi, G. (1961). Some thoughts on risk distribution and the Law of Torts. *Yale Law Journal, 70*, 499.
82. Coase, R. (1960). The problem of social cost. *Journal of Law & Economics, 3*, 1.
83. Denning, A. (1980). *Due Process of Law*. OUP.
84. European Convention on Human Rights, as Amended (1950).
85. Perel, M., & Elkin-Koren, N. (2016). Accountability in algorithmic copyright enforcement. *Stanford Technical Law Review, 19*, 473.
86. Council of Europe, Committee of Experts on Human Rights Dimensions of Automated Data Processing and Different Forms of Artificial Intelligence (MSI-AUT) (2018) *Draft Recommendation of the Committee of Ministers to member States on human rights impacts of algorithmic systems*, MSI-AUT(2018)06 (pp. 6–7). https://rm.coe.int/draft-recommendation-on-human-rights-impacts-of-algorithmic-systems/16808ef256
87. Koene, A., et al. (2019). *A governance framework for algorithmic accountability and transparency*. European Parliament Research Center.
88. Rieke, A., Bogen, M., & Robinson, D. (2018). *Public scrutiny of automated decisions: Early lessons and emerging methods. An upturn and Omidyar network report* (pp. 23–28). https://www.issuelab.org/resources/30226/30226.pdf
89. Binns, R. (2018). Algorithmic accountability and public reason. *Philosophy & Technology, 31*, 543–556.
90. Maggiolino, M. (2019). EU trade secrets and algorithmic transparency. Bocconi Legal Studies Research Paper No. 3363178. https://papers.ssrn.com/sol3/papers.cfm?abstract_id=3363178
91. Wexler, R. (2018). Life, liberty, and trade secrets: Intellectual property in the criminal justice system. *Stanford Law Review, 70*, 1343–1429.
92. Moore, T. (2017). *Trade secrets and algorithms as barriers to social justice*. Center for Democracy and Technology.
93. Kroll, J. et al. (2017). Accountable algorithms. *University of Pennsylvania Law Review, 165*, 633, 658
94. Diakopoulos, N. (2016). Accountability in algorithmic decision-making. *Communications of the ACM, 69*(2), 56–62.
95. Barocas, S., & Selbst, A. D. (2016). Big Data's disparate impact. *California Law Review, 104*, 671–732.

96. O'Neil, C. (2016). *Weapons of math destruction: How big data increases inequality and threatens democracy*. Crown Publishing Group.
97. Doshi-Velez, F., Kortz, M., & Budish, R., et al. (2017). Accountability of AI under the law: The role of explanation. arXiv:1711.01134 [cs.AI]. https://arxiv.org/abs/1711.01134
98. *Times Newspapers Ltd (nos. 1 and 2) v the United Kingdom*, App no 3002/03 and 23676/03, 10 March 2009.
99. *Ahmet Yildirim v Turkey*, ECtHR, App no 3111/10, 18 December 2012.
100. *Guseva v. Bulgaria*, ECtHR, App no 6987/07, 17 February 2015.
101. *Cengiz and Others v. Turkey*, ECtHR, App no 48226/10 and 14027/11, 1 December 2015.
102. Geiger, C. (2007). Author's right, copyright and the public's right to information: A complex relationship. In F. Macmillan (Ed.), *New directions in copyright law* (Vol. 5). Edward Elgar.
103. Lucchi, N. (2011). Access to network services and protection of constitutional rights: Recognizing the essential role of internet access for the freedom of expression. *Cardozo Journal of International and Comparative Law, 19*(3), 645.
104. Land, M. (2013). Toward an international law of the internet. *Harvard International Law Journal, 54*(2), 393.
105. Conley, M., & Patterson, C. (2000). *Human rights and the internet*. Macmillan.
106. Ermert, M. (2009). *Council of Europe: Access to internet is a fundamental right*. IPWatch.
107. BBC News. (2010, March 8). Internet access is a fundamental right. *BBC News*. http://news.bbc.co.uk/2/hi/technology/8548190.stm
108. French Constitutional Council. (2009). Decision no 2009–580 DC of 10 June 2009.
109. European Commission. (2013). Staff working document, impact assessment accompanying the document proposal for a regulation of the European Parliament and of the Council laying down measures concerning the European single market for electronic communications and to achieve a Connected Continent, and amending Directives 2002/20/EC, 2002/21/EC and 2002/22/EC and Regulations (EC) No 1211/2009 and (EU) No 531/2012, SWD (2013) 331 final.
110. Mara, K. (2010, May 10). *ITU-UNESCO broadband commission aims at global internet access*. IPWatch.
111. Nacion. (2010, September 8) Acceso a Internet es un derecho fundamental. *Nacion*. http://www.nacion.com/2010-09-08/ElPais/NotasSecundarias/ElPais2514038.aspx
112. BBC News. (2010, July 1) Finland makes broadband a legal right. *BBC News*. http://www.bbc.co.uk/news/10461048
113. *Nikowitz and Verlagsgruppe News GmbH v Austria*, ECtHR, App no 5266/03, 22 February 2007.
114. *Colaço Mestre and SIC – Sociedade Independente de Comunicação, SA v Portugal*, App no 11182/03 and 11319/03, 26 April 2007.
115. *Ressiot and Others v France*, ECtHR, App no 15054/07 and 15066/07, 28 June 2012.
116. *Sapan v Turkey*, ECtHR, App no 44102/04, 8 June 2010.
117. *Verlagsgruppe News GmbH and Bobi v Austria*, App no 59631/09, 4 December 2012.
118. C-131/12, *Google Spain SL and Google Inc. v Agencia Española de Protección de Datos (AEPD) and Mario Costeja González* (2014) ECLI:EU:C:2014:317.
119. Peguera, M. (2015). The shaky ground of the right to be delisted. *Vanderbilt Journal of Entertainment & Technology Law, 15*, 507.
120. Rosen, J. (2015). The right to be forgotten. *Stanford Law Review Online, 64*, 88.
121. Kulk, S., Zuiderveen Borgesius, F. (2014). Google Spain v. González: Did the court forget about freedom of expression? *European Journal of Risk Regulation, 3*, 389.
122. Zittrain, J. (2014, May 14). Don't force google to forget. *NYTimes*. http://www.nytimes.com/2014/05/15/opinion/dont-force-google-to-forget.html?_r=0
123. Article 29 Data Protection Working Party. (2014). Guidelines on the Implementation of the CJEU Judgment on Google Spain v. Costeja. 14/EN WP 225. http://ec.europa.eu/justice/data-protection/article-29/documentation/opinion-recommendation/files/2014/wp225_en.pdf
124. C-426/11, Opinion of Advocate General Cruz Villalón, *Alemo-Herron and Others* (2013) EU:C:2013:82.

125. C-283/11, *Sky Österreich* [2013] EU:C:2013:28.
126. T-587/13, *Schwerdt v OHIM - Iberamigo (cat&clean)* (2015) EU:T:2015:37.
127. Groussot, X., Pétursson, G. T., & Pierce, J. (2017). Weak right, Strong Court—The freedom to conduct business and the EU charter of fundamental rights. In S. Douglas-Scott & N. Hatzis (Eds.), *Research handbook on EU law and human rights* (pp. 326–344). Edward Elgar.
128. *EMI Records Ltd & Ors v British Sky Broadcasting Ltd & Ors* [2013] EWHC 379 (Ch) [107].
129. Directive 2004/48/EC of the European Parliament and of the Council on the enforcement of intellectual property rights (2004) OJ L157.
130. Suzor, N. (2019). *Lawless: The secret rules that govern our digital lives.* CUP.
131. Gillespie, T. (2018). *Custodians of the Internet: Platforms, content moderation, and the hidden decisions that shape social media.* Yale University Press.
132. Diakopoulos, N., & Koliska, M. (2016). Algorithmic transparency in the news media. *Digital Journalism.*
133. Diakopoulos, N. (2016). Accountability in algorithmic decision making. *Communications of the ACM, 59*(2), 56–62.
134. Wu, T. (2019). Will artificial intelligence eat the law? The rise of hybrid social-ordering systems. *Columbia Law Review, 119*(1), 1–29.
135. Re, R., & Solow-Niederman, A. (2019). Developing artificially intelligent justice. *Stanford Technical Law Review, 22*, 242.
136. Volokh, E. (2019). Chief justice robots. *Duke Law Journal, 68*, 1135.
137. Wagner, B. (2020). Algorithmic accountability: Towards accountable systems. In G. Frosio (Ed.), *The Oxford handbook of online intermediary liability* (pp. 679–688). OUP.
138. Norman, D. (2013). *The design of everyday things: Revised and Expanded Edition.* Basic Books.
139. Diakopoulos, N. (2015). Algorithmic accountability. *Digital Journalism, 3*, 398.
140. Veale, M., Van Kleek, M., Binns, R. (2018). *Fairness and accountability design needs for algorithmic support in high-stakes public sector decision-making.* arXiv:1802.01029 [cs]:1–6.
141. Wagner, B. (2018). *Algorithms and human rights: Study on the human rights dimensions of automated data processing techniques and possible regulatory implications.* Council of Europe, DGI(2017)12. https://rm.coe.int/algorithms-and-human-rights-study-on-the-human-rights-dimension-of-aut/1680796d10
142. Perel, M., & Elkin-Koren, N. (2017). Black box tinkering: Beyond disclosure in algorithmic enforcement. *Florida Law Review, 69*, 181.
143. Elkin-Koren, N., Perel, M. (2020). Guarding the guardians: Content moderation by online intermediaries and the rule of law. In G. Frosio (Ed.), *The Oxford handbook of online intermediary liability* (pp. 669–678). OUP.
144. Wagner, B. (2018). Ethics as an escape from regulation: From ethics-washing to ethics-shopping? In M. Hildebrandt (Ed.), *Being profiling. Cogitas ergo sum.* Amsterdam University Press.
145. Kaye D (2018) *Report of the Special Rapporteur on the promotion and protection of the right to freedom of opinion and expression.* A/HRC/38/35. Available via UN Documents. https://documents-dds-ny.un.org/doc/UNDOC/GEN/G18/096/72/PDF/G1809672.pdf?OpenElement
146. Mostert, F. (2020). 'Digital due process': A need for online justice. *JIPLP, 15*(5), 378–389.
147. Redeker, D., Gill, L., & Gasser, U. (2018). Towards digital constitutionalism? Mapping attempts to craft an Internet Bill of Rights. *International Commercial Gazzette, 80*(4), 302–319.
148. Manila Principles on Intermediary Liability, Intro. https://www.manilaprinciples.org
149. Ranking Digital Rights. https://rankingdigitalrights.org
150. Peukert, A., et al. (2022). European copyright society: Comment on copyright and the digital services act proposal. *IIC, 53*, 369.
151. Regulation 2022/2065/EU of the European Parliament and of the Council of 19 October 2022 on a Single Market for Digital Services and amending Directive 2000/31/EC (Digital Services Act), 2022 OJ L 277/1.

152. Windwekr, S., & Schmonn, C. (2020, July 27). Our EU policy principles: Procedural justice. *EFF*. https://www.eff.org/deeplinks/2020/07/our-eu-policy-principles-procedural-justice.
153. European Commission (2021) Proposal for a regulation of the European Parliament and of the Council on laying down harmonised rules on artificial intelligence (Artificial Intelligence Act) and amending certain Union legislative acts, COM(2021)0206 – C9–0146/2021 – 2021/0106(COD).
154. European Commission High-Level Expert Group on Artificial Intelligence. (2019). Ethics guidelines for Trustworthy AI. https://ec.europa.eu/newsroom/dae/document.cfm?doc_id=60419
155. Clark, C. (1999). The answer to the machine is in the machine. In B. Hugenholtz (Ed.), The future of copyright in a digital environment (p. 139). Kluwer Law International.;

Chapter 10
The Challenges of Introducing Massively Parallel Sequencing into the UK Forensic Market

David Hartshorne, Amy Roeder, Paul Elsmore, Andrew McDonald, and Jaimie Greenham

Abstract The introduction of any new forensic science technique into the Criminal Justice System requires extensive validation and accreditation as well as compliance with the UK's regulatory requirements. In May 2019 Cellmark Forensic Services, an established UK forensic science laboratory and accredited provider of forensic DNA testing services to the majority of police forces in England and Wales, initiated a project to introduce Massively Parallel Sequencing (MPS) into the UK forensic market. Almost two and a half years later, in September 2021, Cellmark became the first UK laboratory to achieve ISO17025 accreditation for MPS. This chapter describes the process involved and discusses the challenges faced, including a 12 month delay due to the COVID-19 pandemic, in making this next generation DNA profiling technology available to UK policing.

10.1 Existing Landscape

In this chapter the challenges of introducing Massively Parallel Sequencing (MPS), also known as Next Generation Sequencing (NGS), into the UK forensic marketplace are explored. With its ability to analyse DNA at the sequence level and capacity to target relatively large numbers of genetic markers in a single reaction, MPS is a huge technological leap forward from the electrophoretic size-separation DNA techniques routinely used in forensic science [1, 2]. However, despite the advantages offered by a new methodology, there are many challenges to introducing a new forensic technique into the Criminal Justice System (CJS) in the UK.

Any scientific technique used to assist in the investigation and prosecution of a criminal offence must undergo extensive testing and validation [3, 4]. In the UK any new forensic method must satisfy the necessary legal, ethical and regulatory requirements and requires an education programme to assist with its understanding

D. Hartshorne (✉) · A. Roeder · P. Elsmore · A. McDonald · J. Greenham
Cellmark Forensic Services, 16 Blacklands Way, Abingdon OX14 1DY, Oxon, UK
e-mail: communications@cellmark.co.uk

S. Francese and R. S. P. King (eds.), *Driving Forensic Innovation in the 21st Century*,
https://doi.org/10.1007/978-3-031-56556-4_10

in the court room. In addition to scientific and legal considerations, the costs and timescales associated with the introduction of a new forensic DNA technology in particular, mean that it must offer significant improvements, advantages or added value to what is currently available. Careful consideration must also be given to the business case economics, assessing not only what will assist investigators, but in practice what they will choose to use and what level of pricing will be acceptable and commercially sustainable.

Some of these challenges are peculiar to the forensic 'market' in England and Wales, particularly in relation to pricing. Unlike most of the rest of the world, in England and Wales police investigators access the majority of their forensic laboratory analyses, interpretation and reporting (in particular DNA analysis) from private Forensic Science Providers (FSPs). Forensic science delivery in England and Wales is highly regulated with stringent requirements for accreditation to international quality standards (primarily ISO17025, or ISO17020 for forensic science delivered at a crime scene) by the UK Accreditation Service (UKAS) [4]. In addition, delivery into the Criminal Justice System is overseen by the Forensic Science Regulator, a position first established by the UK government in 2007 [5] which gained statutory powers in 2023, following the enactment of the Forensic Science Regulator Act 2021 [6].

To understand why the police forces in England and Wales are largely served by private FSPs, it is necessary to look back briefly at the history of forensic services provision in these countries. Prior to the 1990s almost all forensic work was delivered by the UK Government's Forensic Science Service (FSS). However, this started to change when in 2002 the Association of Chief Police Officers removed the FSS's preferred status and in 2005 it became a government owned company (GovCo) on a potential journey to privatisation [7]. A pricing structure, which had been introduced by the FSS to charge the 43 police forces in England and Wales for their submitted forensic work allowed individual police forces to compare prices and start to source equivalent services from alternative providers.

Cellmark was established in 1987 to commercialise the DNA fingerprinting discoveries made by Professor Sir Alec Jeffreys at the University of Leicester [8, 9]. Although initially the Company was primarily focused on introducing DNA technology into the family courts for the resolution of paternity and relationship analysis, Cellmark was also involved in working with the Home Office and FSS laboratories in some of the very early criminal cases involving DNA analysis. However, the DNA methodology was not suitable for the majority of forensic samples due to the amount of DNA required and that the DNA fingerprints were not suitable for databasing [10]. The introduction of PCR (Polymerase Chain Reaction) 'amplified' forensic DNA analysis in the early 1990s [11], the establishment of the UK National DNA Database (NDNAD) in 1995 [12], and the provision of additional funding by the government under the DNA Expansion Programme from 2000–2005 [13] allowed private FSPs to develop alternative services to those offered by the FSS to serve the police forces in England and Wales.

During the 2000s a regulated forensic marketplace developed with individual police forces, or groups of forces, tendering their forensic work in open competition and awarding contracts based on quality, accreditation, service delivery and price.

In part, it was the loss of market share during this period that led to the decision to close the then loss-making FSS in December 2010 [14]. The FSS shut its doors to new work in 2011 and finally closed in March 2012. The three main FSPs expanded rapidly to accommodate the FSS's workload during 2011, largely by employing FSS scientists.

The introduction of PCR based Short Tandem Repeat (STR) DNA analysis during the 1990s transformed forensic science, providing rapid and sensitive identification technology with results that could be readily databased. The STR marker systems used in the laboratory developed rapidly in the first 10 years following its introduction and became one of the most valuable types of forensic evidence available to forensic scientists and investigators. The four STR marker system (the Quad) [11] introduced in 1994 was quickly replaced a year later by the Second Generation Multiplex (SGM) comprising six STRs [15]. SGM profiles were the first to be loaded to the NDNAD when it became operational in 1995, but by 1999 forensic laboratories in England and Wales were loading profiles generated using AmpFℓSTR™ SGM Plus™ (SGM Plus™, Applied Biosystems), a 10 STR multiplex (plus Amelogenin) which provided greater discrimination power [16]. Complete DNA profiles generated with this assay have reported random match probabilities in the region of one in a billion [17].

While STR profiling provides the police with powerful identification technology to match a suspect with evidence found at a crime scene, without a suspect to compare to, a DNA profile on its own has limited intelligence value. However, when there is a national database of profiles to compare against, it becomes a hugely powerful investigative tool. The UK government therefore actively sought to increase the size of the NDNAD by providing additional funding to the police through the DNA Expansion Programme, which operated from 2000–2005 [13]. This programme accelerated the growth of the NDNAD, initially with samples taken from persons charged with or convicted of a recordable offence and after April 2004 from anyone *arrested* for a recordable offence.[1] Currently, the NDNAD has DNA profiles from approximately six million individuals and because of the high level of recidivism, over 60% of the profiles from crime scene samples that are loaded onto the NDNAD match a subject profile [18].

The pioneering days of forensic DNA science and its introduction into the criminal courts in England and Wales have been summarised here in a few short paragraphs. What has not been discussed is the scientific, legislative, legal and operational challenges that accompanied the introduction of this DNA technology, which is now such an everyday part of policing, criminal investigation and the apprehension and prosecution of offenders through the court systems. The adoption of STR profiling in the UK has undoubtedly been a great success story, but care must be taken not to assume that that any new forensic technology that follows, particularly new DNA technology, will enjoy the same level of uptake and will not face considerable challenges. Indeed, it is partly because of the previous successes of STR profiling and the UK NDNAD that the introduction of successor technologies is particularly challenging.

[1] A recordable offence is generally an offence that could result in imprisonment.

As an example, it is worth remembering the history of the more recent STR multiplex transition. In 2014, approximately fifteen years after the introduction of SGM Plus™, all forensic providers in England and Wales transitioned to DNA-17 multiplexes (16 STRs plus Amelogenin) which provide greater discrimination and therefore higher statistical certainty [19]. These multiplexes were engineered to perform better on degraded DNA samples and the PCR chemistry was improved to deliver both enhanced sensitivity and reduced susceptibility to contaminants. At the same time, modifications were made to the NDNAD software to accommodate the additional markers including the development of the associated searching algorithms.

The DNA-17 introduction required coordinated activity by the NDNAD, FSPs, the police and prosecutors. For the FSPs, this involved laboratory method development, validation, development of relevant allelic frequency databases, software modifications, re-accreditation by UKAS, staff-retraining for laboratory analysis, profile interpretation and reporting as well as external training for the police, prosecutors and the judiciary. The replacement of SGM Plus™ with DNA-17 was a major and costly endeavour for FSPs.

From the perspective of the police, the positive impact of the DNA-17 introduction was an increase in detection sensitivity, meaning that DNA information could be obtained from samples containing less DNA, more degraded DNA or both. However, with increased sensitivity came a significant increase in the number of DNA profiles where more than one DNA contributor was apparent. These mixed source DNA profiles required more complex analysis and interpretation by highly trained reporting scientists and, despite the development of software to aid profile interpretation, every profile took longer to analyse. Additional interpretation time translated to higher costs and therefore increased prices. Plus, the higher number of mixed profiles increased the police's reliance on FSPs for the initial reporting of DNA profile matches (some single source and non-complex profile matches were previously reported by the police).

The introduction of DNA-17 multiplexes represented a significant improvement in forensic technology and had a major impact on the investigation of many cases. However, some of the responses from policing were somewhat muted because in many situations there was no discernible operational benefit compared to SGM Plus™ (which was itself highly sensitive and discriminating) and most cases had cost and time implications due to the more complex profile interpretation. The DNA-17 introduction also coincided with a period of financial austerity in the UK when policing budgets were cut and hence, costs became an even more important consideration. As a result, there has been little enthusiasm to move to a multiplex with more STRs, despite the fact that the available multiplexes may be more technically advanced or offer even greater discriminating power.

In England and Wales, the introduction of any new forensic DNA technology therefore faces a number of significant challenges. Policing benefits from an existing infrastructure that delivers timely (and when required very rapid), highly sensitive, quality accredited and, importantly, low-priced expert forensic DNA analysis. For any technology to replace the current STR systems, the benefits must outweigh the investment that has already been made in what is a highly successful system.

With DNA profiles from approximately six million individuals and approximately 680,000 DNA profiles from crime scene samples already on the NDNAD [18] any new technology must be compatible with and augment the existing marker systems. In addition, it must be cost competitive.

MPS technology allows more STRs to be analysed in a single reaction compared to the current DNA-17 system and offers additional benefits [1, 2]. For example, STR results are analysed at the sequence level, which has the potential to help resolve complex mixtures by revealing STR profile differences that cannot be distinguished by measuring marker size alone. MPS also makes it possible to combine STRs with phenotypic and biogeographic ancestry markers (information which could assist an investigator by revealing information about the potential appearance of an unknown offender) in the same reaction; thereby, maximizing the information gained from what is often a very limited amount of sample material.

Accordingly, Cellmark Forensic Services took the decision to invest in MPS technology and in September 2021 became the first FSP in the UK to achieve ISO17025 accreditation for the use of MPS in forensic casework. This chapter concentrates on the work involved in completing the technical validation and achieving ISO17025 accreditation. The extensive engagement undertaken with stakeholders across the CJS to facilitate the introduction of this new technology within the UK's regulatory framework is also discussed. There is no doubt that MPS is a considerable technical advance for forensic DNA analysis but given the established low-cost forensic DNA services that exist for policing, it will be the economics of operational delivery that are likely to be the most significant challenges for the widespread adoption of this technology.

10.2 SNP Analysis and MPS Technology

In the forensic context, MPS has a number of potential advantages over conventional capillary electrophoresis (CE) forensic DNA testing [1, 2]. There is no need to carry out sequential DNA analyses (e.g. autosomal DNA analysis followed by Y-STR analysis) as a much larger number of markers can be included in each assay. STR alleles with the same length, but different DNA sequences can be differentiated which, in turn, can allow for better deconvolution of complex mixed DNA profiles. Large numbers of single nucleotide polymorphisms (SNPs) and STRs can be included in the same assay. SNPs can be more effective than STRs for the analysis of highly degraded DNA. In addition to the use of SNPs for identification purposes, there are also SNP marker panels that can be used for estimations of an individual's most likely external visible characteristics, such as hair and eye colour, and biogeographic ancestry.

The widespread use of SNPs by forensic laboratories internationally has been limited in part because the CE systems used for conventional STR analysis are not suitable for genotyping large numbers of SNP loci and by the lack of forensically relevant commercial kits. Furthermore, established forensic databases currently consist of STR profiles. MPS technology presents an opportunity for SNPs and STRs to be analysed simultaneously potentially making SNP technology more accessible to forensic laboratories.

The ForenSeq® DNA Signature Prep kit (Verogen) was launched by Illumina in 2015 [20]. This kit, designed for the Illumina MiSeq FGx® MPS platform contains 27 autosomal STRs, 24 Y-chromosome STRs, 7 X-chromosome STRs, 94 identity SNPs, 22 phenotypic SNPs (for hair and eye colour) and 56 biogeographical ancestry SNPs, all within a single reaction. This kit allows forensic laboratories the option of incorporating SNP analysis with conventional STR testing. Standard forensic STR markers are included in the assay allowing for comparisons with results obtained using traditional forensic STR multiplexes. The increased number of STRs improves the level of coverage against most countries' national DNA databases (of particular value in cases where the perpetrator and crime sample are on different countries' databases).

10.3 Verogen Partnership

In 2017, Verogen, offered Cellmark an opportunity to evaluate the performance of the Forenseq DNA Signature Prep kit on the Illumina MiSeq FGx system. Following completion of a pilot study, discussions on how Cellmark and Verogen might continue to collaborate progressed and ultimately led to a collaboration agreement to achieve a number of goals, including: (i) establishment of a UKAS ISO17025 accredited ForenSeq DNA Signature Prep Kit service offering at Cellmark Forensic Services; (ii) to work with policing to introduce MPS into casework and with the NDNAD to support the future acceptance of MPS DNA data; and (iii) to position and promote Cellmark as a MPS centre of excellence. Key milestones included the installation of a MiSeq FGx system, a comprehensive validation of the ForenSeq DNA Signature Prep kit and for Cellmark to seek ISO17025 accreditation for the service.

Verogen delivered and installed an Illumina MiSeq FGx system to Cellmark and provided training to Cellmark's Research and Development scientists. The collaboration was announced in a press release on the 8th May 2019.

10.4 Validation of the ForenSeq® DNA Signature Prep Kit on the Illumina MiSeq FGx® System

All technology evaluations at Cellmark progress through a structured and documented ISO9001 accredited design and development process which is recorded in Cellmark's electronic Quality Management System (QMS). Prior to commencing the validation of the ForenSeq DNA Signature Prep Kit on the MiSeq FGx DNA sequencing platform, a validation plan was written outlining the end user requirements for the assay, the work to be carried out for the validation and the acceptance criteria that would be used to determine if the assay was 'fit for purpose'. This was submitted via the QMS for approval by members of staff with relevant technical experience, operational process management and also the Company's Quality Director. Once this document was approved the validation work began.

Using product documentation provided by Verogen as guides [21–23], Standard Operating Procedures (SOPs) were written for all stages of the sequencing process, interpretation of the data and maintenance of the equipment. In addition to a step-by-step guide to performing the procedure, each SOP contained supporting information which included: references to related SOPs and documents relevant to the procedure, Control of Substances Hazardous to Health Regulations 2002 (COSHH) assessments; where the procedures were to be performed (accreditation for a process is specific to the laboratory where it is carried out) and the materials and equipment required for the procedure.

10.4.1 Sample Selection

Accessing samples for any forensic validation exercise is often a challenging part of the process. Any new technology, test or procedure must be validated using samples representative of the sample types that will be submitted in live forensic cases. Appropriate consent, as outlined in the Human Tissue Act 2004 [24], must be obtained from sample donors. The use of forensic casework material in validation work (from reported forensic cases) is restricted and a set of criteria must be met before the use of these samples. The Forensic Science Regulator has published a document, FSR-P-300 that addresses the use of casework samples for validation purposes [25]. This protocol recognises that:

> Where methods are not completely validated before use in casework the result may be that the final stages of validation occurs on casework samples – but not in the controlled environment normally employed for validation. The release of methods which have not been appropriately tested therefore poses a real and significant risk to the Criminal Justice System (CJS)

FSR-P-300 was agreed between the Crown Prosecution Service (CPS), the National Police Chiefs' Council (NPCC) and the Forensic Science Regulator (FSR) and describes an environment in which the CPS agrees that the use of casework material for validation purposes by an FSP is acceptable under circumstances, defined in the protocol. These circumstances include a requirement that the FSP has relevant ISO 17025 and/or ISO17020 accreditation for the validation being performed; that quality systems are in place which implement the provisions of the protocol; and that the FSR, NPCC and CPS have agreed that the FSP's quality systems properly implement the provisions of the protocol. In 2019, Cellmark submitted an application for approval under FSR-P-300 for the use of certain casework material in this validation work and received approval from the CPS, NPCC and FSR.

For validation of the ForenSeq DNA Signature Prep Kit a relatively large range of sample types were required. Broadly, three categories of samples were used for the validation. The first group comprised of samples for which the identity of the donor was known. Since Cellmark was particularly interested in evaluating how informative the phenotypic and biogeographic ancestry SNP panels would be, a selection of 'ground truth' samples were required. An internal notice was therefore placed asking for staff volunteers to provide samples for the validation work. The notice contained information on the assay, the sample type needed and the information (biogeographic ancestry, hair and eye colour) that would be required from each volunteer. On providing a sample, each donor was required to provide the above ancestry and phenotype information and to sign a consent form which detailed how the data was to be used. The second group consisted of mock or simulated casework samples that were similar to what might be encountered in forensic casework. Some of these samples were originally provided for another study and informed consent was obtained from the sample donors for use of the samples for this validation. Bone, muscle and tooth samples were approved for use as outlined in FSR-P-300 and by the police forces that had originally submitted the samples. The third group were samples from related individuals (family groups) that were tested to assess the ability of the ForenSeq DNA Signature Prep Kit to resolve close family relationships. These were samples on FTA cards that had originally been submitted for paternity/immigration testing and were provided under terms and conditions which allow for the anonymised use of the samples for research purposes after the original relationship analysis has been completed and reported.

10.4.2 Laboratory Work

The validation work consisted of experiments designed to test the reproducibility, accuracy and sensitivity of the assay as well as to thoroughly evaluate relevant software and equipment parameters. All DNA extraction, DNA quantitation and STR-PCR methods that were used throughout the validation exercise were Cellmark's existing UKAS accredited procedures.

The ForenSeq DNA Signature Prep Kits are configured so that for each sample, the operator can choose to sequence just the identity markers (autosomal, Y and X STRs, and identity SNPs) or to sequence the identity, ancestry and phenotypic markers. There are also two capacity options (relatively high or low sample numbers) for batching the samples for sequencing on the MiSeq FGx. Both marker panels, sample capacity options and combinations thereof were validated. Allelic drop-in/allelic drop-out, loci that were more challenging (failure to amplify in good quality samples or prone to allele imbalances), allelic stutter and isometric alleles (alleles with the same length but different DNA sequences) were also reviewed.

The reliability of using the Forenseq® Universal Analysis Software (UAS) as an expert interpretation system was evaluated by reviewing the number of sequences obtained for each allele and exporting data from the sequencing software and manually checking the exported results for every SNP and STR against the results displayed within the software to ensure concordance.

The accuracy and reproducibility of the assay was analysed by testing samples with both marker panel options, resequencing of PCR products and replicate testing of samples. The autosomal STR and Y chromosome STR results were also compared to results obtained using validated commercially available CE-based STR kits. The accuracy of the biogeographical ancestry and phenotypic predictions was evaluated using donor samples with a range of biogeographical ancestries, eye and hair colours. The sensitivity of the assay was tested to determine what levels of information would be obtained when sub-optimal amounts of input DNA are used in the assay. The kit manufacturer recommends adding 1 ng of sample DNA to the assay [21]. This input amount is not possible for some forensic samples. It is therefore important to have guidelines to determine whether sufficient levels of information are likely to be obtained from lower DNA input amounts, in order to be able to justify the use of the technology on what might be a limited amount sample material recovered in a forensic case. Results from serial dilutions were also used to provide information for the development of interpretation guidelines for live casework.

It is not uncommon for the DNA to be degraded in forensic samples. To demonstrate the effect that DNA degradation had on the assay, samples were thermally degraded and then sequenced. The results from the degraded samples were compared to sequencing and CE STR (where applicable) results from non-degraded samples from the same donor. The remainder of the validation work consisted of evaluating mock forensic casework samples (bone, muscle, teeth, hair, mock sexual assault), samples from putative related individuals (family groups) and samples with more than one known DNA contributor. The putative family groups were evaluated because it was anticipated that due to the increased number of markers and ability to differentiate between isometric alleles, MPS would be useful for resolving complex family relationships once suitable allele frequency databases had been generated. Although deconvolution of complex mixtures was outside the scope of the validation, several two and three-person mixed DNA samples of known donors and proportions were sequenced and the number of contributors was assessed.

10.4.3 Interpretation and Reporting Guidelines

As the laboratory work was progressing, interpretation and reporting guidelines were being developed for genetic profiles generated with the Forenseq DNA Signature Prep kit. Due to the novel nature of the use of MPS in forensic casework, there were challenges in developing robust reporting guidelines, a key element to the UKAS accreditation assessment. Aside from the bone, muscle and tooth samples, the validation work carried out was based on either good quality DNA from donors or samples mocked up to mimic items that might be expected in forensic casework. However good the validation work, past experience has indicated that genuine forensic casework samples can perform differently to those used in a validation study. With very little in the way of published guidance available within the forensic community for the reporting of MPS results, it was necessary to assess the validation data and follow, where possible, a similar approach to that used for conventional DNA results generated using CE. In addition to a reporting guidelines document, necessary procedures were created to assist the reporting scientist in interpretation of the DNA profiles and subsequent peer checks, in accordance with FSR guidance on cognitive bias [26], so that the process followed was as similar as possible to the reporting of conventional DNA results.

10.4.4 Validation Documentation

Once all the laboratory work and analyses were completed, the information was written up as a validation report that also detailed how the work had met the acceptance criteria set out in the validation plan and provided recommendations on the use of the assay for live samples. As outlined in the FSR document FSR-G-201 [3] an implementation plan, Statement of Completion and Failure Modes and Effects Analysis (FMEA) were required. The implementation plan described how the assay would be transferred from R&D to operational staff and requirements for running the assay in an operational setting. The document detailed how staff would be trained and their competence assessed in the laboratory processes and data interpretation. The plan also listed the required SOPs, where the laboratory work was to take place, information on required quality controls, how materials and supplies used in the process would be sourced and stocked and how the required equipment was to be calibrated and maintained. Finally, a brief description of the assay, potential uses in the criminal justice system and a plan for communication to customers and the relevant regulatory bodies was included. The Statement of Completion provided information about the assay in layman's terms, the intended use of the assay and caveats for use of the assay. The FMEA encompassed the entire laboratory and interpretation process. In addition to a list of cause/effect/controls/correction analysis for the various aspects of the operational use of this assay, the document included potential risks to the criminal justice system should some aspect of the assay fail when used on casework samples and recommendations and caveats regarding the use of the method. These documents were submitted via the QMS system for internal review and approval.

Once the validation was approved, an internal Cellmark auditor assessed all aspects of the laboratory process before providing feedback and raising several actions in the QMS. Where necessary, changes were made to the laboratory process and responses to the actions were recorded in the QMS.

10.5 Accreditation Process

To initiate the ISO17025 accreditation process an AC-4 application document for the assay to be added to Cellmark's scope of accreditation was submitted to the UKAS in September 2019. All the relevant SOPs, the validation report, implementation plan and a Statement of Completion were also submitted. UKAS had not previously undertaken an accreditation of MPS for forensic applications and the documentation therefore underwent a desktop assessment so that UKAS personnel could best determine what approach was required for the site assessment. On the 10th of February 2020, UKAS provided Cellmark with areas that required clarification prior to the onsite visit. The clarification responses were recorded in Cellmark's QMS and submitted to UKAS for review at the end of March 2020. Unfortunately, due to the COVID-19 pandemic, over a year elapsed between the desktop assessment and the onsite visit.

The UKAS onsite visit occurred over 3 days at the end of June 2021. The UKAS team comprised four individuals: the lead assessor/assessment manager, two technical assessors for laboratory and interpretation/reporting and a representative from the Forensic Information Database Service (FINDS) to evaluate the impact and utility of the method for the NDNAD. The laboratory applying for the ISO17025 accreditation pays for the time of the UKAS assessors for both the desktop assessments as well as on-site visits. The assessment of a novel technology necessarily requires additional time and, in this case, additional assessors which can add significantly to the costs of bringing a new technology to the forensic marketplace.

The entire laboratory process was completed in the presence of the assessor along with review of the laboratory SOPs and the validation documents. Examples of the use of the Forenseq DNA Signature Prep in a small number of forensic cases were also required for review. This posed a challenge as until a new technique has been both validated in-house and accredited by UKAS, its use in live casework is generally not permitted. However, after reviewing a number of completed cases (e.g. unknown human remains cases or criminal cases where the case had been through the court system) where sufficient DNA remained for MPS analysis, the required number of cases were identified. Approval was sought from the submitting police forces in line with the FSR guidelines [23]. Once approval was received, the samples were re-analysed using the Forenseq DNA Signature Prep assay and the results interpreted following the reporting guidelines. The UKAS assessor reviewed all of the documented procedures for the process and checked whether these had been followed in the case examples provided. This work became a key part of the accreditation assessment as it demonstrated both how the results would be interpreted and would be reported back to the police.

Following the assessment visit, Cellmark was sent a list of improvement actions to address. These actions and Cellmark's responses to them were recorded in QMS. After undergoing internal approval, these responses were returned to UKAS for review in September 2021. Extension to scope (ISO17025 accreditation) was granted by UKAS at the end of September 2021. Following notification, a customer communication was sent to the 43 police forces in England and Wales and other law enforcement agencies in the UK, announcing the availability of the service. Further information was provided at regular meetings with individual police forces.

10.6 Stakeholder Engagement

In addition to the validation and accreditation activities, it was important to engage with stakeholders and police customers about the plans to provide a new service. Cellmark therefore organised and attended a series of events between May 2019 and March 2020 to explain and seek feedback on the new technology and its potential applications. The first stakeholder engagement day was organised in May 2019. Representatives from the Forensic Science Regulator's office (including the Forensic Science Regulator), FINDS, and UKAS were invited to Cellmark's Abingdon site to learn about the technology, its applications and the validation. A senior representative from Verogen provided an introduction to MPS and the Forenseq DNA Signature Prep kit and highlighted how the technology was being adopted by the international forensic community. Attendees were asked to provide feedback on the information presented and insight on the necessary steps for introduction of the technology into the forensic marketplace.

Following the stakeholder engagement day, a meeting was held with FINDS in October 2019. As FINDS has responsibility for the NDNAD and the UK Missing Persons DNA Database (MPDD) [27], discussions were focussed on the potential for the results generated with the Forenseq DNA Signature Prep kit to be used in conjunction with the databases. Although the NDNAD infrastructure is not easily adaptable, a system to load the length-based genotypes of the DNA-17 loci was developed, thereby making the format identical to DNA-17 results. These results are loaded under a specific code which identifies them as being generated using the Forenseq DNA Signature Prep kit. The infrastructure of the MPDD was updated to allow for the capture of all autosomal STR results and the estimations for the most likely eye colour, hair colour and ancestry. The MPDD primarily consists of unidentified human remains, therefore, providing the additional detail could assist with potential identifications.

Cellmark presented at the Forensic Science Advisory Council (FSAC) meeting in December 2019. The FSAC is a specialist working group established to support and advise the FSR on a range of matters including the procedures for validating and approving new technologies and applications in the field of forensic science [28]. This meeting was attended by representatives from a wide range of organisations including the Chartered Society of Forensic Sciences, the Criminal Bar Association, the National Police Chiefs Council (NPCC) Forensic Science Portfolio, UKAS, the Crown Prosecution Service (CPS), Association of Forensic Science Providers, Forensic Science Northern Ireland, Scottish Police Authority and British Association in Forensic Medicine. The purpose of the presentation was to provide an overview of the technology and the validation and to identify the steps needed for introduction into forensic casework. Subsequently, actions were undertaken by the FSR to discuss further with the FSR DNA Specialist Group, the judiciary, and CPS and to approach the Biometrics and Forensics Ethics Group (BFEG).

The BFEG is a non-departmental government advisory body and one of its roles is to advise ministers and other stakeholders, such as the FINDS on ethical issues relating to the collection, retention and use of biometric information, including DNA [29]. This group was familiar with MPS, as the predecessor to this group, the NDNAD Ethics Group had published a document on the ethical dimensions of MPS in relation to the criminal investigations [30]. Cellmark presented information on the potential use of the Forenseq DNA Signature Prep kit profiles at a BFEG meeting in March 2020. The following discussion included concerns raised about: (i) the current absence of a South Asian population data set for determining ancestral origin (ii) placing people into geographical groups that may not represent their origin, for example individuals classified as of East Asian origin who had lived in Europe for many generations (iii) the reliability of the phenotypic and ancestral markers (iv) the limited amount of information generated from some phenotypic and ancestral markers used and the association with some traits, such as Asian ancestry and dark hair (v) the estimation of ancestry from values at the edges of population clusters would be less certain and would vary depending on the data used to train the algorithm (vi) a risk of excessive data collection and (vii) the risk of incorrect judgements being made by police based on the intelligence information provided by phenotypic and ancestral estimates. It was however recognised that the MPS technology itself was robust and had been proven over a decade of use in non-forensic applications and that over time the population frequency databases used to estimate biogeographic ancestry would be improved. It was also recognised that any reported results would clearly explain the limitations of the phenotypic and biogeographic ancestry estimates and make it clear that the results were for intelligence purposes only.

Parallel to the above discussions several presentations to various police audiences were delivered including technology experience events hosted by Cellmark (June 2019 and February 2020), the National Review Officers Conference (October 2019) and the NPCC Homicide Working Groups National Conference for Senior Investigating Officers (November 2019).

10.7 Training Forensic Personnel

After accreditation was received, the responsibility for performing and interpreting the results obtained with the Forenseq DNA Signature Prep kit transferred to the operational forensic teams. The transition to service delivery for a new technique requires that operational personnel are trained in the laboratory techniques and that results are reported by personnel competent in the work.

For the laboratory work, gaining competency required theoretical knowledge of the technique, understanding the laboratory protocols, shadowing experienced people in the laboratory during the process, performing the laboratory work under supervision by experienced personnel and finally completing the work at an acceptable level without input from the trainer. Once all of these activities were completed successfully the trainees were signed-off as being competent to run batches of samples.

The pool of experienced, court trained DNA reporting scientists identified to report forensic casework results generated using the Forenseq DNA Signature Prep kit was kept to a minimum to allow these individuals to gain a maximum amount of experience before gradually expanding the reporting team. These reporting scientists had been involved during the validation process so had a good level of understanding of the laboratory techniques prior to the service launch. Reporters gaining competency are each required to complete a training plan involving extensive background reading, the preparation of at least five reviewed case reports and satisfactory performance in a viva interview. All scientists involved in delivering forensic services must demonstrate and maintain ongoing competency and, like all Cellmark forensic work, every MPS report is subject to peer review.

10.8 Additional Casework Study

It had become clear from the engagement events with police forces prior to launch that it was the potential for the new capability of phenotypic and biogeographic ancestry estimations that most interested investigators. However, in addition, Cellmark felt that the potential to identify isometric alleles, also a new capability, would be valuable, particularly for deconvoluting mixed DNA source samples. Therefore, to support the launch of the service and provide additional data on the applications of the technology, twelve samples from existing forensic cases were identified. With traditional CE based STR profiling methodology, these samples had generated partial DNA profiles that were considered suitable for a speculative search of the NDNAD but searches had not been undertaken because another sample in the case with apparently the same (but more complete) DNA profile was loaded or searched instead. Given the selection criteria, no change in reporting outcome was expected for these cases because a 'better' alternative sample in the case had already been searched or reported. Once permission was obtained from the relevant police forces, the samples were DNA profiled using the Forenseq DNA Signature Prep kit to investigate the additional STR information this kit could provide. The expectation was that, for some of the samples, the additional information obtained from the MPS analysis would allow a more complete profile to be determined, improving the possible identification power of a speculative search or even reaching the threshold that would theoretically allow a permanent load to the NDNAD. The study demonstrated that the MPS profiling of samples already analysed with traditional CE methods could give significant improvements with the possibility of real changes to case outcomes in terms of increased intelligence information. Once the analyses had been completed, the results were reported to the relevant police forces.

10.9 Early Engagement

Reporting scientists provided police forces with awareness training in how MPS might be able to assist their investigations. Over the course of the year following the launch of MPS into casework, several presentations were given to police which included over 200 attendees, representing almost all UK police forces as well as some police forces from overseas. There was considerable interest by the police in the use of MPS following the awareness presentations and this resulted in the submission of a number of cases. These were mostly unidentified human remains cases but also included some cases where a DNA profile of the offender had been obtained but there had been no significant leads from the NDNAD, either through direct searching or using familial searching. For many of these cases, having an ancestry prediction was considered to be a valuable additional piece of information that might assist the investigation.

10.10 Live Casework Examples

An early example of the use of MPS involved the ancestry determination of a murder victim. Following the discovery of dismembered human remains, conventional DNA analysis was undertaken and the individual's DNA profile was determined. There was no match on the NDNAD and the DNA profile had remained on the MPDD for several years. The police were following various lines of inquiry but there was some doubt as to where the victim was from. Much of the police focus was spent on intelligence that indicated that the individual was from East Asia. With some of the DNA extract remaining from the initial analysis of one of the bones, analysis was undertaken using the Forenseq DNA Signature Prep kit. The data indicated that the individual's ancestry was most likely to be European with no indication that it was East Asian, South Asian or African Caribbean. This information changed the focus of the police investigation.

In another case, MPS has been used in an attempt to identify a male washed up on the shore of northern France in 1984. Efforts to identify this male failed and his remains were buried in a cemetery in the nearby town. Locate International, a UK registered charity dedicated to helping families of unsolved missing person cases find their loved ones, became involved as there was a potential link to a man who had drowned off the coast of East Anglia in England. The body was exhumed and one of the bones was submitted to Cellmark for traditional DNA analysis. This analysis indicated that the unknown male could not be the person who had drowned off East Anglia in 1984. In an effort to assist in identifying the unknown male, Locate

International requested that Cellmark undertake analysis using the Forenseq DNA Signature Prep kit to provide intelligence about the individual's possible appearance. The most likely estimations for ancestry, eye colour and hair colour for the unidentified human remains were incorporated into a facial image generated by the Centre for Anatomy and Human Identification at the University of Dundee which was used in a media campaign to try and identify the individual (Fig. 10.1).

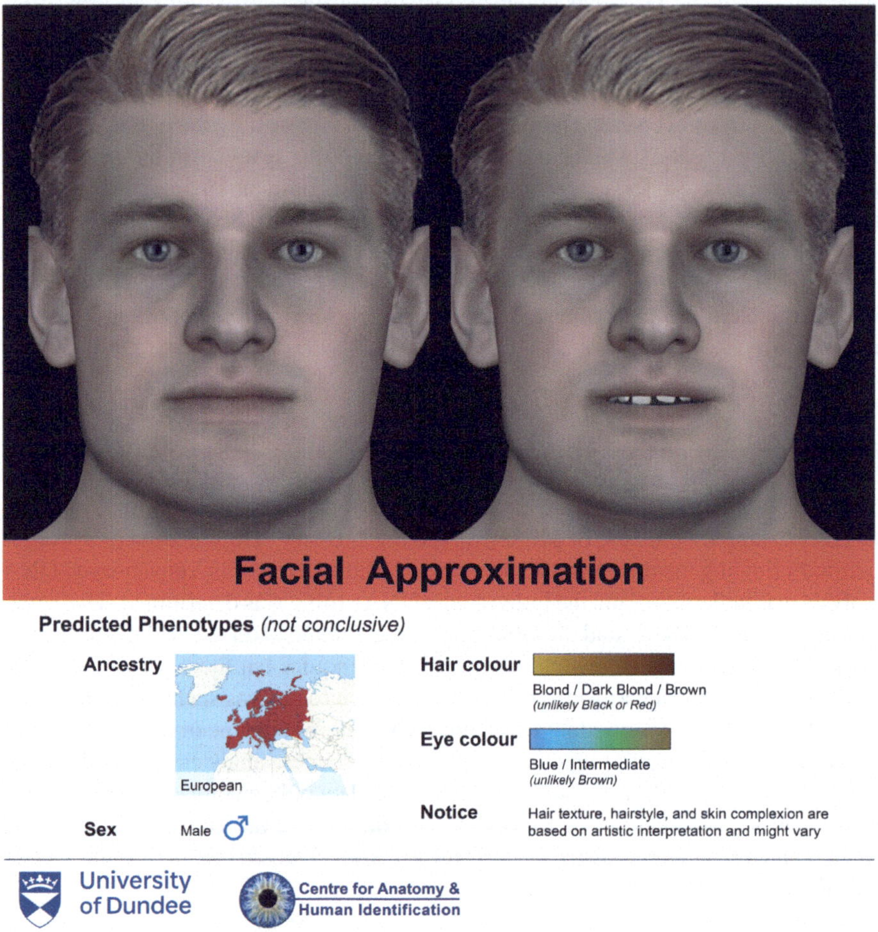

Fig. 10.1 Image used in a media campaign by Locate International to try and identify unidentified human remains, incorporating the most likely estimations for ancestry, eye and hair colour produced using MPS analysis carried out at Cellmark Forensic Services. Courtesy of Locate International and University of Dundee

10.11 Conclusions

The description of the work involved in the development and introduction of an MPS-based service by Cellmark demonstrates the considerable investment required in terms of expenditure on capital equipment, the huge amount of staff time required throughout the validation and accreditation process, the time spent in stakeholder engagement and in staff training, as well as the costs of the accreditation process itself. This is not just one-off expenditure but continues with equipment service costs, ongoing accreditation costs as well as continued training and competency assessments. The entire process from the start of our validation to the launch of an accredited service took almost two and a half years and although there was approximately 12 months delay due to the COVID-19 pandemic, it was a lengthy process even when supported throughout by the technology manufacturer.

Along with the technical requirements, this chapter has described the extensive engagement with key stakeholders that was undertaken to educate, inform and gain acceptance for a new technology being introduced into the UK Criminal Justice System. Indeed it is still early days. The majority of the work so far carried out has been to provide useful intelligence information. The evidential use of MPS has yet to be tested through the UK courts. However, a robust and comprehensive validation and accreditation process has been followed and, as a result, any FSP that follows with their own introduction of MPS, will undoubtedly find it easier to cross the divide to operational service delivery.

MPS is a remarkable technology but unfortunately it remains expensive to use unless large volumes of samples are tested, due to the relatively high cost of the flow cells (a single use consumable where the sequencing reactions take place). These flow cells can be used to sequence multiple samples at the same time (which reduces the per sample cost). However, the processing of a relatively small number of samples in a short timeframe to meet an investigative requirement places the cost per sample at a price point which is multiple times the cost of CE STR analysis. In the UK marketplace, where forensic provision is managed through carefully controlled police budgets, cost will continue to be a significant challenge to the introduction of this technology. In addition to the stakeholder engagement undertaken, ongoing awareness training and marketing of the new service will continue to be required to allow the transition to a sufficient, regular sample volume that will tip the economics of service delivery in the direction of sustainability.

It is also important to consider that further commercial marker panels that provide additional intelligence information will help to drive uptake of this technology, although each new marker set will require a separate validation. As the MPS applications develop further (age estimation, more detailed ancestry estimations, estimations for additional external visible characteristics etc.), it will provide forensic DNA scientists with the potential to deliver even more valuable intelligence to investigators.

A potentially significant application of MPS is its use for Forensic Investigative Genetic Genealogy (FIGG). FIGG utilises large numbers of SNP markers to identify possible relatives on genealogy DNA databases where permission to search has been granted to investigators. Although still in its infancy in Europe, there have already been some notable success in the US using FIGG [31]. There is much debate in the forensic community regarding the use of FIGG, particularly concerning ethical issues, consent, data security and the setting of scientific standards. However, FIGG has the potential to make a very significant impact on law enforcement agencies by providing intelligence leads for both the identification of unknown offenders and unidentified human remains. If approved for use more widely by the forensic community and an appropriate regulatory framework is established, FIGG could become one of the most significant advances in forensic investigation for decades.

References

1. Ballard, D., Winkler-Galicki, J., & Wesoly, J. (2020). Massive parallel sequencing in forensics: Advantages, issues, technicalities, and prospects. *International Journal of Legal Medicine, 134*, 1291–1303.
2. Bruijns, B., Tiggelaar, R., & Gardeniers, H. (2018). Massively parallel sequencing techniques for forensics: A review. *Electrophoresis, 39*, 2642–2654.
3. Forensic Science Regulator. (2020). Forensic Science Regulator guidance validation FSR-G-201 Issue 2. Validation Guidance (publishing.service.gov.uk). Accessed 24 October 2023.
4. Forensic Science Regulator. (2023). Code of practice version 1. Code of Practice (publishing.service.gov.uk). Accessed 24 October 2023.
5. House of Commons. (2007). Official Report—12 July 2007. Forensic Science Regulator—Hansard—UK Parliament. Accessed 24 October 2023.
6. Forensic Science Regulator Act 2021. (2021). Forensic Science Regulator Act 2021 (legislation.gov.uk). Accessed 24 October 2023.
7. House of Commons Science and Technology Committee. (2005). Forensic science on trial. https://publications.parliament.uk/pa/cm200405/cmselect/cmsctech/96/96i.pdf. Accessed 24 October 2023.
8. Jeffreys, A. J., Wilson, V., & Thein, S. L. (1985). Hypervariable 'minisatellite' regions in human DNA. *Nature, 314*, 67–73.
9. Jeffreys, A. J., Wilson, V., & Thein, S. L. (1985). Individual-specific 'fingerprints' of human DNA. *Nature, 316*, 76–79.
10. Roewer, L. (2013). DNA fingerprinting in forensics: Past, present, future. *Investigative genetics, 4*, 22.
11. Kimpton, C., Fisher, D., Watson, S., et al. (1994). Evaluation of an automated DNA profiling system employing multiplex amplification of four tetrameric STR loci. *International Journal of Legal Medicine, 106*, 302–311.
12. Martin, P. D., Schmitter, H., & Schneider, P. M. (2001). A brief history of the formation of DNA databases in forensic science within Europe. *Forensic Science International, 119*, 225–231.
13. Home Office. (2005). DNA expansion programme 2000–2005: Reporting achievement. [ARCHIVED CONTENT] (nationalarchives.gov.uk). Accessed 24 October 2023.
14. Science and Technology Committee. (2011). Seventh Report—The Forensic Science Service. House of Commons—The Forensic Science Service - Science and Technology Committee (parliament.uk). Accessed 24 October 2023.
15. Sparkes, R., Kimpton, C., & Watson, S et al. (1996). The validation of a 7-locus multiplex STR test for use in forensic casework. *International Journal of Legal Medicine, 109*, 186–194.
16. Forensic Science Service. (2003). The National DNA Database® annual report 2002–2003. NDNAD_Annual_Report_02_03.pdf (genewatch.org). Accessed 25 October 2023.
17. Human Genetics Commission. (2009). Nothing to hide, nothing to fear? Nothing to Hide, Nothing to Fear (statewatch.org). Accessed 25 October 2023.

18. Home Office. (2023). National DNA database (NDNAD) statistics as of 30/09/2023. National DNA Database statistics—GOV.UK (www.gov.uk). Accessed 25 October 2023.
19. Home Office. (2015). National DNA database strategy board annual report 2014/15. National DNA Database Strategy Board Annual Report 2014/15 (publishing.service.gov.uk). Accessed 25 October 2023.
20. Verogen. (2022). ForenSeq DNA Signature Prep Kit reference guide. ForenSeq DNA Signature Prep Kit Reference Guide PCR1 (VD2018005) (verogen.com). Accessed 25 October 2023.
21. Verogen. (2018). ForenSeq™ DNA Signature Prep reference guide.
22. Verogen. (2018). ForenSeq™ instrument reference guide.
23. Verogen. (2018). ForenSeq™ Universal Analysis Software guide.
24. Human Tissue Act 2004. (2004). Human Tissue Act 2004. Human Tissue Act 2004 (legislation.gov.uk). Accessed 23 October 2023.
25. Forensic Science Regulator. (2020). Forensic Science Regulator protocol: validation—Use of casework material FSR-P-300 Issue 2. Validation—Use of Casework Material (publishing.service.gov.uk). Accessed 23 October 2023.
26. Forensic Science Regulator. (2020). Forensic Science Regulator guidance cognitive bias effects relevant to forensic science examinations FSR-G-2017 Issue 2. Guidance on Cognitive Bias (publishing.service.gov.uk). Accessed 25 October 2023.
27. Home Office .(2020). National DNA database strategy board biennial report 2018–2020. NDNAD Biennial Report 2018 to 2020 (Print) (publishing.service.gov.uk). Accessed 25 October 2023.
28. Forensic Science Regulator. (2020). Forensic science regulator terms of reference, forensic science advisory council FSR-T-C01 Issue 3. FSAC Terms of Reference Issue 3 (publishing.service.gov.uk). Accessed 23 October 2023.
29. Gov.UK. (2023). Biometrics and forensic ethics group biometrics and forensics ethics group—GOV.UK (www.gov.uk). Accessed 23 October 2023.
30. National DNA Database Ethics Group. (2017). Ethical dimensions of the application of next generation sequencing technologies to criminal investigations. ethical dimensions of NGS technologies to criminal investigations (publishing.service.gov.uk). Accessed 23 October 2023.
31. Greytak, E. M., Moore, C., & Armentrout, S. L. (2019). Genetic genealogy for cold case and active investigations. *Forensic Science International, 299*, 103–113.

Chapter 11
Regulatory Considerations for Translational Forensic Science

Gillian Tully

Abstract To be effectively deployed in operational forensic science, innovative methods must meet the regulatory standards for their jurisdiction. This chapter will consider how the balance between agility in introducing innovative scientific approaches to criminal casework and the requirement to comply with such standards can be reached, primarily drawing on experience in England and Wales. It considers how regulators and courts must balance the risk of failing to use new technologies in a timely manner, against the risk of novel and/or insufficiently tested methods giving rise to unreliable evidence. Demonstration of reliability through validation of methods for their specific purpose, followed by careful implementation and third-party accreditation is discussed, alongside the role of the court in considering admissibility. Practicalities, including the importance of collaboration between researchers and end users, clarity of regulatory requirements, costs, funding and mechanisms for translation are presented.

11.1 Regulation

11.1.1 Forensic Science Regulation in Its Broadest Sense

Few jurisdictions have the formal role of 'Forensic Science Regulator' to develop and set quality standards for forensic science; England and Wales can be considered an outlier, with an independent, statutory regulator. Some, including many European states, have legislation requiring accreditation of elements of forensic science. The United States of America (US) uses the Organization of Scientific Area Committees (OSAC) to:

> Strengthen … the nation's use of forensic science by facilitating the development of technically sound standards and guidelines and encouraging their use throughout the forensic science community. [1]

G. Tully (✉)
King's Forensics, King's College London, 150 Stamford Street, London SE1 9NH, UK
e-mail: gillian.tully@kcl.ac.uk

S. Francese and R. S. P. King (eds.), *Driving Forensic Innovation in the 21st Century*,
https://doi.org/10.1007/978-3-031-56556-4_11

In Australia and New Zealand, the National Institute of Forensic Science facilitates standardisation to reduce risk and has the strategic intent to:

> Deliver high quality and innovative products, services, and advice to enhance capability, efficiency, and reliability of the forensic sciences for police, justice, and the community. [2]

In addition to quality standards, there are often legal and procedural rules governing expert and/or scientific evidence, whether written or unwritten. For example, the Criminal Procedure Rules Committee in England and Wales sets rules for criminal court procedure [3], which are supplemented by the Criminal Practice Directions [4], issued by the Lord Chief Justice. Similarly, the Netherlands has a Code of Criminal Procedure, which contains rules to ensure that prosecutions are conducted fairly; an updated version is close to implementation [5]. The situation in the US is more complex, with both State and Federal laws.

Despite jurisdictional differences, standards relating to quality and/or reliability are common to the application of science in a criminal justice setting.

11.2 England and Wales as an Example

11.2.1 The Forensic Science Regulator

The role of Forensic Science Regulator was established on a non-statutory basis in 2007, with the role being:

> to advise Government and the Criminal Justice System on quality standards in the provision of forensic science. This will involve identifying the requirement for new or improved quality standards; leading on the development of new standards where necessary; providing advice and guidance so that providers will be able to demonstrate compliance with common standards, for example, in procurement and in courts; ensuring that satisfactory arrangements exist to provide assurance and monitoring of the standards and reporting on quality standards generally. [6]

In 2021, the Forensic Science Regulator Act [7] was passed into law, and the Regulator became a Statutory Regulator in July 2022, followed by approval of a statutory Code of Practice by both Houses of Parliament in February 2023, which came into effect on 2nd October 2023.

The Regulator does not assume the role of approving methods for use in forensic science, which could cause a bottleneck by decision-making going through a single point. Instead, the Regulator sets out, in the Code of Practice [8], a structured approach to validation of methods, where validation is defined as.

> The process of providing objective evidence that a method, process or device is fit for the specific purpose intended.

Responsibility for compliance with the Code of Practice sits with each organisation providing forensic science activities in the Criminal Justice System (CJS), but there is a requirement to demonstrate such compliance through the mechanism of independent accreditation. For major or novel technologies, innovators are advised to inform the Regulator, who may "advise on the most expedient method of ensuring that the CJS requirements are understood" [8, para 30.2.5]. There are exceptions to the requirement for accreditation for methods that are infrequently used; this can also be applied to novel methods, for which there is insufficient evidence of routine operation to seek accreditation.

11.2.2 Criminal Procedure Rules and Criminal Practice Directions

In 2011, the Law Commission recommended that a statutory admissibility test be established for expert opinion evidence [9], but this recommendation was not accepted by the Government [10]. As a result, the Criminal Procedure Rules [3] and Criminal Practice Directions [4] were modified in an attempt to address as many of the Law Commission's proposals as possible, short of changing the law. The Criminal Practice Directions now contain details of the factors that a court should take into account when considering admissibility of expert evidence, particularly scientific expert evidence. These are:

a. the extent and quality of the data on which the expert opinion is based;
b. the validity of the methodology employed by the expert;
c. if the expert's opinion relies on an inference from any findings, whether the opinion properly explains how safe or unsafe the inference is (whether by reference to statistical significance or in other appropriate terms);
d. if the expert's opinion relies on the results of the use of any method (for instance, a test, measurement or survey), whether the opinion takes proper account of matters, such as the degree of precision or margin of uncertainty, affecting the accuracy or reliability of those results;
e. the extent to which any material upon which the expert's opinion is based has been reviewed by others with relevant expertise (for instance, in peer-reviewed publications), and the views of those others on that material;
f. the extent to which the expert's opinion is based on material falling outside the expert's own field of expertise;
g. the completeness of the information which was available to the expert, and whether the expert took account of all relevant information in arriving at the opinion (including information as to the context of any facts to which the opinion relates);
h. if there is a range of expert opinion on the matter in question, where in the range the expert's own opinion lies and whether the expert's preference has been properly explained; and
i. whether the expert's methods followed established practice in the field and, if they did not, whether the reason for the divergence has been properly explained.

Factors that may flag concerns about expert evidence are also considered, including adverse judicial comment, adverse findings, disciplinary proceedings or other criticism by a professional, regulatory or registration body and lack of accreditation or commitment to prescribed standards, or the opinion:

> being based on a hypothesis which has not been subjected to sufficient scrutiny (including, where appropriate, experimental or other testing).

11.2.3 The Overall System

The system for assuring that novel scientific methods are only admitted as evidence when sufficiently reliable is therefore two-fold:

1. That the method should be compliant with the Forensic Science Regulator's Code of Practice, including validation of methods; and
2. That the Court should scrutinise reliability in accordance with the Criminal Practice Directions.

As an additional safeguard in the adversarial system, there is of course the potential for evidence to be robustly challenged by whichever party is not seeking to introduce it.

The safeguards against preventing progress of innovative methods include:

1. the exception, within the Regulator's Code of Practice [8], from the requirement for accreditation for infrequently used methods, which may also be applied to novel methods; and
2. the discretion of the Court to admit any expert evidence that meets the requirement of being "sufficiently reliable to be admitted" [4].

Indeed, it has been argued that unvalidated evidence could, and should, be admitted, in certain circumstances, providing that the lack of validation should be made clear to jurors 'up front' [11].

So at least from a theoretical, systematic perspective, there is a balance between the need to enable successful innovation to be applied effectively in the CJS and the need to protect the CJS from unreliable evidence or untested evidence, the limitations of which may be unknown.

11.3 Risks

11.3.1 Learning from the Past: Drift from the Intended Purpose

Numerous examples, within and outside of forensic science, illustrate the extent to which a failure to effectively test methods and understand their limitations *for the specific purpose intended* prior to operational deployment can have negative, even catastrophic, consequences. Perhaps the most widely used example is the Challenger space shuttle disaster in 1986. While the immediate cause of the explosion which destroyed the shuttle, killing all those on board, was an O-ring from the solid rocket booster, the interesting issue is why that failed. In summary, it failed because the launch temperature was well outside the range of temperatures at which the O-ring had been tested.

Allowing presumptive tests in forensic science to be interpreted beyond their specific purpose has contributed to miscarriages of justice. The most famous example is that of the "Birmingham six" [12]. One of the two critical pieces of evidence was the alleged identification of components of commercial explosives on the hands of some of the defendants. At the first trial, in 1975, a forensic scientist testified to being 99% certain of the presence of nitroglycerine on two swabs, based on a presumptive test, the Griess test. Although the results from those particular swabs were negative for nitroglycerine using subsequent, more sensitive analysis by gas chromatography/mass spectrometry (GCMS), a weak positive result for one of the expected ions on a different swab was sufficient for the scientist to revise his level of certainty to 100%. This level of certainty did not reflect the potential for false positive results using the Greiss test, nor the lack of reproducibility of results between the Greiss test and the more sensitive GCMS analysis: the Greiss test was used beyond *the specific purpose intended*, which was as a presumptive test. Subsequent evaluations were hampered by the lack of a written protocol or contemporaneous notes to know exactly how the Greiss test had been performed, and the GCMS analysis had only been set to detect one of the 3 expected ions; without the full set of results, the single ion was of limited significance.

Considering the interpretative, rather than analytical parts of forensic science, going beyond what has been demonstrated to be scientifically valid was illustrated by the invalid testimony on the strength of microscopic hair examination [13]. Indeed, whether the practice of 'identification' can ever be scientifically justified remains a topic of some debate (see, e.g., [14]).

Morgan [15] conducted a systematic review of instances in the US where forensic science contributed to miscarriages of justice. A number of the issues were concluded to have been the result of analyses and/or interpretation which was not scientifically valid or reliable, including some where the practitioners involved believed that they were "on the cutting edge of forensic practice and felt that they were being punished for advocating innovations in their fields." Morgan found that an inadequate scientific foundation was prevalent across a range of disciplines, with practitioners exceeding the limits of science. His work also concluded that there is "a limited basis for police investigators and courts to accept or reject new methods", going on to recommend guidelines for validation and use of new technologies. Importantly, Morgan's data review also supports innovation as a driver for improvement, contributing to a reduction in wrongful convictions involving forensic science.

11.3.2 Managing Risks in a Regulatory Framework

One of the principles of effective regulation [16] is that regulatory objectives should support the desired policy outcomes; this will inevitably involve some degree of balance between different objectives. At the top level the desired outcome of forensic science regulation is to reduce the occurrence of miscarriages of justice. To achieve that outcome, it is necessary to balance the need to encourage innovation, which can improve the science delivered for the CJS, with the need to ensure that novel methods are properly validated, such that their strengths and limitations are understood by their users, including investigators and courts. Or in risk terms, the need to balance the risk of not introducing a new and potentially better method, with the risk of introducing it without the proper testing.

If this balance is to be achieved, it is important to avoid a regulatory bottleneck, where promising new innovations are held up awaiting approval by a single individual or organisation. If a regulator were to insist on approving all new methods prior to their use in forensic casework, this could lead to just such a bottleneck. Criminal casework does not wait while innovation is considered by a regulator: in reality, cases in which the new method could have contributed novel or improved intelligence or evidence will proceed without it: decisions on whether or not to charge a suspect will be made and court cases will proceed. Further, it may be difficult to draw a clear distinction between incremental improvements and new methods needing regulatory approval, when in reality there is a continuum.

A way to manage the balance of risks without creating a bottleneck is to establish a methodology for validation of methods to be used in the CJS for scientists to follow, supported by a means to monitor compliance over time. In England and Wales, the Forensic Science Regulator's Code of Practice [8] sets out an ordered approach to validation (illustrated in Fig. 11.1); a similar approach, although without the risk assessment element, has been documented by the European Network of Forensic Science Institutes (ENFSI) [17].

The methodology is based on a clear statement of user requirements, translated to a testable technical specification. In the Forensic Science Regulator's Code of Practice, risk is the guiding principle: a risk assessment establishes the scale of the validation work required and the areas requiring particular focus. Clear acceptance criteria are needed, based on the technical specification and any control measures identified through the risk assessment; these are set prior to any experimental work being carried out, to avoid post hoc rationalisation of results. Evaluation of whether the method meets the acceptance criteria is carried out by an individual independent of method development or validation; this individual could be from within the organisation conducting the validation, if sufficient skills are available, or could be an external expert if required. There is a requirement for a clear statement of what the method has been validated for and any caveats and limitations on its use. All of the records relating to the validation of a method must be collated into a validation library, which must be retained in an accessible format and may be disclosable in criminal proceedings.

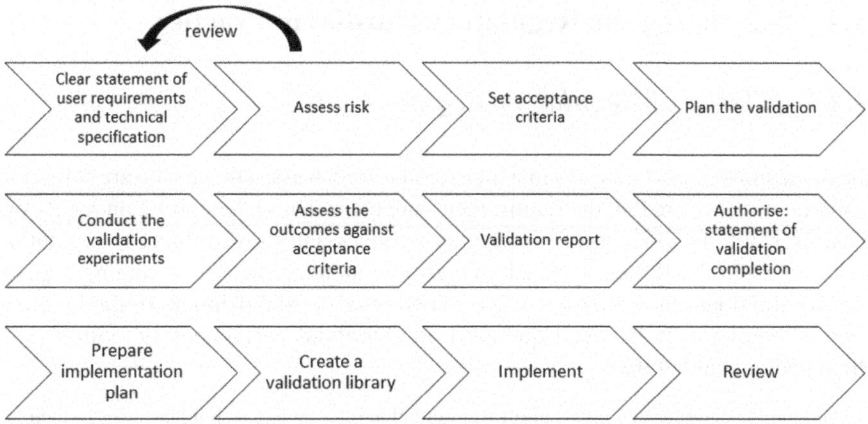

Fig. 11.1 Structured validation process as set out in the forensic science regulator's code of practice [8]

In the general course of events, if the method is to be used on a regular basis and is part of a forensic science activity for which the regulator has set a requirement for independent accreditation to a specified standard, that accreditation would be sought as soon as practicable. However, it is not generally mandatory that accreditation be achieved prior to the first use of the method, since a body of operational data may be required in order to satisfy the assessment body that the method meets the requirements of the standard, and/or a method may be used only infrequently in the CJS. In such instances, a procedure for infrequently used methods is applied, wherein the unit adopting the new technology ensures that the method has been validated, the practitioners are competent and that those receiving reports of results from the method are aware of its status as a novel and unaccredited (but validated) method.

It is then open to the courts to scrutinise the admissibility of the evidence, on the basis of the admissibility considerations in the Criminal Practice Directions [4]. It is also open to defence lawyers and scientists instructed by the defence to challenge the admissibility and/or weight of the evidence. If the validation process set out in the Regulator's Code of Practice has been effectively applied and the practitioners are competent, there should be ample objective evidence on which any challenge can be decided.

Of course, in practice, there are a host of challenges, including the availability of skills and resources to conduct the validation process, the effectiveness and cost of the accreditation process and the extent to which the courts (including the defence) are willing and/or able to challenge new methods. These challenges will be considered throughout the following sections.

11.4 Negotiating the Regulatory Hurdles in Practice

11.4.1 Clarity of Regulatory Requirements

One of the most important ways in which regulators can assist those who are subject to regulation is to ensure that the requirements are clear. Those depending on regulators to assure safety or efficacy of products or services and those subject to regulation can be left in limbo if there is a lack of clarity or an unpredictably changing regime.

In his judgment in *R. v. Hoey* in 2007 [18], prior to establishment of the Forensic Science Regulator, Judge Weir quoted from a previous parliamentary inquiry [19], which had concluded that:

> The absence of an agreed protocol for the validation of scientific techniques prior to their being admitted in court is entirely unsatisfactory. Judges are not well placed to determine scientific validity without input from scientists.

This comment related to the scientific validation of low template DNA analysis, the admissibility of which had been challenged, illustrating the importance of a clear process for validation from an end user perspective.

As an innovator in any sector, there are challenges in clearing regulatory hurdles, but if the requirements are opaque, or the goalposts constantly changing, it becomes virtually impossible to plan and achieve compliance efficiently. Conversely, if there is an overly prescriptive approach, requiring every method to be tested with at least a certain number of samples and against specified performance characteristics, there is a risk that validation becomes a 'tick-box' exercise, rather than a scientifically designed, risk-based study, directly relevant to the specific intended use.

A standard that sets out the required approach to validation, without specifying exact experiments or sample numbers, is a way to provide clarity without being overly prescriptive.

11.4.2 Collaboration

If an innovative method is to be adopted in forensic science practice, the first and most obvious issue is that there must be a need for it: it must meet some form of user or customer requirement. The most ingenious novel method, if it does not provide operational advantages within the timeliness and cost requirements of the system in which it is intended to operate, is unlikely to ever be adopted. While it could be argued that justice should not be constrained by tawdry financial and time considerations, reality dictates that a hugely expensive and time-consuming method will not be used for 'volume crime' cases such as opportunistic residential burglaries or bicycle theft.

Ideally, there should be a balance of technology push, and end user pull, across the spectrum of forensic science research and development. Technology push is important because users may not be aware of the art of the possible. User pull is important if we are to avoid too many solutions looking for (non- or minimally-existent) problems. The optimal way to ensure that an innovation will be adopted is to collaborate with potential users, at an early stage and then throughout its development. This collaboration then feeds directly into the validation and implementation aspects of research translation into practice. As outlined in Fig. 11.1 and Sect. 11.3.2, the validation process is predicated on a user requirement; collaboration assists with ensuring that the user requirement is well designed, and the innovation therefore meets a specified need.

The next question is who should be responsible for the validation? If a method has been developed in a research organisation (whether that be an academic institution or a commercial company), should it be the research organisation or the forensic science unit who validates the method? Ultimately, any forensic science unit adopting the innovation will need to satisfy itself that there is an adequate body of objective evidence to demonstrate the validity of the method for its intended purpose, and that the method works in the hands of its practitioners. The forensic unit may not have the resources or the expertise to carry out all of the validation required for a novel method. However, if validation is carried out by the researcher, the details of the validation undertaken, and the data obtained, will need to be made available to the adopting forensic unit(s). If innovators wish to make their methods attractive to potential users, providing a package of validation (often called developmental validation) to end users will reduce the barriers to that method being adopted. Figure 11.2 illustrates the role of the various parties throughout the research, development, validation and implementation pathway.

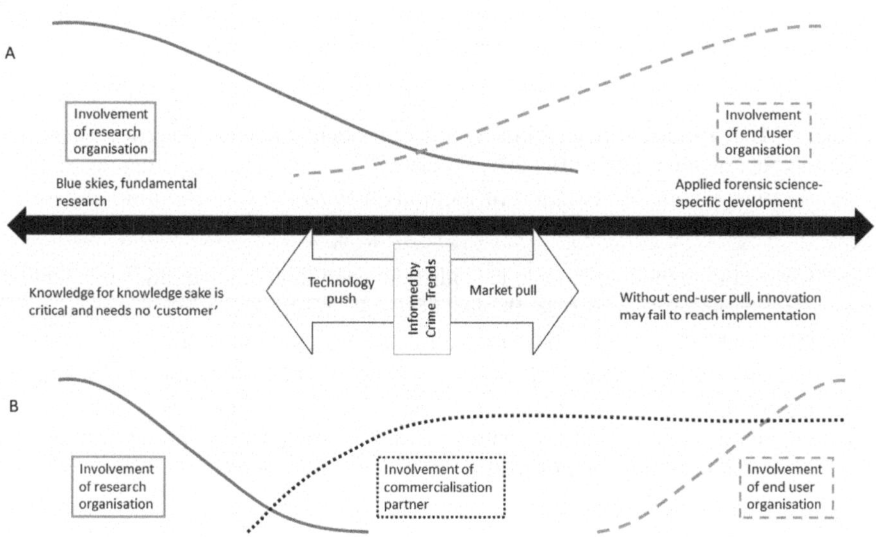

Fig. 11.2 The role of researchers, innovators and end users in research, innovation and crossing the valley of death. **a** Translation from research to end user without a commercialisation partner. **b** Translation via a commercialisation organisation

The fundamental problem for innovations coming from academia in particular is how these translational activities are funded; see Sect. 11.4.5.

11.4.3 Implementation

Implementation of new technologies or methods from a research or development environment into routine casework use involves more than installing equipment and training staff. The Forensic Science Regulator's Code of Practice [8] sets out what should be considered (Box 11.1). Ensuring any new technology is carefully implemented, considering all of the relevant aspects set out in Box 11.1, reduces the potential for poor performance on transfer of a method from a research environment into a casework environment. Post-implementation review provides an opportunity to ensure that any provisos on authorisation of the method for use in casework have been addressed, that any unforeseen issues that have arisen since authorisation of the method have been captured, with corrective actions having been undertaken where required, and checked for effectiveness. As with validation, the process is scalable: if a new version of a software tool is being implemented into an existing digital forensics method, the implementation plan will be short, primarily accounting for issues such as ensuring all workstations have the old versions removed and the new versions installed, and that staff are familiarised with any changes and the outcome of the validation. At the other end of the scale, implementing a new automated workflow for an analytical process may involve building work, air handling alterations, training of multiple staff, pilot running, a ramp-up scheme and regular review of uncertainty of measurement until a steady state has been reached.

Box 11.1: Implementation Plan Requirements of Forensic Science Regulator's Statutory Code of Practice (issue 1)[1] 30.20.1 The forensic unit shall have a plan for implementation of methods new to the forensic unit. Where relevant, this plan shall address:

a. whether the new method can provide new analytical opportunities relevant to revisiting old cases. If so, the forensic unit should determine if any action is warranted, such as communicating the benefits and risks to previous commissioning parties (this may be a general communication on the new capability);
b. the standard operating procedure (including the process for assessment/interpretation/reporting of results) or instructions for use;

[1] The text in Box 11.1 is subject to Crown Copyright.

c. requirements for practitioner training, competence assessment, and ongoing monitoring of practitioner competence;
d. integration of the method with what is already in place;
e. the steps required to include the method in the scope of accreditation (if needed);
f. the monitoring mechanisms to be used to demonstrate that the method remains under satisfactory control during its use. The forensic unit will also assist with any post-implementation review, including:
    i. managing planned increases in volume (i.e. any ramp up from validation studies levels), whether through a phased approach or piloting of the validated method using casework;
    ii. controlling changes in workflow.
g. the protocols for calibration, monitoring and maintenance of any equipment;
h. the supply and traceability of any standards/reference materials;
i. the supply and quality control of key materials, consumables and reagents;
j. the item/exhibit handling and any anti-contamination protocols;
k. the accommodation plan;
l. any specific health and safety, environmental protection, data protection, and information security arrangements;
m. the communication plan; and
n. the schedule for post-implementation review.

11.4.4 Accreditation

Accreditation to an international standard (often ISO/IEC 17,025:2017 or ISO 17020:2012) is a common requirement for forensic science laboratories in many jurisdictions. The European Network of Forensic Science Institutes (ENFSI) aims that members have achieved or are taking steps towards at least 50% of their fields of expertise to be accredited and that a continuing increase in the scope of accreditation should be demonstrated by the institute each year [20]. The Forensic Science Regulator requires accreditation for many disciplines, as the primary means of demonstrating compliance with the Code of Practice [8].

Accreditation is not a silver bullet that solves all the quality issues with forensic science (see, e.g. [21]), but it does provide independent, third-party assessment of an organisation's systematic approach to quality and has been demonstrated to find weaknesses in areas where forensic science units believed themselves to be compliant [22].

Achieving accreditation for a new method is the responsibility of the forensic unit implementing the method. Accreditation is not simply about the analytical or technological aspects of an innovative product; it is a systematic approach to ensuring quality, through management oversight, scientific validation including understanding of limitations and uncertainty, competence of staff, ongoing monitoring of method performance and ensuring performance is understood, for example through participation in proficiency tests and/or interlaboratory comparisons.

One downside of accreditation is its very visible cost, which can provide a disincentive for organisations to adopt new technologies; this is considered further in Sect. 11.4.5.

11.4.5 Financial Considerations

There is frequently a gap between innovative research that is appealing to academic funders and operational funding for casework. While this issue has been highlighted, e.g., via parliamentary committee [23], there is no obvious solution yet and a more detailed consideration is beyond the scope of this chapter.

Where an innovation originates in, or is commercialised by, a commercial technology provider, that entity tends to be the primary investor in at least the developmental validation stage. Some commercial technology providers also sell validation services on behalf of end users (e.g., [24,25]), which reduces abstraction of end user staff from casework, although it carries a financial cost. Such technology providers have been the route by which the majority of forensic genetics innovation has been successfully translated into operational practice in recent years.

A notable exception is the STRmix™ expert software for interpreting DNA mixtures, which was developed by the New Zealand Government's Institute of Environmental Science and Research (ESR), with Forensic Science South Australia [26]. The software was initially used in-house and subsequently commercialised, achieving highly successful market penetration in numerous jurisdictions. There are in the region of 40 publications describing the biological model, mathematics, performance and validation of STRmix™ (for a full list see [27]). These have been critically important to support its use in the face of significant challenge, particularly in the US. If STRmix™ is challenged in a case, additional access is granted to defence teams, including access to a 2-month, time-limited version of the software, to validation records, and to user manuals. The investment in research, development, commercialisation and ongoing maintenance of this product will have been large but will have been offset by the commercial success of the product.

Similar to forensic genetics, the primary route for digital forensics innovation to reach end users has been through commercial providers of software and hardware tools, although digital tool providers have not engaged with end user validation requirements in a substantive manner as yet.

Generalising, the costs of translation of research via a technology provider do not disappear but are passed on to end users through the pricing of products, making it less visible as a separate cost.

The cost of extending the scope of accreditation can provide a disincentive for organisations to adopt new technologies, although taking a longer-term view, it is entirely possible that a structured approach to quality management saves cost over the lifetime of a method, with fewer challenges, errors and retrospective reviews. However, there is little robust data on which to evaluate lifetime costs and economic value of accreditation. Analysis of accreditation costs in the UK has, however, shown that the extent to which an organisation is ready for its assessment, with, for example, a well-embedded quality management system, high quality validation and objective evidence of staff competence, has a vast impact on the cost of external assessments. The costs paid by similarly sized organisations for a similar scope of accreditation differed by as much as £8700, depending on the number of non-conformances raised and whether extra visit(s) were required to satisfy the accreditation body [22] For context, the assessment costs included in [22] ranged from £4.2 to £16.5k. To minimise the cost of accreditation for a new method, effective validation and implementation should lead to a correctly timed assessment, at the point when the forensic science unit can demonstrate that the method is operating successfully in a steady state.

11.5 Court Scrutiny in Practice

Numerous authors have pointed to an apparent reluctance on behalf of courts to apply the principles on admissibility of expert evidence as set out in the Criminal Procedure Rules and Practice Directions (e.g. [11,28]). There are indeed few cases from the Court of Appeal which refer to the rules on expert evidence, which has been hypothesised to be due to one, or more, of the following reasons (reproduced from [29][2]):

a. Part 19 is well understood by lawyers, is easy to apply and is being applied effectively (either by discouraging lawyers from attempting to adduce evidence of dubious reliability and/or by facilitating the exclusion of such evidence when it is adduced).
b. Lawyers find competence challenges relatively easy to make but find challenges to underlying methodology more challenging/more difficult to identify and are not making such challenges when evidence of dubious reliability is adduced.
c. Limited funding has reduced the likelihood that lawyers will be able to adduce expert evidence from less well-established areas of expertise, so there isn't too much to challenge.
d. Scientific reports are insufficiently transparent regarding the limitations of the analysis or conclusions to enable effective challenge; and
e. Reports are being presented in such a way as to appear factual, when in fact there is a great deal of inference, uncertainty and opinion behind what is concluded.

Without further research, it is impossible to tie down the reasons and it remains to be seen whether the Forensic Science Regulator's Code coming into effect on a

[2] The quoted text is subject to Crown Copyright.

statutory basis from October 2023 alters the position. The current level of scrutiny and challenge in court certainly does not appear to be a barrier to introduction of innovative new technologies.

11.6 Summary and Forward Look

In England and Wales, the Forensic Science Regulator's statutory Code of Practice came into effect on 2nd October 2023. The code is admissible in evidence in criminal (and civil) proceedings in England and Wales, and a court may take into account a failure to act in accordance with the code in determining a question in such proceedings [7]. For researchers, technology providers and those seeking to adopt new technologies, the code sets out the required approach to validation and implementation, which should minimise translational costs by ensuring that the goalposts are clear and are not ever-changing.

However, the Forensic Science Regulator is not an economic regulator and so the adoption of new technologies, their pricing and the money that is available from those funding provision of forensic science (in England and Wales this is largely the 43 territorial police forces and, to a much smaller extent, the Legal Aid Agency) is unregulated. Arguably, a lack of funding has been the most significant factor limiting the direct translation of forensic science research into practice and unless there is a change in policy at governmental level, there is no additional funding in sight. However, commercialisation via technology providers (e.g. consumables kits, hardware and software for a range of forensic genetics methods) and via investment from the originating research organisation (e.g. ESR's commercialisation of STRmix™) have both proved successful, meeting regulatory challenges effectively, and have in common that the methods have a strong end user pull.

References

1. National Institute of Standards and Technology. (2023). *The Organization of Scientific Area Committees for Forensic Science*. Available May 30, 2023 from https://www.nist.gov/organization-scientific-area-committees-forensic-science
2. Australia New Zealand Policing Advisory Agency. *About NIFS*. Available May 30, 2023 from https://www.anzpaa.org.au/forensic-science/about-nifs/about-nifs
3. *The Criminal Procedure Rules 2020*. Available May 30, 2023 from https://www.legislation.gov.uk/uksi/2020/759/contents/made
4. Lord Chief Justice of England and Wales. *Criminal Practice Directions 2023*. Available May 30, 2023 from https://assets.publishing.service.gov.uk/government/uploads/system/uploads/attachment_data/file/1159603/criminal-practice-directions-2023.pdf
5. Government of the Netherlands. (2023). *New Code of Criminal Procedure*. Available May 30, 2023 from Contents of the new Code of Criminal Procedure | Modernisation of the Code of Criminal Procedure | Government.nl

6. Hansard. (2007). *Forensic Science Regulator*. Available May 30, 2023 from https://hansard.parliament.uk/Commons/2007-07-12/debates/07071262000011/ForensicScienceRegulator
7. Forensic Science Regulator Act. (2021). UK. Available May 30, 2023 from https://www.legislation.gov.uk/ukpga/2021/14/contents
8. Forensic Science Regulator. (2023). *Code of Practice*. Available May 30, 2023 from https://assets.publishing.service.gov.uk/government/uploads/system/uploads/attachment_data/file/1141863/FINAL_Code_of_Practice.pdf
9. Law Commission. (2011). *Expert Evidence in Criminal Proceedings in England and Wales*. Available May 30, 2023 from https://www.lawcom.gov.uk/app/uploads/2015/03/lc325_Expert_Evidence_Report.pdf
10. Ministry of Justice. (2013). *Government response to Law Commission report on expert evidence (Law Comm No 325)*. Available May 30, 2023 from https://www.gov.uk/government/publications/government-response-to-law-commission-report-on-expert-evidence
11. Ward, T. (2018). Admissibility, reliability and common law epistemology. In P. Roberts & M. Stockdale (Eds.), *Forensic Science Evidence and Expert Witness Testimony: Reliability Through Reform?* (pp. 106–129). Edward Elgar.
12. *Regina v McIlkenny & Ors*. 1991, EWCA Crim 2.
13. Federal Bureau of Investigation. (2015). *FBI Testimony on Microscopic Hair Analysis Contained Errors in at Least 90 Percent of Cases in Ongoing Review*. Available May 30, 2023 from https://www.fbi.gov/news/press-releases/fbi-testimony-on-microscopic-hair-analysis-contained-errors-in-at-least-90-percent-of-cases-in-ongoing-review
14. Biedermann, A. (2022). The strange persistence of (source) "identification" claims in forensic literature through descriptivism, diagnosticism and machinism. *Forensic science International: Synergy, 4*, 100222. https://doi.org/10.1016/j.fsisyn.2022.100222
15. Morgan, J. (2023). Wrongful convictions and claims of false or misleading forensic evidence. *Journal of Forensic Sciences, 68*, 908–961. https://doi.org/10.1111/1556-4029.15233
16. National Audit Office. (2021). *Principles of Effective Regulation*. Available May 30, 2023 from https://www.nao.org.uk/wp-content/uploads/2021/05/Principles-of-effective-regulation-SOff-interactive-accessible.pdf
17. European Network of Forensic Science Institutes. (2023). *Guidelines for the single laboratory Validation of Instrumental and Human Based Methods in Forensic Science*. Available May 30, 2023 from Guidance-QCC-VAL-002.pdf (enfsi.eu)
18. *Queen v Sean Hoey*. 2007, NICC 49
19. House of Commons Science and Technology Committee. (2005). *Forensic Science on Trial*. Seventh Report of Session 2004–2005. Available May 30, 2023 from https://www.gov.uk/government/publications/forensic-science-on-trial
20. European Network of Forensic Science Institutes. (2011). *Scope of Accreditation*. Available May 30, 2023 from https://enfsi.eu/wp-content/uploads/2016/09/policy_on_scope_of_accreditation.pdf
21. Ross, A., & Neuteboom, W. (2022). ISO-accreditation—Is that all there is for forensic science? *Australian Journal of Forensic Sciences, 54*(1), 2–14. https://doi.org/10.1080/00450618.2020.1819414
22. Tully, G., Cohen, N., Compton, D., Davies, G., Isbell, R., & Watson, T. (2020). Quality standards for digital forensics: Learning from experience in England & Wales. *Forensic Science International Digital Investigation, 32*, 200905. https://doi.org/10.1016/j.fsidi.2020.200905
23. House of Commons Science and Technology Committee. (2013). *Forensic Science*. Second report of session 2013–14, evidence, 30 January 2013, Q46.
24. ThermoFisher Scientific. *Human Identification Professional Services*. Available May 30, 2023 from https://www.thermofisher.com/uk/en/home/industrial/forensics/human-identification/human-identification-professional-services.html
25. Promega Corporation. *Genetic Identity Validation Services and Resources*. Available May 30, 2023 from https://www.promega.co.uk/products/forensic-dna-analysis-ce/validation-resources/

26. STRmix^{TM}. *STRmix^{TM} Empowering Forensic Science.* Available May 30, 2023 from https://www.strmix.com/
27. STRmix^{TM}. *Published Data.* Available May 30, 2023 from https://www.strmix.com/strmix/published-data/
28. Davies, G., & Piasecki, E. (2016). No more Laissex Faire? Expert evidence, rule changes and reliability: Can more effective training for the Bar and Judiciary prevent miscarriages of justice? *Journal of Criminal Law, 8*, 327.
29. Tully, G. (2023). *Forensic Science Regulator Annual Report 17 November 2019–16 November 2020.* Available May 30, 2023 from FSR Annual Report 2019–2020 (publishing.service.gov.uk)

Chapter 12
Translational Forensic Science, a U.S. Perspective

Max M. Houck

Abstract Forensic science is a mainstay in the U.S. criminal justice system. Because of its centrality and importance, forensic science needs to have well-researched, validated, and practicable methods that promote public safety. The process of translating forensic methods from research to casework to a public benefit has been especially problematic in the United States. Forensic science is constrained as a science by its history of police administration and its utility in criminal investigations. Moreover, forensic science is perceived to be "merely applied" and not truly contributing to basic research. This perception is misguided, due in part to how basic and applied research have been traditionally defined. Therefore, translational research does not exist in the general sense for forensic science as it does in, for example, the medical sciences. In this chapter, the external factors in the U.S. that have shaped what "gets researched" and makes it to the laboratory bench, and why some methods never get translated, while others that should not be translated are, will be discussed.

12.1 Introduction

Forensic science is central to modern criminal justice systems. It supports investigations, demonstrates associations between people, places, and things involved in criminal activity, and exonerates the innocent. Forensic services are sciences integral to a just society governed through rule of law and they are arguably a public good, accessible to all. This means that forensic science methods need to be well-researched, validated, made usable by forensic service providers, and beneficial to public safety and the public at large. Translating forensic methods from the research laboratory, to the service laboratory, to public safety, has generally been problematic around the world and specifically in the United States.

For many forensic methods that are applied appropriately, *that* the methods work is not the issue; *how* they can work and how much good they do is the central obstacle. To challenge a situation, it is important to first ask "why," then generate

M. M. Houck (✉)
Global Forensic and Justice Center, Florida International University, Miami, USA
e-mail: mhouck@fiu.edu

S. Francese and R. S. P. King (eds.), *Driving Forensic Innovation in the 21st Century*,
https://doi.org/10.1007/978-3-031-56556-4_12

multiple hypotheses or ideas to answer the "what if" questions of creativity, and ultimately get to the heart of the issue by asking "how" and "so what" [1]. Forensic science, either in individual research projects or in the profession at large, seems to be stuck at the "what if" stage, rarely making it to the "how" and "so what." Methods, upon methods, upon methods, have been published and, for many of them, how they work is not always well understood [2, 3]. Moreover, it is difficult to determine how many methods reach the casework laboratory bench. If a methodological concept is synonymous with, and embedded within, the corresponding set of actions taken with those methods [4] and that no measurement can be taken without theory [5], then forensic science must be operating on some set of theories [6, 7]. Forensic science is judged by some, particularly in the U.S., to not be a "real science" because of its lack of discipline-supporting philosophies. Why forensic science has been arrested at the "what if" questions for too long, prohibited or influenced by its policing administration (double meaning intended), to really approach the "how" and "so what" questions appropriately like a science ought to. As Cole notes,

> Few forensic scientists live in this (research) economy in which reputational rewards are allocated in the form of citations for prestigious scientific publications. Rather, they operate in a much more bureaucratic structure within police organizational hierarchies with productivity requirements. Their products are not scientific paper, but reports, which are not cited, but merely consumed and then discarded by the criminal justice system. These reports are not shared with peers in the conventional sense, and they rarely, if ever, generate reputational rewards for their authors [8].

A 2018 article by ProPublica questioning the validity of bloodstain pattern analysis exemplified the problems with translating forensic research in the U.S. One person pioneered the method [9] through a U.S. government grant, applied it in cases, taught it to others, who then applied it and taught others to the point where it is a recognised applied method. U.S. Courts across varying jurisdictions (local, state, federal, and civil) over the years considered it to be sufficiently scientific but the method had not been independently tested to answer the "how" questions. Decades later, questions arose about the method's suitability, applicability, and validity [10]. One U.S. federal judge attempted to rally challenges based on the criticism, to no avail, calling it an "institutional failure" [11] without success. Yet, after millions of dollars in research funding into bloodstain pattern analysis (BPA), the same "how" questions persist. The field got an opportunity to answer the "how" questions, but missed its chance. One practitioner quoted in the article said that the millions of dollars in academic research had had no practical influence on the discipline or the method as applied: "These are great academic studies," he said, "but what do they lend to real-world problems?" The scientist who conducted that research agreed but continues his research endeavours into BPA nevertheless [11]. This essential tension between academic–and by extension, scientific–research and practical application in a law enforcement environment, sets forensic science apart from other translational efforts. While medicine strives to move research from academic to clinical for the benefit of the patient (the core idea of translational research), forensic science fights with itself about what to research, what to do with the results, and how to apply them.

The problems forensic science faces in the U.S. arise more from environmental, cultural, and historical reasons than from issues with the methods, although those do play a role. This chapter will explore the external factors that have shaped what gets researched and makes it to the laboratory bench, and why some methods never get translated while others, that should not be translated, are. Although these factors obtain generally in forensic science across the world, their effects are seen more keenly in the U.S. [10].

12.2 Basic, Applied, and Translational

The history of the dichotomy between basic research and applied research goes back to ancient Greece. The Greeks had one word for scientific knowledge (*episteme*) and another for technical arts (*techne*). *Episteme* was not perceived as the foundation for *techne*. Scientific knowledge, like mathematics, astronomy, and natural philosophy, were seen as ends in themselves worth pursuing for the joy of learning. Plato conceptualised this knowledge as a higher form of intellectualism and mundane daily life was just a poor reflection of this pure state of knowing. The idea was transferred by scholars through the centuries to 19th-century Germany, where the modern research university was created. These institutions were a place for scientists to freely pursue scholarship without regard for what kind of knowledge it was. Ultimately, this model was imported to the U.S. in the late 1800s [12].

Basic Science

Vannevar Bush, who headed up the U.S. Office of Scientific Research and Development (OSRD) and was an advisor to President Roosevelt, established the modern American research model at the end of World War II. The U.S. government significantly increased research funding during World War II, resulting in outcomes still famous today: like radar, penicillin, malaria drugs, the proximity fuse, and the atomic bomb. In the waning years of the war, scientists and engineers wanted to continue with the government funded research while avoiding any micromanagement. Bush's response was a letter to President Roosevelt (at the President's request) outlining Bush's vision for the future of scientific research. The report, '*Science, The Endless Frontier*', stated that basic scientific research would eventually result in practical benefits:

> Advances in science when put to practical use mean more jobs, higher wages, shorter hours, more abundant crops, more leisure for recreation, for study, for learning how to live without the deadening drudgery which has been the burden of the common man for ages past. Advances in science will also bring higher standards of living, will lead to the prevention or cure of diseases, will promote conservation of our limited national resources, and will assure means of defence against aggression [13]

Bush, however, was adamant that any practical benefits were a side effect of basic research and basic research could not be directly focused on producing those benefits. "*Basic research is performed without thought of practical ends.* "*... The scientist* *doing basic research may not be at all interested in the practical applications of his work, yet the further progress of industrial development would eventually stagnate if basic scientific research were long neglected*" [14].

Above all else, the "*freedom of inquiry must be preserved.*" The broad inclination of scientists to explore the world and pursue a variety of phenomena is what pushes progress. The freedom of inquiry, as Bush put it, produces discoveries about the physical world that may lead to innovations in technology that end up benefiting society but those desired benefits cannot be what drives basic research. Bush therefore implored the President to invest in research without regard for any practical results. In doing so, the reward would be far greater than targeting research funds to intentionally practical research ideas. Funnel money into science and it will repay that investment multiple times over. Give scientists freedom to explore what they find interesting and what is discovered will be beyond what could have been imagined.

The influence of *Science—The Endless Frontier* came largely from its timing. Presented at the end of the war (issued less than two weeks after the atomic bombing of Hiroshima), with victory accompanied by numerous technologies that aided that victory, the value of science, research, and technology was lost on no one. The U.S. had completed a shift from an agrarian society to an industrial one, so Bush's vague phrase "basic research" resounded with both politicians, who wanted progress and votes, and researchers, who wanted stable funding for their work. Research that had been previously ignored was now of national and political importance [15].

In the years since, U.S. society has come to have a more pragmatic view of research outcomes. Scientific funding has become more competitive and, therefore, less willing to accept fuzzy notions of basic research that might someday mean something to someone. Some tried to replace the term "basic" with contenders like "transformative" or "fundamental," but the core idea had drifted from Bush's philosophical rallying cry. Basic research is now considered to be "*directed toward greater knowledge or understanding of the fundamental aspects of phenomena and is performed without thought of practical ends. It results in general knowledge and understanding of nature and its laws*" [16]. For example, basic biomedical research explores disease processes without consideration for finding a potential solution, like a vaccine or medicine.

Applied Research

Applied research is a type of systematic investigation seeking a practical application for an existing issue. By comparison with the previous example, applied researchers would use the results of basic research into disease processes, along with other sources, to seek out a vaccine or medicine for a specific disease. Applied research is predicated on the use of other research communities' accumulated theories, knowledge, methods, and techniques, to seek an answer for a specific purpose. As opposed to basic research, applied research lives in the messy world outside the laboratory. It needs to address the uncertainty inherent in the real world, like non-random samples, skewed data, and unforeseen influences. Existing hand-in-hand with its problem, applied research has to adjust its working hypotheses, or core questions, to better address its context. Additionally, applied research is often bound to its literature, residing in specialised academic journals that only cover a single discipline.

Translational Research

Relevant to this discussion is that translational research is related to applied research. Translational research seeks to translate, or convert, results from basic research into outcomes that directly benefit humans. The term "translational" has gained use in science and technology, but particularly in biology and the medical sciences. Because of this conceptual positioning, translational research can be thought of as a form of applied research. The adjective "translational" refers to the "translation" (the term derives from the Latin for "carrying over") of basic scientific findings in a laboratory setting into potential treatments for disease.

Is the dichotomy between basic and applied (with translational thrown into the mix) meaningful? Under Bush's traditional model, scientific discovery from basic research efforts comes first. Engineers and applied researchers then take those results, apply them, and create new knowledge that is directly useful and beneficial. This model implies a one-way path to innovation and discovery when, in fact, they are highly nonlinear and entangled [17]. Discovery goes both ways and technologies draw on scientific knowledge and scientists gain understanding from new technologies and applications. A compromise argues that basic and applied research are not diametrically opposed, but instead are orthogonal [18]. Rather than seeing a one-dimensional relationship with basic research at one end and applied research at the other, consider the relationship to be a matrix the axes of which are "fundamental knowledge" and "considerations of use." The 2 × 2 matrix is shown in Fig. 12.1.

The upper left quadrant contains the classic interpretation of basic research: pursuit of fundamental knowledge about the world without regard for the utility of what is discovered. The research of scientists like Niels Bohr, a physicist who made fundamental contributions about atomic structure and quantum theory, is offered as an example of this type of research [19]. The lower right quadrant contains the classic definition of applied research, that is, solving a specific problem or problems, for example, the work of Thomas Edison, the inventor whose efforts produced the phonograph, the motion picture camera, early versions of the electric light bulb, among many other inventions [20]. The upper right quadrant, however, is the novel aspect

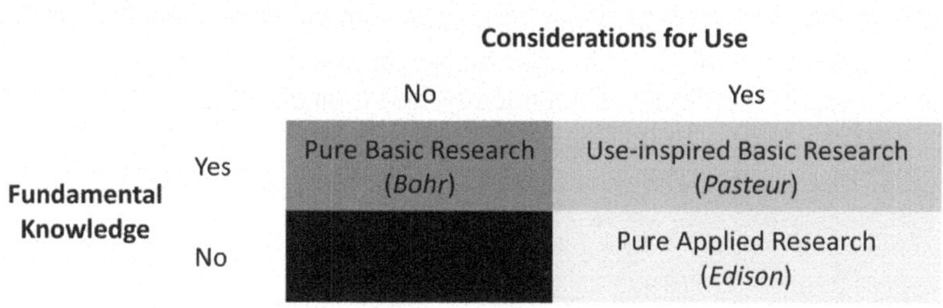

Fig. 12.1 Pasteur's Quadrant, a 2 × 2 matrix to demonstrate the relationship between basic and applied research. Redrawn from [18]

of this argument. Applied research, as has been noted, can be inspired by basic research and vice versa. Louis Pasteur, a French chemist, was consulted about the process of fermentation and the production of alcohol by a local wine manufacturer in Lille. First approaching it as applied research to solve an industrial quality problem, Pasteur discovered the role of bacteria and yeast in fermentation and spoilage, leading to a breakthrough in the understanding of microbiology. He developed a method of heating liquids, like milk, to temperatures between 60 and 100 °C to kill bacteria and prevent spoilage. Later in his career, Pasteur was conducting basic research into the diseases of livestock. A failed experiment led him to formulate the first engineered vaccine, a milestone in the application of science to medicine [21]. Given his predilection to ignore the artificial boundaries between "basic" and "applied," Pasteur said, "There does not exist a category of science to which one can give the name applied science. There are sciences and the applications of science, bound together as the fruit of the tree which bears it" [22]. Therefore, Pasteur's name is fitting as an example of this quadrant.

Other examples of Pasteur's Quadrant abound in the history of science and technology. For example, the case of the transistor defies simple categorization as "basic" or "applied" research [23]. The goal to integrate semiconductor materials to electronic circuits required a series of researchers over decades of development conducting both basic and applied research in various phases and multiple laboratories. Investigations into fundamental physics, materials science, electronics, and technologies were required to produce the actual device. The transistor is a good example of a practical goal that required basic, fundamental research in tandem to attain it. Another good example is the Michelson-Morely experiment in 1887 that used basic research to detect the luminiferous ether, a suspected medium thought to carry light waves. The result was that the hypothesis of the ether's existence was rejected but resulted in the creation of a new instrument, an interferometer, as well as laying the foundation for exploring the theory of relativity [24]. Arguably, like these examples, forensic science fits into Pasteur's Quadrant as a science with applications. Most forensic methods have, at least in part, a premise or grounding in basic science, like biology or chemistry, which has been focused on a specific issue to be addressed, such as DNA from crime scene blood samples or the quantification of active substances in a tablet or white powder. Perhaps because of Bush's statement originating at a crucial time of U.S. scientific growth, the strict dichotomy between basic and applied research has persisted more strongly there and, ultimately, affected the perception of forensic science as strictly applied. Nevertheless, this perception has set forensic science apart from other sciences, culturally, academically, and financially [25].

12.3 How Translational Research Works

The goal of translational research in forensic science is to create bridges or steps to connect basic and applied research by converting—or translating—laboratory observations and results into interventions that improve individual and public health; the concept of translational research is grounded in medical research and the healthcare practice. Translational research strives to understand both the scientific and operational principles that underlie each stage of the process. Although traditionally displayed as "basic to applied," translational research recognizes that successful dissemination of research outcomes may require multiple communication strategies. The process combines the discovery of *how* a method works with the understanding of *why* it works. A priority, therefore, is to demonstrate the potential for real-world implementation in an environment of limited resources.

The translational science spectrum (Fig. 12.2) represents each stage of research along the path from basic research into the biological and chemical foundations of health and disease to treatments that improve the health of patients and the public. Translational research involves two broad phases: One is the translation of basic research to the development of trials and studies in humans and then translating those results from the clinic to public health and epidemiological decisions. The second phase of translation cost-effectiveness of prevention and treatment strategies is also an important part of translational science. These broad phases are broken down into five individual stages, labelled T0 through T4. Although the spectrum runs left to right, the spectrum is not strictly linear because each phase builds upon and provides feedback to the others (white arrows at the top).

T0 research is basic scientific research that seeks greater knowledge or understanding of the fundamental mechanisms of phenomena in biology and chemistry without regard to any practical ends. T0 research yields general knowledge and understanding

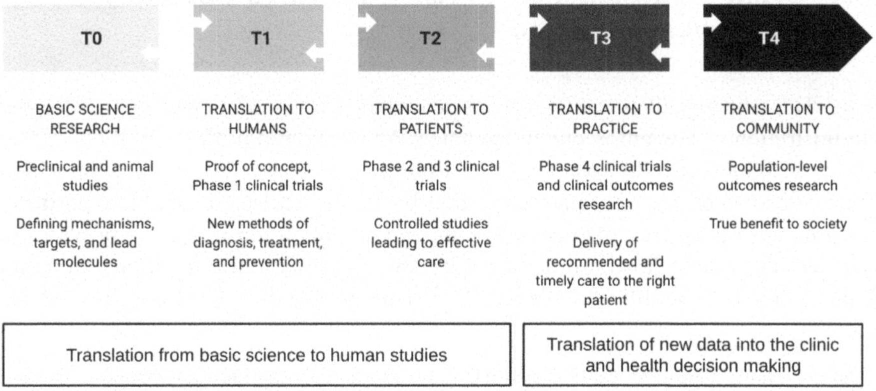

Fig. 12.2 Translational research spectrum, with stages from T0 (basic research) to T4 (public health)

of the world and its laws. Each stage of the translational research spectrum is built upon and adds to basic research.

T1 research is applied research that systematically investigates one or more solutions or practical applications of science to solve a problem. Based on the accumulated findings, theories, and methods of other sciences, T1 research is syncretic, using and weaving various techniques for a specific purpose. In medicine, T1 research is pre-clinical research and attempts to connect the basic science of disease with human medicine. Researchers attempt to understand the basis of a disease or disorder to better discover effective interventions and test them using cell or animal models, human or animal tissues, or computer-assisted simulations.

T2 research is clinical research that seeks to better understand a disease in humans and then track it back to findings in cell or animal models. T2 research can also be the testing and refinement of new technologies or interventions to determine their efficacy or safety in humans. Most clinical research (that is, trials) are hoping to obtain data to support regulatory approval for an intervention.

T3 research is implementation in a clinical setting, adopting interventions that have been demonstrated to be useful and applying them in clinical care for the general population. Gaps between clinical applications and outcomes are identified at this stage. The data at this stage involves many more subjects and so the interpretations and implications are better understood.

T4 research, the final stage, translates to public health. In T4 research, health outcomes at the population level are studied to identify and evaluate the effects of diseases, as well as prevention, diagnosis and treatment. At the T4 stage, the research is translated into actionable information at the community level.

12.4 What "Translational" Forensic Research Currently Looks like in the U.S.

In the U.S., nearly all forensic service providers are governmental and under the administration of law enforcement agencies. As a captured profession, the forensic service providers are disadvantaged in a number of ways [26–28], one of which is that the science providers are governed by non-scientists. Thus, their purpose, mission, and values are not necessarily aligned and the forensic service provider in a subservient role to law enforcement [26–28]. As Shils notes, the motivation and goals of the non-scientific manager and "consumer" are different from those of the scientist:

> Non-scientific managers of scientists working in industry, military, and government institutions were, nonetheless, less expert and his criterion of the scientists success was like the patients and the clients, not the promulgation of some new scientific phenomenon but the bringing about of a situation advantageous to the "consumer" of the scientist's service. The case of the "consumer" of the services of clergymen, physicians, and lawyers, the consumer

> required salvation and peace of mind, physical health, and a decision in his favour by the court. In the case of the "applied scientist," the "consumer" too knew what he wanted. He wanted something other than a scientific proposition. He wanted what would flow from it [29, p. 475].

The capture of professional forensic science by law enforcement has permanently shaped the forensic scientific research effort and its outcomes. The result has been research that is more technical than theoretical, more practical than philosophical, more applied than basic. Cole [30] summarises the contrasting social attributes of research science and forensic science as follows (Fig. 12.3).

The way in which academic research funding is allocated for forensic research may have also disadvantaged the profession's research. Morrison, in testimony before the House of Lords Select Committee on Science and Technology, said that "*forensic science research often focuses on applying existing science and technology to forensic problems and on empirical validation under casework conditions, foci which the granting agencies' and journals' reviewers often do not perceive as innovative.*" Additional testimony from another scientist said this led researchers to "find that the best way they can make progress is to disguise their work, "piggy back" it onto another project, or undertake it as consultancy activity through casework, which may

Social Dimension	Research Science	Forensic science
Time-frame	Open-ended	Limited
Data	Intentionally collected/generated (in most cases); in principle, unlimited	Adventitiously produced; inherently limited
Knowledge claims	General	Specific
Product	Papers and other scientific communications	Reports, affidavits, testimony
Reward structure	Prestige	Bureaucratic
Productivity goals	Volume and impact	Volume and speed
Accountability mechanisms	Scholarly peer review	Legal adversarialism
Audience	Peer scientists, 'core set'	Legal actors, the state
Reporting of results	Conservative, statistical, ambiguous	Ambitious, colloquial, unambiguous
Data sharing	Unlimited, in principle	Treated warily, sometimes prohibited by legal actors
Research agenda	Driven by 'research programmes', 'paradigms'	Driven by demands of courts, law enforcement, and the state
Valid feedback	Sometimes	Rarely

Fig. 12.3 The contrasting social attributes of research science and forensic science (from [30])

result in an embargo or prohibition on publication of their results" [31]. This is also true in the U.S., where a report by the National Institute of Justice stated:

> While agencies acknowledge the importance of research, they face multiple competing funding priorities. Research, which does not immediately translate to faster or more efficient casework, can be one of the first items defunded in times of budgetary austerity, and forensic personnel who contribute to research may be re-allocated to address increasing workloads. Continuous development of a national forensic science research infrastructure is hindered by a lack of dedicated federal grant funding needed to advance the speed, accuracy, and scope of forensic analysis for all types of evidence [32].

The "customer's" goal, as noted by Shils, is the product and not what develops it, or from Pasteur's perspective, the application and not the science. To be obvious, the "customers" are the police, the attorneys and the courts. Even as early as 1963, Paul Kirk, a pioneer in forensic science research and education, commented that the forensic research literature was largely technical and cautioned that research should not be limited to the merely applied [33]. *Contra* Kirk, Kind lamented that professional scientists advanced their careers, in part, through publication, which distracted them from practical casework. He went on to criticise the forensic research at that time as being of little practical value to casework and felt that the "forensic" description was tacked on to justify carrying it out. Although he conceded that the research may have had some value in a "pure science or commercial context," it offered little help to the scientist on the bench working criminal cases [34]. Forensic research efforts are focused on new instruments and technology or improving casework because the funding system rewards applied, short-term projects and not deeper considerations into how forensic science functions [2]. The environmental factors, particularly in the U.S., have altered what research is considered, proposed, and funded, if conducted at all. Projects are seen as either directed to solve a case-related problem (applied) or of little to no use by being too esoteric (*a al* Kind) or too basic [2]. While many research publications are indeed valid, they offer little to the forensic discipline or profession [3]. What good is research that results in the detection of a trace element in some evidentiary material when the instrument costs more than a laboratory can afford? Some in the field say that forensic scientists, and not governments or other disciplines, should decide what research is needed [2] but the granting agencies would have to listen to the researchers and not the forensic service providers' parent agencies. In the U.S., it is those parent agencies that hold political power, both over the captured service providers and with the funding agencies [26, 27].

Given the U.S. environment, what would translational forensic research look like? Based on Fig. 12.2, a suggested interpretation of the current status of forensic translational research is offered in Fig. 12.4. T0 is little populated in the forensic science literature. Discoveries in other sciences either infiltrate or are brought into the forensic fold. Typically, the defining mechanisms, targets, and lead molecules have already been explicated in the native science. T1 research is proof of concept research with the goal of translating existing research into a method or method development process. New ways of detecting, classifying, or interpreting an existing type of evidence are explored. T2 research validates existing methods and demonstrates their potential to produce reliable outcomes. Moving the method to applicability in casework-like

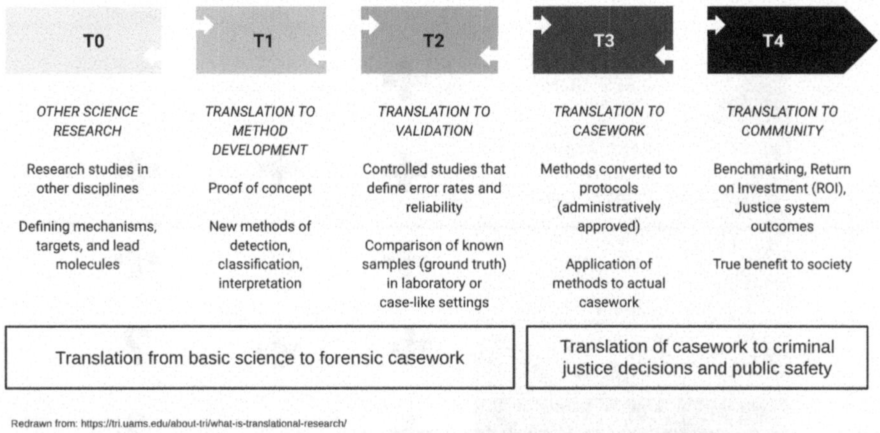

Fig. 12.4 Interpretation of the current status of forensic research in a translational format

settings is a core component of T2 research. T3 research demonstrates the direct application of the science to actual casework: T3 research is about applying, T2 is about proving its potential for application. T3 research compares items of known origin to blinded or anonymized samples to evaluate how well the outcomes comport with ground truth. T4 research is a recent addition to forensic research and, like T0, some of it occurs outside the fuzzy-but-identified boundaries of the forensic discipline.

A few examples will illustrate the patchwork approach of translational research in the forensic sciences. Forensic DNA analysis is probably the only research agenda to run from T0 through to T4 in forensic science (Fig. 12.5). Originating in the biological sciences [35] and applied to issues of human identification [36], DNA analysis went through a messy but necessary vetting process to become fit for forensic casework. Microscopical hair comparisons, by contrast, had no research in other sciences upon which to base its premises. Mammalogists use hairs to classify mammals [37] and dermatologists examine hairs to research disease and metabolism [38] but neither attempt to compare known hair samples to hairs of unknown origin for purposes of association or exclusion of sources like forensic science has [39].

Nevertheless, the concept was translated to the development of a method (T1) and validations were attempted over the years (T2) (for example, see the discussion starting with Gaudette [40]. Regardless of the outcome of the purported validations, including by DNA analysis [41], the method was applied to casework until a recent review raised questions about the method's practical validity [42]. The translation of microscopical hair comparisons to improved public safety remains questionable, given the number of wrongful convictions involving forensic hair comparisons.[1] A final example is that of a preliminary study of the efficacy of eugenol on the

[1] For current information about the number of exonerations, see www.law.umich.edu/special/exoneration/Pages/about.aspx.

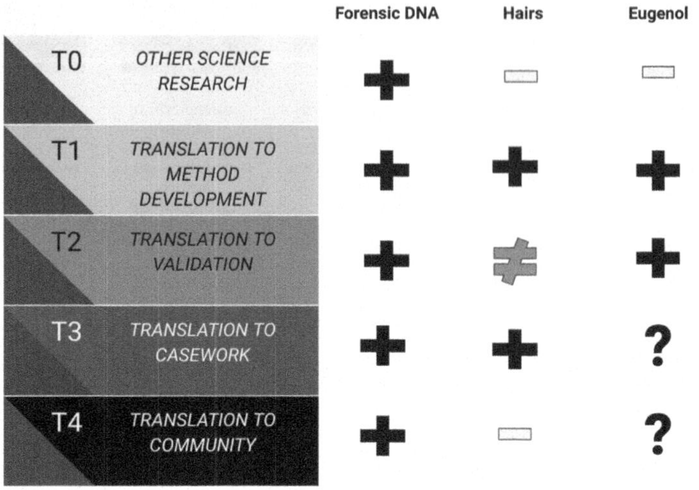

Fig. 12.5 A matrix of forensic research examples in the context of the structure of Fig. 12.3

recovery of obliterated characters on polymers [43]. The utility of using eugenol (4-allyl-2-methoxy-phenol), the main component of clove oil, to revisualise obliterated characters on plastic or polymeric surfaces, like automotive or electronic parts, was mentioned briefly in the literature but never explored until recently. The process was investigated and developed to a validated methodology (T1 and T2) but there is no indication that it has been used in casework or what the benefit of the method to the community at large may be (T3 and T4). In fact, no formal mechanism exists to determine if any laboratories are using this method and what the impact may be to public safety.

Research efforts like Project FORESIGHT, which benchmarks forensic service providers' costs and performance, work from inside the discipline to evaluate jurisdictions' return on investment (ROI) into forensic provision [44–46]. Other efforts, like Doleac's work on the economics of crime, work from the outside to evaluate the effectiveness and efficiency of various forensic-adjacent effects on public safety [47, 48]. These research efforts promote a better understanding of forensic science's benefit to society (T4) but much more work could be done in this area.

With very few exceptions, forensic science lacks a dedicated, supported translational pipeline to move fundamental research through the translational stages to fully benefit public safety and society. It could be argued that translational research, as a process, does not yet properly exist in the forensic discipline. This leads to a discussion of what is being done to build and reinforce this translational pipeline in the U.S.

12.5 What Translational Forensic Research Could Look Like in the U.S.

Various entities at the U.S. federal level, from the National Academy of Sciences National Research Council (NAS/NRC) [10] to the President's Council of Advisors on Science and Technology (PCAST) [49] to the now-defunct National Forensic Science Commission [50], have called for more science and more research to shore up the forensic methods applied in the pursuit of investigations and justice.

The U.S. has little regulatory governance over forensic science provision. With just over 400 forensic laboratories and an unknown-but-large number of forensic service providers (like fingerprint or crime scene units in smaller jurisdictions) scattered across the 18,000 policing agencies at the local, state, and federal levels, accounting is noticeably problematic [51]. As of 2016, 17 states and the District of Columbia have state boards dedicated to the oversight of forensic science practice in their state and the majority of these created statutorily [52]. Only 9 states have passed legislation mandating accreditation of their forensic science service providers. The legislation and oversight requirements vary greatly from state to state. The majority of forensic laboratories are accredited under ISO 17025 and some forensic service providers are accredited under ISO 17020; unless the jurisdiction has mandated accreditation, the process is voluntary. Standards for forensic science methods have existed for some time, starting with ASTM Committee E-30 in the early 1970s, International, and continuing with the U.S. National Institute of Standards and Technology's (NIST) efforts with the Office of Scientific Advisory Committees (OSAC), but these are voluntary standards and forensic service providers are free to ignore them, seemingly without penalty. The forensic profession has also failed to self-regulate, as do most professions, like doctors and lawyers [8].

The two main agencies that support what could be translational forensic research in the U.S. are the National Institute of Justice (NIJ) and NIST. NIJ has stated that new forensic technologies and methodologies be practitioner driven and adopted in forensic testing [32]. In their opinion, universities and other researchers must collaborate with operational laboratories to identify practical casework needs, and only then conduct research to solve or support those needs. One of NIJ's concerns is finding private sector companies to commercialise research outcomes to the wider forensic community. Despite market estimates that range from USD 4.9 billion to over 44 billion, the forensic market is actually quite small. These estimates include technologies that would not be identified as core forensic laboratory activities: like license plate readers, facial recognition, and CCTV cameras. With only around 400 forensic laboratories and an unknown number of forensic service providers (like fingerprint or crime scene units–that are not properly laboratories–in police agencies) in the U.S., the forensic market is probably well below even the lowest estimate to be found in various reports. This environment makes it difficult to fund product development of technologies to what amounts to a niche market in science.

Several NIJ funding opportunities attempt to address translational research goals, including the Research and Development in Forensic Science for Criminal Justice

Purposes grant program and the Research and Evaluation for the Testing and Interpretation of Physical Evidence in Publicly Funded Forensic Laboratories grant program. The Research and Development in Forensic Science for Criminal Justice Purposes program directs basic research findings, fosters research and development in broader scientific fields with applications to forensic science, and supports ongoing forensic science research for criminal justice purposes. Proposals address the stated challenges and needs of the forensic science industry based on professional and community input, including technical working groups and the Organisation of Scientific Area Committees (see below). The Research and Evaluation for the Testing and Interpretation of Physical Evidence in Publicly Funded Forensic Laboratories program funds projects that direct research and evaluation outcomes toward the identification of the more efficient, accurate, reliable, and cost-effective methods for the identification, analysis, and interpretation of physical evidence. Funded projects identify and inform the forensic community of better practices through the evaluation of existing laboratory protocols or applications. The goal is to have a direct impact on laboratory effectiveness, efficiency, and decision making, especially in policy issues. Although it is only one agency, NIJ is the closest to promoting T0-T4 translational research efforts in the U.S.

NIST offers resources that support and promote equity in the criminal justice system by strengthening the science that underlies forensic methods and practices. The agency has a series of studies that explore and describe the basis for forensic methods through a review of the published scientific literature and other relevant sources of data that address questions of validity and reliability. The Science Foundation Reviews identify the science that supports (or does not) forensic methods, documents and evaluates the empirical evidence for their reliability through the exploration of the capabilities and limitations. The Reviews are also intended to identify knowledge gaps and areas for future research. As such, they can identify T0-T3 research and provide bridges to the next stage or stages. Amongst other projects, NIST also administers the Organization of Scientific Area Committees for Forensic Science (OSAC), which facilitate the development of science-based standards and guidelines for a broad array of forensic disciplines, providing a potential linkage to T4 research.

12.6 Conclusions

Although forensic science is central to the U.S. criminal justice system, it lacks a distinct process to translate basic research to public safety (T0-T4). Being captured within policing agencies has limited forensic science's development as a science because of its parent agencies' focus on practicality and utility. As Cole notes:

> Forensic science is structured in such a way that valid feedback is rare. To be sure, there are odd occasions in which independent data does resist forensic science. Forensic scientists may occasionally come to conclusions that are refuted by mundane, common sense evidence. [...] Forensic results may also occasionally be refuted or challenged by the results of another

> type of forensic analysis. Again, there are no records to indicate how often such events occur. [...] In short, justice systems desire results, but they have no way of determining the accuracy of the results they receive. This differs from academic or industrial science [30].

To date, despite some slow progress, forensic science has failed to correctly identify, and ultimately conduct, the kind of research that would support the knowledge claims that they make [53]. As David Stoney, a forensic professional of long standing, noted:

> In the 1990s, forensic scientists were doing work in the field, but not many others...Not many people cared about forensic science, the public wasn't engaged with it, and certainly other scientists weren't engaged. They viewed forensic science as merely an interesting application of science, without any intellectual foundation of its own [54].

Because of the capture of the forensic profession by police, they are production-oriented; this is compounded by high caseloads and lowered resources. As a result, as Stoney says, forensic laboratories "are not a bed for the intellectual development of forensic science" [54]. Formative and foundational research is being conducted by non-forensic professionals–that is, other scientists and legal critics–and this research is making a slow sea-change for the discipline. What is impeding the later translational stages of forensic research are two factors: resistance of the forensic profession to change and time it takes for other sciences to gain an appreciation for what forensic science is and what it could be. Science is a conservative endeavour and policing is much more so; therefore, it is no wonder that forensic science would double-down on resisting change, either procedurally or scientifically. Given the popularity of forensic applications in popular media, it is no wonder that other sciences might have a skewed view of forensic science and see it either as merely an application of other scientific disciplines or one that is complete and infallible. To see forensic science as a separate science that has its own specific challenges and a need for intellectual development takes effort and most non-forensic scientists, as expected, are focussing on their careers and research.

Forensic science methods need to be based in science (T0), well-researched (T1), validated (T2), and transferable to casework (T3) in order to promote public safety (T4). The U.S. history of forensic science as a captured profession and the perception of it as "merely applied" have hampered the growth and intellectual development of the discipline and the profession. Translational research generally does not exist in forensic science although some governmental agencies are trying to promote this process. Forensic science needs to adopt a translational research mindset to better support its methods, their applications, and their benefit to society.

References

1. Berger, W. (2014). *A more beautiful question: The power of inquiry to spark breakthrough ideas*. Bloomsbury Publishing USA.
2. Weyermann, C., Willis, S., Margot, P., & Roux, C. (2023). Towards more relevance in forensic science research and development. *Forensic Science International, 3*, 111592.

3. Roux, C., & Céline, W. (2021). From research integrity to research relevance to advance forensic science. *Forensic Sciences Research, 6*(4), 292–294.
4. Bridgman, P. W. (1927). *The logic of modern physics*. Macmillan.
5. Deming, W. E. (2018). Out of the crisis, reissue. MIT Press.
6. Houck, M. M. (2010). *An investigation into the foundational principles of forensic science (Undergraduate thesis)*.
7. Houck, M. (2005). Production taxonomies as the foundation of forensic significance. In *Forensic Science: The Nexus of Science and the Law*. National Academy of Sciences.
8. Cole, S. A. (2017). Who will regulate American Forensic Science. *Seton Hall Law Review, 48*.
9. MacDonell, H. L., & Bialousz, L. F. (1979). *Laboratory manual on the geometric interpretation of human bloodstain evidence*. Laboratory of Forensic Science.
10. National Research Council. (2009). *Strengthening Forensic Science in the United States: A path forward*. National Academies Press.
11. Smith, L. (2018). *How a dubious forensic science spread like a virus*. ProPublica. December 13, 2018.
12. Perkin, H. (2006). History of universities. In J. J. F. Forest & P. G. Altbach (Eds.), *International handbook of higher education* (pp. 159–205). Springer.
13. Bush, V. (1945). *The endless frontier*. National Science Foundation–EUA Washington.
14. Bush V. Science. (1945). The endless frontier. *Transactions of the Kansas Academy of Science (1903-), 48*(3), 231.
15. Pielke, R. (2010). In retrospect: Science—The endless frontier. *Nature, 466*(7309), 922–923.
16. Cohrs, R. J., Martin, T., Ghahramani, P., Bidaut, L., Higgins, P. J., & Shahzad, A. (2014). Translational medicine definition by the European society for translational medicine. *EJMCM, 2*(3), 86.
17. Narayanamurti, V., & Odumosu, T. (2016). *Cycles of invention and discovery: Rethinking the endless frontier*. Harvard University Press.
18. Stokes, D. E. (2011). *Pasteur's quadrant: Basic science and technological innovation*. Brookings Institution Press.
19. Blaedel, N., & French, A. P. (1989). Harmony and unity: The life of Niels Bohr. *Physics Today, 42*(9), 91–92.
20. Stross, R. E. (2007). *The Wizard of Menlo Park: How Thomas Alva Edison invented the modern world*. Crown.
21. Robbins, L. E. (2001). *Louis Pasteur and the hidden world of microbes*. Oxford University Press.
22. Pasteur, L. (1871). *Pourquoi la France n'a pas trouve des hommes superieurs au moment du peril*. Revue Scientifique Andrews.
23. Nelson, R. R. (1962). The link between science and invention: The case of the transistor. In *The rate and direction of inventive activity: Economic and social factors* (pp. 549–584). Princeton University Press.
24. Consoli, M., & Pluchino, A. (2018). *Michelson–Morley experiments: An enigma for physics and the history of science*. World Scientific.
25. Hamlin, C. (2013). Forensic cultures in historical perspective: Technologies of witness, testimony, judgment (and justice?). *Studies in History and Philosophy of Biological and Biomedical Sciences, 44*(1), 4–15.
26. Houck, M. M. (2019). Tigers, black swans, and unicorns: The need for feedback and oversight. *Forensic Science International: Synergy, 17*(1), 79–82.
27. Houck, M. M. (2019). Asymmetric politics and forensic intelligence. *Forensic Science International: Synergy, 18*(1), 283–284.
28. Bechky, B. A. (2020). *Blood, powder, and residue*. Princeton University Press.
29. Shils, E. (1968). The profession of science. *Advancement of Science, 24*(122), 469–480.
30. Cole, S. A. (2013). Forensic culture as epistemic culture: The sociology of forensic science. *Studies in History and Philosophy of Biological and Biomedical Sciences, 44*(1), 36–46.
31. Science, C., & Select, T. (2019). *Forensic science and the criminal justice system: A blueprint for change*. House of Lords.

32. Justice, D. O. (2019). *Needs assessment of forensic laboratories and medical examiner/coroner offices: A report to congress.*
33. Kirk, P. L. (1963). The ontogeny of criminalistics. *Journal of Criminal Law, Criminology and Police Science, 54.*
34. Kind, S. S. (1987). The scientific investigation of crime. *The Scientific Investigation of Crime.*
35. Watson, J. D., & Crick, F. H. (1953). The structure of DNA. *Cold Spring Harbor Symposia on Quantitative Biology, 18*, 123–131.
36. Gitschier, J. (2009). The Eureka moment: An interview with Sir Alec Jeffreys. *PLoS Genetics, 5*(12), e1000765.
37. Vaughan, T. A, Ryan, J. M., & Czaplewski, N. J. (2013). Mammalogy. Jones & Bartlett Publishers.
38. Sinclair, R. D., Banfield, C. C., & Dawber, R. P. (1999). *Handbook of diseases of the hair and scalp.* Blackwell Science.
39. Hicks, J. W. (1977). *Microscopy of hairs: A practical guide and manual.* Department of Justice, Federal Bureau of Investigation.
40. Gaudette, B. C. (1976). Probabilities and human pubic hair comparisons. *Journal of Forensic Sciences, 21*(3), 514–517.
41. Houck, M. M., & Budowle, B. (2002). Correlation of microscopic and mitochondrial DNA hair comparisons. *Journal of Forensic Sciences, 47*(5), 964–967.
42. Cole, S. A., & Duster, T. (2016). Microscopic hair comparison and the sociology of science. *Contexts, 15*(1), 28–35.
43. Burke, K., Lewis, S., Bett, J., Southurst, T., Lim, K., & Gutowski, S. (2007). *Preliminary investigations into using Eugenol to recover erased characters on polymers.*
44. Houck, M. M., Riley, R. A., Speaker, P. J., & Witt, T. S. (2009). FORESIGHT: A business approach to improving forensic science services. *Forensic Science Policy & Management: An International Journal, 1*(2), 85–95.
45. Speaker, P. J. (2019). The jurisdictional return on investment from processing the backlog of untested sexual assault kits. *Forensic Science International, 20*(1), 18–23.
46. Houck, M. M., & Speaker, P. (2020). Project FORESIGHT: A ten-year retrospective. *Forensic Science International: Synergy, 12*(2), 275–281.
47. Anker, A. S. T., Doleac, J. L., & Landersø, R. (2021). The effects of DNA databases on the deterrence and detection of offenders. *American Economic Journal: Applied Economics., 13*(4), 194–225.
48. Doleac, J. L. (2017). The effects of DNA databases on crime. *American Economic Journal: Applied Economics, 9*(1), 165–201.
49. Lander, E. S. (2016). *Forensic science in criminal courts: Ensuring scientific validity of feature-comparison methods.* Executive Office of the President.
50. Hsu, S. (2017). *Sessions orders Justice Department to end Forensic Science Commission, suspend review policy.* The Washington Post.
51. Childs, R. A., Witt, T. S., & Nur-tegin, K. (2009). Survey of forensic service providers. *Forensic Science Policy & Management: An International Journal, 1*(1), 49–56.
52. Melbourn, H., Smith, G., McFarland, J., Rogers, M., Wieland, K., DeWilde, D., et al. (2019). Mandatory certification of forensic science practitioners in the United States: A supportive perspective. *Forensic Science International: Synergy, 7*(1), 161–169.
53. Risinger, D. M. (2017). The irrelevance, and central relevance, of the boundary between science and non-science in the evaluation of expert witness reliability. In P. Roberts (Ed.), *Expert evidence and scientific proof in criminal trials* (pp. 117–160). Routledge.
54. National Institute of Justice. (2022). *The slow but steady March towards a more reliable forensic science (Internet).* nij.ojp.gov. (cited June 2, 2023). Available from: https://nij.ojp.gov/topics/articles/slow-steady-march-towards-more-reliable-forensic-science#citation--0

The manufacturer's authorised representative in the EU is Springer Nature Customer Service Centre GmbH, Europaplatz 3, 69115 Heidelberg, Germany. If you have any concerns regarding our products, please contact ProductSafety@springernature.com

Printed and bound by CPI Group (UK) Ltd, Croydon, CR0 4YY
30/09/2026
02225569-0008